**7**

# Communicating in Groups

## Applications and Skills

# Communicating in Groups
## Applications and Skills

Katherine Adams
California State University, Fresno

Gloria J. Galanes
Missouri State University

 McGraw-Hill
Higher Education

Boston   Burr Ridge, IL   Dubuque, IA   New York   San Francisco   St. Louis
Bangkok   Bogotá   Caracas   Kuala Lumpur   Lisbon   London   Madrid   Mexico City
Milan   Montreal   New Delhi   Santiago   Seoul   Singapore   Sydney   Taipei   Toronto

The McGraw-Hill Companies

# McGraw-Hill
# Higher Education

Published by McGraw-Hill, an imprint of The McGraw-Hill Companies, Inc., 1221 Avenue of the Americas, New York, NY 10020. Copyright © 2009, 2006, 2003, 2000, 1997, 1994, 1991. All rights reserved. No part of this publication may be reproduced or distributed in any form or by any means, or stored in a database or retrieval system, without the prior written consent of The McGraw-Hill Companies, Inc., including, but not limited to, in any network or other electronic storage or transmission, or broadcast for distance learning.

This book is printed on acid-free paper.

1 2 3 4 5 6 7 8 9 0 DOC/DOC 0 9 8

ISBN: 978-0-07-338500-6
MHID: 0-07-338500-X

Editor in Chief: *Mike Ryan*
Publisher: *Frank Mortimer*
Sponsoring Editor: *Suzanne Earth*
Developmental Editor: *Phil Butcher*
Marketing Manager: *Leslie Oberhuber*
Production Editor: *David Blatty*
Manuscript Editor: *Margaret Moore*
Design Manager: *Margarite Reynolds*
Production Supervisor: *Tandra Jorgensen*
Composition: *10/12 Garamond Regular by Macmillan Publishing Solutions*
Printing: *45# New Era Matte, R. R. Donnelley & Sons/Crawfordsville, IN*

Cover art: © Tim Hall/Digital Vision/Getty Images

**Library of Congress Cataloging-in-Publication Data**

Adams, Katherine L.
  Communicating in groups : applications and skills / Katherine Adams, Gloria Galanes.—
7th ed.
      p.   cm.
  Includes bibliographical references and index.
  ISBN-13: 978-0-07-338500-6 (alk. paper)
  ISBN-10: 0-07-338500-X (alk. paper)
  1. Small groups. 2. Interpersonal relations. I. Galanes, Gloria J. II. Title.
  HM736.A33 2009
  302.3'4—dc22                                          2007051521

The Internet addresses listed in the text were accurate at the time of publication. The inclusion of a Web site does not indicate an endorsement by the authors or McGraw-Hill, and McGraw-Hill does not guarantee the accuracy of the information presented at these sites.

www.mhhe.com

*We dedicate this book to our students,*
*who teach us as much as we teach them.*

# BRIEF CONTENTS

**PART ONE**
## Orientation to Small Group Systems    1

**1**  Small Groups as the Heart of Society    2

**2**  Groups as Structured Open Systems    28

**PART TWO**
## Foundations of Small Group Communicating    51

**3**  Communication Principles for Group Members    52

**4**  Using Verbal and Nonverbal Messages in Small Group Communication    74

**PART THREE**
## From Individuals to Group    103

**5**  Becoming a Group    104

**6**  Working with Diversity in the Small Group    138

**PART FOUR**
## Understanding and Improving Group Throughput Processes    177

**7**  Creative and Critical Thinking in the Small Group    178

**8**  Group Problem-Solving Procedures    216

**9**  Managing Conflicts Productively    250

**10**  Applying Leadership Principles    276

**PART FIVE**
## Small Group Public Presentations    313

**11**  Planning, Organizing, and Presenting Small Group Oral Presentations    314

Appendix: Techniques for Observing Problem-Solving Groups    A-1

References    R-1

Bibliography    B-1

Index    I-1

# CONTENTS

Preface   xiv

## PART ONE
## Orientation to Small Group Systems   1

### CHAPTER 1
### Small Groups as the Heart of Society   2

Groups in Your Life   5

Groups as Problem Solvers   6

Participating in Groups   6

Groups versus Individuals as Problem Solvers   8

When a Group Is a Good Choice   9

When a Group Is Not a Good Choice   9

Groups, Small Groups, Teams, and Small Group Communication   11

Groups   11

Small Groups   12

Small Groups versus Teams   13

Small Group Communication   14

Groups and Technology   15

Classifying Groups by Their Major Purpose   16

Primary or Secondary Groups   16

Types of Secondary Groups   17

Being an Ethical Group Member   21

The Participant-Observer Perspective   24

### CHAPTER 2
### Groups as Structured Open Systems   28

What Is a Theory?   30

Overview of General Systems Theory   30

The Small Group as a System   32

Definition of a System   32

Concepts Vital to Understanding Systems   33

Characteristics of Systems   40

Organizations as Systems of Groups   46

## PART TWO
## Foundations of Small Group Communicating   51

### CHAPTER 3
### Communication Principles for Group Members   52

Communication: What's That?   55

Communication Is Symbolic   55

Communication Is Personal   56

Communication Is a Transactional Process   56

Communication Is a Sender and Receiver Phenomenon   58

Communication Involves Content and Relationship Dimensions   60

Implications for Small Group Communication   61

Listening: Receiving, Interpreting, and
Responding to Messages from Other
Group Members   63
   Listening Defined   63

Listening Preferences   64
Habits of Poor Listeners   65
Listening Actively   69

**CHAPTER 4**
**Using Verbal and Nonverbal Messages in Small Group Communication   74**

Creating Messages in a Small Group   76
How Communication Structures the
Small Group   77
Using Language to Help the Group
Progress   78
   Following the Rules   79
   Adjusting to the Symbolic Nature
   of Language   80
   Using Emotive Words Cautiously   82
   Organizing Remarks   83
Making Sure the Discussion Question Is
Clear and Appropriate   85

Using Language to Focus a Group's Discussion:
An Application   86
Nonverbal Behaviors in Small Group
Communication   90
   Principles of Nonverbal
   Communication   90
   Functions of Nonverbal
   Behaviors   91
   Categories of Nonverbal
   Behaviors   94
Nonverbal Behavior in Computer-Mediated
Groups   100

**PART THREE**
From Individuals to Group   103

**CHAPTER 5**
**Becoming a Group   104**

The Life Cycle of a Group   106
Challenges in Group Development   107
   A Group's Major Functions   107
   Social Tensions in Groups   108
   Phase Models in Group Development   112
Group Socialization of Members   113
   Stages of Group Socialization   115
Group Roles   118
   Types of Roles   118
   Role Functions in a Small Group   119
   The Emergence of Roles in a Group   121
   Managing Group Roles   123

Rules and Norms   123
   Development of Group
   Norms   125
   Enforcement of Group Norms   126
   Changing a Group Norm   128
Development of a Group's
Climate   129
   Trust   130
   Cohesiveness   132
   Supportiveness   133
Ethical Behavior during Group
Formation   135

**CHAPTER 6**
**Working with Diversity in the Small Group   138**

What Is Diversity?   140
Diverse Member Characteristics   142

Differences in Motives for Joining
a Group   142

Diversity of Learning Styles   143

Personality Differences   146

Cultural Diversity   150

Dimensions of Culture   150

Racial and Ethnic Differences   155

Gender Differences   159

Generational Differences   161

Working with Diversity/Bridging
Differences   167

Creating a Group Identity through
Fantasy   168

Using SYMLOG to "Picture" Diversity   169

**PART FOUR**

# Understanding and Improving Group Throughput Processes   177

**CHAPTER 7**

## Creative and Critical Thinking in the Small Group   178

What Is Creative Thinking?   180

Enhancing Group Creativity   183

Brainstorming   184

Synectics   185

Mind Mapping   187

What Makes Thinking "Critical"?   189

Enhancing Critical Thinking in a Group   189

Having the Right Attitude   191

Gathering Information   193

Evaluating Information   197

Checking for Errors in Reasoning   203

Avoiding Groupthink   208

**CHAPTER 8**

## Group Problem-Solving Procedures   216

A Systematic Procedure as the Basis
for Problem Solving   219

Capturing the Problem in Problem
Solving   220

How Do We Know a Problem When
We See One?   220

Area of Freedom   221

Characteristics of Problems   222

Identifying Problems with a Problem
Census   223

Effective Problem Solving and Decision
Making   227

The Procedural Model of Problem Solving
(P-MOPS)   228

Applications of P-MOPS   244

**CHAPTER 9**

## Managing Conflicts Productively   250

What Is Conflict?   252

Myths about Conflict   252

Types of Conflict   256

Substantive Conflict   256

Affective Conflict   256

Procedural Conflict   257

Computer-Mediated Communication
(CMC) and Conflict Types   258

Managing Conflict in the
Group   259

Conflict Management Styles   259

Expressing Disagreement Ethically   265

Maximizing Your Chances to Influence
the Group   267

The Nominal Group Technique   268

Steps in Principled Negotiation   270

**CHAPTER 10**

**Applying Leadership Principles    276**

Leadership and Leaders    278

    What Is Leadership?    278

    Sources of Power and Influence    278

    What Is a Leader?    280

Myths about Leadership    283

Current Ideas about Leadership    286

    The Functional Concept of Group
    Leadership    286

    The Contingency Concept of Group
    Leadership    287

What Good Leaders Do    290

    What Group Members Expect Leaders
    to Do    291

    Performing Administrative Duties    292

    Leading Group Discussions    297

    Developing the Group    303

Encouraging Distributed
Leadership    306

Ethical Guidelines for Group
Leaders    309


**PART FIVE**

Small Group Public Presentations    313


**CHAPTER 11**

**Planning, Organizing, and Presenting Small Group Oral Presentations    314**

The Planning Stage    316

    Your Audience    316

    Your Occasion    317

    Your Purpose    317

    Your Subject or Topic    318

    Member Strengths and Fears    318

    Supplemental Logistics    319

    Types of Group Oral Presentations    319

The Organizing Stage    322

    Delegating Duties    323

    Gathering Verbal and Visual Materials    323

    Organizing Materials and the Presentation    326

The Presenting Stage    330

    Checking Your Language    330

    Practice Aloud    331

What Makes a Good Oral Presentation?    332


Appendix: Techniques for Observing Problem-Solving Groups    A-1

References    R-1

Bibliography    B-1

Index    I-1

# FEATURES

## CASES

1.1  The Best Friends Animal Society   3
2.1  The Jamaican Winter Olympic
      Bobsled Team   29
3.1  Students for Alternative Medicine   53
4.1  The Search for a New Dean   75
5.1  The *Man of La Mancha* Cast
      and Crew   105
6.1  The Misfit   139
7.1  Ozarks Greenways, Inc.   179
7.2  Problems at NASA   190
7.3  The Class Project   208
8.1  The Merger   217
8.2  The School Board Breaks a Deadlock   239
9.1  The Cask and Cleaver Work Crew   251
10.1  The College Service Club   277
11.1  Food for the Homeless   315
A.1  Consulting to the Technical College
      Executive Committee   A-1

## APPLY NOW

Individual or Group?   11
How Small Is Small?   13
Meeting Member Needs and Handling
   Membership Changes   16
What's in a Name?   21
Bona Fide Groups: The Jamaican Bobsled
   Team   38
CNN's Reporting Disaster: What Happened?   45
CNN and *Time* as a System of Groups   48
Communication and the Students for
   Alternative Medicine   62
Students for Alternative Medicine
   and Listening   64
Poor Listening Habits and
   Misunderstandings   70

What Are Our Questions?   89
What If . . . ?   93
The Public Affairs Web Page Committee   101
Managing Tertiary Tensions   111
Integrating a New Member   114
Creating a Space for Yourself in the
   Group   122
Changing a Norm You Believe Is Harmful   130
Handling Different Motives and Orientations
   toward Work   144
Balancing the Church Board   150
Euro-Disney Stumbles   154
Mom's in My Group!   166
Using SYMLOG to Help a Group   172
Creative Fund-Raising for the College   183
Creating Suggestions for Crossing Kansas
   Expressway   186
Should You Support Mary Alice Beasley
   for School Board?   201
Gun Control   207
Improving Airport Security   221
Characteristics of OPT's Problem   225
Moving to New Facilities   244
Helping the Cask and Cleaver Crew   271
Should He Go Back to School?   273
Informal Leadership in the Group   282
Which Contingency Style Is Most
   Appropriate?   291
Red Ribbon Committee and Sober
   Graduation   302
Marcos and His Fraternity   305
The Great Leader   306
What Type of Group Presentation Should
   the Group Make to the Restaurant
   Association?   322
Preparing an Individual Presentation   333
Using the Canons to Evaluate   334

## ETHICAL DILEMMAS

Would You Falsify Data?   25
When to Code Switch and When
   Not to?   78
What Do You Do When Emotive Words
   Are Offensive?   82
When Is It OK to Be Deviant?   128
Can You Be Trusted?   131
Different Voices for Making Ethical
   Decisions   157
What Would You Do?   204
Your Needs or the Team's
   Needs?   310

## MEDIA AND TECHNOLOGY

The Instinctive Need to Group Together   7
The Influence of Computer-Mediated
   Communication on the System   42
CMC and Communication Richness   59
The Symbolic Nature of Avatars   92
Norm Enforcement in Internet Groups   126
Diminishing Implicit Assumptions of
   Group Diversity   160
Terrorism, TV, and Groupthink   213
Using Chat Rooms for GSS   237
Group Leaders and the Use of Technology   298
Using Presentation Technology   326

**PREFACE**

*People can be motivated to be good not by telling them that hell is a place where they will burn, but by telling them it is an unending committee meeting. On judgment day, the Lord will divide people by telling those on His right hand to enter His kingdom and those on His left to break into small groups.*

**Rev. Robert Kennedy**

This quote, given to us by a student, expresses precisely how many people feel about participating in groups. In fact, it describes some of our own experiences! But the quote's sentiment focuses attention on the torture that participating in small groups can produce—and it ignores the uplifting, energizing effect that can also occur through group participation. Group participation *can* feel like torture, but it can also be incredibly rewarding and a lot of fun. Both of us have had the experience of being in a group that so excited us, made us feel alive, gave us a way to express ourselves, helped us connect with others, and so enabled us to accomplish a tremendous amount of work, that we didn't want to see the group end. Yes, that is a rare occurrence. But in this book, we hope to give students tools to help them attain those ideals by providing insight about how groups work and practical suggestions for applying those insights.

   This book is designed for the first- or second-year student who may not have had a prior communication course and who may never take a subsequent course—but who *must* work in groups because that is the nature of corporate, educational, and civic participation in this day and age. Two overarching goals guide our writing. First, being able to work effectively in groups is not a luxury—it's a necessity. Our introductory students want to cut to the chase; they want to know what works *right now.* That is the reason for our distinctly *practical* focus in *Communicating in Groups.* Although this text uses the same research foundation as our more advanced text, *Effective Group Discussion,* we strive here to provide information in a way that is both useful and immediately usable. Second, we want students to recognize that effective group work is, to a great extent, a matter of *communication behavior,* not a matter of personality or fate. Thus, it is to a great extent within their own control. We want students to start thinking about their own communicative choices in groups and to have the tools to make wise choices so they can make the groups they belong to as rewarding and productive as possible.

   To meet our goals, we have chosen to use an informal writing style and to provide many examples from our own and others' experiences. We also report research findings in much less detail, with more synthesis and distillation of findings, fewer footnotes, and less evaluation of competing theories than in our other text. This allows readers to focus on what is usually more important to them—the practical application of the research. Finally, we refer to ourselves, Kathy and Gloria, frequently throughout the text. We think of our readers as individuals with whom we are on a first-name basis, and we encourage you to think of us the same way, as if we were members of the same small group.

# Overview of the Text

With each revision, the hardest thing we have to do is decide what to retain and what to cut out. We try to focus on what we believe are the most important concepts, particularly those that will be most useful and practical for students to understand. In this edition, we continue to cover the influence new communication technologies have on small group communication, add material on cultural dynamics in small groups, and use general systems theory as our structural framework because we believe it provides a framework that is easy to grasp. As before, the chapters are ordered in a way that is logical to us but that does not preclude other methods of organizing a small group course. Each chapter is self-contained and can be read in an order different from what we provide here.

**Part One** provides basic information students need to understand how groups function. Chapter 1 introduces some basic terms encountered throughout the book, shows how to classify groups according to their major purpose, and introduces the concept of ethical behavior of group members. Chapter 2 presents general systems theory as a framework for understanding the complexity of group communication. We provide specific illustrations of systems concepts throughout the rest of the book as well.

**Part Two** provides the foundation for understanding communication in groups. Chapter 3, which may present review material for some readers, discusses basic communication theory, including what communication is, what constitutes effective listening, and how people interpret what they see and hear. Chapter 4 discusses the specifics of verbal and nonverbal messages.

**Part Three** explores in detail how we move from being individuals to connecting as a group. Chapter 5 explains how a group develops as a team from an initial collection of individuals. Chapter 6 focuses on how groups can work effectively with multiple levels of diversity: member motivation, learning styles, personality, culture, gender, and ethnicity.

**Part Four** focuses on the group's throughput processes. Chapter 7 discusses the creative and critical thinking skills necessary for effective group problem solving. We believe creative and critical thinking are at the heart of the group problem-solving process and that students should know something about these processes before understanding problem solving in general. Chapter 8 describes the problem-solving process and introduces the procedural model of problem solving as a helpful guideline to follow. Chapter 9 explains why group conflicts occur and how they can be managed so that the group benefits instead of suffers. Chapter 10 provides a comprehensive picture of leadership and also gives suggestions for applying leadership principles effectively and ethically.

**Part Five** presents information about oral presentations, the culmination of much group effort. In Chapter 11 students will learn about the types of oral presentations, ways to prepare effective presentations, and criteria for evaluating presentations.

Finally, the **Appendix** presents information about a number of techniques a member or outside observer can use to gather information about a problem-solving group and help it improve its performance.

# New to This Edition

- Moved the chapters on group development and diversity into a new section so the material is addressed earlier than in previous editions.

- Moved material on groupthink into Chapter 5, "Becoming a Group," and Chapter 7, "Creative and Critical Thinking in the Small Group," so that it could be covered in relation to cohesiveness and critical thinking.

- Integrated the National Communication Association's Credo for Ethical Communication into every chapter.

- Provided a stronger bridge between defining the group problem and problem analysis.

- Added new material on types of conflict including new information on computer-mediated communication and group conflict.

- Added new sources of power and included leadership styles commonly referenced in organizations.

- Integrated material across chapters with updated material from small group research.

# Features

***Case Studies:***   Establish the main ideas of the chapter by providing realistic scenarios for student application, and utilizing a variety of group contexts, such as business, health care, social groups, and civic organizations.

***Apply Now Boxes:***   Make concepts practical to everyday life, throughout the text.

***Ethical Dilemma Boxes:***   Encourage critical evaluation of typical ethical scenarios faced by groups, and stimulate discussion of their causes, controversies, issues, and solutions.

***Media and Technology Boxes:***   Look at how media and technology are changing the ways in which small groups can interact. Topics include online support groups, synchronous and asynchronous computer-mediated communication, terrorism, television, and groupthink.

***Online Learning Center:***   Icons prompt students to use the book-specific website www.mhhe.com/adamsgalanes7 where they will find a variety of resources and activities for teaching and study.

# Resources for Instructors

***Instructor's Manual:***   This manual provides exercises, sample syllabi, writing assignments, a list of transparency masters, and a test bank to help faculty, from first-time small group instructors to experienced ones, structure the course in ways that correspond with their teaching goals. The manual is on the book's website, www.mhhe.com/adamsgalanes7, and on the Instructor's Resources CD.

***Videos:***   *Communicating in Groups: Short Takes* provides numerous brief video examples to help students visualize a number of concepts. (0-697-34989-6)

# Acknowledgments

We wish to thank the reviewers, all of whom did a conscientious job of reading the manuscript and providing helpful suggestions. We appreciate their thoughtful suggestions and have incorporated many of them in this seventh edition.

Jerel Cowan, *University of Central Oklahoma*

Ann Marie Jablonowski, *Owens Community College*

Karen Krumrey-Fulks, *Lane Community College*

Suzanne McCorkle, *Boise State University*

Jim L. Query, Jr., *University of Houston*

Dr. Margaret Sargent, *Southern Connecticut State University*

Janice Xu, *Western Connecticut State University*

**Katherine Adams**
**Gloria J. Galanes**

## PART ONE

# Orientation to Small Group Systems

art One introduces you to the study of small groups. In Chapter 1 we explain why small groups are important to understand, and we define many of the terms you will encounter in your study of small groups. We discuss the types of small groups you are likely to experience, we address the ethics of small group communication, and we explain the participant-observer perspective used throughout the book. Chapter 2 presents you with a framework, general systems theory, to help organize the many concepts important to understanding how groups function.

# Small Groups as the Heart of Society

## CHAPTER OUTLINE

Groups in Your Life

Groups versus Individuals as
Problem Solvers

Groups, Small Groups, Teams, and
Small Group Communication

Classifying Groups by Their
Major Purpose

Being an Ethical Group Member

The Participant-Observer Perspective

## CHAPTER OBJECTIVES

**After reading this chapter you should be able to:**

1. Explain why groups play a vital role in the personal and professional lives of individuals.

2. List criteria for determining whether a group or an individual should be used to solve a problem.

3. Define a group, a small group, a team, and small group communication.

4. Differentiate between small group communication, public communication, interpersonal communication, and intrapersonal communication.

5. Explain and give examples of primary groups.

6. Explain and give examples of secondary groups.

7. Compare and contrast the different organizational groups.

8. Explain the four ethical standards any member of a group should be held to.

9. Explain and give examples of a member being an effective participant-observer.

## The Best Friends Animal Society

**CASE 1.1**

Sinjin the cat was near death when he arrived at Best Friends Animal Sanctuary in Angel Canyon, Utah.[1] Someone had set him on fire after dousing him with gasoline, badly burning three-quarters of his body. The care at Best Friends, however, pulled him through; Sinjin the one-eyed cat became a sleek, confident creature who loved his treats! Best Friends Animal Society runs the largest animal sanctuary in the world, with over 1,500 resident animals at any one time. Best Friends has been a prime mover in the No More Homeless Pets movement, advocates spay-neuter programs and no-kill animal shelters, provides consultation services for animal lovers all over the world who want to set up no-kill shelters and spay-neuter programs in their communities, offers internships for veterinary students, runs a large volunteer program, provides wildlife rehabilitation, schedules educational programs and seminars, and, of course, takes in abandoned animals. What does this have to do with small groups? Best Friends Animal Society started out, nearly 40 years ago, as a small group of friends on a quest for spiritual fulfillment.

In the 1960s a group of friends from Great Britain traveled together to the Bahamas, Mexico, the United States, and Europe seeking a meaningful life. The one belief that bound these diverse individuals together was what members called the Universal Law and what we know as the Golden Rule: "As you give, so shall you receive. So do unto others as you would have them do unto you."[2] The "others" included animals. Although the group members ended up living in different places, they stayed in touch, with love of animals the constant that united them. In 1982 the opportunity arose to buy 3,000 acres in Angel Canyon for an animal sanctuary. Of the 27 members who met to discuss buying the land, a core group of 20 pooled their personal resources to establish what would ultimately become Best Friends. The group included an architect, an artist, a real estate professional, several community organizers, and workers from another animal sanctuary run by some of the members. Over the years the group has learned (among other things) to build dwellings, fund-raise, tend sick and injured animals, and communicate with the media. The sanctuary is now one of the best known in the world. Several of the original members remain active, but new members have joined to contribute their expertise and energy.

The true story of Best Friends illustrates vividly what Margaret Mead said: "Never doubt that a small group of thoughtful, committed citizens can change the world. Indeed, it is the only thing that ever has."[3] This group of individuals, bound by a vision of a better world in which animals are respected and loved, shows what a small group can accomplish that an individual could never hope to achieve alone. The group demonstrates qualities that characterize effective group behavior: Members had a vision for what they wanted to accomplish; they appreciated and used the many different talents of their members; they trusted each other to work for the good of the group (and the animals); leadership was shared among them, as different needs and challenges arose; and the group continued to learn and develop by setting new goals that would increasingly stretch the abilities of its members. Throughout this text we will share what we know about how groups can achieve success like this. The glue that holds a group together and enables it to do its work is *communication*. That will be our focus: how you can communicate effectively to help a group succeed.

The group that formed and continues to oversee Best Friends is a voluntary group of members who choose to work together. However, many of the groups you belong to, especially where you work, may not be voluntary. You may be assigned to a group because you have a particular expertise your employer believes is important to the group's task or because small groups are an essential component of a course in which you are enrolled. No matter what the reason, you must be able to work well in teams, task forces, committees, and all kinds of special problem-solving groups if you want to succeed in the organized world of today. In fact, Monster Campus, part of Monster.com's website geared to college students, notes that teamwork is one of the seven "hot skills" most employers want, no matter their size or type of industry.[4] Moreover, Monster Campus reminds students that they can develop this skill during college.

Teams of all kinds, especially multidisciplinary teams, are becoming more common in all areas of American life: business, industry, education, health care, the nonprofit sector, and government. For example, some of the biggest companies in the United States, including every Fortune 500 company, has some version of small groups and teams in place.[5] Companies use teams in a number of ways. For instance, Motorola has more than 5,000 teams operating. Eastman Kodak forms process teams to follow a product through the design, manufacture, and marketing processes. Ritz-Carlton Hotels employees can choose to participate in team-based work in addition to their regular jobs, and 5 percent of the Texas Instruments workforce participates in self-directed work teams (described later in this chapter).

But there's a dark side to small group work. In one study of 179 teams, only 13 percent were rated highly effective.[6] A *Newsweek* article highlights some of the problems.[7] The article reports that one survey estimates managers spend one to one-and-a-half days in meetings each week—and half of that is wasted time. Some companies, including Nestlé USA and SC Johnson, ban meetings on Fridays. One management consultant estimates that the average meeting in a large company costs approximately $15,000. If meeting time isn't used effectively, that waste can be staggeringly expensive.

We take the position that effective small group work—whether in meetings, on teams, on committees, and so forth—cannot be left to chance. When individuals come together, particularly individuals from differing backgrounds, perspectives, and areas of expertise, teamwork doesn't just happen. Training in *how* to be an effective team member is essential. If you want to succeed as a team member, you must learn how small groups function and what you personally can do to help ensure team success. Chapter 1 will help you start this process by asking you to consider how important groups are in your own life and by introducing you to concepts central to understanding small group processes, the variety of groups you will encounter, and the importance of being an ethical participant-observer in groups.

## Groups in Your Life

Lawrence Frey, a leading advocate for the study of small groups in their natural settings, believes that the small group is *the* most important social formation: "From birth to death, small groups are interwoven into the fabric of our lives."[8] Small groups usher us in when we are born and out when we die, and they are present at every phase in between. The first group you encounter is your family, and in many ways this group forms the foundation for other groups that follow. Think about your family of origin for a moment, and consider how much of your identity—who you think you are—was formed by that initial group. Development and maintenance of identity remain important functions that only groups can provide for us. This is obvious when we consider groups such as fraternities or sororities, spiritually based groups (churches, synagogues, other religious organizations, and even spiritually guided activist groups like Best Friends), gangs, book clubs, and poker clubs. Groups formed at work also contribute to who we think we are. Are you a member of a union, for example? A management group? A classroom group? A neighborhood coalition trying to prevent a zoning change in your neighborhood? Each of these groups, though not expressly formed as an identity-supporting group, will affect how you see yourself in relation to other people.

Professionally, the higher you go in any organization (government, service, manufacturing, education, communication, the military, or whatever), the more time you will spend working as a member of small groups. No matter what specific group you are in, you need to know how to behave in ways that are appropriate and helpful to the group and to any larger organization to which the group may be attached. If you don't work well in groups, you are more likely to be laid off or frozen at a low-level job. A survey of 750 leading American companies asked businesspeople to describe characteristics of the ideal MBA (Master of Business Administration) graduate.[9] The top preference was possession of good oral and written communication skills (listed by 83.5 percent of respondents). The fourth-ranked preference, the ability to work in teams, was listed by 71.4 percent. These communication skills far surpassed even cutting-edge knowledge of the company's field (14.8 percent) and previous work experience (31.9 percent) in importance. Clearly, knowing how to work in a small group can be of practical benefit to you.

Even as a student, you may be surprised to discover how many groups you belong to. For most students the list goes up to 8, 10, 15, or even 20 or more small groups. Why do most of us belong to so many groups? Humans are social beings with powerful genetic needs to belong to small groups. We need to affiliate with others of our kind, just as do many other animals. A baby is dependent on others for its care for a long time before it develops self-reliance. Plus, one lone adult cannot provide everything a baby needs. This function is provided by different kinds of small groups, sometimes families with father and mother, but also groupings of the "Full House" sort, kibbutzim, extended family groupings that include a grandmother or aunts, or other child care groups. This famous African proverb emphasizes the key role of groups: "It takes a village to raise a child."

## GROUPS AS PROBLEM SOLVERS

You are constantly solving problems: how to find a job, where to eat lunch, how to keep your car running on a limited budget, and even how to keep your company on the cutting edge of its industry in a turbulent economic climate. Life can properly be called an unending series of problem-solving episodes. Solving any problem means coming up with a plan (even if it takes only a split second) and executing it. Planning solutions to problems used to be both the privilege and the responsibility of high-status people: generals, monarchs, dictators, managers, directors, and teachers. Carrying out the solutions was usually the work of lower-ranked people: infantrymen, secretaries, workers, students, and other subordinates. But things are changing. As you can see from the information provided earlier about the number of companies using teams and groups, more and more planning is done by groups—you won't be able to escape it, even in your classrooms! Because you are reading this text, chances are you are in a course requiring participation in small groups. All kinds of courses, not just communication courses, use small group participation as a way to learn actively. If you want to participate in planning and not just carry out assignments planned by others, you will need to be able to work effectively in groups.

## PARTICIPATING IN GROUPS

We emphasize how groups can become better problem solvers, but that cannot be accomplished by focusing only on the rational side of human behavior. To understand how groups operate, you must know something about human feelings and behavior. Effective group problem solving depends on how well members understand and manage such things as informational resources, how members feel about each other and about the task of the group, how skilled they are at expressing themselves and listening to others, and how well they collectively process the information they have to work with.

Group members must make sure they have the materials (information, tangible resources, time, and so forth) to complete the task, but they also must learn to manage their interpersonal relationships effectively enough to complete the task well. Thus, communication in groups performs two key functions: It accomplishes the group's task, and it creates "the social fabric of a group by promoting relationships between and among members."[10] This function—the group's relational communication—is just as important as the task-oriented functions of group work.

Samantha Glen's book about Best Friends describes several vivid examples of communication that convey just how much members of this group care about each other and how they express it.[11] At various times several members of the Best Friends core group encountered problems that seemed overwhelming and faced the real threat of burnout as they tried, in the early days, to keep the sanctuary running with little help, less money, and the ever-growing population of animals others had thrown away. In one encounter Faith lost it when she publicly confronted a prominent, well-respected local man who had adopted a puppy from the sanctuary but then abandoned it by the side of the road. Fellow group member, Michael, gently but firmly made Faith face the fact that she was

## The Instinctive Need to Group Together

Go to
**www.mhhe.com/
adamsgalanes7**
for additional
weblink activities.

**MEDIA AND TECHNOLOGY**

Some scholars have assessed situations in which a collection of individuals begin to group together. Such effort is common in face-to-face interaction where a particular force, problem, or crisis has created the need for individuals to group. Yet little is known about how and why individuals with nothing apparently in common or with no mediating force begin to group. A good example is in a computer-mediated environment.

To examine this unique grouping process, Tom Postmes, Russell Spears, and Martin Lea collected data on students who volunteered to complete a computerized statistics course, which offered participants e-mail options for contacting staff. Participants also used the function to send about 1,200 e-mail messages to fellow students. The messages were later classified into nine categories reflecting both task and relational functions (e.g., requests, complaints, reactions, humor, emotion, personal revelations). The researchers found that 11 groups formed, in which members spent most of their time (74 percent) interacting about socio-personal topics (reactions to contributions of other group members, humorous contributions, displays of affection and emotion). Despite having little impact on the successful completion of the course, these students grouped together to fulfill their need for relational interaction with fellow classmates.

SOURCE: T. Postmes, R. Spears, and M. Lea, "The Formation of Group Norms in Computer-Mediated Communication," *Human Communication Research* 26 (2001), pp. 341–71.

getting burned out and needed help. His obvious concern allowed Faith to realize how deep her exhaustion was and to accept help from the others. In another example the group's veterinarian, Bill, brought two gifts to the sanctuary: an Airstream trailer, accepted in lieu of payment from a client, that would serve as dedicated space for an operating table, and a goat to keep Sparkle the horse company while her leg healed. Faith, expressing the whole group's gratitude, said to Bill, "We love you, you know."[12] This comment may not be typical of what you hear in most work groups, but communication that conveys appreciation, gratitude, and liking goes a long way in creating a group that is also a community, and that can be a deeply satisfying experience. The Best Friends group succeeded because members focused on *both* task and relationship aspects of working in teams. Organizational and work skills *and* people skills are essential. We hope our book furthers your understanding of and your knack for effective group participation.

Participation in a group always requires trade-offs. You give up the freedom to do what you want when you want for the advantages of affiliating with others to produce the kind of work possible only when several people coordinate their efforts. However, when individuals must coordinate their efforts, tensions always arise. This is true in all small groups, from a classroom work group to a task force of engineers designing a rocket. This is what *Communicating in Groups* is about: knowing what produces tensions in a group (both in the individuals and in the group as a whole), and knowing how to manage the tensions so that the group's decisions are the best that can be made, the members gain from the group, and the organization that gave birth to the group is improved by the group's work.

# Groups versus Individuals as Problem Solvers

If group work is so tricky and has such potential for problems, why not have individuals plan the solutions to all problems? The benefits of having a group tackle a problem *can* (but not necessarily *will*) outweigh the costs in time and tensions.

Research into the effectiveness of solutions developed by small groups, compared to those planned by individuals acting alone, has shown that groups can be far superior for solving many types of problems.[13] Groups tend to do much better than individuals when several alternative solutions are possible, none of which is known to be superior or "correct." They also are better at conjunctive tasks, where no one person has all the information needed to solve a problem, but each member has some needed information.[14] These are the very sorts of problems most groups and organizations face. For example, which of several designs for a car is most likely to sell well? What benefit options should be available to employees? How can the federal government give citizens a tax cut and still provide sufficient funds for social programs and the homeland defense?

Many college courses require small group activity of some sort. When instructors move from teacher-centered to more student-centered instruction, they use small groups. Collaborative or cooperative learning rests on the consistent use of student groups.[15] Instructional experts Robert Powell and Dana Caseau support the notion that groups are better at collaborative tasks.[16] When student groups tackle a variety of collaborative tasks in the classroom, they become active, not passive, learners. Students can improve problem solving, critical and creative thinking, and social skills in small group learning contexts. Powell and Caseau point out that group activity is a preferred way to learn for some (e.g., Latinos, Native Americans, African Americans, and females).

The following story illustrates how a group's greater resources can help the problem-solving process. Gloria participated on a steering committee to help integrate a public television station into the university where she teaches. (This case introduces Chapter 8.) This large committee also included a lawyer, the general manager of the TV station, the general manager of the university's public radio station, the director of development, the vice president overseeing physical plant matters, the vice president for finance, and several other administrators. This committee had six months to complete its work. The lawyer drew up the documents for the Federal Communications Commission (FCC) to approve the license transfer to the university. The vice president overseeing the physical plant worked with others to determine how space needed to be modified to accommodate the station's master control units, other equipment, and personnel. The finance vice president kept track of the budget. The TV station manager served a liaison function with her employees and met with them to determine what new equipment was needed. The radio station manager helped the TV station manager and others rewrite job descriptions so that they would be compatible with the university's human resources designations. Many, many other tasks had to be completed in the time allotted for the transfer. No one person possessed the necessary expertise (to say nothing of the time and energy) to accomplish this highly complex task. Also, an enormous amount of coordination had to occur for this task to be accomplished successfully, and for that, everybody's people skills were needed.

After the major planning tasks were completed, smaller, more focused committees took over the remaining tasks and handled implementation.

## WHEN A GROUP IS A GOOD CHOICE

For several reasons groups working on problems with multiple solutions typically make higher-quality decisions than do individuals. Groups usually have a much larger number of possible solutions from which to choose. Group members can help each other think critically by correcting one another's misinformation, faulty assumptions, and invalid reasoning. Several people can often think of issues to be handled in the process of solving a problem that might be overlooked by any one member. In addition, several people can conduct more thorough investigative research than one person working alone. Group members often counteract each other's tendencies to engage in self-defeating behavior.[17]

A recent example, mentioned on the *Today Show,* illustrates the value of group problem solving. Doctors at the University of Michigan studied the value of a multidisciplinary team approach to providing breast cancer patients with a second opinion.[18] Patients who were diagnosed with breast cancer and whose doctors had recommended a course of treatment were referred for a second opinion to a team that included a variety of cancer treatment specialists: a radiologist, surgeon, pathologist, medical oncologist, and radiation oncologist. The team met, usually with the patient, to discuss options. Over half the time, the team recommended an approach different from the one the original physician had. Sometimes, a team member was aware of new treatment protocols or techniques the original doctor hadn't known. Other times, the original doctor had not followed national treatment guidelines. Having qualified, dedicated team members work together to address an important issue can produce better results.

A further advantage to having a team work out a problem is that group members who are involved in solving a problem or planning a procedure usually understand that procedure and work hard to implement it. In addition, people are more likely to accept a solution they had a hand in designing. Satisfaction, loyalty, commitment, and learning tend to be higher when people have a voice. These principles have resulted in such small group techniques as quality control circles, self-managed work groups, and collaborative learning groups.

## WHEN A GROUP IS NOT A GOOD CHOICE

Not all problems are suitable for groups, nor is group decision making always a wise or productive use of time. When a problem has a best or correct solution (such as in an arithmetic or accounting task), a skilled person working alone often performs better than a group of less knowledgeable people, even if the group includes the highly skilled person as a member. Coordinating the work of several persons when conditions are changing rapidly (as in a weather disaster, battle, or ballgame) may be done best by one person (a commander, chief, or coach). Likewise, if small groups have certain social, procedural, or personality-mix problems, the output may be inferior, even though members may produce it with confidence in the results. Much of this book addresses how to apply small group theory—based as much as possible on scientific research—to make sure that groups work on the kinds of problems for which they are best suited, and to do so in ways likely to produce a high-quality solution (see Table 1.1).

## Problems Appropriate for Groups versus Individuals

**TABLE 1.1**

### Problems Suitable for a Group

- The problem is complex; one person is not likely to have all relevant information.
- There are several acceptable solutions, and one best solution does not exist.
- Acceptance of the solution by those who are affected is critical.
- Sufficient time exists for a group to meet and discuss and analyze the problem.

### Problems Suitable for an Individual

- There is a best solution, and a recognized expert is most qualified to determine that solution.
- Conditions are changing rapidly (such as during a fire or natural disaster), and coordination is best done by one person.
- Time is short and a decision must be made quickly.
- Group members have personality, procedural, or social problems that make it difficult or impossible for them to work as a team on the solution.

"You take two of these at the first sign of the onset of boardroom turbulence."

Many organization members have come to dread participation in groups. © The New Yorker Collection; 1985 Donald Reilly from cartoonbank.com. All Rights Reserved.

## Individual or Group?

What would you do if you were president of a university and your governing board approved the acquisition and license transfer to the university of the public television station in your town? As president you have the power to make this happen by appointing a high-level person to coordinate the many tasks that need to be done, or you can appoint a committee to accomplish the same thing.

1. How would you weigh the factors (time, energy, expertise) in making your decision?

2. What are the advantages and disadvantages of having your appointee placed in charge of this effort compared with having an appointed committee placed in charge?

3. The members of the committee actually in charge of overseeing the project spent untold hours making sure that no important detail was left undone. What benefits do you think they may have gained by working on this time-consuming project?

Your experiences in task-oriented groups may have been unpleasant ones. In fact, you may dread hearing a teacher tell you that you'll be working on a group project. Unfortunately, this kind of **grouphate** is common, probably because many groups do not function as well as they should. If this is how you feel about group participation, it is especially important for you to become familiar with group processes, ways to handle problems, and procedures that can help you solve group problems.

Thus far, we have seen that small groups are commonly involved in problem solving. We now introduce you to the types of small groups that engage in problem solving and the situations that create them. We will first define terms necessary to understand group communication. We encourage you to use our definitions when you think about, discuss, and complete assignments about small groups as you read this book.

# Groups, Small Groups, Teams, and Small Group Communication

Before we discuss small group communication, you must first understand how we conceptualize the terms *group, team,* and *small group.*

## GROUPS

What is a group? On the surface the answer may appear simple. However, scholars from disciplines such as sociology, social psychology, and communication have all tried to pinpoint the essential features of a group. Marvin Shaw, an important early small group theorist, defines a **group** as "persons who are interacting with one another in such a manner that each person influences and is influenced by each other person."[19] The essence of "groupness" is that members have interdependent relationships, act interdependently toward a common purpose, and are aware that, together, they act as part of a unit. Just putting a bunch of people in the same place does not mean that a group has been created; it takes time for members to develop their interdependent relationships.

The following example will illustrate what we mean. At a recent communication convention, one of us stood waiting for a streetcar late at night. Three other conventioneers, identified by their badges, stood at the same stop. At this point a group as we define it had *not* been formed; what existed was a collection of individuals who happened to be in the same place at the same time. This was not a group because no interaction had occurred, members were not particularly aware of each other as individuals, there was no *common* purpose (although there were four individual goals that happened to be similar), and no mutual influence had occurred. There was no sense of collective identity, and members had no attachment to each other or to the group.

After about 15 minutes with no streetcar in sight, one person mentioned, to no one in particular, that the streetcar was "awfully late." Others chimed in about the unreliability of the streetcar system, the lateness of the hour, the city's reputation for being unsafe late at night, and the fact that they had other places where they needed to be. We introduced each other and chitchatted about the convention. At this point the collection of individuals began to form into a group. This process started with our mutual awareness of the other individuals and the dawning realization that perhaps we were all in the same boat. However, we still lacked mutual influence and common purpose. Those came when one of us suggested that we share a cab to our various hotels, which were close together. That suggestion—the first attempt at mutual influence by one member—helped us become an actual group of people whose individual goals merged into a common goal, that of getting to our hotels as quickly as possible. Even though this group was short-lived and relatively unimportant, it met all the criteria for being a group: We interacted with and mutually influenced one another, became interdependent, had a common purpose, and were aware, for the short time we were together, that we acted as a unit to achieve our mutual goal.

Groups can range in size from very small (three) to very large. In this book we are concerned only with small groups. The principles that pertain to small groups do not necessarily hold true for large ones, and vice versa. Techniques appropriate for groups of 3–7 members may be disastrous if tried in groups of 30, 70, or more. Likewise, communication techniques and procedures appropriate in large group meetings may be harmful to the effective functioning of small groups. For instance, parliamentary procedures developed for large group meetings (e.g., Robert's Rules of Order) are not meant to help small groups accomplish their tasks efficiently.

## SMALL GROUPS

*Small*, pertaining to groups, has usually been defined either by an arbitrary number or in terms of human perception. We prefer to define it in terms of psychological perception: A **small group** refers to a group in which individual members perceive each other and are aware of each other as individuals when they interact. This definition is precise only for a given point in time. A committee of five new members may be perceptually large until after each member has had a chance to speak repeatedly, but the initial Best Friends group of 20 seemed perceptually small because members had known each other well and had worked together on other projects over many years. At the point when they met to discuss buying Angel Canyon, members knew and could describe every other member and could also say something about what each person contributed to the discussion. That is the idea of *small* group as we use it.

More practically, small groups usually consist of three to seven members. This seems to be the ideal range, so long as members possess sufficient knowledge and skills to do the job facing the group and have a diversity of perspectives and information relevant to the task. The more members, the more likely there will be inequity and communication overload for some members. We intentionally exclude the dyad (two-person group) from our definition of small group because dyads function differently. For example, dyads do not form networks or leadership hierarchies. Groups have continuity that dyads do not. If one member leaves a dyad, the dyad disbands, but members often leave small groups, sometimes to be replaced by new members, and the group itself continues. Some members of the original Best Friends group of 20 have left the group, and new members have joined; Best Friends, however, endures.

### How Small Is Small?

**APPLY NOW**

The Best Friends core group consisted of 20 people who committed their personal resources to buy Angel Canyon and create an animal sanctuary.

1. What evidence suggests that this group is actually a group and not a collection of individuals?
2. Would you classify this group as "small"? Why or why not?
3. What kinds of problems might a group of this size encounter? What kinds of advantages might it have over a smaller group?
4. Why is this story used as an example of *small* group communication?

In this book we focus on continuing small groups, in which the members "meet more or less regularly in face-to-face interaction, . . . possess a common identity or exclusiveness of purpose, and . . . share a set of standards governing their activity."[20] Task forces, work crews, sport teams, committees, quality circles, and classroom groups are examples of such groups. One-meeting groups in which members have a sense of shared purpose, interact face-to-face, share at least some standards and procedures for governing their interaction, and have a sense of each other as group members also qualify as small groups by our definition. So do virtual groups whose members seldom or never meet face-to-face.

## SMALL GROUPS VERSUS TEAMS

Is there a difference between a small group and a team? Although we use the terms interchangeably, some people believe there is a difference. For example, Steven Beebe and John Masterson say that a team is more highly structured than a typical small group.[21] They identify four characteristics that differentiate teams from groups: Team member responsibilities are more clearly spelled out (such as positions on a sports team); team rules and operating procedures are explicitly defined; team goals are clear and specific (e.g., to increase sales by 15 percent over the previous year); and teams openly discuss how members will work together. In our view these characteristics are positive ones that we think would benefit most groups. Most committees, for example, can improve their performance if members discuss how they will operate together, what group procedures they will use, and what their specific goals will be.

Others believe that a team represents a particularly effective small group. For example, Frank LaFasto and Carl Larson, over a lifetime of working with a variety of groups, have described five dimensions that matter most for a team to be effective.[22] Team members are collaborative and easy to work with; relationships among members are easy and supportive; group processes and procedures are aligned well with what the team wants to achieve; team leaders help team members accomplish their goals rather than getting in the way; and the team's parent organization encourages and supports the team rather than interfering and creating obstacles to its success. Their book explores in detail specific practices, for each dimension, that help a team succeed.

Although others distinguish between groups and teams, we do not differentiate between them. We use the terms interchangeably throughout this book because, in everyday life, distinctions between groups and teams are not as clear as they have been described here. For example, your company might set up teams of employees, but those teams may not be more clearly structured or more effective than if they were called something else—say, *committees* or *groups*. In our own lives we have participated in various task forces or committees that possess all the characteristics of highly effective teams, but were not called *teams*. Similarly, we have participated in teams that performed miserably or were loosely organized. Just because they were called *teams* did not mean that those teams operated differently from any other run-of-the-mill groups.

We hope, though, that you will pay careful attention to the dimensions that differentiate *effective* groups or teams from *ineffective* ones. There are clear differences! A major purpose of this book is to help you understand what helps create an effective group and what you, as group member or leader, can do to help your team succeed.

## SMALL GROUP COMMUNICATION

Our definitions of *group* and *small group* have emphasized the process of members communicating with each other to become interdependent. Groups cannot exist without communication. More importantly, regardless of why you are in a group or what its purpose is, group work requires communication. Thus, to undertake the study of small group dynamics means you must tackle the complexities of communication.[23]

**Communication** refers to the perception, interpretation, and response of people to messages produced by other people. The definition states that group members send verbal and nonverbal messages—words, gestures, facial expressions, and so forth—and that the other group members observe, interpret, and respond to these messages. This implies that members of a group pay attention to each other and coordinate their communication behavior to accomplish the group's assignment. It is the members' communication with each other—their perceiving, interpreting, and responding to one another's signals—that creates the interdependence necessary for individuals to be called a group. We develop this concept in detail in Chapter 3.

**Small group communication** refers to the part of the field of group dynamics that focuses on the exchange of verbal and nonverbal information among group members. Small group communication requires interacting. As members create, perceive, interpret, and respond to messages, they are engaging in small group communication. This is different from public speaking to large groups (audiences), participating in a large assembly (i.e., a legislature or convention), communicating in a more-or-less-intimate dyad, or talking with one other person in assigned roles such as waiter and customer. While basic communication principles are common no matter what the setting, our emphasis in *Communicating in Groups* is communication that occurs within the group. We also touch on the presentational skills group members need when they publicly share a group's output.

Small group communication is different from the communication that occurs in other contexts, such as interpersonal communication, public communication, and intrapersonal communication. It is more complex than interpersonal communication, which focuses on the communication between individuals as unique persons, as in a dyad. For instance, in a dyad, only one interpersonal relationship is possible, but in a five-person group 10 unique interpersonal relationships exist. In addition, a main reason people form groups is to get something done, to accomplish a task, which is not usually the main reason for forming interpersonal relationships. Compared to public communication, such as giving a speech, small group communication is more informal and spontaneous. In a public speaking situation, usually the speaker's role (speaking) is clearly differentiated from the audience's role (listening), but in a small group these roles are interchangeable. In addition, a public speaker usually has planned his or her remarks, whereas a small group member responds relatively spontaneously to the group interaction. In a small group verbal feedback is immediate, but it is usually delayed in a public situation, although much nonverbal feedback is instantaneous in both contexts. However, group members may find themselves in various kinds of public presentations, and some of these, such as symposiums, involve group member speeches. These will be discussed in Chapter 11. Finally, intrapersonal communication, the communication that occurs within an individual human being (such as thinking and self-talk), is always present in all communication contexts, including small groups.

## GROUPS AND TECHNOLOGY

When we have talked about communication in groups, we have specified face-to-face communication. Most small group communication research studies small group dynamics when members are present with each other in the same place and time. However, technology is becoming a critical component of how group members communicate and has modified how we define *group*. Some groups blend face-to-face communication with computer-mediated communication, while others never meet face-to-face. Often, such groups do have a sense of belonging and identity, have a shared purpose, and do their work through the exchange of signals—both verbal and nonverbal (e.g., in the form of emoticons, which we discuss in Chapter 4). More importantly, members of computer-mediated groups often perceive themselves to be part of a group. They find ways to work around computers' limitations by conveying *social presence,* or the extent to which computer-mediated communication is socially and emotionally similar to face-to-face communication.[24]

John Cragan and David Wright, two small group theorists, call groups that use technology **cyborg decision-making groups.**[25] The machine, or cyborg, part of these groups includes audiovisual equipment, computers, e-mail, and interactive software.

Four different meeting environments are possible with technology. The most common meet in the "same time and place" and may use an LCD projector or even interactive software to facilitate discussion dynamics. The second type of meeting is the "different time but same place" meeting. Members of a group work alone with stored group messages and may do things like coordinate work problems across different shifts (e.g., emergency room nurses). The third cyborg meeting occurs when group members communicate with each other at the "same time but not face-to-face." A small group from a class may coordinate an assignment outside of class by talking with each other on a conference call or in a chat room. Electronic bulletin boards illustrate the fourth kind of cyborg meeting: "different time and place."

We will address the impact of technology on small group dynamics throughout the book. Thus, we consider many computer-mediated groups in our definition.

# Classifying Groups by Their Major Purpose

How a specific small group functions in part reflects the purpose for which the group exists. We have classified small groups according to the reasons they exist.

## PRIMARY OR SECONDARY GROUPS

Many small group writers accept the theory proposed by psychologist Will C. Schutz that three major forces motivate human interaction. These are the needs for inclusion, affection, and control. The first two concern needs for belonging and caring from other people. The third, control, refers to the need for power or control over the world in which we exist, including the people we encounter.[26] A group is classified by sociologists as primary or secondary depending upon which of these needs is the major reason it exists.

### Meeting Member Needs and Handling Membership Changes

**APPLY NOW**

The membership of Best Friends has changed over the years. Some of the people who started the group have moved on to other things while new members have found their place at Best Friends. Membership changes can present unique challenges to a group.

1. Why might a member who was initially fully committed to a group's goals and willing to work hard on behalf of a group choose to leave the group?

2. Why might a new member choose to join?

3. What challenges does member fluctuation present for group members, existing and new?

4. What can current members do to make new members feel welcomed and part of the group?

**GLOSSARY**

**Primary Groups**

*Groups formed to meet primary needs for inclusion and affection*

**Primary Groups.**    **Primary groups** form to meet the first two types of needs, inclusion and affection. They may accomplish work, but that is not their primary objective. Loving, caring, avoiding feelings of loneliness, sharing, feeling cared about—these are the motives for which we willingly give up some freedom as individuals to be members of primary groups. We are all familiar with families, friendship groups, sororities and fraternities, drinking buddies, cliques, gangs, and those many small groups that seem to form spontaneously to meet interpersonal needs for inclusion and affection. As we mentioned earlier, your family is probably your first group and mirrors, in many ways, the many groups you belong to now. The communication patterns you learned in your first group likely affect the way you communicate in groups now.[27] In addition, many of the needs that were met by your first group are now met by other groups you belong to.

**Secondary Groups.**   **Secondary groups,** or task groups, exist mainly to meet control needs: solving all sorts of problems. A secondary group may create or implement a plan (solution) to provide control. Control, in this sense, may include supplying physical needs, such as providing water, food, and shelter to victims of Hurricane Katrina, preventing the spread of AIDS in sub-Saharan Africa, or combating global warming, or even more mundane matters such as fixing a flat tire or designing a computer program to organize recipes. This book is mostly about secondary groups. Task forces, committees, work crews, quality circles, and learning groups are all secondary groups.

No group is purely primary or secondary in its functioning (see Figure 1.1). Primary groups encounter and solve problems. Secondary groups supply members with a sense of inclusion and often with affection. In fact, sometimes the most productive and satisfying secondary groups have strong primary components, such that members feel included, appreciated, and even cared for. Think of the best group you ever belonged to. Chances are, not only was this group productive, but you also formed close friendships with the other members. Most likely, a number of your psychological needs—for inclusion, affection, and control—were met. Our motives for joining groups are often mixed; we may want to participate in solving a problem, but experiencing pleasure in the interaction with others is also a main reason for our involvement.[28]

## TYPES OF SECONDARY GROUPS

Secondary groups tackle a range of tasks. They may be formed for one specific job or a variety of related tasks. Examples include support groups, learning groups, organizational groups (such as committees, work teams, self-managed work teams, and quality control circles), and activity groups.

**Support Groups.**   **Support groups** exist to help members understand and address personal issues or problems. Support groups may be called therapy or personal growth

**FIGURE 1.1    Groups with Both Primary and Secondary Characteristics**

Purely primary — Purely secondary

Family · Close friends · Poker club / Ski club · AA support group · Therapy group · Class project group · Learning group · Committee at work · Quality circle · Task force · Production group groups. Regardless of what they are called, their purpose is not to solve a problem *as a group* but to help individual members address or solve personal issues or cope with personal problems. Groups based on the well-known 12-step process developed by Alcoholics Anonymous are examples of support groups, as are groups such as breast cancer support groups, anger management groups for abusive spouses, and so forth. The premise of these groups is that individuals can better understand and cope with their own problems if they interact with others with similar problems.

For example, one of our friends, after completing treatment for ovarian cancer, started a support group—only the second such group in Missouri—for women diagnosed with the same disease. The treatment prognosis for such women is usually not optimistic, so Joy believed it was especially important for such women to support each other. She felt the need to talk with others who had been through the same experience, particularly those women whose treatments had been successful. But more importantly, she was eager to share her experiences and her message of hope to women newly diagnosed. In another example, during the aftermath of the World Trade Center attacks on September 11, 2001, police officers, firefighters, and rescue workers assembled in New York City. Although these people came to help rescue efforts and clean up the devastation, they also provided emotional support to each other and to shocked New Yorkers. Primary and secondary functions were equally important.

The easy availability of computers has made it possible for people to form support groups of members who never meet face-to-face, yet who experience strong support and comfort from their computer contacts. In a recent study comparing online and face-to-face

*"O.K., who else has experienced the best-friend relationship as inadequate?"*

For more information on finding groups on the Internet, go to the Online Learning Center at **www.mhhe.com/ adamsgalanes7** support groups, Kevin Wright found that people benefited from both types.[29] Online groups have the advantages of providing 24-hour access, greater participant diversity of experience and information, and freedom to discuss risky topics. The online support networks also tended to be larger, thereby providing members with more resources. Interestingly, the online support groups did not evolve into face-to-face groups.

## Learning Groups.

**Learning groups** of many sorts, as we mentioned earlier, exist to help members understand or control events in their lives and the world around them. Your class is a learning group (probably a large one) that may be further organized into several small learning groups. Learning groups of people from preschool to retirement age discuss all sorts of interests. Study groups are types of learning groups. So are cohort groups; many universities group students into cohorts, whose members enter a particular program together and stay together throughout their course of study. Cohorts are encouraged to study together and to help each other learn, much like the group of young doctors in *Grey's Anatomy*. In a study of adult undergraduate learning cohorts, researchers found a significant relationship between the level of group development and the individual achievement, measured by grade point average, of the members.[30] Not all groups achieved equally, which further emphasizes the importance of understanding group communication and development.

Although this book does not specifically focus on support or learning groups, learning is a first step in many problem-solving groups, and personal affirmation and support are crucial by-products of effective group interaction in all kinds of groups.

## Organizational Groups.

Organizations such as corporations, schools, agencies, legislatures, bureaus, large departments, hospitals, and even social clubs create problem-solving groups to serve them. **Organizational groups** include any such problem-solving group formed within the context of a larger organization.

### Committees.

Most **committees** are created by larger organizations to perform a service for the organization. The organization commits a problem or task to the small group (committee) created for that purpose. For example, at Kathy's university, a fact-finding committee was asked to investigate the possibility of establishing an honor code and report its findings to the faculty and president. Occasionally, a special committee is empowered both to select a plan and to execute it, though in most cases problem-solving committees do not go beyond making recommendations. Instead, they are usually advisory, reporting to an executive or a board that has final authority and responsibility for deciding. A different committee is created to carry out the chosen plan, or an individual may be assigned to execute the solution. Committees in organizations may be standing, ad hoc, or conference.

A *standing committee* is a permanent committee. Often, an organization's bylaws include a procedure for creating it and a description of its purpose and area of freedom to act. For example, a membership committee may be responsible for recruiting new members and for screening the applicants' qualifications. "Standing" implies that a committee continues indefinitely. However, its membership is usually changed by election or appointment on a periodic basis.

*Ad hoc committees* are created to perform one special assignment and then go out of existence. The end product might be a report of findings or recommended solutions—for example, evaluations of several sites for a new plant or suggestions about how to cut

---

**GLOSSARY**

**Learning Groups**

*Secondary groups whose members meet to understand and learn about a particular topic*

**Organizational Groups**

*Groups created by organizations, usually to solve organizational problems*

**Committee**

*A type of secondary group that performs a specific service for an organization*

costs. This report is often delivered in writing and orally to the person(s) who created the special committee. A couple of years ago, one of us headed a faculty ad hoc committee formed to prevent the loss of a department's graduate program. This committee put together a plan to build the graduate program, which included a newly designed graduate curriculum, a plan for recruitment, and the policy for a newly formed department graduate committee. This plan was presented orally and in writing to the dean of graduate studies. Its work thus completed, the committee disbanded.

Such groups are often called task forces, with members selected because their knowledge and skills are thought necessary to do the group's work. Presidents have created many task forces to investigate and make recommendations on such national concerns as illegal drug traffic, acid rain, the condition of national parks, health care, waste in government expenditures, and disease epidemics.

*Conference committees* are composed of members who represent other groups that must find common ground to accomplish their work. For example, the U.S. Senate passed the Patient's Bill of Rights. However, that bill did not become law as it stands. The House of Representatives crafted its own version of a Patient's Bill of Rights that differed in key respects from the Senate's bill. A conference committee composed of both representatives and senators formed to reconcile differences in the two bills. We will use the term *conference* to refer only to such groups of representatives, never as a synonym for committee or task force.

**Quality Control Circles.**   American, foreign, and multinational companies (such as Xerox, Procter & Gamble, Westinghouse, Ford, General Motors, Dow Chemical, and Paul Revere Insurance Group) use **quality control circles.** *Quality control circle* or *quality circle* is a generic name for small groups of company employees who volunteer to tackle any issue that may affect job performance. All such circles are concerned with the quality and quantity of their work output and attempt to improve their competitiveness with other organizations. They can be found in all types of organizations, ranging from manufacturing and service organizations, to state governments, to school systems, to voluntary organizations, and sometimes to individual families. They help involve employees in the organization's decision-making loops.

If instituted properly, quality circles can improve company effectiveness by increasing worker productivity, identifying quality control problems and possible solutions, and enhancing worker involvement. For instance, quality circles helped one international hotel chain cut losses on unused fruit baskets by over $5,500 per quarter.[31] However, for quality circles to produce these kinds of benefits, careful planning is required. The organization must prepare before introducing quality circles and train employees in how to participate.

However, a number of problems can occur with quality circles. Sometimes unions see them as a ploy to increase production without improving wages or benefits. Managers can be threatened if they perceive that suggestions from quality circles undermine their managerial prerogatives. Quality circle programs stagnate if the company fails to act promptly on suggestions provided by the quality circle or explain why a suggestion is not being implemented. Quality circles often work best in conjunction with an overall organizational development program that supports the concept of employee participation.

**Self-Managed Work Teams.**   Sometimes called autonomous work groups or modules, **self-managed work teams** are groups of peers who manage their own work schedules and procedures within certain prescribed limits. Members are highly trained and cross-trained—each is able to perform several tasks for the team. The process is similar to having a team of people building a house: "When you need more carpenters, the painters can put down their brushes and pick up hammers for a couple of hours. Or the carpenter goes and helps the plumber when he's behind."[32] Not only is this efficient, but it also helps workers develop a variety of skills and reduces boredom and frustration. Self-managed work teams have been used with great success at such companies as Procter & Gamble, Sherwin-Williams, GM, and TRW.

A self-managed work team elects its own leader, who is a co-worker, not a supervisor or manager. The leader acts as a coordinator, not a boss. The organization establishes the work group's area of freedom, but often these groups have a great deal of latitude in how they operate. Some work groups establish their own schedules and annual budgets, prepare their own reports, develop specifications for jobs and procedures, solve technical problems that occur while completing jobs, and even prepare bids in attempting to attract new company business. For example, at one office furniture manufacturer, the custom-orders team has complete authority to bid jobs under $10,000, custom-design the furniture for the client, and schedule its manufacture. For complex jobs the whole team goes to the client's office to listen and offer suggestions. The team's success has made the custom-order portion of the business extremely profitable.[33]

### What's in a Name?

**APPLY NOW**

The SC Johnson Company has a meeting-intensive culture that has spawned its own vocabulary to describe various kinds of meetings. *Generals* are weekly one-on-one meetings that bosses hold with their subordinates. *Nice-to-knows* are optional informational meetings that employees often skip, and *huddles* are meetings designed to provide quick updates.

  **1.** What kinds of group meetings do you attend?
  **2.** What nicknames would you give to them?

Companies that have effectively instituted such programs report that self-managing work teams have a 20–40 percent edge in productivity over more traditional work systems.[34] They require less supervision and surveillance, produce higher-quality products, have less lost time, and generally produce high morale and job satisfaction.

## Being an Ethical Group Member

Throughout this chapter we have emphasized how important it is for you to understand small groups so you can be a valuable participant in them. You want to be the kind of group member others can count on, thus making the small group experience a satisfactory and successful one for all members. In most small group communication classes, we have found one or two project groups plagued by irresponsible members who want credit

**GLOSSARY**

**Ethics**

*Standards and rules for appropriate group member and leader behavior*

for the work but are unwilling to do their share of the work. They fail to show up for meetings, they miss report deadlines, they disappear with essential information, or they are absent from rehearsals for presentations. Such individuals are the biggest source of animosity among group members and are responsible for derailing many projects. Other problem members include bullies, know-it-alls, and individuals who are just plain insensitive to the needs of others.

Ideally, everyone in a group wants to be a member others can count on. Groups require collaborative, cohesive behavior from members. Members thus need to know the kind of behavior that is expected of responsible, ethical members. **Ethics** refers to the "rules or standards for right conduct or practice,"[35] that is, what is considered appropriate behavior in certain contexts. Our professional association, the National Communication Association, has developed a credo that describes guidelines for ethical communication in all contexts (see Figure 1.2). We have used this credo as the basis for developing principles of ethical communication in small groups. The way you communicate with fellow group members has consequences for yourself and others, sometimes vital consequences. The way you interact with each other determines, in large part, whether your groups succeed or fail and whether your group outcomes are winners or train wrecks. Therefore, you must pay attention to whether your communication in groups meets the standards of ethical behavior we present here. In a small group, ethical behavior concerns members' willingness to communicate, treatment of fellow members, treatment of information, and commitment to the group.

1. **Members must be willing to communicate and share ideas, information, and perspectives within the group.**

   Groups succeed because several heads are better than one. However, this advantage will not be realized if group members are unwilling to speak up or engage in group dialogue. Being silent deprives the group of your voice. Even if you do not feel comfortable talking, there are multiple ways to contribute, such as encouraging other members, being attentive during discussion, and volunteering for work that needs to be done outside of meetings.

2. **Group members should treat their fellow members with respect and consideration.**

   If members are to respect each other, they must operate from the belief that all group members have the same rights. Egalitarian attitudes encourage all members to contribute fully to the task at hand and value good ideas no matter who contributes them. To do otherwise undermines the potential effectiveness of the group. If members do not contribute their voices and resources to a group because they fear being scorned or belittled, then the discussion process is derailed. Treating others with respect is a cultural value embedded in our democratic traditions and is the right thing to do. Even when members disagree with each other, they should learn to do so without being offensive or personalizing the disagreement.

3. **Group members should use their best critical thinking skills when they evaluate information, ideas, and proposals in a group.**

   They should evaluate information in a thorough and unbiased way. Earlier, we noted that an advantage to group processes is that members can correct each other's misinformation and faulty reasoning. In fact, it is unethical for them *not* to do so,

| **FIGURE 1.2** | **National Communication Association Credo for Ethical Communication** |
|---|---|

Questions of right and wrong arise whenever people communicate. Ethical communication is fundamental to responsible thinking, decision making, and the development of relationships and communities within and across contexts, cultures, channels, and media. Moreover, ethical communication enhances human worth and dignity by fostering truthfulness, fairness, responsibility, personal integrity, and respect for self and others. We believe that unethical communication threatens the quality of all communication and consequently the well-being of individuals and the society in which we live. Therefore we, the members of the National Communication Association, endorse and are committed to practicing the following principles of ethical communication:

We advocate truthfulness, accuracy, honesty, and reason as essential to the integrity of communication.

We endorse freedom of expression, diversity of perspective, and tolerance of dissent to achieve the informed and responsible decision making fundamental to a civil society.

We strive to understand and respect other communicators before evaluating and responding to their messages.

We promote access to communication resources and opportunities as necessary to fulfill human potential and contribute to the well-being of families, communities, and society.

We promote communication climates of caring and mutual understanding that respect the unique needs and characteristics of individual communicators.

We condemn communication that degrades individuals and humanity through distortion, intimidation, coercion, and violence, and through the expression of intolerance and hatred.

We are committed to the courageous expression of personal convictions in pursuit of fairness and justice.

We advocate sharing information, opinions, and feelings when facing significant choices while also respecting privacy and confidentiality.

We accept responsibility for the short- and long-term consequences for our own communication and expect the same of others.

SOURCE: National Communication Association. Accessed January 6, 2007: www.natcom.org/nca/Template2.asp?bid=514

because decisions are only as good as the information and reasoning on which they are based. Perhaps the lives of the *Columbia* space shuttle crew could have been saved had NASA officials paid attention to safety warnings more thoroughly and with less bias. Tragically, important information about the structural integrity of the shuttle was ignored. Group members must make a conscientious effort to find and present all relevant information and points of view, must not falsify data or information, and must evaluate all the information in an objective manner. This is the heart of effective group problem solving.

4. **Members must demonstrate a commitment to the group.**

   For as long as they are in the group, members should place the good of the group ahead of their own individual goals. Committed, responsible members are highly involved in the activity of the group. All members are needed, and there is no room for freeloaders. If a group you belong to makes a decision you cannot support, then it may be better for you to leave the group. Some people are unable or unwilling to commit to a group, and they make horrible team members. Committed members support the group's actions and decisions, even if they sometimes are not what any one member would do alone.

Remember, groups exist because members' identities are intertwined with a recognized and valued group identity. Group member communication matters because it affects other members as well as the group. Whenever you are faced with choosing how to behave in your small group, following these four principles should help you. Stand back and consider the impact of your communication on others and the group because membership in groups is not only about participation but also about observation. We turn now to the participant-observer perspective.

## The Participant-Observer Perspective

Earlier, we asked you to consider all the groups to which you belong. Even as you learn about the principles of communicating in groups from reading this book, you will continue to be a member of these groups. We hope you will want to use the principles and techniques you learn to improve the functioning of your groups. This means that you will be in the role of a **participant-observer,** someone who is a regular member of the group and, at the same time, actively observes the group and adapts to its processes and procedures. This is especially important for the group leader or leaders. Because most group members have not been trained to be effective group participants, it is especially important for you to learn something about small group communication so you can monitor the groups' discussions and help your groups perform as well as possible. A skilled participant-observer can help a group by supplying information, procedural suggestions, and interpersonal communication skills needed by the group. This is an important focus of this book—to help you become a more valuable group member as you sharpen your skills in observing small group processes.

We encourage you to become a participant-observer for the groups you are in. As you read this book, try to think of examples from your own group experiences that illustrate the principles described in the text. Start paying attention in a conscious way to the processes of small group communication. In addition, use the case study and application boxes in each chapter to improve your awareness of group dynamics. As you learn more about communicating effectively in groups, you will feel more comfortable making suggestions to serve the groups to which you belong. We provide additional information about the participant-observer and other types of observers in the Appendix.

### GLOSSARY

**Participant-Observer (Perspective)**

*A group member who participates but also observes the group and adapts as necessary*

## Would You Falsify Data?

ETHICAL DILEMMA

Your five-member class project group has been assigned to serve as consultants to another group. You are charged with observing this group, gathering data about it, evaluating the group's communication, and making recommendations to improve the group's functioning. The problem is that each of your project group members is very busy, and you're having a hard time agreeing on a time to observe the other group. Two of you are graduating at the end of the semester, and one of you, planning to spend the summer working in Europe, is scrambling to get all assignments finished in time to leave. Two members suggest making up data for your final project. The chances of getting caught are slim, and this "solution" would save you all several hours of observation and work. You personally strongly object to this form of cheating. For one thing, you don't want to chance having a plagiarism charge against you. But mainly you object to this form of lying, and you don't want to damage your relationship with your professor.

1. Do you speak or remain silent?
2. If you speak, what do you say?
3. What do you do if the entire group—except you—is in favor of falsifying data?
4. Do you talk to the teacher? Why or why not?

## RESOURCES FOR REVIEW AND DISCUSSION

SUMMARY

- People in modern society need to be able to function effectively in small groups if they want to succeed and if they want to be full participants in contemporary organizational life.

- Small group members participating in decision making create and consider more issues, correct each other's misinformation, accept solutions more often, and are more loyal to the organization than members who don't participate in decisions.

- Perceptual awareness makes a group "small"; the group must be small enough for each member to participate and for each member to be conscious of and aware of the other members.

- Groups can be classified according to their purpose. Groups can satisfy inclusion, affection, and control needs.

- Ethical group members are willing to communicate, treat others with respect, evaluate information thoroughly, and demonstrate commitment to the group.

- Participant-observers, members who know something about the small group process, can help a group succeed.

1. List all the groups to which you belong. Be sure to include family groups, friendship and other social groups, activity groups, committees, work teams, athletic teams, classroom groups, study groups, political action groups, and interest groups. Categorize them into primary or secondary groups (recognizing that no group is solely one or the other). Discuss your list with the class or in small groups.

2. Ask several individuals to define *group*. Bring your definitions to class, and together or in small groups, share those definitions. Report aspects of the definitions that are similar and that differ. Compare and contrast them to the one presented in this text. Decide, as a class, on your working definition of *group*.

3. Break up into small groups. Devise your own list of ethical standards for group members. You can do this for a general class discussion, or you can develop a class list of standards that will be used for all future group work in the class. If the class is structured around a major group project, then individual groups can create their lists relevant to the standards of the group members.

Go to **www.mhhe.com/adamsgalanes7** and **www.mhhe.com/groups** for self-quizzes and weblinks.

Committee
Communication
Cyborg Decision-Making
  Groups
Ethics
Group

Grouphate
Learning Groups
Organizational Groups
Participant-Observer
  (Perspective)
Primary Groups

Quality Control Circles
Secondary Groups
Self-Managed Work Teams
Small Group
Small Group Communication
Support Groups

**www.mhhe.com/adamsgalanes7**

Use the flashcards and crossword puzzles on the Online Learning Center to further your knowledge of these key terms.

# Groups as Structured Open Systems

## CHAPTER OUTLINE

What Is a Theory?

Overview of General Systems Theory

The Small Group as a System

Organizations as Systems of Groups

## CHAPTER OBJECTIVES

**After reading this chapter you should be able to:**

1. Explain what a theory is and why systems theory is a useful perspective for studying small group communication.

2. Define and give examples of a system.

3. Define inputs, throughput process, and outputs of a group system.

4. Explain why communication is at the heart of a group's throughput process.

5. Describe the role of the group's environment.

6. Compare and contrast open and closed systems.

7. Describe what interdependence means to the functioning of a small group system.

8. Explain the role of feedback in helping a system adapt to changing circumstances.

9. Explain why all groups experience multiple causes and multiple paths.

10. Explain why nonsummativity is a systemic characteristic of groups.

11. Explain how modern organizations are composed of networks of groups.

## The Jamaican Winter Olympic Bobsled Team

**CASE 2.1**

A Jamaican Olympic bobsled team is about as unlikely as a Popsicle stand in the middle of the Mohave Desert—but that is the true story told in the film *Cool Runnings!* With only three months to find equipment, secure financial backing, and qualify for the Winter Olympics in Calgary, Alberta, Canada, in 1988, four of the most incompatible, untrained Jamaicans come together to compete for an Olympic gold medal. Sanka is the best pushcart driver in all Jamaica; his friend Derice is Jamaica's beloved track sprinter; Yul is a moody, angry sprinter; and Junior is a wealthy sprinter who tripped both Derice and Yul in the Olympic track qualifiers. Junior's mistake cost Derice his chance to follow his dad's legacy and compete for Olympic gold in track. Not to be denied, Derice searches for another way to try for a medal. He hears about Irving Blitzer, a former Olympic medalist in the bobsled, who believed track sprinters would make outstanding bobsledders. Irv had been stripped of both his medals for cheating and had left the sport in disgrace. Derice finds Irv in Jamaica and pleads with him to coach the first Jamaican bobsled team. Sanka signs on as a favor for his friend, Yul joins to get off the island, and Junior joins to get away from his domineering father.

This unlikely collection of three track sprinters, one pushcart driver, and a disgraced coach has no money, no sled, no ice and snow to practice on, no fan support, skeptical and cruel responses from fellow bobsledders, and animosity among team members. Any betting person would predict from these initial factors that they would fail. Even the Jamaican Olympic committee would not give them the money to go to Canada for the bobsled trials. Facing one obstacle after another, these athletes slowly emerge as a cohesive team and find themselves in the Olympics. During the last run for gold, this unlikely Jamaican bobsled team crashes before the finish line because of a loose runner on the sled. Injured but not deterred, they pick up their sled, named "Cool Runnings," and walk over the finish line to the cheers of the other bobsledders and all of Jamaica. What does "Cool Runnings" mean? It translates into "peace be the journey."[1]

The story of *Cool Runnings* illustrates several important aspects of systems theory. We will return to the story throughout the chapter to provide examples of how various elements of systems theory apply to the Jamaican bobsled team. First, we consider what a theory is, examine an overview of general systems theory, and look at how it furnishes a useful and popular framework for examining small group communication.

# What Is a Theory?

Most students tune out when they know a discussion about theory is looming. Many people believe theories are boring, irrelevant, and unnecessary. However, the truth is that all of us use theories every day, although we probably do not think about it. Em Griffin, in his introductory communication theory text, defines a **theory** as a "map of reality,"[2] something that helps us navigate unfamiliar terrain and make decisions. Like a map a theory describes relationships between elements (for example, Kansas City is 180 miles northwest of Springfield) and shows you how to get from one element to another (from Springfield, take Route 13 to Clinton, Route 7 to Harrison, and Route 71 to Kansas City). This helps make a drive from Springfield to Kansas City predictable and orderly.

Good theories are practical and reliable: You can—and do—use them to improve your decision making. For example, assume you've agreed to meet your friends for a "Thank God It's Friday" celebration, but you're short of funds. You will have to cash Friday's paycheck before you can join the group. But you know that if you wait until 5:00 P.M. on Friday, you'll be stuck in a long line at the bank's drive-through because everybody else who got paid on Friday will be doing the same thing! So you ask your boss if you can leave at 4:00 P.M. to beat the rush. You have just formulated a theory, used it to predict events, and made a decision about how to act. Your theory probably goes something like this: (1) Long lines at the bank are related to the number of people trying to deposit or cash paychecks; (2) in your city many people receive paychecks on Fridays; (3) the workday for most businesses ends between 4:30 and 5:00 P.M.; therefore, (4) you'll be held up at the bank if you wait until 5:00 P.M. to cash your check. Solution: Leave at 4:00 and beat the crowd. You have just theorized about the relationship between the day of the week, the time, and the likelihood of a crowd and taken appropriate action, and you've used your own implicit theory to help you.

There are many theories that have a bearing on small group communication. Some of these are broad in scope, which means they apply to all or most groups; other theories are more limited, applying in particular group situations or to a few clearly defined phenomena. We will discuss a number of theories throughout this book. These theories will be useful in helping you assess what is working well in a group and why, what isn't working and why, and what you might do about it. The theory we turn to now, general systems theory, is a comprehensive theory that applies to all living organisms, including social systems such as groups. We use this theory as a broad framework for organizing the many elements that constitute a small group.

# Overview of General Systems Theory

General systems theory was developed by a biologist, Ludwig von Bertalanffy, as a way to examine and explain complex living organisms. Because living organisms, including groups, are constantly changing, they are difficult to study. Only processes and relationships display any constancy. Think for a moment about your own body, one of the most complex of all organisms. Although it appears to operate as a single unit, in reality it is composed of many smaller units that work interdependently to sustain your life. For example, when you walk across the room, your muscular, skeletal, nervous, circulatory, and respiratory systems all cooperate in moving you to your destination. Even if you are sitting still, your body is involved in constant activity—your eyelids are blinking, your heart is beating, you are breathing automatically, and so forth. Your individual cells constantly change as they take in nourishment through the blood, restore themselves, and excrete waste through the cell walls. This complicated, continuous process is hard to capture. Fortunately, systems theory provides us with a way of examining and describing how a system's parts are interrelated, even while they are continuously changing. Systems theory reminds us that when we want to understand any living entity—such as a group—we not only study its component parts but also examine how the parts operate together to understand the organism as a *whole*.

Although a group is composed of individual members, those members are *inter*dependent; each one influences and is influenced by the others. When the members start to interact, they form a social system that becomes an entity of its own, distinguishable from all other groups. The members' shared patterns of communication create and maintain a unique group culture that constantly evolves as the members interact to complete the work of the group. We explore this interaction in depth in subsequent chapters.

Systems theory has helped social scientists, family therapists, business professionals, and others by providing a useful framework for looking at groups. Many individual elements affect the dynamics of a group—the reason the group was formed, the personalities of group members, the information members have, the type of leadership, the way the group handles conflict, and how successful the group has been in accomplishing its

*"I guess we'd be considered a family. We're living together, we love each other, and we haven't eaten the children yet."*

Social systems are composed of interrelated parts. © The New Yorker Collection; 1995 Sam Gross from cartoonbank.com. All Rights Reserved.

### GLOSSARY

**System**

*A set of elements that functions as a whole because of interdependent relationships*

assigned task, to name only a few. *But no single element functions alone;* the elements interact continuously. Systems theory concepts warn us not to oversimplify our description of group interaction. All parts interact to produce the entity called a "small group."

Characterizing a group as a social system was a significant advance in small group communication theory. The assumption that *communication* connects the relevant parts of a system is fundamental to understanding a small group as a system. This moves the role of communication to the forefront of small group theory. We now take a closer look at the underlying principles of systems theory.

# The Small Group as a System

Several concepts are important to understanding a small group as a system. We will use the Jamaican bobsled case study we presented at the beginning of the chapter to illustrate these concepts.

## DEFINITION OF A SYSTEM

A **system** consists of elements that function interdependently. The system, in our case a small group, also functions interdependently with the environment in which it operates as part of a larger system. Not only is a group made up of several elements that influence one another, but the group also both affects and is affected by its surroundings. The systems components—such as the members of a group—are interdependent, mutually influencing one another and also the environment in which the group operates. Without mutual influence the group is merely a collection of parts with no interdependence.

Think back to that unlikely Jamaican bobsled team (see also Figure 2.1). Several elements and their unique interaction affected the team. Consider first the members themselves, with their various abilities. A winning bobsled team needs a driver and three strong runners to push the sled—and this team had them. Sanka was loyal to Derice and was, after all, the best pushcart driver in all of Jamaica. Yul was strong and fast. Junior was also quick and sharp. And Derice was born to compete in the Olympics—both fast and driven.

A second element was the team's game plan. For example, how should the coach match these abilities with the various positions? Should the pushcart driver be the driver of the sled? The team's first conflict involved this very issue. Sanka thought he should be the driver, yet the coach pointed out that the driver had to be focused at all times and was responsible not only for the course but also for the lives of the others. So Derice was selected as the driver, and Sanka became the brakeman. The other two were the middlemen.

The third element was the leadership within the team. Derice, for instance, had to figure out how to manage the hard feelings between Yul and Junior. In addition, Yul had a personal motive that had nothing to do with the team—he wanted to use the "team" to get off the island.

The fourth element was Irv's ability to assess the team's competency, earn members' trust, and motivate them to find their own style of sledding. Notice also the interaction of the team with its surroundings. The attitudes of the Jamaicans, their families, other Olympic bobsledders and coaches, as well as the media, at first thwarted then later inspired the team. In return, the team's success influenced the entire country of Jamaica and the rest of the winter Olympic community.

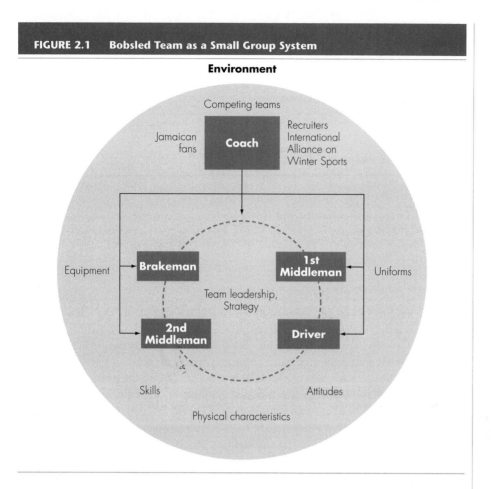

**FIGURE 2.1    Bobsled Team as a Small Group System**

## CONCEPTS VITAL TO UNDERSTANDING SYSTEMS

To understand systems theory, you need to understand four basic concepts true of all systems: inputs, throughput processes, outputs, and environment. Our explanations of these are based on scholarly work by Daniel Katz and Robert Kahn.[3]

**Inputs.**    Elements involved in a group's dynamics can be classified into three broad categories: inputs, throughputs, and outputs. **Inputs** consist of all the factors—people, information, energies, and other resources such as computer programs designed to facilitate group problem solving—that are brought into the group from the outside (see Table 2.1). Inputs are the "raw materials" that initially form the group and that are used by members to perform their work. For example, the abilities of the bobsled players—whether they were smart or not, whether they were relatively fast or slow, how well they "read" the subtle nature of the course—were all input characteristics that the players brought with them to the group and that influenced how well the team performed during a run. Other inputs included the instructions on how to synchronize the movements of all four bobsledders and their sled, the continuous stream of information that Irv gathered about the strengths and weaknesses of opposing teams, the three-month

| TABLE 2.1 | **Examples of Small Group Inputs** | |
|---|---|---|

| **Members** | **Resources** | **Environmental Factors** |
|---|---|---|
| Personalities and characteristics (e.g., age, gender) | Information about task | Physical surroundings |
| | Knowledge and expertise | Degree of support from parent group or organization |
| Needs | Time available for group work | |
| Attitudes | Tangible resources (e.g., money, materials) | |
| Values | Computer software | |
| Abilities and skills | | |

time limit they had to qualify for the Olympics, and the attitudes of the team members toward each other, the sport, and their coach.

Perhaps your class has been divided into groups to complete a group project. Examples of inputs to your project group include the group's purpose (beginning with the assignment your instructor gave you), the members' attitudes toward the project, the abilities and experiences of the members, the information members have or are able to find about the topic, and the physical or social features of the environment that may affect the group, such as classroom noise that makes it hard to hear other members.

**Throughput Processes.**   The **throughput processes** are the activities the group engages in as it goes about its work (see Table 2.2). These activities transform the inputs into something else by doing something with them, just as a car manufacturer turns the inputs of metal, plastic, and rubber into a car. A group's throughput processes refer to *how* the group works, including how roles, rules, and leadership develop; how members handle conflict; and how members evaluate the information they receive. Communication is *the* central activity in this transformation process. During this activity members are aware of one another; are simultaneously sending, interpreting, and receiving messages designed to influence; and are affected by one another. For example, it is through communication that a group receives information (an input), then discusses that information, argues about its credibility, and finally decides to incorporate it into the final report. The discussion, debate about credibility, and process of deciding to include the information are examples of the group's throughput processes.

In our bobsled team example, the coach's placement of Derice as the driver instead of Sanka, the obvious choice, is an example of a throughput process. The informal leadership of Sanka, whose enthusiasm motivated the other members, was also part of the team's throughput processes. Significant for this team was how Yul and Junior reconciled their differences and developed a mutual respect across socioeconomic lines.

In another example, members of your classroom group may have developed the habit of examining critically all the information they bring to meetings and arguing openly before

| TABLE 2.2 | **Examples of Small Group Throughput Processes** |
|---|---|

**MEMBERS' BEHAVIORS**

Degree of encouragement for presenting ideas

Demonstration of members' willingness to work

Dogmatic or otherwise stifling behaviors

Methods of expressing and resolving disagreements

Degree to which cohesiveness is expressed

**GROUP NORMS**

Support for using critical thinking skills to test ideas versus uncritical acceptance of ideas

Support for open disagreement versus suppression of conflict

Support for relative equality among members versus strict hierarchy

**COMMUNICATION NETWORKS**

Extent to which each member talks to every other member

Extent to which participation is distributed evenly

**STATUS RELATIONSHIPS**

Type of leadership

Degree to which power and influence are shared

**PROCEDURES**

Communication

Decision making and problem solving

Method for implementing solutions

they reach any decision. This style of handling conflict is an example of a throughput process. Thorough and critical evaluation of information will have a different effect on the group's decisions than if the members uncritically accept any and all information.

Recall from Chapter 1 that all four ethical principles for group members are anchored in the National Communication Association's Credo for Ethical Communication and demonstrate how effective communicators interact. Whether you are showing a willingness to communicate, displaying respect for others, critically assessing information, or demonstrating commitment to your group, you are engaging in a variety of *communicative* behaviors—all four standards are grounded in *what* and *how* you communicate to others. Group communication is the focus of Part Two of our text.

**Outputs.**    **Outputs** are the "results," the products of the group's throughput processes (see Table 2.3). They include tangible outcomes, such as decisions the group has made and

**GLOSSARY**

**Outputs**

*Those tangible and intangible products or achievements of the group system emerging from throughput processes*

| TABLE 2.3 | Examples of Small Group Outputs |
| --- | --- |

| Tangible Outcomes | Intangible Outcomes |
| --- | --- |
| Reports | Feelings among members (cohesiveness, trust; disharmony, dislike) |
| Recommendations | |
| Solutions and decisions | Personal growth of members |
| | Personal satisfaction of members |
| Physical objects (e.g., table decorations, assembled cars) | Modifications in throughput procedures (e.g., alterations in the status relationships, use of different conflict resolution strategies) |

written reports. However, they also include less obvious results, such as cohesiveness, member satisfaction, personal growth of individual members, and changes in the group's structure. In our bobsled example, a clear result of the members' respect for each other was, although not a gold medal, pride in themselves and adulation from their country. Other outputs included the sledders' increased cohesiveness and new skills, Junior's independence from his father, Yul's pride in the team, and Derice's realization that a gold medal does not make one a whole person.

Although we hope that the outputs of a small group's interaction are positive and helpful, some outputs are destructive to both the group itself and the organization that established the group. Hasty decisions, dissatisfaction of group members, and shoddy products are examples of destructive outputs. Harmful group outputs are like toxic waste, dangerous to everyone involved, including the organization to which the group belongs.

Input, throughput, and output elements are interdependent. Small group systems are evolving, changing all the time. Outputs thus reenter the group system as inputs affecting throughput variables and influencing new outputs. For example, if a group member enters the group unwilling to communicate to other members, this input affects the overall group communication by creating a climate of suspicion (throughput), which leads to low group satisfaction among other members (output). The members' subsequent lack of commitment to each other becomes a new input variable, which continues to destroy the group's climate (throughput), leading to a group report that is never finished (output). This downward pattern will continue unless group members notice the problems and adjust their communication to change the climate of the group. We will take up the issue of group feedback after we discuss the relationship a small group has with its environment.

**Environment.**    A group does not exist apart from its surroundings, or **environment,** which consists of everything outside the group that affects the group. Groups are not like lead boxes that keep things from getting in or out. The "walls" between a group and its environment are porous, allowing information in and out as well as providing the opportunity for mutual influence between the group and its environment. In our example, the Jamaican fans and the other bobsledders influenced the team's morale and enthusiasm. Notice also that the team affected its environment as well. When the other bobsledders discovered the courage of this Jamaican team, their disrespect turned into support, and those who had rejected the coach for his past cheating accepted him back into the bobsled fraternity.

Your classroom group's immediate environment is the classroom. Your group is affected by whether the classroom is pleasant or ugly, noisy or quiet. In addition, what your friends in other classes say or do may cause your group to change a procedure, a topic, an approach, and so forth. These friends and their classes are part of your group's environment, too.

The effect of a group's environment, or its context, is an important but understudied factor in how well a group operates.[4] The small group system is linked to its environment, which in turn affects communication processes within the small group itself. To understand a small group in depth, we must consider the group's environment. Linda Putnam and Cynthia Stohl, two leading scholars of group communication, call this a **bona fide group perspective.**[5] They emphasize that groups not only are influenced by their environments but also help *shape* those same environments. This interdependence occurs for several reasons. First, members of groups often belong to other groups that simultaneously influence and are influenced by them. Second, groups typically have to coordinate their actions with other groups within the same parent organization or across organizations. Third, there is frequent internal and external communication over interpretation of group goals, the extent of the group's authority, and support for group actions that helps define a group's accountability for its task. Finally, members bring to their groups a variety of interests, ways of speaking, and mental models of effective group problem solving. This in turn affects how members create their sense of "group."

All group interaction directly and indirectly reflects this back-and-forth relationship between the group and its environment. For example, a student group on campus decided to investigate traffic safety when a student was killed crossing a street on her way to class. Although the group had not known the victim, they wanted her death to result in positive actions that would make the campus safer. The student's death—part of the group's environment—was the catalyst for motivating the group to act. The street where the student died, bordering the east side of the campus, was under control of the city; the students did not have the authority to decide, on their own, what safety measures should be taken, but they could recommend various courses of action. The group's written report and recommendations were summarized in an oral report given to on-campus groups that included staff from the offices of Student Affairs, Administrative Services, and the president. In addition, several off-campus groups, including the city offices of Planning and Development, Traffic Engineering, and Street Maintenance, heard the group's presentation and received the written report. These groups—also part of the student group's environment—had to be persuaded to adopt the group's recommendations before any changes could be implemented. In order to produce a compelling report, the group had to research local and state laws about changing street configurations and present their information professionally, in the format preferred by these various groups. The city ultimately accepted the students' recommendations to build a retaining wall down the center of the street and reduce the speed limit. The group's work thus brought about a lasting change to its environment. This story illustrates the complexity of group work and the mutual influence operating between a group and its environment. Nowhere is this complexity of interconnected group work seen more clearly than in modern organizations, yet this interaction between a group and its environment is often ignored.

## Bona Fide Groups: The Jamaican Bobsled Team

**APPLY NOW**

The Jamaican Olympic bobsled team was not an isolated group, separate from its environment. As a bona fide group it was connected to its environment, and vice versa. Four reasons explain the interdependence between this bobsled team and its environment. Using the information from the case study at the beginning of the chapter, surmise possible answers to the following questions:

1. For each member of the team (sledders and coach), what were all the possible groups these individuals could belong to while they were members of the team (e.g., the coach was a banished member of the Olympic bobsled fraternity)?

2. Bona fide groups are faced with coordinating their actions with other groups. Considering the list of groups for each member of the team, what actions would have had to be coordinated (e.g., Junior was supposed to leave the country and attend school to be an accountant)?

3. What kind of internal and external communication about team goals, team authority, and support existed for this team (e.g., the governing body of winter sports disqualified the team after it successfully qualified)? With each example, discuss how the communication impacted the group.

4. How was the unique nature of *this* Olympic team shaped by the interests and past team experiences brought to it by each member?

Once you have compiled some answers to these questions, examine the complicated manner in which this bobsled team was interdependently connected with its environment.

Benjamin Broome and Luann Fulbright asked real-life group members within larger organizations to list which factors hurt their group efforts.[6] They found that organizational factors beyond a group's control often had strong negative effects on the group's performance. For example, three categories emerged: individual (e.g., member motivation and interest), group (e.g., group leadership), and organizational (e.g., assistance from the organization, including continuing informational support as needed). These findings emphasize the complexity of the group process and suggest that outcomes depend on input factors relating to members, on throughput processes such as leadership, and on environmental factors often beyond the group's control. This and other studies of actual organizational groups support the overall utility of the systems framework, which remind us to pay attention to the group's environment.[7]

Interestingly, for groups dealing with complex tasks in a very uncertain environment, how often members interact with others in the surrounding environment is more crucial to their performance than how they communicate within the group.[8] This demonstrates how important it is for groups to match their internal abilities to process information with the external informational demands of their environment.

Most of the research in small group communication has focused on groups whose members meet face-to-face with easily identifiable environments (e.g., an office space or a small group course). We began to speculate in Chapter 1 about how traditional group processes may change when members do not meet face-to-face and do not communicate with each other in real time. In our global world many companies now collaborate on tasks with the help of computer technology that allows the members of multiple groups to interact with each other without being on the same site. For instance, the Boeing 767 airplane is the result of collaboration among Boeing engineers, who designed the fuel system and cockpit; Aeritalia SAI engineers, who developed the fins and rudder; and multiple Japanese firms, whose responsibility was the main body of the plane.[9]

Modern organizations are also rapidly changing. More and more, they are composed of employees who may not work in the same place or at the same time. Some employees belong to **virtual groups** whose members complete most or all of their work without meeting face-to-face. Members of such groups may work online at the same time or participate in telephone conference calls for their group work, or they may work asynchronously, at different times, as each individual's schedule permits. The group's "location" is actually an electronic network of members who may see each other infrequently or perhaps not at all. Members of these work groups may contact each other only via electronic mail (e-mail), text messaging, or videoconferencing. Some of these virtual groups contain members from different organizations who form a temporary alliance to attain a particular purpose.[10] These groups commonly appear in such industries as telecommunications, aerospace, auto manufacturing, electronics, and computers. For example, MoveOn.org is a liberal advocacy group with a membership in the millions,[11] but this organization does not have an office. A small staff works from the home in different cities by communicating mostly by e-mail and instant messaging.

Bona fide group theorists have begun to study such virtual groups. They posit that collaboration is primarily a communicative phenomenon. How then do group members manage their roles, multiple contexts, boundaries, and tasks when they perform most of their work without meeting face-to-face? Traditional small group concepts are thrown into new light. For instance, traditional groups manage their knowledge internally and can more easily find out where to get needed information; in contrast, virtual groups often assume tasks that are so innovative and multidimensional as to be beyond the knowledge of any member. In addition, members may have no clue whom to contact for information. In collaborating groups, members have loyalties and responsibilities to other groups and organizations, which can reduce their commitment to the collaborating group. Formal positions of power (for example, chair, secretary, vice-chair) often don't exist, which means that power positions must be continually negotiated. Decision-making procedures are often created internally in traditional groups, but, in virtual groups, such procedures are affected by the norms of parent companies, cultural changes, orders given by external agents, and even decisions made outside the group. For example, UNIX, a computer desktop environment, is the result of collaboration among a variety of computer companies. Any decisions made by one or more of those companies on products unrelated to UNIX could have affected the decisions made during the UNIX collaboration.

**GLOSSARY**

**Virtual Group**

*A group in which members do not communicate with each other in the same time and place*

## CHARACTERISTICS OF SYSTEMS

The paragraphs that follow describe several important characteristics of social systems, including groups. These characteristics help explain how a system functions, both inter-nally and with the surrounding environment.

**Open and Closed Systems.** Whether a system is relatively open or closed is determined by the amount of interaction the system has with its environment. A **closed system** (we know of no completely closed human system) has little interaction with its environment, whereas an **open system** has a great deal. The model in Figure 2.2 illustrates

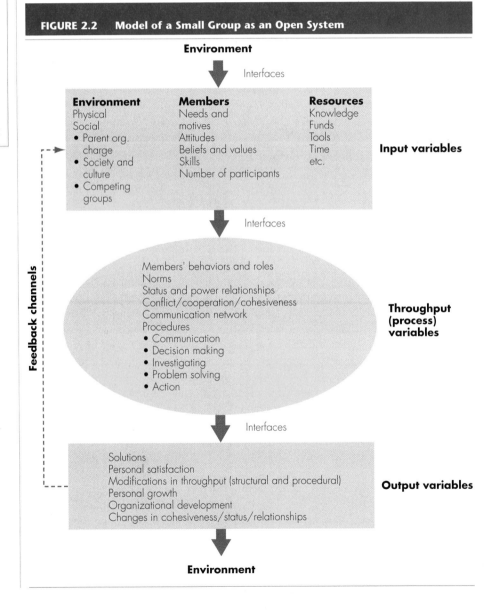

**FIGURE 2.2 Model of a Small Group as an Open System**

Environment

Interfaces

| **Environment**<br>Physical<br>Social<br>• Parent org. charge<br>• Society and culture<br>• Competing groups | **Members**<br>Needs and motives<br>Attitudes<br>Beliefs and values<br>Skills<br>Number of participants | **Resources**<br>Knowledge<br>Funds<br>Tools<br>Time<br>etc. | **Input variables** |

Interfaces

Members' behaviors and roles
Norms
Status and power relationships
Conflict/cooperation/cohesiveness
Communication network
Procedures
• Communication
• Decision making
• Investigating
• Problem solving
• Action

**Throughput (process) variables**

Interfaces

Solutions
Personal satisfaction
Modifications in throughput (structural and procedural)
Personal growth
Organizational development
Changes in cohesiveness/status/relationships

**Output variables**

Environment

**Feedback channels**

that inputs entering an open group system are worked on and communicatively transformed during the throughput process to be sent out from the system as outputs. The model also illustrates that the environment's response becomes feedback that is recycled to the group as further inputs. The group-environment interchange should be apparent from the model. The fact that the United States is an exceptionally open system made it easier for the 9/11 terrorists to enter the country, train as student pilots, and travel freely from state to state. Groups too are open systems experiencing varying levels of interchange with their environment. Our bobsled team had a moderate amount of interaction with its surroundings. The team was affected by the fans' reactions, and the fans and general public were influenced by the team's successes as well. Your classroom groups also experience degrees of openness with their environments. You may not learn what another group has been doing until group presentations because its members had little interaction with other class members and the instructor. Other groups may often interact with each other in class, getting ideas from those outside groups, and may meet regularly with the instructor to clarify requirements for group projects and presentations. These groups choose more open exchanges with their environments.

Openness has advantages and disadvantages. For example, some American companies, resisting the changes brought by "outsiders," prefer to stay as closed to outside influence as possible. This enables managers to maintain more control over what happens internally, but it also cuts off the company from information that might improve its operation and profits. Classroom groups that remain relatively closed in an effort to control information may miss valuable information and ideas that could have improved their critical thinking. Groups that choose to be more open with their environments may have more information to coordinate and may run the risk of becoming overloaded; however, they can take advantage of that information in their critical thinking and in carrying out their task.

Openness and free interchange with the environment are distinct advantages for most groups. For example, Pacific Gas & Electric (PG&E), a large utility company in California, engaged in a planning and marketing process that deliberately solicited customer feedback at every step in the process.[12] Called "Voice of the Customer," the process first sought to determine how satisfied PG&E residential customers were with the company's overall service, which services customers felt were most important, and how the company might improve its services in those key areas. Among other things, customers complained about being kept on hold for a long time, experiencing unpredictable scheduling of service, and being transferred to several offices in the course of solving a problem. The company's restructuring of its service delivery processes, accomplished in teams of employees, sought and used customer feedback throughout the process. Success with the residential pilot program led to the same approach with business and commercial customers. PG&E deliberately increased its openness to consumers, with profitable results.

**Interdependence.**   **Interdependence** refers to the fact that each element of a system simultaneously influences and is influenced by the other elements. Just as the system as a whole is affected by its environment, so are the system's individual components affected by each other. Geese fly farther *together* than any individual bird can fly. They can do this by taking advantage of the draft each bird's wings create together. Within small groups one element, idea, behavior, or person can change the functioning of the entire group. In our bobsled story, we saw how the sledders' abilities determined, in part, the coach's strategy, and how the personality of individual players such as Sanka, the eternal optimist, could spur a team to greater effort, which in turn increased the likelihood of team success.

Another characteristic of interdependence among elements of a small group is the interdependent goal toward which all group members work. The members of the group rely on each other as they strive to reach their objective; one member cannot reach the objective alone. As with the bobsled team, group members win and lose as a group. Sports teams cannot have one member win and the rest of the team lose. So it is with most small groups as they work to accomplish a task as a group. If one member is to achieve the goal, then all members must achieve it. For example, if your project group is required to give a presentation to the rest of the class, the goal is reached for all members when all are satisfied with the completed presentation. Interdependence is a key characteristic to look for in determining whether a collection of individuals has become a group.

## The Influence of Computer-Mediated Communication on the System

Go to
**www.mhhe.com/
adamsgalanes7**
for additional
weblink activities.

**MEDIA AND TECHNOLOGY**

The integration of technology, and the potential for various modes of computer-mediated communication (CMC), has begun to influence the way we view small group systems. Technological advances have increased the potential for group members to interact more freely with the environment by opening the lines of communication between those inside and outside of the group. For instance, an input such as the time a member can allocate to the group has become less restrictive as technology has allowed interaction any time or place. The Internet also has increased group access to information about the task (i.e., search engines), increased the flow of information (i.e., e-mail and instant messaging), and allowed for telecommuting opportunities (i.e., netmeeting and group computer software systems). What other group inputs described in this chapter may be enhanced as a result of an increased reliance on technology? What about throughputs and outputs?

Although each of these resources functions to create a more open group system, integration of technology also has a variety of drawbacks that may discourage its use. Think about how the types of inputs you bring to the group (personality, abilities, and expertise) are influenced by your physical presence. If you were relegated to working off-site for a group meeting, would it be possible for you to exert the same input? In an examination of telecommuting, Mallia found that individuals using this approach lose status within the group. They also reduce their prospects for upward mobility in an organizational hierarchy chain because of the lack of face-to-face interaction. Can you think of other disadvantages that may result for a group or organization fostering CMC interaction?

To learn more about the advantages and disadvantages of the integration of technology into an organization or group, visit **www.gilgordon .com** for a comprehensive list of available resources on the subject.

**Feedback.**   One valuable feature of human systems is that they are able to adapt to changing conditions and circumstances. In part, they can do this through the use of **feedback,** the part of the system's output that is returned to the system as input. Feedback enables the system to monitor its progress toward the goal and make corrections when needed. In our bobsled story, Irv saw that his arrangement of sledders was successful. This feedback indicated that what he was doing was working, so he didn't need to change their positions. In another example, during practice runs and after studying pictures of the course, Derice made adjustments in the team's movements for more successful runs.

As we pointed out earlier, open systems interact freely with their environments. Feedback is the environment's response to a system's output. Coming in the form of information or tangible resources, it helps the system determine whether it needs to make adjustments to reach its goals. For instance, the critical response you receive from your instructor on group assignments provides your group with information on how well you are accomplishing your group task. Your project group can assess this information and decide which changes need to be made and how they should be made. The uncertainty group members experience motivates them to seek feedback and gives the feedback its value.[13] You might ask, Are we on the right track? Did we select the best service organization to work with for our project? Is our group report comprehensive enough? Are our meetings getting us anywhere? These and countless other questions reflect the uncertainties in group work and prompt you to search for feedback to help you answer the numerous questions raised during group work.

However, not all feedback is equally useful. Group members evaluate feedback along various dimensions including characteristics of the feedback and the source of the feedback.[14] Is the feedback relevant, clear, and accurate? More importantly, the group must judge the information relevant to its task. Clear, accurate, and relevant feedback is more beneficial to a group than feedback that is ambiguous, false or not grounded in sound reasoning, or irrelevant.

Critical feedback, regardless of its clarity and accuracy, is hard to give and receive. However, it is necessary for effective group problem solving. The best way to give it is to sandwich it between favorable feedback and pose it as a *group* issue, not a personal one.[15] For example, assume that Irv noticed that the bobsled team was not bonding enough to be a championship team. Rather than tell members he was disappointed in them, he could have asked them how they could work together to be more cohesive. He might have done this by first sharing with them how much their track speed had increased, then observed that, when pressed, they seemed to fall apart, but that they had become closer than when they first met as a group of individuals interested in going to the Olympics. The critical observation that they seemed to fall apart under pressure was sandwiched between two more favorable observations.

Feedback is evaluated by its content as well as its source. Originally, Irv did not have much credibility with his bobsled team because he had left the sport in disgrace. His feedback about who should play what role on the team and how members should work toward the medal was not received well initially. He had to earn the team's respect for his feedback to have any credibility. Groups receive feedback from a variety of sources and must ascertain how trustworthy it is, how responsive it is to the needs of the group, and what is the status of the person giving the feedback.[16]

For more information on multiple paths in a tangled web, go to the Online Learning Center at **www.mhhe.com/ adamsgalanes7**

**Multiple Causes, Multiple Paths.**     One feature of all living systems, including small groups, is complexity. This complexity and the fact that group members have choices about their behaviors make it impossible to predict where a group will end up. The concept of *equifinality* (literally, "equal ends") suggests that groups can start out at very different places but end up at the same place. For example, the bobsled team with which we began this chapter held its own with more experienced groups. The factor of experience didn't seem to matter because the Jamaican team ended up performing well. The concept of *multifinality* (literally, "different ends") suggests that groups starting out the same may end up in very different places. For example, given two experienced, successful sports teams, one may end up losing many of its games while the other wins a championship. Too many variables and moment-to-moment decisions can lead the groups in different directions, even if both started out similarly.

It is important to remember that, with groups, many factors combine to produce the final outcome, a concept we refer to as **multiple causes.** As an example of multiple causes, the Jamaican bobsled team had high morale at the end of the Olympics. This occurred for several reasons: They became medal contenders, the country supported them, they had a leader who was well liked and effective, and all the members contributed to the team's success. Too often, individuals try to pinpoint a single cause for a group outcome. For example, you may have heard someone say, "We would have come up with an excellent proposal if our chair had listened to our suggestions. As it was, everybody hated the group." The behavior of the group's chair certainly contributed to the group's low morale, but other factors probably had an impact as well. Perhaps members did not like each other, the task was not an interesting one, or the group did not have sufficient time or information to do its best. All these factors likely interacted to produce the dissatisfaction.

A related principle of groups is that there is usually more than one appropriate way to reach a particular goal or endpoint. This principle is indicated by the concept of **multiple paths.** For example, there are a number of ways to plan a fun party, and a variety of ways to develop a respectable undergraduate curriculum for communication majors. Which is the "right" way? Various ways are right—the most effective approach depends on the characteristics of all the participants. Also, the concept of multiple paths implies that two or more groups could come up with similar solutions to a problem, even though each group had members with different abilities and areas of expertise, leadership styles, and ways of resolving differences of opinion. Like multiple causes, the concept of multiple paths encourages us to recognize the complexity of small groups.

**Nonsummativity.**     **Nonsummativity** refers to the concept that a system is not the sum of its parts. Sometimes, as with the Jamaican bobsled team, a small group performs better than the sum of its parts, and sometimes it performs much worse than expected. The Los Angeles Lakers were favored to be the National Basketball Association's 2004 champions—even at the start of the season. They had arguably the two best players in the league and had acquired two other outstanding players. Yet they lost to the Detroit Pistons, a team whose roster did not match the Lakers' in talent or salary. How could this be? A small group is an entity of its own and takes on a life of its own, so it can perform better—or worse—than anyone predicts.

Small group researchers have long been aware of this phenomenon. Groups often achieve an *assembly effect,* or a positive synergy, in which the output is superior to the averaging of the outputs of the individual members. For instance, we heard a television story about a Tucson, Arizona, Little League team called the Diamondbacks that won the 1998 championship, 26–0. What was so unusual about this team winning the championship? The team was made up of all the kids who were not picked for the other teams, the "leftovers"! On the other hand, groups can often experience what some have called *process loss,* or negative synergy. For example, even groups of intelligent, knowledgeable individuals can make an extremely poor decision, such as the NASA scientists and managers who decided to launch the space shuttles *Challenger* and *Columbia* on their fatal trips.

## CNN's Reporting Disaster: What Happened?

**APPLY NOW**

CNN, during its premiere of *NewsStand: CNN & Time,* a television news venture with *Time* magazine, reported in the lead story, "Valley of Death," that the United States had used lethal nerve gas in 1970 as part of a secret mission to kill American defectors in Laos. This report was broadcast June 7, 1998, on *NewsStand: CNN & Time* and reported in *Time* despite several oral and written complaints from journalists in both news organizations questioning the validity of the story. A military consultant resigned in protest. On July 3, 1998, the *Fresno* (California) *Bee* reported CNN's retraction of the story by Tom Johnson, CNN News Group chair, president, and CEO. Johnson admitted to serious faults with the broadcast and apologized, saying that CNN was not able to confirm the story. *Time's* managing editor admitted that he, too, could not confirm the story.

A group of television producers and print journalists conducted 200 interviews as they worked together for eight months on the story. The group was headed by two successful producers and included an award-winning documentary producer and a Pulitzer Prize–winning journalist. An independent investigation into the validity of the story concluded that the group members had not intentionally made up the story. Instead, the reporting team drew conclusions based on questionable evidence, led sources into thinking that their suspicions could be supported by unseen evidence, and made decisions based on interview responses to a variety of hypothetical questions. The CNN investigation concluded that those involved in putting together the story so firmly believed what they were reporting that they ignored information contrary to what they were finding.

How could a team of talented individuals, after an eight-month investigation and in the face of cautionary criticism, produce a report that ended in people being fired, resigning, and facing reprimands—not to mention embarrassing two highly respected news organizations? Using the concepts of open and closed systems, interdependence, feedback, multiple causes/paths, and nonsummativity, develop your own "systems" explanation for this reporting disaster. You can do this in groups or as a class.

Although no one knows exactly why one group experiences positive synergy and another negative synergy, it may have something to do with how much ambiguity the group faces, whether the group encounters obstacles during its problem-solving process, and how it deals with those obstacles.[17] The Jamaican team faced numerous obstacles: a short time in which to train and qualify, little money, members with no experience, a country with no snow, a coach lacking respect, ridicule from others, ouster from the Olympics, possible loss of one member, and the list goes on. Yet the team members worked together to overcome each obstacle, finding new pride in themselves and their own style of sledding. Communication among members is the key to making the most, instead of the least, of group members' abilities. Group members must understand the problem-solving process and be taught how to use communication that facilitates effective discussion and problem solving.

Systems theory's contribution to small group communication research and to our understanding of the process of small group interaction is obvious. However, the theory is not without its detractors. Any theory is a human construction and therefore limited in scope—it gives *a* particular view, not *the* view. Some, for instance, have questioned whether systems theory research is merely a descriptive framework but not a useful explanatory one.[18] Others take issue with the systems theory assumption of *homeostasis,* or dynamic balance—the idea that systems are self-maintaining and work toward keeping on track. This emphasis on balance, some argue, draws attention to system stability rather than change. However, we have chosen systems theory as our theoretical framework because of its centrality in small group research and its focus on patterns and wholes. Even so, you should know that it is but one theory used by scholars to understand small group communication.

# Organizations as Systems of Groups

Much of the work of both corporate and nonprofit America is done in and by small groups. Most organizations are interlocking systems of groups (see Figure 2.3). Think for a moment of how automakers design, build, and market their cars. Although many individual engineers are involved in the design of specific car parts, an engineering team is typically responsible for seeing that the individual parts come together into a car that works the way it is supposed to. Decades ago a single manager could oversee the production of cars, but today manufacturing teams have that responsibility. Marketing, too, is a complex activity that usually involves a team of researchers, artists, copywriters, photographers, and other specialists.

In companies such as Kraft and Procter & Gamble, for example, many employees work in self-managed teams to design, produce, and market their company's products. In addition, quality control circles and special project teams are composed of individuals from numerous departments and divisions. Many other products could not be manufactured and many types of services could not be offered without the functioning of large systems composed of interdependent small groups.

You can see from these examples that complex organizations have small groups as primary components. The principle of larger systems being composed of many subsystems (progressively smaller groups) has many important implications. First, knowing something about how groups function and how to be an effective group member is essential if you hope to survive and prosper in modern society. Second, because there are so many parts

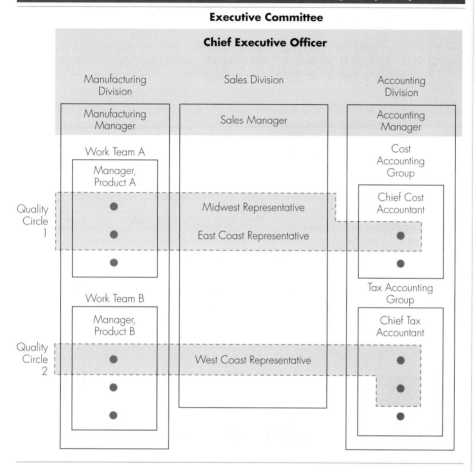

**FIGURE 2.3    An Organization as a System of Interlocking Group Subsystems**

to a system, careful coordination and extensive communication among the parts are essential. The individual groups within an organization must find ways of sharing information with each other to avoid duplicating effort or allowing important matters to fall through the cracks. This spotlights the central role of communication, both within each group and among groups, to the effective functioning of modern organizations and society. This extra-group communication has received relatively little attention from researchers, even though it is very important to the long-term survival of the group.[19]

The usefulness of the systems perspective should be clear. We can use that perspective to help us identify and describe the individual components of groups, as long as we remember that each part functions in relation to all the other parts of the system; what affects one part affects all the other parts. This is true whether the system being studied is a person, a single group with several members, or a large organization composed of numerous interlocking groups.

## CNN and *Time* as a System of Groups

**APPLY NOW**

The previous application example describes the rather complex system of groups that can make up the modern news organization. CNN, or the Cable News Network, together with *Time* produced *NewsStand: CNN & Time*. Both CNN and *Time* are owned by Time Warner. Using this information, and the information in the previous application example, construct your own diagram of the system of interlocking group subsystems. Then discuss the role of "extra-group" communication in this example. What went wrong? At which level? What could they have done differently? Is there a way to guarantee a valid, successful story all the time?

### RESOURCES FOR REVIEW AND DISCUSSION

**SUMMARY**

- A theory is a "map of reality" that helps us describe relationships, explain how phenomena operate, and make decisions about what to do.

- General systems theory is a useful framework for studying small groups because it reminds us that systems are complex, with all parts of the system being interdependent.

- All systems use inputs to engage in throughput processes and produce outputs. Feedback helps systems monitor their performance, which cannot be predicted by summing the individual performances of the components.

- All systems try to survive by adapting to changing conditions. Open systems freely exchange resources with their environments, but closed systems do not.

- Modern organizations can be pictured as complex systems of interlocking and interdependent small groups.

**EXERCISES**

1. Bring to class a box of toothpicks and glue. Take out 12 toothpicks and use the glue to create some form out of the toothpicks. After you have finished, display your creation. Discuss all the creations and the concept of nonsummativity. Then move from discussing toothpicks to behaviors and from creations to small groups.

2. Select classmates to form one primary group: a family. Select parents, children, and any other members you want. Then select members of the class to be other individuals who may be involved in the family's life, such as a pastor, professor, and boss. With a ball of string, loosely connect all of these individuals to relevant individuals, and as you do so create a story about them. For instance, only one spouse may work and so is connected to the boss, the other spouse, and a parent. A child may be connected to only one parent, and so on. Then instruct the various individuals to role-play their parts by

periodically pulling on the strings and requesting something of the individual. Use this activity to show the concept of interdependence.

3. Bring a large muffin to class. Use the muffin to discuss inputs, throughputs, and outputs. Make a list of the inputs for making the muffin. Discuss the kinds of throughputs necessary for the creation of the muffin, and then point out the output. Discuss how the environment

may influence the muffin. After this discussion, compare the making of a muffin, as a relatively closed system, to the creation of a group, a relatively open system. How are they similar and how are they different?

 Go to **www.mhhe.com/adamsgalanes7** and **www.mhhe.com/groups** for self-quizzes and weblinks.

| | | |
|---|---|---|
| Bona Fide Group Perspective | Interdependence | Outputs |
| Closed System | Multiple Causes | System |
| Environment | Multiple Paths | Theory |
| Feedback | Nonsummativity | Throughput Processes |
| Inputs | Open System | Virtual Group |

 **www.mhhe.com/adamsgalanes7**

Use the flashcards and crossword puzzles on the Online Learning Center to further your knowledge of these key terms.

# Foundations
# of Small Group
# Communicating

For groups to function effectively, they must create and sustain a solid foundation that supports members' efforts. Part Two focuses on this foundation, the communication process itself. As discussed in Chapters 1 and 2, communication is at the heart of group throughput processes, so your understanding of this process is essential. Chapter 3 presents basic communication principles you should understand to be an effective group member, and Chapter 4 focuses on verbal and nonverbal messages that constitute member interaction.

# 3

# Communication Principles for Group Members

## CHAPTER OUTLINE

Communication: What's That?

Implications for Small Group Communication

Listening: Receiving, Interpreting, and Responding to Messages from Other Group Members

## CHAPTER OBJECTIVES

**After reading this chapter you should be able to:**

*1.* Define *communication.*

*2.* List and explain the five major characteristics of communication.

*3.* Explain the three major implications derived from the five major characteristics of communication.

*4.* Explain the ethical principles relevant to understanding the communication process and improving listening behavior.

*5.* Describe the difference between listening and hearing.

*6.* List and explain the seven habits of poor listeners.

*7.* Explain why listening is active behavior.

*8.* Describe paraphrasing as a technique for active listening.

## Students for Alternative Medicine

Students for Alternative Medicine is a group of nursing students interested in alternatives to traditional Western medicine. Each month, the group sponsors a seminar, open to everyone, where the featured speaker is a practitioner of some form of alternative medicine. The group operates with a small budget and usually relies on volunteers to present the seminars; volunteers are given a token gift, such as a T-shirt with the group's logo, but are generally not paid an honorarium. The group's executive committee is responsible for scheduling and publicizing speakers.

At one meeting, member Rhea suggested that they invite Chief Robert, a Cherokee medicine man, to address the group. She further suggested that, as compensation for his talk, they buy Chief Robert a piece of equipment he wanted for his work. Members agreed that Chief Robert, a prominent local healer, deserved a substantial gift, but the equipment was expensive ($200), and paying him would set a precedent for future speakers, which the group could not afford. Wade, chair of the executive committee, said, "I don't know how we'll be able to afford something like that, though I agree that he's certainly worth the money." Rhea then said, "OK, that sounds good to me." The group went on to discuss other matters, and Chief Robert was forgotten. At their next group meeting, Sonya reported that publicity for Chief Robert's seminar was proceeding well, and the upcoming Sunday paper was planning a feature story on him and the seminar. Rhea noted how pleased she was that they had agreed to buy the chief his equipment and especially how grateful he was for their generosity. At that point the meeting exploded into cries of "What? What do you mean buy his equipment? We didn't agree to buy that for him!" Members had misunderstood each other, and as a result Rhea had obligated them to a $200 gift that would come close to wiping out their savings. However, at this point, members believed they couldn't back out. It took them several meetings to overcome their anger and begin to trust each other again.

*"Frances tells me you're a communications major."*

Scenes like this occur every day in small groups and illustrate what can happen when people fail to understand each other. To function effectively as a team, members must learn to put their thoughts and feelings into messages that other members can interpret and respond to. However, glitches can (and often do) occur in this *creating–sending–receiving–interpreting–responding* cycle called *communication.* In our example Wade said, "He's certainly worth the money." He meant, "It would be great to pay him and all of our speakers—they do such a wonderful job—but there's no way our budget can handle it, so let's stick to T-shirts." Rhea heard his words yet interpreted them to mean, "We don't have money to pay all our speakers, and it will be hard to come up with that amount for Chief Robert, but, of all the speakers we've had, he is certainly worth the expense, so we'll figure out some way to pay him." She said, "OK," meaning, "Great, I'll tell him we'll make an exception in his case." Wade heard her, yet he *interpreted* her meaning as, "I see what you mean about the expense, and I agree with you." These collective failures in message interpretation between group members cost the group time, money, and energy. Unfortunately, this misunderstanding within a small group is not unusual. We know you can think of plenty of instances you have experienced in your own groups!

The primary purpose of Chapter 3 is to help you understand in more detail communication, which is central to group dynamics. To do so enables you to think analytically and critically about communication in your groups. A secondary purpose is to help you improve your own contribution to your group's communication. Communicating effectively takes conscious thought and hard work. In this chapter and the next, we focus both on the process and on how you as a group member can communicate more effectively.

# Communication: What's That?

The word *communication* has been used in dozens of slightly different ways by different writers. We use **communication** to refer to the perception, interpretation, and response of people to messages produced by other people. There are five major characteristics to this seemingly simple definition.

## COMMUNICATION IS SYMBOLIC

Messages, including gestures, sounds, actions, and words, are symbolic.[1] The symbolic nature of communication is central to any definition of communication.[2] A **symbol** is anything (e.g., a gesture, sound, action, object, or word) that arbitrarily represents something else with which it has no natural or direct relationship. For instance, there's no natural reason we call something we sit in a *chair* instead of *pig* or *une chaise*. There is no natural reason why you have the name you do or the student group in Case 3.1 is called "Students for Alternative Medicine." In addition, most of our symbols stand for concepts that have no tangible form, such as a *relationship, cohesiveness, love,* and *democracy.* Even the concept of *communication* holds no tangible form.

There is no inherent or direct relationship between any word and what it represents. For instance, even within a single language, the same food might be called *dinner, supper,* or the *evening meal* by different people. We noted in Chapter 1 that a collection of people can be called a *collective,* a *group,* a *team,* a *collaborative,* or a *committee.* New symbols are constantly being created to represent new things or ideas: *bioterrorism, interface, identity theft,* and *user-friendly.* There is no limit to how many symbols we can invent and use to communicate. Even Homer Simpson has created a symbol for something gone wrong or something really foolish; *d'oh* has been selected for official entry into the *Oxford English Dictionary.*

Symbols, due to their arbitrary representations, are convenient for thinking and communicating because we do not need to have the items actually present to represent them to other people.[3] Groups can discuss their observations about people, places, and things without their presence. In Case 3.1 the members can talk meaningfully about a speaker none of them has met. Symbols free us from the constraints of the here and now. Group members can call up memories of past meetings to reinforce group norms, and they can fantasize about possible new directions to take as a group. Symbol use in communication allows group members to travel simultaneously in the past, present, and future. In addition, symbols allow group members to name individual and group experiences. Naming our experiences is the primary way we have of infusing that experience with meaning. The name you give your group carries with it a complex set of meanings. Small groups in our classes often think of names that tell others what topic they are working on, such as Students for Alternative Medicine. Some groups think of names that capture their unique qualities (e.g., The Researchers), and others name their groups for their goals (e.g., The A+s). Symbols allow us to engage in self-reflection because we can use all sorts of labels to describe our self-concepts and feelings. If a group member refers to another as a "leader," that label is associated with a set of assumptions for how to behave, which may come to define what the other group members expect of the labeled leader.

Symbols can take a variety of forms. Words are the most common, but we also use numbers, pictographs (such as the international signs for cars and restrooms), Morse code, emoticons such as those used in e-mail to convey feelings or objects, and gestures like those we use for *OK.*

## GLOSSARY

**Communication**

*The process of creating, sending, receiving, and interpreting messages between people*

**Symbol**

*Anything that arbitrarily stands for something else*

As convenient and helpful as symbols are, they also have liabilities. Because symbols are arbitrary, *their meaning must be interpreted.* Dangers come from misusing and misunderstanding symbols. Two people can use a symbol to represent different concepts and therefore misinterpret each other without knowing it, as Rhea and Wade did. For example, when you say, "I love you," do you mean the same thing as your boyfriend or girlfriend does? A person may believe that there is a relationship between symbols and tangible events when none really exists. In addition, a symbol can evoke different responses than a communicator intended. Liars can manipulate us easily with symbols. In what some called "tortuous linguistic negotiation,"[4] the United States in the spring of 2001 sent a carefully worded letter to China in hopes of securing the release of the crew of the downed U.S. EP-3E surveillance plane from China's Hainan Island. The Americans attempted to offer regrets to China without offering a formal apology for an incident the United States considered an *accident.* Thus, in the letter, U.S. officials used the phrase *feichang wanxi,* or *extreme sympathy,* which the Chinese interpreted as *shenbiao qianti,* or *deep apology.* Misunderstandings and multiple interpretations are likely in small group communication, which makes it necessary to monitor the communication processes in our groups more thoughtfully than we normally do in our everyday conversations.

## COMMUNICATION IS PERSONAL

Because communication is symbolic, meanings are in people, not in the words themselves. Words can and do have different meanings for different people. Even when two people agree on the dictionary definition of a word, they may disagree vehemently about what that word means to them. For instance, to your group an *excellent* group report may mean one that is free of typographical errors and turned in on time. To your teacher *excellent* may be reserved for a group report that not only is grammatically perfect but also shows considerable insight and creativity. You both are using the same word, but not meaning the same thing. This fact leads directly to the next principle of communication.

## COMMUNICATION IS A TRANSACTIONAL PROCESS

It is not a thing or state. First, let's address the notion of process. Communication is an extremely complex process involving human senses, feelings, meanings, and cultural experiences, not just a simple matter of nouns and verbs. During the process with no clearly marked beginning and end, one person experiences a perception or feeling and expresses this experience by putting it, consciously or not, into words and/or nonverbal messages, which others can perceive and respond to. Talking about communication as if it were a simple signal-response event, with nothing likely to go wrong, is naive. It is more complex than any computer circuitry.

The word we use to capture this kind of complex process is *transactional.* The communication process is often modeled with components that include a source, message, channel, receiver, and response (or feedback). Communication can be pictured as a one-way or a linear process, with feedback similar to a tennis game. The server sends the message, and the receiver lobs a response back. This is misleading, however, because communication is a *multidirectional transactional* process. We have tried to capture this multidirectional transactional process in Figure 3.1, which was inspired by a model originally created by Frank Dance[5] and by models of the double-helix structure of the DNA molecule. Pictorial models that accurately depict the communication process are notoriously hard to create

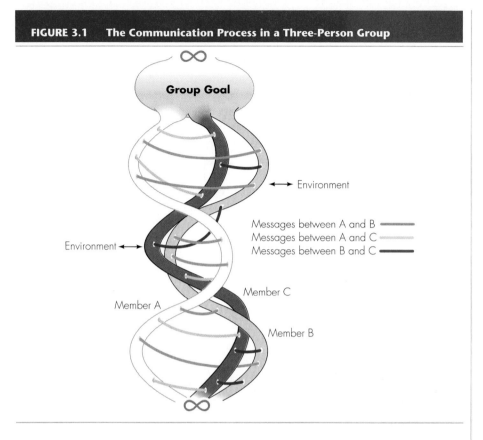

**FIGURE 3.1     The Communication Process in a Three-Person Group**

Group Goal

Environment

Messages between A and B ━━━━━
Messages between A and C ━━━━━
Messages between B and C ━━━━━

Environment

Member C

Member A

Member B

because the process itself is messy and complex. In this model three members—A, B, and C—come together (shown at the bottom of the model) to form a group with a distinct group goal (shown at the top of the model). Because group communication has no clear beginnings or endings, the infinity symbol is located at the top and bottom of the model. Each member is represented by a strand with a distinct shade, which suggests that each member brings his or her own unique personality, values, experiences, perspective, and so forth to the group. During their interaction each member sends messages to the other two members. Messages between members A and B are represented with a gray line; messages between A and C are represented by a light green line; messages between B and C are represented by a dark green line. The members are not represented as either senders or receivers because they are both simultaneously. The helix itself represents the group and is created by the interaction. Without the interaction each member would be just a separate strand, but with the interaction the strands are connected to one another, just as group members are. From the bottom up, the interaction among members keeps moving forward; it is irreversible, with each current interaction influenced by every interaction that has already occurred. Once a message is expressed, it becomes part of the group and cannot be taken back. The environment surrounds both the helix and the individual members; the double-headed arrow from the environment to the members and the group suggests the mutual influence between environment, members, and group. This model is

**GLOSSARY**

**Transactional**

*The idea that while communicating, all interactants mutually and simultaneously define both themselves and others*

itself a symbol because it stands for something else (the group communication process) and uses pictorial symbols to represent the verbal symbols describing the process. This is what symbols allow us to do!

**Transactional** has two major meanings relevant to communication among members of a small group. First, communicating is a simultaneous, multidirectional process. That is, regardless of who is speaking at any given moment, *every* member is simultaneously sending verbal and nonverbal messages that every other member (including the speaker) could potentially receive and interpret. The implication is clear: To be most effective as a group member, you must be aware of actions from all members, even when you are speaking. For example, a speaker may notice from facial expressions that group members are reacting negatively to her suggestions and thus modify her ideas as she speaks. Communication, rather than being a linear, one-way process, occurs among all members simultaneously. This illustrates the complex, transactional nature of communication.

Second, *transactional* implies that members together create mutual understanding for what words and concepts mean and that members can consciously help each other in this process. For example, consider the following exchange between a friend of ours upgrading his computer system and the computer salesperson helping him. Notice how Noah helps the salesperson help *him* understand.

| | |
|---|---|
| **Salesperson:** | You'll want to upgrade to Windows so you won't have to go directly through DOS. |
| **Noah:** | What's Windows? |
| **Salesperson:** | It's a graphic interface that makes computing a lot easier. |
| **Noah:** | Graphic—does that mean it works with pictures? |
| **Salesperson:** | Right. We call them icons. Windows interfaces between the user and the computer. |
| **Noah:** | But why would you want something between you and the computer? |
| **Salesperson:** | Well, instead of having to talk to the computer in a difficult language that doesn't seem logical to get it to do what you want, you use pictures to talk to the computer. It's more natural, more like the way people actually think. |
| **Noah:** | Oh, I see now. Windows is like a translator between me and the computer and, because it works with icons, it will be easier for me to use. |

In this instance Noah was able to get the computer salesperson to explain the concepts in ways that made sense to Noah. However, it took some careful listening on his part and a considerable amount of *transacting* for the salesperson's meaning to become clear to Noah. Meanings are not so much *re*ceived intact from each person, but instead *con*ceived or created in context between persons.

## COMMUNICATION IS A SENDER AND RECEIVER PHENOMENON

Of course, something must be sent, but if there is no receiver, there is no communication. Talking makes no sense unless someone is listening, and vice versa. If you are talking while no one is listening, no communication has occurred. Neither does it occur if you are listening for something that has not been sent. Many people believe that communication means only the sending of messages, so the best way to improve communication is to improve the quality of the messages being sent. However, paying attention only to the sending part of communication overlooks the transactional nature of communicating, especially how a person receives and interprets messages. Thus, *both* sender and receiver are responsible for the effectiveness of any particular communication as you can see in the previous example with Noah. The sender is responsible for being as clear as possible, and the receiver is responsible for attending to the sender, trying to understand what the sender means, and asking questions to help the sender clarify the message.

In fact, the last principle of the National Communication Association's Credo for Ethical Communication, discussed in Chapter 1 and displayed in Figure 1.2, speaks to this. The principle calls for all communicators to accept responsibility for the short- and long-term consequences of their communication. Whether you are sending or receiving a message, you are responsible for monitoring your communication behavior to give your

## CMC and Communication Richness

**MEDIA AND TECHNOLOGY**

Businesses and organizations are increasingly relying on computer-mediated communication (CMC). Therefore, it is important to understand how different forms of CMC influence how one's message is received. Richard Daft and Robert Lengel developed the concept of *media richness* to describe the extent to which different media reduce the uncertainty behind different types of messages. From this theoretical perspective a medium's richness is determined by four factors: the *personal focus,* or the amount of personal information the medium carries; the *medium's capacity* for immediate feedback; the *number of cues* and senses involved; and the medium's *use of natural language.* A rich medium, such as face-to-face interaction, would possess all four factors to a large extent, whereas a lean medium, such as e-mail, is much more limited in the number of cues, personal information, and immediacy of feedback afforded by the medium. The concept of media richness directs our attention more to the decision-making processes that individuals go through as they match their communication objectives to the medium that facilitates optimal understanding.

Another factor that influences the effectiveness of a medium is whether the communication is synchronous or asynchronous. With *synchronous communication* members interact in real time, and each participant is simultaneously a sender and a receiver. With *asynchronous communication* delays occur in the communication interaction, and each participant must take turns being the sender and receiver. E-mail is asynchronous communication because this medium does not allow for interactive, real-time communication between people.

SOURCE: R. Daft and R. Lengel, "Organizational Information Requirements, Media Richness and Structural Design," *Research in Organizational Behavior* 6 (1984), pp. 191–233.

Go to
**www.mhhe.com/
adamsgalanes7**
for additional
weblink activities.

group its best chance of succeeding. The communication problems between Wade and Rhea in Case 3.1 resulted from messages that were unclear as sent but were also never clarified by the receivers and thus were interpreted according to what receivers *wanted* to believe. Group members behaving ethically would have tried to clarify Wade's and Rhea's communication before it had a chance to harm the group.

## COMMUNICATION INVOLVES CONTENT AND RELATIONSHIP DIMENSIONS

For more information on the relational dimension of words, go to the Online Learning Center at **www.mhhe.com/ adamsgalanes7**

Both are essential.[6] The **content dimension** of a message involves the message's ideas or the *what* of the message. When you listen to a teacher's lecture, the content of her or his messages is what you record in your notes. When you listen to a research report from a group member, you often attend to the ideas the member is summarizing for the group. These may be recorded in the group's minutes. The **relational dimension** of a message is *how* the message is expressed and recognizes that content is never expressed in a vacuum. Every time you send a message, you express ideas, and you simultaneously express how you perceive the relationship between yourself and others present. For instance, the teacher's lecture can be given in a variety of ways: boring, passionate, exciting, straightforward, authoritative, and so forth. Does the teacher talk down to you as if you are a child who must be told what to think, or does the teacher share the information with you as if you are someone with your own valid experiences and knowledge? You usually do not write this dimension in your notes, yet you may talk about it to your friends during and after a lecture: "I really like how Professor Jones treats us like we have something to say, too," or "Man, I am insulted by the way Professor Jones treats us like we are children with no opinions worth listening to!" These same messages are processed in small groups as members offer how it is they see themselves in relation to each other through their messages. We often focus more explicitly on the content of messages; however, the relational aspects of messages are always present and just as integral to the communication dynamics of groups.

We cannot stress enough how important it is to pay attention to the relational elements of messages. Ethical communicators, according to the NCA's credo, strive to understand and respect other communicators before evaluating and responding to their messages and also work to promote a climate of caring and understanding. In small groups they avoid condemning or belittling others because that creates a toxic atmosphere preventing all members from doing their best work on behalf of the group. You cannot work creatively and enthusiastically when you are being attacked or ridiculed by others. As group members you have a responsibility to consider *how* you talk to each other. We urge you to monitor your behavior to avoid sending relational messages that poison the group's climate.

Our discussion thus far has focused on communication in traditional, face-to-face groups, but the growing use of computers for small group problem solving continues to change the nature of communication in small groups. We showed in Chapter 1 that with the help of computers, members can get messages to each other during meetings or outside meeting times. Members do not have to hold meetings face-to-face. They can be in different places and "talk" to each other simultaneously or receive messages at their own leisure. Using computers to interact with others inside or outside the group is called **computer-mediated communication,** or CMC. We will explore CMC further in

## GLOSSARY

**Content Dimension**

*The ideas or "what" of a message*

**Relational Dimension**

*The "how" of a message expressing the perceived relationship between communicators*

**Computer-Mediated Communication (CMC)**

*Any interaction via computer technology, such as chat rooms*

Chapter 4 and other chapters. CMC is a symbolic, personal, and transactional process, yet there is much we still must learn about its nature in comparison to face-to-face communication.

Although skills in expression are essential to effective small group communication, most small group members need to pay closer attention to how they *listen* and *interpret* than how they express themselves. This is true whether they are communicating face-to-face or doing so through computers. Usually, the *receiving* as well as the *relational* aspects of communication fail to get adequate attention.

## Implications for Small Group Communication

The five communication principles just described have several implications that are particularly relevant for small groups. We explain three of the most important ones here.

1.  **Making group communication productive is the responsibility of every member.**

    There is a great tendency to blame another person when a statement is ignored, misunderstood, forgotten, or not heard. "If he had just listened to me," or "If she weren't so (boring, arrogant, dominating, nasty, prejudiced, ignorant, etc.) I'd have paid more attention" are typical statements group members use to blame others and disclaim any responsibility for miscommunicating. But communication is a transactional, multidirectional activity. For example, the responsibility for glitches in the Students for Alternative Medicine's meeting was not Wade's or Rhea's alone. If you don't understand, you can (and should) say so. If you can't hear, you can ask the others to talk louder. If you failed to note an assignment for which you are responsible, you have the obligation to ask. Do not expect others to read your mind and supply you with information you are missing. In short, everyone must constantly monitor how the communication process is working and correct problems as needed.

2.  **Perfect understanding among group members is impossible.**

    Because of all the communication characteristics we discussed earlier—that it is symbolic, personal, transactional, multidimensional, and so forth—perfect understanding cannot occur. Since we have different words in our vocabularies and different experiences with words, our associations with words and gestures differ. Hence, some degree of difference in meaning always exists between two or more people responding to each other's messages. Fortunately, perfect understanding isn't necessary. In a group you need only communicate well enough to coordinate your behavior toward a common goal. When you can do this, you are communicating well enough for group success, even though you haven't achieved perfect understanding.

3.  **Disagreement and conflict are not necessarily signs of a breakdown in communication.**

    People often say that conflicts can be avoided if people would communicate better. This vastly oversimplifies the truth. Although some small group conflicts are due to misunderstandings or lack of information that might be solved through communication, many conflicts result from group members having different values, goals, beliefs, or personal objectives. (We elaborate on several of these in Chapter 9.)

## Communication and the Students for Alternative Medicine

The Students for Alternative Medicine is composed of people with a common interest: alternatives to Western medicine. It is an organized, productive group. However, as we saw, even groups composed of members with a common interest can encounter communication problems. Perfect understanding is never possible in small groups. Reflecting on the five characteristics of communication in small groups, consider the following:

1. Which symbols do you think were the most problematic for the group? Why?

2. What different forms did the symbols take in this case study?

3. Explain how there is no definite beginning and ending to their story.

4. How was the communication among the members transactional?

5. How did the group members work together to create the misunderstanding?

6. Change the script of the meeting, and show how the members together could have produced a better outcome.

7. List what you think are the content issues and then list what you believe are the relational issues expressed in how the messages may have been expressed.

8. How can the conflict between Wade and Rhea be seen transactionally, or as one with no clear cause but as mutually created by both of them?

In addition, conflict may occur not over *what* ideas were expressed but rather over *how* they were expressed. Thus, no breakdown or misunderstanding occurs—members are quite clear about what the conflict involves; in this case matters are made worse if miscommunication is blamed while the gist of the conflict is ignored.

Coordinating the efforts of group members in a functioning system is more dependent on good listening than on good speaking skills, although we often concentrate on speaking. No matter the skill of the speaker, it is the *listener* who determines whether listening will happen. A beneficial group member must be able to synthesize group sentiments and summarize a discussion cogently. But that is not possible if members were not listening well enough to recall what others said or to think carefully about what they meant. For example, at one time it was estimated that 15 million meetings occurred in the United States every morning. In just one six-person group, 30 minutes of time is wasted every time 5 minutes of information is repeated.[7] Imagine the total waste in all these groups! You can probably see why a national survey of 1,000 personnel managers identified *listening* as the second most important skill that influences their hiring decisions.[8]

# Listening: Receiving, Interpreting, and Responding to Messages from Other Group Members

If a small group is to operate effectively, members must understand each other. Listening is the central component of this process.[9] Both members and leaders of small groups must be good listeners. Members who are perceived as poor listeners are not likely to be chosen as group leaders, and leaders usually are perceived as good listeners.[10] Thus, as a good listener, you will not only be helpful to your group but be influential as well.

We have urged you to behave as an ethical communicator in a group by striving to understand others, taking responsibility for the consequences of your own behavior, and working to create an accepting climate. Listening effectively is one of the best tools you can use to accomplish these things. If you can motivate yourself to *want* to achieve better understanding of your fellow group members, the information you now provide about good listening will help you achieve that.

## LISTENING DEFINED

Many people use *hearing* and *listening* as if they were synonyms, but we agree with Lyman Steil and colleagues that **listening** is a four-step process that begins with perceiving a message, then interpreting it, deciding what it means, and finally responding to it.[11] Such listening is not passive but active. Listening is behavior over which you can exert considerable control.

Most people do not listen well. The majority of participants in half-hour discussions we observed could not list the ideas proposed as possible solutions, the major issues discussed, or the decisions reached. When we ask students to paraphrase previous speakers' ideas, more than half the time they cannot do so (and we expect that college students are not much worse at such listening than are other people). In short, most of the time individuals listen rather badly. As respondents they often give the speaker little or no overt feedback. This provides the speaker little opportunity to assess whether the message was understood as intended. This also implies that what the speaker said wasn't worth a response.[12]

Effective listening requires that the listener hear what the speaker said, interpret it accurately, and respond appropriately. Usually, hearing what the speaker said presents little problem. Group members are accustomed to asking a member to repeat a statement they weren't able to hear. However, the interpretation and response steps can be tricky because of the nature of symbolic communication we discussed earlier. Different people mean different things with the same words and actions. Major factors that influence what words and actions mean to us include our culture, gender, age, sexual orientation, learning style, and personalities. We take a closer look at such diversity in small group interaction in Chapter 6. In addition, the relational dimension of messages in groups gives members all sorts of information about how they see themselves in relationship to each other. This requires that members listen "between the lines" for this information, because it often is not directly stated but found in *how* (e.g., tone) the message is expressed. When members of the Students for Alternative Medicine expressed their displeasure with Rhea, they did so with raised voices and harsh tones. How they expressed disappointment in her behavior could have sent the message that they no longer respected her choices or did not trust what she said.

**GLOSSARY**

**People-Oriented Listener**

*A listener who is concerned about how her or his listening behaviors affect relationships*

Steps can be taken to become a more competent listener in small groups. In the next sections we describe four listening preferences and several of the bad habits of poor listeners, as well as providing suggestions for improving your listening behavior.

## LISTENING PREFERENCES

Over time and in a multitude of conversations, we all develop listening preferences. When do you enjoy listening? When is listening difficult for you? Who are the people you like listening to? What do you focus on when you listen? Why do you choose to listen? Our preferences can greatly affect the quality of communication in a small group.

There are four general listening preferences: people-, action-, content-, and time-oriented.[13] No one preference is right or wrong; each has its advantages and disadvantages. Being an effective group member means identifying your own preference and those of the other members. It also means shifting your preference to meet the needs of the group.

**People-oriented listeners** are focused on how their listening behaviors affect relationships. These are the members others go to when they want someone to listen. They are

## Students for Alternative Medicine and Listening

**APPLY NOW**

Earlier you met two members of the Students for Alternative Medicine's executive committee: Wade and Rhea. Now let's meet three other members: Sonya, Bob, and Eric. Each of these members has his or her own listening preferences, some of which may be seen in the case study. Rhea is a people-oriented listener, and Wade is an action- and content-oriented listener. Sonya is a content-oriented listener, Bob is a time-oriented listener, and Eric avoids listening situations but is required to show up and vote. Wade and Rhea do not get along at most meetings, often arguing over who should be supported by the group. Wade thinks that Rhea gets too upset when others are upset, and Rhea thinks that Wade is overly critical. Sonya is close friends with Eric, who often votes with Sonya. Bob contributes to the group only when he has something worthwhile to say and does so in a very precise fashion. He gets along well with Rhea and Sonya.

Imagine you are a community member who is interested in bringing Dr. Jessica McGehee, a leading practitioner of holistic medicine, to the attention of the group. You would really like the group to sponsor a seminar with Dr. McGehee. You also know the group is low on funds due to the most recent expenditures, but Dr. McGehee will be in town and will be available. You know a generic presentation to the group will not work, so you decide to tailor your presentation to the listening preferences of the group.

1. Whom would you select as the target of your presentation, and why?
2. What specific strategies would you use in your presentation to appeal to those you believe you need to convince most?

attentive and nonjudgmental. Their listening behaviors may include the use of *we* more often than *I*, and they incorporate emotional appeals into their discussions. For instance, they might be heard telling a human-interest story to calm members who are upset. Showing concern for others is their priority, but people-oriented listeners can attend too much to others' moods and get distracted from the group's task.

The **action-oriented listener** is focused on the job at hand. Such listeners help the group stay on task by paying attention to the details and giving feedback about the goal and how the group may achieve it. They enjoy listening if material is presented in an organized fashion. However, sometimes these listeners may appear overly critical, may tune out when the discussion seems aimless, and may interrupt too much if the discussion gets off track.

The **content-oriented listener** is drawn to the highly credible source and enjoys analyzing the things she or he hears. These listeners dissect information and can show a group the many sides to an issue. At times, though, they can be seen as overly critical and intimidating. In addition, their listening preference slows the group's problem solving because they like to spend considerable time analyzing information. They also minimize nontechnical information such as anecdotes and devalue information from unknown sources.

The **time-oriented listener** is the member who sets meeting times, reminds members of their time constraints, and discourages wordy discussions. These members value time. They discourage discussion as the time nears for the meeting to end and grow impatient with the more creative, spontaneous activities in groups.

No preference is the best. Our preferences are influenced by many factors, including the nature of the relationships among group members and time constraints. Each one has positive and negative tendencies, summarized in Table 3.1. Use them productively and curtail the negative characteristics of each one. Do this by knowing your own and the others' preferences and encouraging the productive use of each preference.

## HABITS OF POOR LISTENERS

The irony of being in a small group is that you spend more time listening, yet because you are among other people, the pressure to listen is not as strongly felt as it is when you are interacting with only one other person.[14] The more people held accountable for the success of the group, the easier it is to get away with poor listening. We all develop poor listening habits, yet effective group discussion is built around recognizing the challenges of good listening. You can do that by recognizing the listening preferences of your group and understanding several common poor listening habits, summarized in Table 3.2.

**Pseudolistening** occurs when a listener fakes active listening by giving the speaker many of the signs that good listeners give, while actually thinking about something else. The pseudolistener nods, smiles, murmurs, and often looks the speaker in the eye. However, he or she may be daydreaming, thinking up an argument instead of trying to understand the speaker's perspective, or working on a personal problem. If you can't find a way to make yourself pay attention with interest, reschedule the discussion: "I am so sorry, but I am distracted today with worry about a project that has run over budget. Could we reschedule our meeting for later in the week?"

**Silent arguing** means the listener forms a quick judgment about the speaker's idea, rejects it without listening to the rest of what the speaker says, and then begins a silent

| TABLE 3.1 | Listening Preferences |
|---|---|

**PEOPLE-ORIENTED LISTENERS**

| Advantages: | Focus on relationships.<br>Show concern for others.<br>Are inclusive and nonjudgmental. |
|---|---|
| Disadvantage: | Can become distracted by others' moods. |
| Example: | "Tell me more about how you would feel if we went ahead with that option." |

**ACTION-ORIENTED LISTENERS**

| Advantages: | Focus on the job.<br>Help the group stay on task.<br>Help the group stay organized. |
|---|---|
| Disadvantage: | May sacrifice relationships in favor of task. |
| Example: | "I know you're upset, but we have a lot of work to do so we'd better get down to business." |

**CONTENT-ORIENTED LISTENERS**

| Advantages: | Help the group analyze information.<br>Look at issues from many sides. |
|---|---|
| Disadvantages: | Seem overly critical.<br>Dismiss anecdotal or nonexpert information. |
| Example: | "We aren't ready to decide yet because we haven't really heard every side of the issue." |

**TIME-ORIENTED LISTENERS**

| Advantages: | Help the group stick to schedule.<br>Discourage rambling discussions. |
|---|---|
| Disadvantage: | May stifle creativity by expressing impatience with spontaneous discussion. |
| Example: | "Let's make up a schedule so we know we can get done by our deadline." |

mental search for arguments about what is wrong with the idea. We tend to listen to that which supports our previous beliefs and to ignore or tune out what contradicts them. You cannot listen well while silently arguing.

**Assuming meaning** occurs when the receiver interprets what the sender said or did through the filter of the receiver's culture, then proceeds to make a judgment about the sender. For example, a Native American may answer a question from a European

| TABLE 3.2 | **Habits of Poor Listeners** |
|---|---|

**PSEUDOLISTENING**
Pretending to listen while thinking about something else or while daydreaming.

**SILENT ARGUING**
Failing to understand what a speaker is saying, then mentally rehearsing objections to the misunderstood notion of the speaker's idea.

**ASSUMING MEANING**
Interpreting the speaker's behavior by using the cultural rules appropriate for the listener.

**MIND ASSAULT**
Insisting that they understand better than the speaker what the speaker meant, even though the speaker protests.

**FOCUSING ON IRRELEVANCIES**
Becoming distracted from a speaker's message by unimportant details such as dress, accent, physical appearance, or things in the environment.

**SIDETRACKING**
Changing the topic because they weren't paying attention to the speaker; not connecting remarks to statements of the previous speaker.

**DEFENSIVE RESPONDING**
Failing to listen or failing to try to understand what a speaker is saying because they feel psychologically threatened by something the speaker said or did; responding with "chips on their shoulders."

American without looking the questioner in the eye; the European American concludes that the Native American is hiding something or lying. However, looking down is a sign of respect in many Native American cultures. The European American's conclusion is in error because it is based on what middle-class European Americans do when answering questions. In other words, the Native American's behavior is being interpreted by the wrong set of rules, and a serious misunderstanding has occurred.

**Mind assault,** a stronger form of assuming meaning, involves insisting that a speaker meant what the listener would have meant by a statement and continuing to insist on this meaning despite protests from the speaker.[15] For example, "I know what you really mean. You don't think our professor will object to our topic. You just want to do something else!" assumes that the listener knows better than the speaker what the speaker meant. With this behavior the listener attempts to dominate or reject the speaker. Instead, good listeners try to understand another as that person wants to be understood, and only then evaluate the other's ideas and motives.

*"I'm sorry—did you say something? I was off creating my own reality."*

Pseudolistening is not an effective way to listen. © The New Yorker Collection; 1999 William Haefeli from cartoonbank.com. All Rights Reserved.

## GLOSSARY

**Focusing on Irrelevancies**

*A poor listening habit of focusing on irrelevancies and not on what the speaker is saying*

**Sidetracking**

*A poor listening habit of responding to another's message in an irrelevant manner*

**Defensive Responding**

*A poor listening habit of responding to another's message defensively because a threat has been perceived*

**Focusing on irrelevancies** occurs when a listener pays attention to something other than what the speaker is saying. Some people pay so much attention to dress, word choices, grammar, face or body details, accent or dialect, or things in the environment that they have little energy to give to the ideas of a speaker. For example, one of our students mispronounced a word during a group presentation. A faculty member smirked and rolled her eyes. She didn't listen to another word the student said, even though the information was valuable, because she had focused on the mistake the student had made. If you are guilty of this bad habit, constantly remind yourself to concentrate on understanding the speaker and not being distracted.

**Sidetracking** takes several forms, all of which result in going off on a tangent. The listener makes a statement that is not connected to what was previously said, thus sidetracking the discussion by starting a new topic. In the student discussions David Berg analyzed, the topic was switched on the average of about every minute.[16] The following example illustrates sidetracking by switching issues, thereby giving irrelevant responses to previous remarks:

**Pete:** We can use our time better if we split up the work. Why don't we each pick the section we want to research?

**Jean:** Did any of you guys happen to see *Borat* last weekend? [a sidetrack]

**Defensive responding** is likely to occur when a listener perceives a threat from another's remark—someone's "hot button" has been pushed. For example, you may be sensitive to the attempts of others to control or dominate what you do (shown in how the message is expressed), so, when Tony says, "Get me a Coke while you are at the machine," you reply, "Get your own blankety-blank drink!" People who listen and respond defensively usually quit trying to understand the other's point of view and thus may miss important qualifications or statements that clarify the speaker's meaning. It is especially important to guard against defensive responses when highly emotive words such as *abortion, right to life, gun control, welfare state,* and *liberal* are used. When you feel yourself getting tense and emotionally aroused, sit back, take a deep breath, and try to paraphrase what the speaker said before you express either support or opposition. That will keep you from listening or responding defensively.

In all the poor listening habits, the listener is focusing attention not on the ideas of the speaker but on something else—a physical characteristic, a habit of speech, a personal belief, a different topic, a personal definition of a symbol, a private relationship with the speaker, a personally held value, or the way the message was expressed. Where and how to focus attention are consistent problems for many, including those who are generally good listeners in other contexts.

## LISTENING ACTIVELY

Listening is active, not passive, behavior. When you pay close attention in an effort to understand what a speaker means, your heart speeds up as your metabolic rate rises. In contrast, heart rates of passive listeners who take no personal responsibility for understanding a speaker slow down. Active listening is partly a matter of choosing to focus on the other person and of selecting what parts of a message to focus on and try to recall.

A good test for **active listening** is to paraphrase (put in your own words) what you think the other person meant. Merely repeating another's words, like a parrot, does not demonstrate that you understood. An effective paraphrase requires the listener to process the information cognitively. When you paraphrase what you thought the speaker said or the relational message you inferred from how it was expressed, you give the speaker a basis for deciding whether you understood the original message adequately or whether you missed or distorted parts of it. The original speaker, after hearing the paraphrase, should accept it if it is accurate or correct the parts that were distorted or omitted, then ask you to try paraphrasing again. Only when the original speaker is completely satisfied that you have understood adequately should you proceed to agree, disagree, elaborate, or change topics. Here is a bit of dialogue that illustrates active listening between two group members discussing medical insurance:

| | |
|---|---|
| **Karla:** | Medical costs are incredibly high. On average it costs about $1,500 per day in the hospital. No wonder 37 percent of our citizens lack hospital insurance! Too many people are making too much money off the illnesses of others. We've gotta stop that! |
| **Jeannie:** | You're saying that the reason so many people lack hospital insurance is that hospital costs are high, and they are so high because a lot of people are paid too much in the health care business. Is that right? [Jeannie attempts to check whether she understands what Karla said by paraphrasing so as to clarify Karla's reasoning.] |
| **Karla:** | Well, basically, but I really don't mean people don't have insurance because the hospital costs so much, but because they can't afford it. |

### GLOSSARY

**Active Listening**

*Listening first to understand another's message before critically judging the message*

| | That may be partly because it costs a lot for the insurance—like $350 a month for a young husband and wife with no kids—and partly because the insurance companies have to pay such high hospital and other medical bills. [Karla corrects the paraphrase and clarifies her own reasoning.] |
|---|---|
| **Jeannie:** | Now let's see if I understand your thinking: 37 percent of our citizens lack hospital insurance because they feel they can't afford it. Part of the reason they can't afford it is that high medical costs have made premiums very high, like $200 a month for a young person. And a lot of people are making more money than you think they should out of the illnesses of others. [Jeannie's second attempt at paraphrasing Karla's statements.] |
| **Karla:** | Right. [Karla confirms the second paraphrase as accurate.] |
| **Jeannie:** | I partly agree and partly disagree. I think . . . [The paraphrase accepted, Jeannie now begins to explain her position on the issue about why so many people lack hospital insurance.] |

Active listeners confirm their understanding *before* they state evaluations. Then, confident of what the speaker meant, active listeners evaluate what they have understood. They may respond by agreeing or disagreeing, saying that the idea is irrelevant to the issue being discussed, that it is logically unsound, that there is no evidence to support it, and so on. In the above example, the group members are focused on clarifying the content of their messages. They could also have focused on their interpretations of how the ideas

## Poor Listening Habits and Misunderstandings

**APPLY NOW**

Reconstruct the Students for Alternative Medicine meeting. Your agenda item is the discussion of whether to sponsor a seminar featuring Chief Robert, a Cherokee medicine man and prominent local leader. Get together with six other members of the class to role-play group members. Before your discussion, hand out envelopes to each member. Four of the envelopes will contain a description of one poor listening habit (pseudolistening, silent arguing, assuming meaning, mind assault, focusing on irrelevancies, or sidetracking). The other three envelopes will instruct the member to practice active, focused listening. Allow yourselves to role-play the meeting for about 25 minutes. Ask your classmates to watch the meeting and take notes on the listening behaviors. After the meeting, discuss how the poor habits were displayed and what their impact was on the discussion.

1. Were any behaviors particularly destructive? How so?
2. How well were the members practicing active, focused listening, and did they reduce the effects of the poor habits? How typical are some of these poor habits?
3. How was the role-play of the meeting different from a real meeting?

were expressed. For instance, if Jeannie had expressed herself as someone who felt superior to the others, they might have asked if she was trying to tell them what to think or just thinking aloud with peers.

One effect of active listening is that the discussion slows down. Most of us are our own best listeners—we like to talk and, given half a chance, we will. We may become impatient, not taking time to paraphrase even when we should. You should listen actively all the time but paraphrase only part of the time—when a controversial issue is being discussed, when you can see some possibility that the speaker has a different meaning from what you think, when you are confused by what the speaker has said, and when there has been a lot of topic switching or misunderstanding. Be on guard against pseudolistening. If you realize you didn't really listen, apologize and ask for a restatement.

## RESOURCES FOR REVIEW AND DISCUSSION

### SUMMARY

- Communication is the process by which we create, receive, interpret, and respond to messages from others; this makes communication an ongoing, transactional, sender-and-receiver-oriented phenomenon for which every group member is responsible.

- Symbols, including words, are arbitrary, which makes perfect understanding between group members impossible and means that effective communication among group members is the responsibility of all members.

- Principles of ethical communication require us to accept responsibility for our part in the group communication process, first by making sure we understand the process and then by learning to listen carefully.

- Listening involves hearing a message, interpreting it, deciding what it means, and responding; group members, who typically display a number of bad listening habits, need to improve this skill the most.

- Active listening, especially paraphrasing, helps members understand others more clearly.

### EXERCISES

1. This exercise is designed to help you distinguish between viewing communication as a one-way, linear process or as transactional. Divide into two large groups. Turn to the Karla and Jeannie dialogue in the text. One group should examine the dialogue from a linear perspective. The other group should examine it from the transactional perspective. Each group can focus on the following questions:

   *a.* When does communication occur in the dialogue?

   *b.* What is the message in this dialogue? Where does the message come from?

   *c.* Who is responsible for clarifying the meaning of the message? How is clarity created in this dialogue?

   *d.* Who is the communicator and who is the listener?

   With your classmates, discuss how different the answers are to these questions depending on the approach used to answer the questions. Remember, although the approach changed how the communication/dialogue was understood, the communication/dialogue did not change.

2. Recall three recent conversations you have had. (If you are taking part in a major group project, think about three recent conversations in your group meetings.) For each conversation write down whom the conversation was with, what you talked about, how well you listened (on a scale of 1 [not well at all] to 10 [very well]), and what some of the reasons were for your good or poor listening (e.g., time of day, boring topic, preoccupied with something else). During class discussion, look for factors common to good and poor listening.

(If you apply this exercise to your group project, create a list of steps you will take to improve your listening in your next meetings.)

3. This exercise is designed to help you apply and practice active listening. Divide into groups of five or six members. Select a controversial topic and practice active listening as you discuss the topic. Remember that paraphrasing is not simply restating the previous remarks. Each group should use the following rules:

*a.* A discussant may not have the floor or add anything to the conversation until she or he paraphrases what the previous speaker has said to that speaker's satisfaction.

*b.* If the paraphrase is not accepted, the discussant may try again until the speaker accepts the paraphrase.

*c.* One member of the group should keep track of the number of times paraphrases were accepted or rejected. Each attempt should be recorded.

After the activity, discuss the difficulties encountered in active listening. Look for the benefits of paraphrasing and the problems that may be encountered. Discuss why it may be so hard for group members to understand others before contributing to the discussion.

 Go to **www.mhhe.com/adamsgalanes7** and **www.mhhe.com/groups** for self-quizzes and weblinks.

---

KEY TERMS • CONCEPTS

| | | |
|---|---|---|
| Action-Oriented Listener | Content-Oriented Listener | Relational Dimension |
| Active Listening | Defensive Responding | Sidetracking |
| Assuming Meaning | Focusing on Irrelevancies | Silent Arguing |
| Communication | Listening | Symbol |
| Computer-Mediated Communication | Mind Assault | Time-Oriented Listener |
| Content Dimension | People-Oriented Listener | Transactional |
| | Pseudolistening | |

 **www.mhhe.com/adamsgalanes7**

Use the flashcards and crossword puzzles on the Online Learning Center to further your knowledge of these key terms.

# 4 CHAPTER

# Using Verbal and Nonverbal Messages in Small Group Communication

## CHAPTER OUTLINE

Creating Messages in a Small Group

How Communication Structures
the Small Group

Using Language to Help
the Group Progress

Making Sure the Discussion Question
Is Clear and Appropriate

Nonverbal Behaviors in Small Group
Communication

Nonverbal Behavior
in Computer-Mediated Groups

## CHAPTER OBJECTIVES

**After reading this chapter you should be able to:**

1. Define the concept *message.*

2. Describe structuration theory and explain its relevance to small group communication.

3. List and explain five ways to use language appropriately in small group interaction.

4. Explain how to use abstract words effectively.

5. Describe how group members can organize their remarks.

6. Explain why it is important to use the right wording for a group's discussion question, and describe seven types of questions commonly used: information, interpretation, value, policy, action, procedure, and relationship.

7. Explain how best to phrase questions in small group interaction.

8. Describe the principles and functions of nonverbal communication.

9. Discuss the significance of the major categories of nonverbal signals to small group communication.

10. Discuss how nonverbal communication is affected during computer-mediated communication and how members compensate for technological limitations.

## The Search for a New Dean

It was the first meeting of the committee charged with conducting the search for a new Arts and Humanities dean at California State University, Fresno (CSUF). As was customary, a student representative was on this search committee along with faculty members and administrators. The committee chair used this organizational meeting to let people talk in an unstructured way about what they wanted in a new dean.

The committee discussed diversity issues and brainstormed ways that qualified minorities and women could be recruited to apply for the dean's position. Several members talked about what they perceived as a general need to increase diversity among administrators because of the large percentage of minority and international students currently at CSUF. Suddenly, Raj, the student, said, "I don't think that's a big issue because our campus is already very diverse." Simultaneously, two faculty members and one administrator exclaimed, "What?"

Feeling somewhat attacked, Raj became defensive, and the meeting threatened to degenerate into a "Yes, it is/No, it isn't" argument. When one member encouraged Raj to explain what he meant, he said, quite reasonably, that the only other campus he had ever visited was a small, church-related school in Fresno that had an even more homogeneous administration. The committee members readily agreed that, from Raj's perspective, the CSUF campus was more diverse administratively than his comparison school. Raj, in turn, agreed that the CSUF campus was less diverse than the schools, such as UCLA, Ohio State, and the University of Maryland, the other committee members were using for comparison.

This brief episode ended well and set the stage for the rest of the committee's meetings, but it could just as easily have alienated Raj and caused the faculty and administrative members to tune him out.

This story, so typical of many small group discussions, illustrates several important points discussed in this chapter. First, many words can be taken in several different ways. For instance, Raj initially responded defensively to the word *what*. He heard the word *what* as meaning, "What on earth are you saying, calling this a diverse administration?" In fact, that is what two of the members *did* mean when they said, "What?" However, the third member, as she explained later, simply hadn't heard Raj, so she said, "What?" as a question, meaning, "Could you please repeat what you said?"

Second, verbal and nonverbal behavior together contribute to our interpretation of what words mean. For example, how did Raj correctly interpret that two of the committee members intended to challenge his opinion? Probably because of the sharp, disbelieving tone of voice they used and the fact that they both whipped their heads around to look at him when they said it. Raj felt attacked because, in a way, he *was* attacked. In another example, the popular phrase "waazzzup?" makes sense only in how the phrase "What's up?" is said and when used in the appropriate context. Finally, this dean search committee story illustrates the most basic principle of all— *communication creates a group.* The verbal and nonverbal messages all group members send create the working atmosphere in the group. The type of verbal and nonverbal messages members allow determines whether the group will be cooperative or hostile and whether it will think carefully or rush to judgment. In our story members' basic goodwill and effective listening skills were able to undo the potential harm done by their reaction to Raj's comment. The group went on to be highly productive, cooperative, and cohesive—and it was the members' communication behaviors that made this happen.

In this chapter we will focus on the verbal and nonverbal messages central to small group communication. The NCA Credo for Ethical Communication, introduced in Chapter 1, directs us to try "to understand and respect other communicators before evaluating and responding to their messages." We will be examining the complexities of group messages in an effort to help you not only understand other group members better but also more effectively evaluate and respond to those messages.

# Creating Messages in a Small Group

In Chapter 3 we talked about messages members send. A **message** is any action, sound, or word in interaction that is interpreted as a whole by another person.[1] Messages can be entirely verbal, nonverbal, or a mixture of verbal and nonverbal. For instance, a nod of the head may be interpreted as agreement or disagreement. When Raj's group members challenged his opinion, they did so by saying "What?" and simultaneously raising their voices, which conveyed to Raj their disagreement with his viewpoint.

The primary way members exchange information and ideas in small groups is by the words they use. While the use of words is obvious in small group communication, verbal and nonverbal messages operate *together* to create meaning; they are indivisible. All communicative acts are expressed via multiple verbal and nonverbal channels, which together create meaning. Think of an orchestra.[2] No single note conveyed by one instrument constitutes the symphony. Notes played together via a multitude of instruments create a symphony. Meaning is found in particular combinations of notes played within a larger symphony. When you document and analyze your group's communication (symphony), you are, in fact, scoring *both* the notes (words) *and* how they are played (nonverbals).

In this chapter we will first explain how any group's communication structures and maintains the group. We will then look at the impact of verbal and nonverbal messages in group interaction, remembering that in practice they are inseparable.

## GLOSSARY

**Message**

*Signals interpreted as a whole by group members*

# How Communication Structures the Small Group

In Chapter 2 we said that communication, the verbal and nonverbal messages members exchange, is *the* essential throughput process within a small group. The way members create and maintain this exchange of messages is called **structuration.** The theory of structuration, applied to small group communication by Marshall Scott Poole, David Siebold, and Robert McPhee, is complex, but the main point is this: Verbal and nonverbal communication among members creates the group norms and operating procedures *and* maintains them once they are established.[3] Group members' communication influences both the content of a discussion and the relationships among members.

The theory contains three important assumptions. First, group members do not come to a group with a clean slate about how to behave. They have been taught what is appropriate by their general culture, by their participation in other groups, and by the organizations they belong to. For example, the faculty and administrative culture at CSUF encourages people to treat each other politely and with respect. Thus, when members of the search committee realized that Raj felt attacked, they were motivated to undo the harm they believe they had created. The members brought into this *particular* group a broad norm, from their common CSUF culture, about how people should behave in groups. Notice also that the group members' attempt to repair the damage had a particularly potent effect on the *relationship* element of their communication within the group. This group was beginning to develop into a respectful, safe group within which members could share ideas. The more members continued to behave respectfully, the more that standard of behavior became entrenched: "This is how we operate in our group."

Second, although people pick up rules and standards for behavior from the general culture, there is no law that forces them to follow those rules. Individuals may choose to ignore norms and rules for behavior. For instance, even if the search committee members knew that Raj felt attacked and that norms of politeness required them to try to heal the breach, they could have decided just as easily that his opinion didn't matter: "Well, he's just a student. He hasn't seen any of the world, so who cares what he thinks." In that case members wouldn't have bothered to take the time to repair the damage; the group's atmosphere would have evolved differently, in both relationship and content terms. Raj would have felt uncomfortable, but so would the others, who then might have hesitated to speak up for fear that someone might attack *them*. The group, then, would have missed out on what could have been productive ideas and suggestions.

The third important assumption of structuration theory is that the group is never finally created; instead, it constantly re-creates itself through communication so that it is always in a state of becoming. Thus, change usually happens incrementally. The search committee's meeting when Raj felt attacked was the committee's first meeting, but what if the meeting had been the tenth meeting, with the norm of attacking members well established? Because group members would have been more set in their communicative ways, it would have been much harder (although not impossible) to move the group to a respectful path. That's what structuration is all about—how communication creates and maintains the group over time.

We especially like the communicative focus of the theory of structuration; it reminds us to look at members' communicative behavior—what they say and do in the group. For instance, Raj didn't feel attacked because he had a paranoid personality. He felt attacked because of the communicative behavior of the other members. Similarly, the other members attempted to rebuild bridges with Raj when they said things such as, "I'm sorry, Raj; I didn't mean to sound so sharp. Why do you think CSUF has a lot of diversity? Tell us about the other campus you visited." Again, it was the communicative behavior that changed an incipient norm, that it's OK to attack others verbally in this group, into a more productive one, that active listening is this group's standard of behavior. We now turn to a discussion of how group members use language to communicate.

# Using Language to Help the Group Progress

Human language consists of symbols—verbal and nonverbal—and rules for using them. The verbal code is the vocabulary, or the set of words, available to the person who uses the language. In print, nonverbal elements include punctuation marks, underlining, *italics,* CAPITALIZATION, **boldfacing,** and s p a c i n g. The rules are the spoken and unspoken guidelines for arranging words: what to capitalize, how to space, where to place punctuation marks, and so on. Collectively, these are the rules of syntax and grammar. Both the codes and the rules vary according to social contexts; communication rules differ for an online chat group, a formal meeting of a city council, and a Jamaican bobsled team. Small groups will use their own rules and codes during group meetings, but they must also learn how to adapt them for group presentations to others. These rules are outlined in more detail in Chapter 11. Suggestions for using language effectively are detailed in the following section and summarized in Table 4.1. The suggestions are followed by an example of using language carefully to word an appropriate discussion question that gets the group started off right. The suggestions in the table and the discussion that follows are appropriate generally for most task groups in the United States. As we will note in Chapter 6, however, different rules apply in different cultures.

## When to Code Switch and When Not to?

We have proposed the necessity of adapting to the different rules for communication, or code switching, when the context of the social system changes. A characteristic of communication competence is being aware that different groups use different rules of communicating and being able to change to meet the expectations and obligations of those different groups. However, the various ways we use language to communicate is highly personal and often resistant to change.

1. When you move from group to group, how easily do you adopt the rules of communicating in that group?
2. Are there times when your personal way of communicating should not be given up?
3. Are there appropriate ways of blending both your own personal style and that of the group?
4. Is adapting to the rules of communicating in a particular group a violation of personal language use?

| | |
|---|---|
| **TABLE 4.1** | **Using Language Appropriately to Help the Group Progress** |

**FOLLOW THE RULES OF STANDARD ENGLISH**

**1.** Use standard sentence structure and vocabulary.

**2.** Use correct grammar.

**3.** Avoid jargon, excess slang, and profanity.

**ADJUST TO THE SYMBOLIC NATURE OF LANGUAGE**

**1.** Guard against bypassing.

**2.** Be as precise and concrete as possible.

**3.** Give specific examples of what you mean when you have to use an abstract term, or use synonyms.

**USE EMOTIVE WORDS CAUTIOUSLY**

**1.** Recognize words that are likely to trigger strong emotional responses in others, and substitute neutral words.

**2.** Never use name-calling.

**ORGANIZE YOUR REMARKS AND THE GROUP'S DISCUSSION PROCESS**

**1.** Relate your statement to the preceding statement.

**2.** Make one point at a time.

**3.** State your case directly and concisely.

**4.** Keep yourself and other members on the topic.

## FOLLOWING THE RULES

Because different groups and cultures have different rules for communicating, you will increase your chances of being accepted and understood if you follow the rules for the group. For example, some groups are formal: Members address each other by title (e.g., Dr. Adams or Ms. Galanes) and use many abstract words with a complex sentence structure. However, these rules would be inappropriate in a self-managed work team in an auto factory, where concrete language with a clear and concise sentence structure is more effective. Virtual groups have even created a language of their own, using abbreviations to save time: <u>LOL</u> (laughing out loud), <u>IMHO</u> (in my humble opinion), <u>TM</u> (text me), and so forth. Be aware of and adapt to appropriate standards of behavior *for the particular group*. For example, in 2001, Rick Ayers's Communication Arts and Sciences English class at Berkeley High School in California created its first slang dictionary.[4] Each entry in the dictionary contains its etymological source, a pronunciation key, and a sentence using the entry—the students have laid out the word or phrase and the rules for its use. "Off the hook"

**GLOSSARY**

**Bypassing**

*Occurs when group members think they have the same meaning for a word or phrase but in actuality do not*

was appropriate for 1999, "off the heazie" for 2000, and "off the hizzle" for 2001. The purpose of this slang dictionary project was to give students an opportunity to use their own rich home language as a viable avenue for creativity in their classroom.

Even as we advise this, however, we note that many of the secondary groups you participate in will take place in the mainstream of the U.S. business, professional, and educational communities. In such cases you should conform to the vocabulary and grammar rules of standard English. This will help other people understand you and increase your influence, because numerous studies have shown that nonstandard dialects and usage lower the credibility of speakers with a variety of listeners. As Rick Ayers recognized, "I want to make them aware of their brilliance, that the way they speak is not wrong, it's just another form of discourse. . . . The trick is teaching them how to translate it into standard English when they need to."[5]

## ADJUSTING TO THE SYMBOLIC NATURE OF LANGUAGE

People who use language effectively in group discussions are keenly aware of its symbolic, personal nature. They realize that words do not have meanings in and of themselves, so they strive to express their ideas in words likely to evoke similar meanings in listeners.

As listeners, they ask themselves, "What does the speaker mean?" rather than, "What do those words mean?" or "What would I mean if I said that?" They are on guard against **bypassing,** in which two or more people have different meanings for a word but do not realize it. Bypassing can lead either to a false agreement or to the perception that a disagreement exists when it really doesn't. For example, the meaning of *patriotism* in the wake of the 9/11 terrorist attacks has become increasingly complicated for many Americans. Imagine yourself in a small group class trying to figure out what your group's community service task is going to be for the semester. Members begin to brainstorm ideas about how they can show their patriotism in their local community. Everyone appears eager to show their patriotism, so they decide that *patriotism* will be their theme. During a subsequent meeting, while the group begins to figure out what to do specifically, Lucinda suggests they organize a peace rally. Other members immediately challenge the idea by claiming it is not right to oppose our country's military actions while we are at war. In addition, they become angry with Lucinda because they thought they had all decided to do a patriotic-theme project. This group bypassed on the meaning of *patriotic,* which led to a false agreement affecting a future meeting.

Words vary from highly concrete to highly abstract. For example, the terms in the following list become more abstract (more vague) as you proceed down the list:

Maria Thomas

Public relations major

California State University, Fresno student

College student

Female

Young person

Human

Efficient communicators know that many words, especially abstract ones, will be interpreted differently by different people. The most concrete forms are those that refer to one and only one thing: *Dr. Galanes' desk, radio personality Howard Stern,* or *golden retriever number PD736251.* However, abstract words and phrases such as *liberal, effective, spiritual, democracy,* and *love* are highly ambiguous and likely to be understood quite differently by different group members.

The level of abstraction matters a lot during discussions. Concrete language helps reduce misunderstanding, but confusion can be rampant when highly abstract words are used. Highly abstract statements (such as "Don't you think this is a matter of historical dialecticism?") consistently disrupt discussions among college students, and the amount of confusion and disarray increases as the statements are made more abstract.[6]

Using abstract words is OK; in fact, having a meaningful discussion without them would be impossible. Many of the ideas group members discuss must include fairly abstract words such as *consensus, criteria, leadership, trust, success,* and *climate.* In addition, we sometimes may choose to be ambiguous in an effort to allow for multiple interpretations while exploring an idea. However, you can take steps to help make your remarks more specific and thus clearer. First, speak as concretely as possible to express what you mean. Don't use jargon to show off. Group members, in addition to their own ethnic cultures, belong to a multitude of co-cultures (e.g., athletes, musicians, computer gamers, bloggers, business professionals, teachers), which use their own jargon. In a group of members with mixed computer literacy and experience, not everyone may know that the *sandbox* refers to the research and development departments of software companies and that *beani* refers to the Macintosh computer key with the cloverleaf sign.

Second, whenever you use a highly abstract term that may be problematic, give concrete examples of what you mean—for instance, "He was a really controlling chair [abstract concept]. He decided, by himself, when the group would meet, what would and would not be on the agenda, who could and could not speak at the meetings, and what the committee should recommend to the president of the fraternity [concrete examples of the abstract idea of *controlling*]."

Third, define highly abstract terms by using synonyms or descriptive terms or by explaining an operation the term refers to. Thus, you might define *drunk driving* as "having a level of .08 percent alcohol in the blood as measured immediately after driving by a machine called a Breathalyzer," which is the DWI definition used in many states. This definition combines both a procedure (i.e., measured by a Breathalyzer) and precise quantification for the term (i.e., .08 percent alcohol in the blood).

Fourth, quantify when possible. Frequently, groups use relative terms for comparisons when precise quantification is possible. For instance, instead of saying, "The chances of developing lung cancer are *higher* [a relative term] if you smoke a pack of cigarettes a day than if you don't smoke," you can state quite precisely what the increase in the percentage of people developing lung cancer will be.

Up to this point, we have focused on what the speaker can do to make communication clear, but remember from Chapter 3 that *both* sender and receiver are responsible for effective communication. Listeners are equally responsible for helping to clarify group messages. As a listener you can ask speakers who use highly abstract language to quantify, give examples, or define their terms with less abstract language: "Sam, when you say that you want us to pick an 'interesting' topic for our debate, I'm not sure what you mean by 'interesting.' Could you give me an example or two of what would be interesting to you?" You can paraphrase in more concrete terms, then ask the speaker to accept or revise the paraphrase. This will help you interpret the speaker's meaning more accurately.

For more information on defining words with precision, go to the Online Learning Center at **www.mhhe.com/ adamsgalanes7**

"Sorry, Chief, but of course I didn't mean 'bimbo' in the pejorative sense."

## What Do You Do When Emotive Words Are Offensive?

**ETHICAL DILEMMA**

Two African American members of your group refer to each other as "nigga" when they greet each other at the beginning of group meetings.[7] You and one other member find the use of the term highly offensive and do not believe any person, no matter her or his color, should use the term. One other member really does not care and does not see the point in making a big deal out of it.

This racial epithet is a highly emotive trigger word in the American culture, and people weigh in with all sorts of opinions on its use.

1. As a group what do you do? How would you discuss this issue?
2. When do the references in personal member greetings become an issue for a group?
3. What new rules might this group create to allow for emotive words yet avoid the consequences of their use?

**GLOSSARY**

**Emotive Words**

*Words that trigger strong emotional responses*

## USING EMOTIVE WORDS CAUTIOUSLY

**Emotive words** are terms that call forth strong feelings. Often these are called *trigger words* because they evoke almost instantaneous emotional responses that could interfere with good listening.

For instance, for some people *feminist* conjures up a very negative image of a bra-burning woman who hates men and is destroying the American family because of her selfish goals. Among the worst trigger words are sexist terms and racial epithets (such as *wetback, feminazi,* or *faggot*). Again, we are calling attention to the importance of monitoring your linguistic choices in group interaction. The nature of your communication not only reflects the kind of communicative climate in your group but, as we pointed out earlier, also re-creates that climate over the course of your group's time together. Are you re-creating the kind of climate you want?

You can improve the quality of thinking during group discussions by avoiding such words yourself and suggesting alternatives when someone else uses one of them. Consider the following two lists. The first has negative emotive terms; the second, neutral ones that denote the same things.

| Negative | Neutral or Positive |
|---|---|
| chick | woman |
| jock | athlete |
| Jew-them-down | negotiate or haggle |
| hillbilly | native of the Ozarks |
| cop | police officer |

Suppose someone said to you, "He's just a failed politician, not a scientist, and he's grandstanding as he looks for a new platform. What could he know about global warming?" You could paraphrase as follows: "So, in other words, you think that the opinions of a nonscientist are not valid on scientific issues such as global warming, and you mistrust his motives?" This helps defuse the trigger words ( *failed politician, grandstanding*) so the group can focus on the merits of the message itself. It also provides the speaker an opportunity to clarify if you have misunderstood. This will defuse the trigger words so that the group can begin a more objective, less emotional evaluation of the person's qualifications.

## ORGANIZING REMARKS

Organization of the discussion in general and of your own remarks in particular is affected by what you say and how you say it. Frequently, discussions jump almost aimlessly from topic to topic, with no one responding to prior comments. It is often hard to tell exactly what issue or question a speaker is addressing, or even what the point is of some remarks. Good organization can do a lot to overcome these communication problems.

Consider the following discussion by a group of students planning publicity for an upcoming career day seminar:

**Lori:** OK, the seminar is planned, so now it's time to start working on the publicity. Any ideas?

**Deidre:** We forgot to include a session on portfolios.

**Tony:** One of the things we could do is send a memo to all the people in the dorms. That worked well last time.

| **Chris:** | I know someone who would do a great job with portfolios, and I'll be glad to call her. |
| **Kevin:** | I think a memo is a really tacky idea, and we ought to do something more professional. |
| **Lori:** | I don't like memos either. I'd be happy if we didn't do one. |

It's hard to tell from that discussion who is responding to what question, or even exactly what is meant. Let's help the individuals organize their remarks so the discussion is more organized as a *group* process:

| **Lori:** | OK, the seminar has been planned, so now it's time to start working on publicity. What ideas do you have for how we could promote the career day seminar? [Not a big change here, but Lori's question to the group is more focused than before. We discuss the importance of forming appropriate focusing questions later in the chapter.] |
| **Deidre:** | Lori, could we postpone our discussion of publicity? I'd like to talk first about something we overlooked in the planning. We forgot to schedule a portfolio session. [First, Deidre responds directly to Lori and Lori's question before suggesting a different initial topic.] |
| **Lori:** | That's a good idea, Deidre. OK, guys, let's spend time making sure the plans are finalized before we talk about publicity. What did you mean by a portfolio session? [Direct response to Deidre, acknowledgment of the legitimacy of her request to postpone discussion of publicity and request for clarification] |
| **Deidre:** | That was the session where someone showed us how to put together a public relations portfolio so that when we apply for jobs we'll be able to show people what kinds of assignments we've completed. It's like a résumé with specific examples of your work. [Direct clarification response from Deidre] |
| **Lori:** | You're right; we need that. Big oversight. Glad you thought of it. [Affirming Deidre's good thinking on behalf of the group's project] |
| **Tony:** | One thing we could do is send a memo to all the people who live in the dorms to let them know about the seminar. [This remark seems to be about publicity and does not appear to respond directly to the portfolio topic.] |
| **Chris:** | That might be a good idea, Tony, but I'm not sure we're ready to go on to that yet. Were we finished with the portfolio session planning? [Chris doesn't ignore Tony or put him down, but he does help the group keep focused on the topic, and he makes it a group issue by using *we*.] |
| **Tony:** | Sorry! I thought we were ready to move on. What do we need to do yet with portfolios? [Apology and direct acknowledgment of the topic under discussion] |

| | |
|---|---|
| **Chris:** | Well, for one thing, we need to figure out who would be a good person to handle that session. [Direct response to Tony, moves the discussion forward] |
| **Kevin:** | I know someone at Walker, Beard, and Korma Public Relations. I'll call and see if she's available, and, if she isn't, maybe she can suggest somebody else. [Direct response to Chris] |
| **Lori:** | OK, Kevin, do I understand you right? You'll take care of getting someone to handle the portfolio session and let us know who that is by next week? [Lori has detected an ambiguity in Kevin's earlier remark ("maybe she can suggest somebody else"), so she helps him clarify.] |
| **Kevin:** | Yes. [Direct answer clears up the ambiguity.] |
| **Lori:** | OK, Kevin will find someone to handle the portfolio sessions. Now, are we ready to turn to publicity? [Group members nod.] That's great. What ideas do we have for publicizing career day? |

In the second version each comment begins with acknowledgment of the prior speaker, often using the other member's name. No one switches topics abruptly. Statements are right to the point. In almost all cases, the speaker stays with one point. Notice, too, that this discussion takes longer—members do not assume they understand but work to make the connections between speakers and topics explicit.

The following is a list of guidelines to facilitate coherent, orderly, and clear discussion:

1. **Relate your statement to the preceding statement.** Sometimes this will have to be done explicitly in a statement; sometimes it can be done with a word or phrase (e.g., Lori: "That's a good idea"; Tony: "Sorry.")

2. **State one point, not give a multipoint speech.** If you talk about two or more issues, the discussion is likely to go off track because no one can predict which issue the next speaker will pick up on, even if she or he responds directly to your remarks. The one major exception to this rule occurs when you present an initial description of a problem or give a planned report that has more than one point. In that case, preparing a handout that includes the main findings, facts, statistics, quotations, formulas, and so on is a good idea.

3. **State the point as directly, concretely, and concisely as possible.** In the dominant culture of the United States, simple declarative sentences are preferable to flowery language and emotive terms. Phrases such as "My point is that . . ." and "This is the idea: . . ." may help focus listeners.

# Making Sure the Discussion Question Is Clear and Appropriate

Thus far, the chapter has been devoted to language, the verbal messages of communication. We now apply the concepts we have discussed about language and verbal communication to the specific issue of a group's discussion question.

## USING LANGUAGE TO FOCUS A GROUP'S DISCUSSION: AN APPLICATION

Language is crucial to both the content and relationship elements of communication, and nowhere is it more important than when the group leader or members formulate the right kind of question to launch the group's discussion. Different types of questions and different ways that questions are phrased lead a group's discussion along different paths, and you want to ensure that your group takes the right path. The **discussion question** is the central question or issue the group must answer. For discussions to be effective, a group's discussion question must be clear, and each member should be able to state what it is. Having a clear discussion question helps the group begin its task in the right way, whatever the task may be.

Unfortunately, many groups start with a vague or limiting question that sends them in the wrong direction. In addition, members are sometimes sloppy about sticking to the question under discussion—they often wander off task or bring up task-related issues, but at the wrong time. A careful analysis of many discussions will show that different members are attempting to answer different questions at the same time. For example, Mary may be trying to evaluate a suggestion Thuy has proposed—to solve the lack of parking spaces on campus—while Sonya is explaining how student parking fees are being spent and LaShonda is presenting her proposal to solve the parking problem. This creates a disorganized discussion with the kind of confused topic switching described earlier.

Establishing an effective question can determine whether the group produces a good or poor solution. Consider the following two discussion questions: "How can we raise money to build another classroom building?" versus "How can we relieve the overcrowding in classrooms?" The first question focuses on an already-decided solution, which may or may not be the best solution to the problem. The second focuses on the problem (overcrowding) without biasing the solution in advance. Building more classrooms may work, but perhaps the problems are due to poor scheduling of existing facilities. Maybe holding classes at off-campus locations such as shopping centers, factories, and offices throughout the city would be more effective in reducing the overcrowding as well as provide better service to students. However, these options will never be discovered if the group is determined to solve the problem by building more classrooms. Thus, how a group states its discussion question influences the entire progress of the group's discussion. As an input the discussion question has a far-reaching effect on the system's throughput process and its subsequent output.

Anytime you feel confused about what is going on during small group meetings, ask yourself or the group what question is being discussed. Get an answer to that question before you proceed, and help the entire group become oriented toward the same goal at the same moment. When you ask a question, be sure the type of answer you seek is clear from the phrasing of the question. Seven types of questions, classified on the basis of the type of response requested, with examples of each type, are described in Table 4.2. While most of these questions pertain to the group's task, thus influencing primarily the content of the group's communication, one category—Relationship Questions—directly addresses the group's relational communication. All these examples should help you appreciate the number of different types of questions you can choose from and the way these questions work to solicit information from other members.

| TABLE 4.2 | **Types of Discussion Questions** |
| --- | --- |

**INFORMATION QUESTIONS**

Ask for specific information or facts, but not interpretations or opinions.

*Examples*

- Why was this meeting called?

- How many thefts were reported on campus last year?

- Where did you learn that?

- What did Jim say was his reason for missing the meeting?

**INTERPRETATION QUESTIONS**

Ask for personal opinions, interpretations, or judgments; they invite discussion.

*Examples*

- What might have caused this increase in the rate of theft?

- What connection might there be between college grades and whether a student has a computer?

- Do you think our presentation should emphasize the need to reduce the deficit or the need to keep inflation down?

**VALUE QUESTIONS**

Ask how good, important, significant, or worthwhile something is in the opinion of the responder. A value question is a type of interpretation question.

*Examples*

- How good a president do you think Ronald Reagan was?

- Is this question important enough to take up the group's time?

- What are the pros and cons of this alternative?

- How good a case did the prosecuting attorney have against O.J.?

- Which of these suits do you think looks best?

- How much do you like this painting?

**POLICY QUESTIONS**

Ask what should be done about an issue; the key word is *should.* Usually, groups have discussed a number of information and interpretation questions before they begin to discuss and decide what policy to take.

*Examples*

- What should the U.S. government do to reduce the federal deficit?

- What should our school's attendance policy be?

- What kinds of skills should be required of all "med tech" graduates?

- What should the Washington, D.C., police do to reduce drug-related crimes?

**ACTION QUESTIONS**

Ask how to implement a decision or policy already decided by the group.

*Examples*

- How will we make this recommendation to the student senate?

- Now that we've decided what food to serve at the banquet, who will see to it that it is prepared and served?

- How can we guarantee that all pilots know about this policy and follow it?

*(continued)*

**TABLE 4.2**        (*Continued*)

**PROCEDURE QUESTIONS**

Ask how the group, or an individual member, does something; what procedure the group will use.

*Examples*

- Should we vote or try to come to consensus?

- What would be the best way to present our proposal to our client?

- What sequence should we use to organize our discussion of this issue?

- How can we divide the work of the committee in a way that's fair to everybody?

**RELATIONSHIP QUESTIONS**

Seek information about how members feel toward each other, the group, their responsibilities to the group, the relative status of members, and their expectations of each other.

*Examples*

- Do we need some introductions, or does everybody know everybody else?

- How do you all feel about our assignment to select an insurance carrier for our medical programs?

- How did you get the authority to decide when we meet?

- Paul, something seems to be bothering you. Is there something that's made you upset?

---

When you reply to a question, be sure you give the kind of response sought by the questioner. The following are a few guidelines to help you phrase questions that focus and facilitate group interaction.

1. **Unless the group has already narrowed a list of alternatives to two, avoid either-or questions.**

   Usually, these grossly oversimplify the issue by treating questions as if there were only two legitimate answers instead of a wide range. In the list that follows, the first question of each pair is poorly worded in either-or terms; the second version is worded as an open-ended question:

   Is our university's central administration diverse? (Implied is a yes or no answer.) How diverse is our university's central administration?

   Should we all take notes or just elect a recorder? (Provides only two options) How should we keep track of all the information in our group meetings?

2. **Word questions as concretely as possible.**

   Double-barreled questions that combine two questions in one are confusing. For example, "Do you think we should increase funding to the public schools by instituting casino gambling in the state?" is a double-barreled question. Listeners may want to respond differently to each part. For example, maybe someone wants to increase funding to the schools but doesn't want to allow casino gambling in the state. Perhaps both issues need to be addressed, but if so, each question should be asked separately: "First, do you think funding to the public schools should be

## What Are Our Questions?

APPLY NOW

In Case 4.1 we described the events of the first meeting of CSUF's dean search committee. During this meeting members talked freely about what they wanted in a new dean. The search they were about to undertake would be a complicated one that would entail developing a recruitment plan, establishing screening and selection criteria, scheduling on-campus interviews, and so forth. Each phase would require a series of questions. For example, during the recruitment phase members would have to consider how to attract a diverse and qualified pool of applicants.

Imagine you are a member of this committee and are helping plan the discussion for subsequent meetings.

1. Think of the phases this committee will experience in the course of its work.

2. Compose a list of discussion questions, including questions of information, value, policy, action, procedure, and relationship, that might help guide the group's discussion in each phase.

You can do this by yourself or you can get together in a group. Once the questions have been written, go over the examples critically, looking for any that may be either-or questions, may not be worded concretely, or may inadvertently suggest an answer.

increased? Second, should we approve a measure to allow casino gambling in our state?"

3. **Avoid suggesting the answer in the question.**

   A question that suggests an answer is not an honest question but an indirect way to make a point. For instance, "Don't you think we should recommend building a new parking garage to relieve the parking problem?" suggests a solution.

4. **Apply critical thinking skills to questions you ask.**

   Guidelines for evaluating information and detecting errors in reasoning are explained in Chapter 7. Use them to evaluate and improve the questions you and others ask during discussions.

Up to now we have been emphasizing the importance of words to the messages processed in small group interaction. However, you will recall from our earlier discussion that nonverbal behaviors also carry a significant communicative load in a group. Entire courses are devoted to nonverbal communication, which is far too broad a topic to be covered in depth here. We have selected the information we think is most relevant to small group communication. While this may be a review for you, we suggest you look at the information if only to remind yourself about just how important nonverbal behavior is to small groups.

**GLOSSARY**

**Nonverbal Behavior**

*Anything in a message that is not the word itself*

# Nonverbal Behaviors in Small Group Communication

**Nonverbal behavior** is anything in a message except the words themselves. However, as we pointed out early in this chapter, our symphonies (communication) are created when we play our notes *together*. Our symphonies use both verbal and nonverbal behaviors simultaneously. Even the words on this page are surrounded by punctuation, with varying degrees of white space, in a chosen typeface and in a particular color, all of which affect how you interpret the words. Likewise, head nods, eyebrow flashes, posture, touch, clothes usually occur within a larger conversational episode containing spoken and written words. Two communication scholars, John Stewart and Carol Logan, believe we make sense of this complexity by using a continuum.[8] At one extreme are primarily verbal behaviors such as written words; in the middle are mixed behaviors such as spoken words, vocalics (e.g., pitch, rate, volume), pauses, and silences; and at the other extreme are primarily nonverbal behaviors that can occur without words such as eye gaze, touch, and facial expressions. Verbal and nonverbal behavior are inseparable, just as two sides of a paper are inseparable.[9]

For the following discussion we will focus on the mixed and primary nonverbal behaviors. These nonverbal behaviors serve a number of purposes. We will explain several important principles of nonverbal behavior, examine key functions performed by these behaviors, and finally explore briefly some common categories of nonverbal behavior that have an impact on small group communication.

## PRINCIPLES OF NONVERBAL COMMUNICATION

Most of the time in a small group, only one person is speaking, but *all* members are sending nonverbal signals *all* the time. Understanding something about nonverbal behaviors is crucial to understanding what is happening in your groups. However, interpreting nonverbal behaviors can be trickier than interpreting verbal signals.

1. **Nonverbal behaviors are ambiguous.**

    Do you think that a smile means someone is happy? In many cultures that is usually the case, but in Japan someone who is feeling quite miserable may smile to avoid upsetting the person to whom he is speaking. Do you think that someone who has her arms folded across her chest is uninterested in hearing what you say? Maybe. But maybe she is merely trying to keep warm. Many factors influence the meaning of nonverbal behaviors, including cultural differences. Nonverbal behaviors should be interpreted in context and in conjunction with the words group members are using.

2. **People cannot stop sending nonverbal behaviors, even when they are not talking.**

    Usually, only one person in a group speaks at a time, but all members continuously process nonverbal behaviors. Even if you choose to be quiet in a group meeting, you will likely leak your feelings nonverbally. For example, a church board member unhappy with the way the church secretary was handling office business chose not to say anything when personnel matters were discussed. However, after the meeting the board chair asked him what was wrong and why he had seemed uninterested at the meeting. This example points out two features of nonverbal behavior. First, even though the member chose not to say anything, he certainly was communicating *something* nonverbally. Second, nonverbal behaviors are easy to misinterpret. The emotion the board member was feeling was anger at the church secretary, but the board chair thought he was uninterested in the meeting. Thus, we shouldn't jump to conclusions without first checking them out.

3. **When verbal and nonverbal behaviors clash, most people believe the nonverbal behaviors.**

   In fact, when a person is trying to interpret what someone else means in a face-to-face interaction, the nonverbal part of the message counts almost twice as much as the verbal.[10] When the verbal and nonverbal behaviors don't fit, most people trust the nonverbal ones because they are less subject to deliberate control. Many nonverbal behaviors, such as sweating, blushing, and shaking, are controlled by primitive structures of the brain over which we have little or no conscious control. You can choose your words, but your nonverbal behavior often gives you away. When you clench your fists, turn red, and scream at another group member, "No, I'm NOT mad!" no one will believe you.

## FUNCTIONS OF NONVERBAL BEHAVIORS

Nonverbal behaviors perform what a friend of ours would call the "heavy lifting" in communication; without nonverbal behaviors we would not know how to "take" the words that people say. "Right," says member Sarah. *How* she says it—a nonverbal behavior—can make that "Right" a statement of agreement ("Yes, you are right and I agree") or one of disagreement (if said sarcastically, as in "Yeah, sure you're right" but meaning exactly the opposite). One of the most important functions of nonverbal behavior is to express *how we feel*. We convey emotions, such as anger, sadness, and happiness, through our nonverbal behaviors. We laugh when we are happy, frown and glare when we are angry, and so forth.

Nonverbal behaviors also perform the important function of indicating *how we perceive our relationships to other people*. For instance, status and liking are conveyed nonverbally. In one recent study people were asked what nonverbal behaviors are exhibited by people who have social power (status) and by those who do not.[11] Those with high social power were perceived to hold themselves more erect, gesture more, invade others' space and be more successful at interrupting others, be more open and expressive, and have speech that was smoother and more confident. Also, whether someone likes another person seems to be strongly associated with that person's nonverbal—but not verbal—behavior.[12] In one study teachers liked students who were nonverbally responsive, such as sitting upright (not slouching), making direct eye contact, having positive facial expressions, and taking notes in class. Interestingly, teachers were also more willing to comply with students' requests (e.g., extending a due date on an assignment) if the students had been nonverbally responsive to the teacher. This applies directly to small group behavior. Most students want others to like them, and liking is clearly linked to nonverbal behavior. In addition, showing signs of liking produces signs of liking in return. Kory Floyd and George Ray found that people interacting with someone who showed them signs of liking (e.g., eye contact, smiling, leaning forward) continued to increase their own liking behavior.[13] Findings like these have clear implications for small groups.

Go to
**www.mhhe.com/
adamsgalanes7**
for additional
weblink activities.

## The Symbolic Nature of Avatars

**MEDIA AND TECHNOLOGY**

In its infancy computer-mediated communication was primarily text based (i.e., typed messages on a computer keyboard). Because CMC relies so heavily on the text to create meaning, it is hard to guess at the qualities of the individuals you are interacting with in a CMC environment. To adapt to this drawback, Internet providers have begun to use *avatars*. An avatar is a visual representation of yourself that you construct and display next to the textual dialogue. Most sites that offer the use of avatars allow you to select things such as gender, hair color, clothing style, facial expression, and even pets that you want depicted in your visual representation. Ambiguity still exists with avatars; however, users are able to select stronger nonverbal characteristics and cues to accompany the textual dialogue.

These websites provide an opportunity to experiment with the construction and implementation of avatars in chat rooms or during instant messaging: **http://avatars.yahoo.com/index.html** and **http://www.121chat.com.** If given an opportunity to create your own avatar to use in a chat room, which types of features would you select, and why? What things should you consider about other people based on the way they present themselves visually? How do you think avatars illustrate the notion discussed in the section on principles of nonverbal communication? Does the potential for CMC interaction using these media contradict some of the face-to-face principles described?

Another function of nonverbal communication is to *supplement* words by emphasizing them or, in effect, repeating them, just as <u>underlined</u> or **boldfaced** words in a text are emphasized. Thus, nonverbals can call special attention to the words they accompany. For instance, a person may say, "Look at the rise in air pollution in the Valley during peak traffic hours" while pointing at a bar graph.

## What If . . . ?

Earlier you met a group of students planning publicity for a career day seminar. In their meeting they discussed adding a portfolio session and then how best to publicize the seminar. Recollect the following dialogue:

**Lori:** You're right; we need that. Big oversight. Glad you thought of it.

**Tony:** One thing we could do is send a memo to all the people who live in the dorms to let them know about the seminar.

**Chris:** That might be a good idea, but I'm not sure we're ready to go on to that yet. Were we finished with the portfolio session planning?

**Tony:** Sorry! I thought we were ready to move on. What do we need to do yet with portfolios?

**Chris:** Well, for one thing, we need to figure out who would be a good person to handle that session.

The goal of this application is to show you how much the context and nonverbal behavior influence the meaning of what we say. Select four trios. Each trio is to role-play the dialogue but from a different relational context. The first trio is composed of close friends who have worked together on several committees. Members of the second trio have never met before, and one member is not sure he or she even wants to be on this committee. The third trio has a highly aggressive member who believes he or she knows how to run this group. The fourth trio is composed of individuals who really dislike each other but are trying to be civil.

During the role-plays, have audience members take notes. Ask them to observe the nonverbal behavior and how it changes the meaning of the conversation. When the trios are through, discuss the principles and the functions of nonverbal behavior. You can even discuss how the trios used such things as gestures, facial expressions, movements, and spacing to create the relational context.

Nonverbal behaviors can *substitute* for spoken or written words. In this case a gesture becomes a symbol, substituting for the more conventional words. For instance, a circled thumb and index finger can express "OK," or a beckoning finger can indicate that you want someone to lean closer to you. Kathy and some of her graduate students bring their two forefingers together to indicate a "shared moment," a gesture they picked up from the movie *Chasing Amy.* Much of the communicating among members must be with unspoken substitutes for spoken words. If you aren't conscious of these behaviors and don't look for them, you will miss many important messages among group members and misinterpret other nonverbal messages. In a sense you will be only half-listening.

Another major function of nonverbal behaviors is to *regulate* the flow of verbal interaction among members. The coordinator of a discussion group may use nods, eye contact, and hand signals to indicate who should speak next. Direct gaze from listeners means, "Continue," whereas looking away is a nonverbal way of saying, "Shut up!" People who want to speak lean forward, slightly open their mouths, extend a hand or finger, and even utter a sound such as "um." Speakers who ignore such cues are judged inconsiderate and rude. One of us observed a group that contained a blind person who obviously could not see such regulating cues. Other members began to judge this member as arrogant and self-centered for "talking out of turn." Some discussion of visible regulatory cues increased the members' sensitivity to the communicative problem experienced by their blind member and helped the group pull together.

Finally, as noted earlier, nonverbal behaviors can *contradict* words we utter. A person who says, "I agree," hesitatingly, with a rising pitch at the end of the words, may be perceived as having reservations, or even as disagreeing. A person who says, "I heard you," but who will not attempt a paraphrase has indicated nonverbally that he probably was not really listening. When you observe nonverbal behaviors that seem to contradict what a person has just said, and it matters to you what the person really thinks, try saying, "I heard you say . . . , but the way you said it bothers me." Then explain the apparent contradiction you perceived, and ask the person to clarify it for you.

## CATEGORIES OF NONVERBAL BEHAVIORS

Several categories of nonverbal behavior are especially important to your understanding of small group communication. Personal appearance, space and seating, facial expressions and eye contact, gestures and body movements, voice, and time cues are among the major types of nonverbal behaviors most relevant to small groups.

**Appearance.**   Members of a group form impressions of each other, accurate or not, long before anyone says anything. Sex, race, height, build, dress, grooming, and other visible cues have been shown to influence responses. Cues such as sex, body shape, and ethnicity particularly affect how group members interact with each other initially.[14] Such personal characteristics as status and wisdom may be associated with a member's age and sex. Members also create impressions of each other's physical characteristics including impressions of clothing, makeup, and other body "artifacts." These impressions may very well determine whether a group member interacts with another member and, if so, what type of interaction they have. For instance, violating societal norms about dress, grooming, makeup, and accessories can arouse suspicion or even mistrust. Dressing noticeably differently from other members will almost certainly be interpreted as a sign that you do not identify with them. You may have to prove yourself in other ways to be accepted. To date, no research has examined the impact of the relative physical attractiveness of group members on group throughput and outcome variables.[15] This is surprising given how much attention is placed on physical attractiveness in American culture at large and in interpersonal communication research specifically.

The appearance of group members matters not only to the other members but also to outsiders. Groups do not operate in a social vacuum; how members appear to others can affect their credibility during group presentations and even their success, as is the case with rock bands. The most famous of them all, The Beatles, wore black clothes early in their career to mimic the color of beetles.[16] When John Lennon was asked how much of their success was due to their sound rather than their appearance, he replied, "We could have managed, looking like we look and making worse records, or we could have managed, looking like the average pop singer and making our noise. But the combination makes a better impact. We have always looked different from the rest of the mob."[17]

**Space and Seating.**   Many scientists have examined how people use space to communicate. The amount of space people prefer between them depends on a variety of factors, including culture and gender. For example, in the United States most business transactions are conducted at what Edward Hall calls *social distance,* which is between four and eight feet.[18] We are comfortable allowing only our intimate friends within a foot or two. However, four feet is much too far for someone from the Arab world or from Latin America. In these countries people transact business at what we consider close personal distance, which often makes Americans very uneasy. In the dominant culture of the United States, females tend to sit closer together than males, as do people of the same age and social status and those who know each other well.

The seating arrangements in groups and even the way furniture is arranged is called **group ecology.**[19] In a group, sitting close together, especially if the room is large enough for members to spread out, indicates that members like each other and share a sense of cohesiveness. A member who sits apart from the others may be signaling that he or she does not feel a part of the group.

Group ecology and group processes such as status, leadership, power, and member participation are linked to each other. Dominant people often claim more than their fair share of space, and a group's leader usually is given more space by the other members than they claim. In addition, group leaders generally sit in a central position, such as at the head of a rectangular table, where they can see as many of the other members as possible. Quite simply, the most central place in a group's ecology allows members who occupy that space more influence, participation, domination, and opportunity to foster attributions of leadership.[20] People who sit across from each other respond to each other more than people sitting side by side or on the edges of each other's vision. The ideal table for most small group discussions is a round table, where members have easy eye contact with each other. If that is not possible, group members are advised to position themselves around the table, whatever shape it happens to be, in something close to a circle or oval.

Violating space norms may spell trouble for group members, depending on their status within the group.[21] High-status members can get away with moving both closer to others and farther away. These violations in expectation actually increase their status. Group members who are high in status or rewarding to others have a kind of insurance with other members with their groups and can deviate from group norms with little or no punishment. Low-status members are not so fortunate because their deviations are framed within the context of their negative status. Thus, if they move closer to others they can be seen as pushy, and if they move farther away they can be seen as aloof, and their attractiveness and persuasiveness diminishes.

Altering seating arrangements may also appear nonconsequential; however, the seating choices you and your group members make indicate how socially accessible you have made yourselves to each other. Social accessibility is important if members are to promote social contact and enhance the more relational group outcomes, such as respect and cohesiveness.[22] For example, a student group one of us advised had developed the custom of having the six-person executive committee meet just before the large organizational meeting. Unfortunately, executive committee members conducted their meeting sitting in the same places they used for the organizational meeting—at a long head table, with all six members on the same side of the table. Members showed signs of frustration, anger, confusion, and so forth, until they took the suggestion to use a round table instead of the head table for the executive meeting. Both the content of the meetings and the relationships among members improved dramatically with that simple space change.

**Facial Expressions and Eye Contact.**   Sitting where you can see every other member of the group is important because it allows you to make eye contact with other members. Eye contact and facial expressions are among the most important nonverbal behaviors for group members, as you can see in the accompanying cartoon. For Americans, making eye contact signals that the channel for communication is open. This is why many students look down at their notebooks when a teacher asks a question—they avoid eye contact so they won't be called on to answer. Prolonged eye contact can signal cooperativeness or competitiveness, depending on the circumstances. Most Americans establish eye contact before speaking and continue it intermittently when talking to someone they like. However, people from other cultures are sometimes offended by Americans' direct gazes, while others prefer to maintain an intense, unbroken stare when conversing, which is uncomfortable for Americans. As with other nonverbal behavior, numerous cultural factors influence what a person considers to be appropriate eye contact. In unified and cohesive groups, members tend to look continuously at each other during a discussion. In hostile or tense groups, members avoid eye contact.

People can accurately determine the type of emotion someone in a photograph is experiencing from looking just at the face and eyes. Anger, sadness, happiness, support, disagreement, interest, liking—all are indicated by facial expressions.[23] In addition, the emotion does not need to be displayed for a long time. People can recognize microexpressions that

Judging from their facial expressions, what do you think Washington, Jefferson, Roosevelt, and Lincoln are thinking? © The New Yorker Collection; 1998 Donald Reilly from cartoonbank.com. All Rights Reserved.

last as little as one-fifteenth of a second, and they can be trained to improve their ability to detect microexpressions.[24] Some people have "poker" faces; their facial expressions change very little. They tend to be trusted less than those whose faces express their feelings more openly. Most of us monitor the facial expressions of others because they provide clues about what is going on in the group. Even if a group member isn't saying anything about your proposal, you can tell by her spontaneous frown and grimace that she doesn't think much of it. That gives you information about what your next steps should be—drop the proposal, modify it, ask the other member directly what she thinks, or speak with her privately after the meeting.

Emotional expression is one example of how mixed messages play together to affect group communication. The face, eyes, and voice as well as the actual words work together to create a wide range of emotions in small group communication. Although we emphasize the role of rationality in group problem solving, emotion does impact group dynamics. Group climate, which we discuss in Chapter 5, is another label for the emotional atmosphere of any group. Positive and negative emotional expressions have interesting implications for member collaboration.

**Movements.**    Movements of the hands, arms, and body signal many feelings and attitudes. For example, people turn directly toward others they like and away from those they dislike. Leaning toward each other indicates a sense of mutual inclusiveness, whereas leaning away signals rejection.[25] When group members feel a sense of unity with each other, they tend to imitate each other's posture and body movements. This takes place automatically, without conscious awareness. Edward Mabry found that body orientation changes significantly from one meeting to another.[26] As group members get to know, like, and trust one another more, they tend to increase their eye contact and angle their bodies more directly toward each other.

Both tension and status can be revealed with movements. Members who are swinging a foot, twisting a lock of hair, or tapping a pencil may be indicating tension. It may be hard for the other members to know whether the movements indicate frustration, impatience, or annoyance with the group's progress. Movement can also indicate who has high status in the group. High-status members tend to be the most relaxed, so they lean back and look around.[27] Members are more likely to imitate the movements of high-status members than those of low-status members.[28]

**Voice.**    Vocal cues include such factors as pitch, speed, fluency, loudness, and pauses. We rely on tone of voice to interpret someone's mood. Someone who says, "Yeah, I could live with that" softly in a questioning tone of voice is not likely to be believed. In addition, listeners tend to judge the status, educational level, ethnicity, and attitudes of speakers on the basis of vocal cues.[29] In the United States people who speak in a monotone have less credibility and are less persuasive than those who speak in a more animated tone of voice. However, those who are extremely animated may appear to be irrational or hysterical.

Those nonverbal signals that regulate interaction express group member involvement, dominance, competition, and cooperativeness.[30] For instance, people make nonverbal backchannel sounds, such as "mm-hmmm" and "uh-huh," to indicate involvement and understanding when listening. Interestingly, cultures vary in the use of the backchannel. Most people from western European backgrounds use the backchannel less frequently than African Americans, Hispanics, or people with southern European backgrounds. If conversational partners do not share the same backchannel norms, they can begin to stereotype each other and develop negative perceptions.[31] In addition, when people from the same culture converse, the fact that they use the backchannel similarly helps increase their recall of the conversation later.[32] However, when people with different backchannel norms converse, they seem to give each other misleading feedback that reduces their later recall. We discuss backchannel differences between African Americans and European Americans in more detail in Chapter 6. Backchannel sounds also may be interpreted differently, seen as showing either interest in or acceptance of what is being said. These differences can cause misunderstandings if group members are not aware of them and thus influence how smoothly members can agree on issues. If, for example, you believe group members agree with your ideas based on their "uh-huhs," only to discover later that they were just trying to show interest in your idea, you'll probably be upset!

*Dialect* refers to regional and social variations in pronunciation, vocabulary, and grammar. The different dialects you hear in your groups can influence perceptions of intelligence, competence, and credibility.[33] Countries such as the United States, Great Britain, and Japan have regional and social class language deviations from the "standard" dialect. Group members who use nonstandard dialects—saying, for example, *dees* instead of *these*—are often given lower status and credibility ratings. General American dialect is rated higher on pleasantness and socio-intellectual status than the dialect of South Boston or the Bronx. Communities of speakers show their uniqueness by creating, among other things, their own dialect. Be very cautious about stereotyping group members with dialects different from your own.

**Timing.**    Time cues are both culture-related and relational. In some other cultures and in co-cultures of this country, no one would expect to get right to work in a group meeting; first, one must get the feel of the other people. Most rural people tackle business at a slower pace than their urban counterparts. In the fast-paced U.S. business world, people who come late to meetings are judged inconsiderate and undisciplined. North Americans will allow only about a five-minute leeway before they expect an apology from someone who is late.[34] In the predominant culture of this country, coming late and leaving early indicates to fellow group members that your time is precious but it's OK to waste theirs. In dozens of case studies of student groups, one consistently late member was the subject of bitter complaints by the others.

Time is a vital commodity during meetings. People who talk little and those who talk excessively have little impact. Excessive talkers are considered rude and selfish. Although they did not protest at the time, many students have complained about fellow project group members who waste time by chattering at length about social matters or other topics irrelevant to the group's purpose. On the other hand, those who talk somewhat more than the average are judged favorably on leadership characteristics.[35] In fact, talkativeness, or speaking time, is considered a strong factor in determining how much power a group member is perceived to have.[36] Likewise, people who structure the group's time so that every item on an agenda can be discussed are appreciated. If you are insensitive to time cues in your group, you will have little influence and will not be completely accepted by the others.

No type of nonverbal behavior can be overlooked if you want to understand what is going on in a group. However, much remains to be discovered about how nonverbal communication operates in small groups; group researchers must broaden their efforts to understand this important phenomenon. Relatively little, for instance, is understood about the influence on group behavior of member touch behavior, artifacts such as clothing, emotion, and different kinds of group contexts (e.g., groups in submarines).[37] Remember also that you cannot state with confidence exactly what someone else is thinking or feeling from nonverbal cues alone. We hope the list of nonverbal behaviors presented here encourages you to increase your awareness and sensitivity, but you should not consider this list exhaustive. We summarize this list, in tongue-in-cheek fashion, in Table 4.3, which reminds you how to behave in a group if you want the others to dislike you.

---

| **TABLE 4.3** | **Nonverbal Behaviors Guaranteed to Get Other Members to Dislike You** |
| --- | --- |

Nonverbal behavior plays an especially important role in creating and maintaining group relationships. Here are several suggestions for getting your fellow group members to dislike you:

**1.** Show the others that you don't like them:
- Don't smile.
- Don't lean forward.
- Don't make eye contact.

**2.** Be unresponsive to the others:
- Slouch.
- Don't pay attention.
- Scowl.
- Text message on your cell phone when someone else is talking.

**3.** Keep a poker face to make the others guess what you're thinking.

**4.** Violate an important group appearance norm:
- If your group dresses casually, wear formal attire.
- If business casual is the norm, wear torn sweats. This is especially important if your group is giving a presentation; that's when you should wear your grungiest clothes.

**5.** Violate your group's space norms:
- If group members sit far apart, move in close to another member (and watch him or her squirm).
- If members sit close to each other, you sit farther apart. It might be especially helpful to turn your body so that you seem to have your back to the group.

**6.** Indicate rejection by leaning away from the group.

**7.** Violate your group's movement norms:
- Gesture wildly.
- Don't gesture at all.
- Get up and leave the room without explanation; when you return, don't tell them where you've been.

*(continued)*

| **TABLE 4.3** | *(Continued)* |

**8.** Violate your group's vocal cues:
  - Talk r-e-a-l-l-y s-l-o-w-l-y.
  - Talkasfastasyoucan.
  - SHOUT.
  - Whisper so others have to ask you to repeat.
  - Use jargon the others won't understand.
  - Refuse to use the jargon or special vocabulary of the group.
  - Overuse the backchannel when others are speaking.
  - Don't give any backchannel cues at all—don't do anything to indicate that you're paying attention.

**9.** Violate your group's norms about timing:
  - Come late to meetings (especially without explanation).
  - Leave meetings early (don't explain this, either).
  - Hog the group's time by talking constantly.
  - Don't say anything at all.

# Nonverbal Behavior in Computer-Mediated Groups

As challenging as it is to understand nonverbal behavior in face-to-face (FtF) groups, it is even more challenging in virtual groups and groups using CMC. CMC can take a variety of forms, including e-mail, chat room discussions, electronic bulletin boards, listservs, net conferencing (audio, video, or computer conferencing), and text messaging, to name a few. New technologies are created all the time, and existing technologies evolve at a rapid rate. The corporate world has embraced computer technologies to enhance group work, with organizations using CMC for strategic planning, assessment, product evaluation, and project coordination, and even to replace or enhance routine meetings.[38] This trend is sure to continue, in part because many employees prefer online to FtF meetings.[39] Such technologies can also save an organization time and money. For example, many universities save travel costs for job candidates by scheduling telephone or video conference calls to interview job candidates. These factors make nonverbal communication in CMC important to study!

Nonverbal communication operates differently in CMC environments. For example, in a **net conference**—any meeting where members are electronically connected by networked computers—nonverbal messages such as facial expressions and body language may be missing entirely or exaggerated, depending on the type of conference.[40] If members are all at keyboards, gestures are reduced. If the net conference provides audio but not video links, members cannot see each other's facial expressions, but they can hear tone of voice. Turn taking may be awkward because there is often a half-second delay in transmission, which can make CMC discussions choppier than FtF. For some tasks, such as brainstorming a list of ideas, these nonverbal challenges may not matter much. However, if the group

## The Public Affairs Web Page Committee

At Missouri State University, where Gloria teaches, a six-member committee has been created to establish policies and review materials for the university's public affairs Web page. Initially, their Webmaster drafted the first version of their report, and committee members commented on the draft from the website. After some discussion the committee decided it would conduct most of its business over the Web due to difficult schedules. In addition, members need to conduct private discussions, so they each have a password accessing the committee's Web page at their convenience.

Pretend you are the Webmaster for this committee. You are familiar with the different kinds of net conferences. You also have extensive knowledge of the advantages and disadvantages of using computer-mediated communication to conduct business as compared to meeting face-to-face. Given that your committee wants to conduct all business over the Web, what would you recommend? Draw up a description of how the Web is to be used by this committee given your expertise. Your suggestions and guidelines will be given to all the members.

needs to achieve consensus on an important decision, CMC can impair a group's sense of sharing, involvement, and team spirit.[41]

Nonverbal communication contributes significantly to a medium's **social presence,** which is the extent to which group members perceive the medium (for example, a telephone, a video conference, computer e-mail) to be like FtF interaction socially and emotionally. Members' perception depends on the degree to which they perceive that other members are actually *there* during the interaction.[42] Asynchronous communication, or communication with a delay between messages (e.g., e-mail), promotes less social presence than synchronous, more simultaneous communication (e.g., electronic chat rooms).

Social presence is influenced not only by the technology but also by the complexity of the group task. Net conferences work better for routine tasks and information sharing. The harder the task, though, the less adequate some CMC can become. However, group members can become very inventive when it comes to creating the same kind of social presence found in FtF communication.[43] For example, group members can choose to sandwich net conferences in between FtF meetings, thereby enhancing their "groupness." Groups can use trained moderators who can help improve the process by doing things like reminding members of the rules for speaking and taking turns. When individuals do not know each other, they use cues such as e-mail names to form impressions of one another, thereby increasing social presence.[44] For instance, the more creative names (e.g., stinkybug) were attributed to white males, while ordinary names (e.g., jsmith) were seen as more productive. **Emoticons,** the typographic symbols used in CMC to convey a variety of emotions (e.g., :-) for happiness or :-( for sadness), are substitutes for the type of nonverbal communication that is conveyed by facial expressions or gestures in FtF. Emoticons help increase the social presence of CMC. Social presence is important to a group, and we are just beginning to learn how groups create social presence within the limitations of technology.

### GLOSSARY

**Social Presence**

*The degree to which a person feels that another is actually present during an interaction*

**Emoticons**

*The typographic symbols used in CMC to convey a variety of emotions*

## RESOURCES FOR REVIEW AND DISCUSSION

**SUMMARY**

- Group members communicate via messages, verbal and nonverbal signals they send and interpret; these messages, as noted by the theory of structuration, both create and maintain the group.

- More accurate interpretation of verbal signals occurs when members use standard English, clarify abstract language, organize their remarks, and use clear and appropriate discussion questions.

- Nonverbal behaviors, more believable because they are harder to control, are especially hard to interpret accurately; they supplement or substitute for verbal communication, regulate the flow, and express feelings.

- Nonverbal categories especially important to understanding small group communication include appearance, use of space, facial expressions, eye contact, movements, vocal cues, and timing.

- Group members increasingly use computers to communicate, and computer use dramatically influences the nature of a group's nonverbal messages in particular.

**EXERCISES**

1. Browse through several magazines for interesting advertisements. Cut out a variety of advertisements and bring them to class. Discuss with your group or your class each of the advertisements. Identify what the audience for each ad is and how the language of the ad is designed to appeal to its audience.

2. Generate a list of words with positive connotations and a list of words with negative connotations. Look at the lists of your classmates, and see if any words appear on the same list or different lists. Compile two lists on the board, and discuss why some words are on each list and why some words may be on both lists. Where do these connotations come from?

What kinds of experiences contribute to these connotations?

3. Tape-record a group meeting. Watch the tape, and note the group's seating arrangements and the space between members. Examine the facial expressions and eye contact, and note voice qualities and timing. When you are finished, discuss your observations. How do you think these nonverbal behaviors contributed to the overall communicative character of this group?

 Go to **www.mhhe.com/adamsgalanes7** and **www.mhhe.com/groups** for self-quizzes and weblinks.

**KEY TERMS • CONCEPTS**

| | | |
|---|---|---|
| Bypassing | Group Ecology | Social Presence |
| Discussion Question | Message | Structuration |
| Emoticons | Net Conference | |
| Emotive Words | Nonverbal Behavior | |

**www.mhhe.com/adamsgalanes7**

 Use the flashcards and crossword puzzles on the Online Learning Center to further your knowledge of these key terms.

# From Individuals to Group

Part Three focuses on the interaction among group members as they begin to merge their own individual personalities, cultures, behaviors, and so forth into a functioning group. Chapter 5 looks at how a group develops from an initial collection of individuals into a team, with roles, norms, and a unique group climate. Chapter 6 continues this discussion of group formation by examining various aspects of diversity among members and exploring how this diversity can be managed so the group can perform at its best.

# Becoming a Group

## CHAPTER OUTLINE

The Life Cycle of a Group

Challenges in Group Development

Group Socialization of Members

Group Roles

Rules and Norms

Development of a Group's Climate

Ethical Behavior during Group
Formation

## CHAPTER OBJECTIVES

**After reading this chapter you should be able to:**

1. Explain why groups have a life cycle.

2. Describe the two major tasks groups must manage and how these create an equilibrium problem for a group.

3. Define primary, secondary, and tertiary tension, and give examples of each.

4. Describe Tuckman's model of group development and Gersick's model of punctuated equilibrium and how each describes phases many groups experience.

5. Describe the communicative dynamics of each stage of group socialization.

6. Describe each of the three main categories of roles in groups.

7. Differentiate between formal and behavioral roles, and describe how behavioral roles emerge during group interaction.

8. Differentiate between rules and norms, and describe the four methods by which norms develop.

9. Explain what you would say and do if you wanted to change a group norm.

10. Describe each of the three main components that contribute to a group's climate.

## The *Man of La Mancha* Cast and Crew

Noel, his church's choir director, broke his back in an airplane crash. To make his hospital time pass more quickly, he imagined the choir performing one of his favorite plays, *Man of La Mancha.* When he got out of the hospital, Noel decided to realize his dream by directing the play; he cast all the roles with choir members and performed the lead role of Don Quixote himself. Geoff, an experienced actor, was sidekick Sancho. Geoff couldn't carry a tune, but his acting experience and his unfailing good humor helped the cast mesh into a cohesive team. Gena, in the role of Aldonza, was also an experienced actress but had never before sung solo; however, she had a good sense of rhythm and was able to coach the dancers. Very few of the choir members could sing well, but they had an amazing array of other talents. Davida, who was both shy and clumsy, nevertheless was an outstanding artist and created two fabulous horse heads out of papier-mâché. She also created a minimal but effective set that could be positioned and removed quickly from the sanctuary. There were not enough men for all the roles, so Noel cast women in several parts, including the Barber and the horses. Delores had no sense of rhythm and could sing only whatever part the person next to her was singing, but she was a whiz at creating costumes out of Salvation Army thrift shop treasures.

The cast had only three weeks to rehearse, from the play's first read-through to opening night. Given the lack of singing and acting talent, lack of experience, lack of money for costumes and set materials, and time constraints, this play should have been a disaster. Instead, it was a great success. Several experienced theatergoers said that, although they had seen more professionally mounted productions of *Man of La Mancha,* this performance had touched them emotionally more than other performances.

The cast and crew had grown into a cohesive team whose output far exceeded reasonable expectations. Members contributed all their talents (singing and otherwise) to make the performance a success. Why did this small group work when all "objective" assessments suggested it would fail?

The mutual influence that occurs when group members communicate with each other is at the heart of any group's throughput process. Recall from Chapter 1 how a collection of individuals comes together to become an effective group, much like the *Man of La Mancha* cast and crew. When members interact with each other in such a way as to create an interdependent purpose, and thus succeed or fail together, they have become a group. In Chapter 2 you studied the key principles of these complex social systems and learned that the process of becoming a group is never finished because social systems are always adapting to feedback. This chapter explores more fully some of the throughput processes indicative of an emerging group. You will study in more detail how groups such as the *Man of La Mancha* cast and crew become an effective group. Groups whose individual members develop into a productive team consistently figure out how to manage their tensions and create and maintain constructive roles, norms, and a supportive group climate. These groups must also develop and support a stable leadership structure. Leadership is so central to group dynamics that it will be covered more completely in Chapter 10.

## The Life Cycle of a Group

Small groups, like all other living systems, conform to the natural order of the universe. Although groups are complex and therefore challenging to study, we know a great deal about how such systems emerge and function. For example, groups as systems have their own **life cycles,** or patterns of development over time. They are always in the process of becoming and are never really finished. Each group creates its own culture, or pattern of values, beliefs, norms, and behaviors that are shared by group members and that in turn shape the group's personality. Many factors weave together to create and sustain these minicultures, such as the content and pattern of group communication and the norms and rules guiding group communication. The cast and crew of the *Man of La Mancha* acted in such a way as to become a theater culture with unique ways of speaking about cast and crew roles, of negotiating the wishes of the director and actors, of effectively complementing each other's talents, and so forth. In their three weeks together they created a history with each other that contained cycles of development reflecting all sorts of tensions, norms, and climates unique to them.

The *Man of La Mancha* cast and crew, as a living system, was driven to survive, which may be difficult or even impossible. Even a casual look at nature tells us that the natural life cycle for any system includes conception and birth, growth, maturity, decline, and finally death. But living organisms fight their eventual deaths as long as possible by adapting through feedback to changing conditions. Human groups usually do everything in their power to help ensure their continuation. The cast and crew in Case 5.1 did not abandon their goal of performing *Man of La Mancha* when they faced only three weeks of rehearsal. They did not quit when they assessed their talent and resources. Instead, they emerged into a cohesive unit capable of carrying off a performance that exceeded reasonable expectations.

When members first come together as a new group, they must sort out a variety of factors before they can become a fully functioning group. For instance, they must get to know each other's strengths and weaknesses. A stable leadership structure must emerge, and roles and norms must be established that all members can agree to follow. When these sorts of processes appear, the group can begin to mature and become productive. Individual members may leave and be replaced by new members, but the group can continue indefinitely as a functioning social unit. However, as with any living organism, the small group will eventually decline and disband, perhaps when it no longer has a purpose, when no new members replace those who leave, or when a competing group destroys or absorbs it. At this point the group has completed its usefulness and is appropriately laid to rest.

# Challenges in Group Development

All groups must resolve certain issues on their way to becoming fully functioning groups and teams. Among those are handling the two key tasks all groups face: managing social tensions and moving smoothly from one stage of development to another.

## A GROUP'S MAJOR FUNCTIONS

All groups face certain demands on their way to maturity. All groups must perform two key functions: making progress on the group's task and managing relationships among members. These two functions, task and socioemotional, must be handled simultaneously, thus producing what group members may experience as a tug-of-war between group task and social demands. When members spend emotional and mental energy on the interpersonal issues, they take away from the energy needed to attend to their work. On the other hand, when members attend to the task at hand, they pay less attention to each other's human needs. Robert F. Bales calls this the **equilibrium problem.**[1] A group's attention must shift between concentrating on its task and concentrating on the relationships between members. First, the group must develop dependable, harmonious relationships that will give it stability. Bales refers to this as the group's *socioemotional* concern. Second, the group must focus on its charge, or *task* concern. Neither one of these concerns can be ignored if the group is to succeed. Both need to be attended to, in some degree, throughout the life of the group.

Task and socioemotional concerns surface at predictable periods in a group's life cycle. Initially, before members have gotten to know each other well and developed smooth working relationships, the group must necessarily spend more time on socioemotional issues. Members work out their relationships with each other in a structuration process during which norms, rules, roles (including leadership), and the group's climate emerge. In Case 5.1, for instance, Geoff could not sing well but had valuable acting experience. Davida had not sung solo but had the dancing skills necessary to help coach the dancers. Both were encouraged to put their talents—whatever they were—to use for the group. The *Man of La Mancha* cast and crew did a particularly good job of working out their relationships effectively and finding a valuable role for everyone.

Notice that, while the individual relationships were being worked out, the group was engaged in rehearsing and preparing for its performances. In other words, it could not ignore its task while members got to know each other. In fact, the group relationships developed *in the process of* working on the group's task. Rarely does a group have the luxury of members getting to know each other well before they have to start working—they

**GLOSSARY**

**Equilibrium Problem**

*The problem created by a group's need to balance task and socioemotional concerns simultaneously*

usually have to get to work right away! Thus, instead of a group's task and socioemotional functions occurring separately and sequentially, the group works on both at the same time (i.e., the equilibrium problem), but at any given time one may be more important than the other.

In groups that mature smoothly and effectively, socioemotional issues are handled appropriately in the beginning so that the group can move on to other things. If the group does a good job of working out its initial socioemotional concerns and relationships among members, then as it matures it can focus more energy on its task. For example, once Davida was given the go-ahead to coach the dancers, then Gina—who also had dance experience—didn't need to compete with her for that role. Davida could then concentrate on perfecting the dance chorus while Gina explored her own character's motivations in depth, and they could all get down to the business of putting on a great show.

One final note: Groups never stop dealing with both main functions. Task concerns are always present, and relationships among members must be monitored, with problems addressed as they arise. One function may be in the foreground at any given moment, but the other hasn't disappeared from view. Both task and socioemotional concerns remain key functions groups must manage.

## SOCIAL TENSIONS IN GROUPS

There are three typical tensions most groups experience. **Primary tension** often characterizes a group's early interactions, as members are getting to know each other. During periods of primary tension, interaction is overly polite, with long, uncomfortable pauses in the conversation.[2] This kind of social tension is similar to *stage fright*.[3] Recall how you typically feel the first time you meet with a new group. Like most people you probably worry whether the others will like you and whether you will belong. You want to be valued by the group, and so does everyone else. This makes most members careful not to say or do something that might offend the other members; behavior is tentative, stiff, and cautious. That is why newly formed groups often seem overly formal and excessively polite.

**Secondary tension** usually occurs later in a group's life cycle.[4] This tension is work related and stems from differing opinions about substantive issues. It is inevitable in task groups because members bring different perspectives to their group's task concerns. Potentially more serious than primary tension, it is often unpredictable and, if not managed well, does not go away with the passage of time.[5] One of the best markers of secondary tension is an abrupt move away from the group's routine. This could happen with a sudden outburst from a member followed by an angry exchange between members and then a rather unpleasant long pause. Poor management of secondary tension potentially threatens the interpersonal health of the group and can evolve into a destructive group climate.

Much of the tension we have observed in groups is not strictly primary or secondary. Instead, groups often become bogged down in arguments that seem to recycle over and over. This inability or even unwillingness to manage issues often represents a power or status struggle between members. This is a modified form of primary tension that can appear on the surface to be secondary tension over content issues. When examined more closely, however, they are struggles over how group members define themselves in relationship to each other. These power struggles produce **tertiary tension** among

## GLOSSARY

**Primary Tension**

*Anxiety arising early in a group's formation, as members work out their relationships and roles*

**Secondary Tension**

*Task-related tension that stems from differing opinions about the substantive work of the group*

**Tertiary Tension**

*Tension that stems from power and status struggles in a group*

"Before we begin this family meeting, how about we go around and say our names and a little something about ourselves."

Primary tension includes very polite conversation with uncomfortable pauses and is usually reserved for strangers. © The New Yorker Collection; 2002 Matthew Diffee from cartoonbank.com. All Rights Reserved.

members. Members struggle over who will decide the rules and procedures for the group. Conflict may occur over how to make decisions, how to resolve conflicts, who has the authority to determine what will happen in the group, who can make assignments, who is an expert at what, what are the rights and privileges of group membership, and so forth. Jury deliberations, for instance, are rife with tertiary tensions.[6] Jurors have been known to pick up their chairs and toss them through windows, engage in fistfights, attempt escapes from heated deliberations, write angry notes to the judge, and shout so loudly they can be heard outside their room. More and more jurors are dismissed for such behavior. These actions have prompted courtrooms to develop booklets for jurors explaining how they can constructively manage diverse opinions during jury deliberation.

One of us observed a classroom group experiencing tertiary tension. The group's assignment was to observe a task group and gather data about it, either through observation or by talking to the members. Mike insisted that the group use his questionnaire as one method of gathering data. Michelle demanded instead that the group use her questionnaire. This endless argument was a thinly masked power struggle. If this really had been only secondary tension, Mike and Michelle could easily have combined their questionnaires. Instead, each demanded to be in charge of deciding the group's procedures while the others frustrated themselves trying to come up with a compromise that neither would accept. This potentially destructive power struggle is an example of tertiary tension.

For a group to perform at its best, social tension must be managed appropriately.

1. **Group members can move through the primary tension stage more quickly if they know each other.**

   The choir described in Case 5.1 had an advantage in that members already knew each other fairly well when they began play rehearsals. A get-acquainted period helps members do this—even when members *do* know each other. Don't hesitate to suggest this, even if your group's designated leader doesn't. The members will be able to accomplish their task much more effectively and quickly if they know where the other members are coming from, what they do on the job, and even what hobbies and outside interests they have. Joking, laughing, and having fun together before getting down to work help as well. So does storytelling. David Ryfe found that one way members get to know each other and form a collective sense of who they are and what they believe is through narrative—telling stories.[7] However, telling stories takes time; thus, it is important for the group's leader or facilitator to allow storytelling to occur without cutting the process off prematurely.

2. **Members can reduce both primary and secondary tension by sharing what they know about the problem at hand.**

   For instance, if a committee is charged with recommending solutions to a campus parking problem, each member's perception of the scope and seriousness of the problem can be shared so that all will have some common understanding of the problem. This mapping process will be described in Chapter 8.

3. **Secondary and tertiary tensions can be managed if group members demonstrate tolerance for disagreement.**

   When group members believe that their opinions and ideas are appreciated, even if these opinions are contrary to the ideas of others, then they feel valued by the group. They also are less likely to demand high status if they already believe the group appreciates them. Showing that you appreciate someone else's thoughtful analysis, even if you don't fully agree, can help. For example, saying, "I see what you mean about the hidden costs of that option, Tom, and that's something I hadn't considered" shows Tom that you were listening and that you appreciate the careful thought he gave to the issue. Statements that acknowledge confidence in the group (e.g., "We'll be able to find an answer—we've done a good job so far") help develop solidarity in the group system.

4. **Humor is also an effective way to handle secondary and tertiary tension in a group.**

   A well-timed, lighthearted comment can move a group past an obstacle that seems insurmountable. Joking and laughing together increase the members' good feelings toward each other. This in turn helps members become more open toward each other, which can lead to resolution of their substantive and status differences. However, *never* joke to change the topic or to put someone in his or her place, because this can destroy the cohesiveness the group has developed.

Tertiary tension is always tricky to handle; indirect methods often don't work. Group members will probably have to address the problem directly by saying something to the offending members. Either a group's designated leader or one of the other members can politely but firmly confront the members involved in the status struggle by pointing out the negative effects the power struggle is having on the rest of the group.

## Managing Tertiary Tensions

**APPLY NOW**

A situation that arose between Gena and Geoff on the set of *Man of La Mancha* illustrates the type of situation that often leads to tertiary tension. Gena had been in several plays and had studied acting informally. She loved the process of uncovering a character from the inside out and discovering the meaning of a scene or a line through the rehearsal period. Geoff was a more experienced actor with some directing experience as well. He had strong ideas about how certain lines should be read and certain scenes played. When he took it upon himself to advise Gena about how to read certain lines, she was both irritated and confused. She liked Geoff and respected his experience, but she had her own preferred way of developing a character. She knew she had several choices about how to handle the emerging conflict with Geoff, with some choices likely to be more effective than others for the entire enterprise. Consider Gena's situation:

1. What were several options Gena had for handling this situation? For example, she could do nothing or she could quit the cast. (List at least five in addition to these two.)

2. How was Geoff likely to react to each of these choices?

3. What were the likely outcomes for the group as a whole of each of these choices?

4. If you were faced with this choice, what would be more important to you—keeping control of "your" character or maintaining harmony among the cast? Are there other things that would be more important to you in this situation than harmony or control? If so, what would those be?

5. What choice would you be likely to make, and why? How effective do you think this choice would be?

Ask two class members to select one of Gena's options and to role-play this situation. After discussion about what worked and what didn't, ask two different class members to role-play a different option. Which communication strategies seem to be more effective? Why?

The process of managing task and socioemotional demands and their accompanying social tensions can be further complicated if a group uses electronic technology as a tool. Many people believe that computer-mediated technology increases a group's task communication while it decreases its socioemotional communication: This occurs because electronic tools keep groups focused on such task-related processes as keeping records, listing ideas, and structuring the problem-solving process. In addition, tools such as e-mail, which provide limited ways to express nonverbal cues, may encourage members not to think of each other as individuals. However, researchers examining groups using CMC have discovered that members find ways to communicate socioemotional information that is the same as the information exchanged in face-to-face groups.[8]

## PHASE MODELS IN GROUP DEVELOPMENT

Small group scholars have observed that many groups experience predictable phases as they develop; several group development models describe such phases. We will discuss two such models: Tuckman's model of group development and Gersick's punctuated equilibrium model.

### Tuckman's Model of Group Development.

Bruce Tuckman's model of group development is one of the best-known models for describing typical stages in how groups develop.[9] This linear model assumes that groups move through five stages from beginning to end. (Initially, the model contained four stages.) *Forming* occurs when group members first meet. Members form initial impressions of one another, start to get a handle on the group's task, and focus on getting along. The group avoids conflict and controversy as it deals with primary tension. Next, *storming* occurs when members start to tackle the group's important issues and strong feelings start to surface. In this stage members argue to defend their points of view. In the *norming* stage, the group has worked through its initial conflicts to establish its rules and norms about how it will operate. Members have gotten to know and appreciate one another's skills and abilities and feel like they are part of a group. During the *performing* stage, group members are able to work smoothly and effectively together. Not every group reaches this stage of development, but for groups that do, members are interdependent, responsibilities shift appropriately, and group identification is high. A fifth stage, *adjourning*, was added to the model later. In this stage, as the group completes its task, members prepare for the group to disband. They may agree to keep in touch, and, in fact, some relationships are likely to continue after the group's life has ended.

Many small group scholars consider phase models too simplistic. There are many factors that can affect whether a group progresses through stages in an orderly way, what stages a group experiences, what order those stages occur in, and how long a stage may last. However, phases such as those in Tuckman's model seem to describe what many people have experienced. Thus, even though these stages are not universal, they do seem to capture the common experiences of many of us.

### Gersick's Model of Punctuated Equilibrium.

Connie Gersick's model of punctuated equilibrium stands in contrast to linear models such as Tuckman's.[10] In her examination of real-time work teams, Gersick discovered that these teams moved back and forth between periods of stability (she referred to this as *inertia*), with members working steadily but unremarkably on the task, and short periods of significant change.

Thus, the *change* punctuated the long periods of stability, or *equilibrium,* to create **punctuated equilibrium.** No matter how long the group had to complete its task, the key punctuation point occurred at the group's midpoint. For example, if the group had six months to complete its task, a significant transition point likely occurred at the three-month point. If the group was given three months, the transition occurred at one and a half months.

Before the midpoint, team members figured out what their charge was and how they would approach the task; they then worked steadily within that framework. At the halfway point, however, the groups suddenly seemed to realize that their time was beginning to run out. Members broke from their routine work to assess what progress was being made toward the group's task; successful teams made adjustments in their work procedures, time lines, and so forth. If constructive changes were not made at this midpoint, they likely wouldn't be made at all because, during the second half of their time frame, teams moved into another long period of stability in how they went about their work. Then, as teams approached the end of their time period, they rushed to meet the expectations of outsiders, such as the boss, the teacher, or the parent organization. If the initial work procedures were appropriate, or the team made the right adjustments at midpoint, the team succeeded. Otherwise, the team failed to achieve its goals.

We see this kind of development all the time in small group communication courses. Initially, groups lay out how to proceed, stick to their plans, and then at midterm or midsemester realize they may or may not have understood the assignment well enough to receive a positive final evaluation. They make all sorts of changes. Some groups effectively correct their path while others do not. Then, as the time nears for group presentations, many groups spend a concentrated time with each other, sometimes all night, preparing for final presentations. When students receive their grades on their written and oral assignments, they experience the consequences of meeting, or not meeting, outside expectations. Groups can become set in their ways very early in their life cycle, resisting change until midway. Then at midpoint they are most open to assess their progress; however, they must be willing to make constructive changes. At the end there is another flurry of activity, and the expectations of outsiders become particularly relevant.

The life cycles of groups are complex and do not occur in clean, discrete stages. However, members can assess how well they are proceeding by paying attention to important factors that affect the group's development. One factor that can alter a group's development is the change brought on by new members in newly formed and existing groups. One common reality is that group membership often changes. We now turn our attention to how both individuals and groups deal with socialization of members.

# Group Socialization of Members

When we hear the word *socialization,* we generally think about someone who is learning to become part of something, such as a group. Just as children are socialized into families and school, group members are also socialized into newly formed and established groups. Carolyn Anderson, Bruce Riddle, and Matthew Martin define group socialization in a way

## Integrating a New Member

One week before a community theater's opening night of *Hotel Paradiso*, leading man Richard, who had been complaining of shortness of breath, was told by his doctor that he needed heart bypass surgery—immediately! The cast was devastated. Members were concerned about Richard, of course, but they also were concerned about watching their six weeks of rehearsals go down the drain. The cast and crew had become a tight, cohesive group. Rehearsals had been going well, with the play promising to be the season's top moneymaker. The director debated canceling the run but prevailed on his talented friend Ted to assume Richard's part. Opening night was delayed for a week to give Ted time to learn the lines and the cast time to integrate a new cast member.

1. If you were the director, what would you do to help the reformulated cast get through its formation phase so members could focus on the play? Is there anything that can speed up the cast's formation phase?

2. If you were Ted, what would you do to help the other cast members feel comfortable with you?

3. If you were the cast members, how would you help Ted feel at ease?

that emphasizes the central role of communication in group processes including the socialization of members.[11] **Group socialization** is a

> *reciprocal process of social influence and change in which both newcomers and/or established members and the group adjust and adapt to one another through verbal and nonverbal communication as they create and re-create a unique culture and group structures, engage in relevant processes and activities, and pursue individual and group goals.*[12]

This definition is lengthy, so let's take it apart and examine what it implies about the process of group socialization. First, the adapting and adjusting that happen when a new group forms or when new members enter an established group occur through *communication* among group members. Anderson, Riddle, and Martin point out that communication is instrumental in reducing the uncertainty that is often felt during this time.[13] For group socialization to be effective, everyone involved must practice open communication, be accepting of the new member, and welcome the positive change new members can bring. For instance, if the community theater cast members had not talked to each other about Ted (see Apply Now), welcomed him into the troupe, and seen his presence as a way to move in new directions, then his willingness to replace Richard would have been a waste.

Second, the definition above recognizes that effective socialization requires a balance between individual member and group goals as well as comparable positive satisfaction levels between the member and the group. Ted, the community theater director, and the other cast members had to have similar goals and levels of comfort if Ted's stepping in for Richard was to be a positive experience.

### GLOSSARY

**Group Socialization**

*The process by which new and/or established members learn to fit together through communication*

Finally, the definition acknowledges socialization as an ongoing process that is not only about the new member but also about the group. When we consider how the community theater group might have handled Ted's entry into the group successfully, we must think about what Ted, the director (or leader), *and* the cast (the group) could have done to manage this kind of group change. Understanding the phases of group socialization may help you to further consider how this community theater group and Ted could best manage his entrance into the cast.

## STAGES OF GROUP SOCIALIZATION

Anderson, Riddle, and Martin describe five stages of group socialization: antecedent, anticipatory, encounter, assimilation, and exit.[14] Each stage has its own unique communication demands. Remember that different groups move through these stages at different speeds and may cycle back through one or more stages; also, behaviors in one stage have a ripple effect on subsequent stages. The stages are summarized in Table 5.1.

In Chapter 2 we discussed group inputs such as member characteristics and their potential impact on group throughput and outputs. In Chapter 3 we talked about the influence

For more information on antecedent socialization in online groups, go to the Online Learning Center at **www.mhhe.com/ adamsgalanes7**

| TABLE 5.1 | Stages of Group Socialization |

| Socialization Stage | Description |
| --- | --- |
| Antecedent | Before new members join the group, new and old members have attitudes, beliefs, motives, and behavior patterns that affect how they will function in the group. |
| Anticipatory | New and old members have expectations about one another; the new members have expectations about the group. Welcoming activities that introduce old and new members (informal dinners, getting-to-know-you meetings) help members overcome primary tension. |
| Encounter | New and old members begin to work together and adjust to one another; the new member's role is negotiated in the group, and old members' roles may change. |
| Assimilation | The new members are fully integrated into the group; role relationships have been worked out. |
| Exit | Members must cope with the loss of a member or the termination of the group. Discussion and formal disbanding activities help members say goodbye. |

In Chapter 6 we will talk about cultural differences and group processes.

Recall our discussion of listening styles in Chapter 3.

## GLOSSARY

**Antecedent Stage**

The stage in group socialization during which members bring previous group experiences, attitudes, beliefs, motives, and communication traits to the process

**Anticipatory Stage**

The stage in group socialization describing individual and group initial expectations of each other

of different listening styles on group interaction and outcomes. In Chapter 6 we will talk about cultural differences and group processes. These individual characteristics play a key role in the **antecedent stage** of group socialization. All members, including Ted in our preceding example, bring to a group their own attitudes, motives, and communication behaviors. This profoundly affects how ready and able they are to engage in the socialization process and how willingly they approach group work and building relationships. Let's take, for instance, the attitude commonly referred to as *grouphate*.[15] Many of the ideas and attitudes people bring to new or existing groups are based on previous experiences in groups. If someone has been a member of groups that have struggled to get anything done, she or he may internalize this experience and, in future groups, show a negative bias toward groups and group work. We hear students in small group classes repeatedly verbalizing their dislike for anything resembling group work because of horrific experiences in the past. This kind of pessimism makes it very difficult for someone with bad group experiences to join a new group and equally difficult for other group members to welcome such a person to the group.

Another antecedent factor that affects group socialization is our disposition or motive for communication. Recall our discussion of listening styles in Chapter 3. Some of us listen in order to sustain the relationships in the group, and others listen to make sure the work gets done. Some focus their listening on meeting a time schedule, and others focus on information only from trusted sources. These listening preferences are also tied to our motives for communicating and influence effective socialization of members. For instance, those members who communicate to build relationships report more satisfaction with groups. Those who communicate to facilitate the work talk more in the group. Members highly motivated for both reasons are generally more willing to engage in the socialization process.[16]

Communication apprehension and verbal aggressiveness are two other antecedent factors influencing group socialization. Individuals or group members who are not comfortable talking in groups—that is, who experience communication apprehension—find it hard to participate actively in socialization. For socialization in groups to be effective, members have to communicate with each other to reduce the uncertainty inherent in the socialization experience. On the other hand, individuals or group members may be quite comfortable talking and may even be verbally aggressive—they attack others when expressing disagreement. This kind of communication typically alienates others and does not promote positive socialization experiences.[17]

The **anticipatory stage** of group socialization involves all the initial expectations members have of each other and the group. These expectations form the basis for what the individual and the group anticipate will happen over the life of the group. Have you ever expected to really like someone and to have a successful meeting with them, only to have your expectations crushed? Suppose the director had really talked Ted up to the cast, who were led to anticipate a master actor and great opening night. In turn, suppose Ted had been told about the great cast he was joining. Both parties would have anticipated a successful experience. However, if their expectations had not been accurate, socialization could have been a disaster. In both examples, the more the group members' expectations differ from their actual experience, the more chance there is for anxiety and even anger between members.

Socialization involves both individual expectations (Ted) and group expectations (cast). Individuals enter new or existing groups with all sorts of expectations, including estimating how well they will be received and how much they will be respected as individuals. Ted may have predicted that he would be well received and, although he was stepping in for Richard, the cast understood that he brought his own interpretation to the role. If his predictions were not met, he would have had a stressful entry into the group, and both he and the group would have had a negative experience—even perhaps an unsuccessful adjustment. For the cast members (in this case comprising an existing group), their anticipatory phase began when Ted agreed to take over for Richard. If cast members were open to the adjustment ahead of them, they were more likely to promote Ted's integration into the group.

We asked you to think about what each party could have done to help welcome Ted (see Apply Now). Group socialization is enhanced when groups systematically have in place ways to welcome new members.[18] In the case of the community theater cast, this could include a meeting with Ted in which members introduced each other and talked about their expectations, an informal dinner with Ted, and a tour of the theater, stage, and dressing rooms. Stewart Sigman calls these kinds of activities *audition practices,* and they help both the new member and the group draw more realistic expectations and experience less primary tension during socialization.[19]

The third stage of group socialization is the **encounter stage.** The learning that occurs in all forms of socialization begins in earnest during this phase. It starts when the expectations of the anticipatory stage meet the realities of the group and lasts for an indefinite period.[20] During the encounter stage the individual and the group are adjusting the group's norms, culture, climate, goals, roles, and leadership structure—topics we discuss later in this chapter.

As we mentioned earlier in our discussion of group socialization, it is important to negotiate a balance between individual and group goals. During this stage members also negotiate their roles in the group. The roles established in a newly forming group can be disrupted later with the addition of a new member. Communication about individual role expectations and careful assessment of what the group needs are necessary if socialization is to be a positive experience. For instance, newcomers who proactively seek information about role expectations are socialized more effectively than those who do not seek this kind of information.[21] We talk more about roles and norms later in the chapter.

The **assimilation stage** is characterized by full integration into the group and its structures.[22] In full integration new members have become comfortable with the group culture and show an active interest in the group's task and relationships. In turn, the existing members demonstrate acceptance of the new member. Members show a productive and supportive blending, enacting communication necessary to sustain the group's culture. If this integration does not occur smoothly, as is often the case, secondary tension can throw the group back into the anticipatory and encounter stages. Do not be surprised if these regressions occur because, over a group's life span, members will often have to negotiate a good fit between themselves and the rest of the group.

The fifth stage of group socialization is the **exit stage.** Earlier we remarked that group socialization is a process that continues over the course of a group's life. This process is experienced at both the individual and the group level and actually ends when a member leaves or when the group ceases to exist. Exiting a group, whether because an individual leaves or a group breaks up, can be a difficult transition and is one that group members often minimize.[23] If a member leaves, such as Richard in the community theater example, the group must deal with why he left, how he left, how his departure changes their communication, and what comes next. When an entire group disbands, members deal with variations of the same issues.

When an individual leaves a group, the departure is often complicated because the member may have left psychologically earlier than she or he left physically. Kathy, one of your authors, watched as a colleague and good friend retired. Almost a year before he actually left the department, he mentally pulled out. Kathy watched his interest in department issues fade, which affected what issues he fought for and how he voted in faculty meetings. Should you or anyone else leave a group voluntarily, it is a good idea to let others know you are leaving, help the group adjust to your departure, and try to remain in some sort of contact after you leave. This can help to avert such things as grouphate.

Group turnover is common. How many times have you watched as a member left, and then found yourself dealing with the loss and the adjustment to a new member? This process can be filled with uncertainty and resentment, or it can be managed quite well. Your group can effectively manage turnover by developing a positive group attitude toward turnover—seeing it as a way to redefine who you are. When an entire group ends, do not treat it lightly—how you disband affects the kind of experiences you take into the next group. Joann Keyton recommends that groups give themselves an opportunity to say good-bye and to process their experience.[24]

Group socialization is a complex process spanning the entire life of a group. Recognizing its characteristics adds depth to our understanding of group phases and acknowledges that groups often do not mature with the original members but must adapt and adjust to members coming and going. The encounter stage of group socialization involves several components of group life including roles, rules and norms, and group climate. We turn now to a discussion of group member roles and their importance to group dynamics.

# Group Roles

Your **role** is the part you play in a group. The role you perform in any particular group is a function of your personality, your behavior, your expectations, the expectations of other members, and any formal titles or instructions you may have been given regarding that group. Just as an actor has a role in a play, so do we all have a part to play in each group we belong to. And just as an actor has different parts in different plays, so do we have a unique position in each group we join.

## TYPES OF ROLES

Member roles are formal or informal. Formal roles are assigned on the basis of a member's formal position or title and are sometimes called *positional* roles. For example, one member may hold the title of secretary for the group. *Secretary* is a formal role that carries with it certain requirements and expectations, which the group's rules will state: "The secretary shall write and distribute to all members minutes of all meetings held by the group. At the end of each year the secretary shall provide a written summary of the group's work during that year to the president of the student senate."

Informal roles, sometimes called *behavioral* roles, are the parts people play that reflect their personality traits, habits, and behaviors in the group. Through trial and error, every member of a group begins to specialize in certain behaviors within the group. For example, one work group included a member who knew how to use databases to find pertinent research reports. She became the group's bibliographer, as well as its prodder by constantly encouraging everyone to finish assignments when promised. Specific roles result from an interplay between the individual's characteristics and other members of the group and emerge from group interaction.

## ROLE FUNCTIONS IN A SMALL GROUP

Members' roles in small groups are categorized according to what they do for the group: How does this behavior help or hinder the group in achieving its goal? Small group roles are typically classified into three main behavior categories: task, maintenance, and individual. The first two are helpful to the group; the third is not.

**Task Roles.**    A **task role** encompasses behaviors that contribute directly to the accomplishment of the group's task. You probably can think of many task-related behaviors you have seen performed in groups. Recently, one of us served on a church building committee trying to find a new place to meet. One member said, "Let's make a list of all the possibilities in our price range." After the committee completed the list, the member said, "Now, let's split up the list and each visit one or two before our next meeting. Who will volunteer to look at the two buildings on Glenstone Avenue?" These remarks, which *suggested procedure* and also helped *coordinate* the work of the group, are examples of task behavior. Some other helpful task roles are:

- **Initiating and orienting:** proposing goals, activities, or plans of action; defining the group's position in relation to the goal. ("Let's get started by assigning ourselves tasks to complete before the next meeting.")
- **Information giving:** offering facts, information, evidence, or personal experience relevant to the group's task. ("Last year, the library spent $50,000 replacing stolen books.")
- **Information seeking:** asking for facts, information, evidence, or relevant personal experience. ("John, how many campus burglaries were reported last year?")
- **Opinion giving:** stating beliefs, values, and judgments; drawing conclusions from evidence. ("I don't think theft of books is the worst problem facing our library.")
- **Clarifying:** making ambiguous statements clearer or interpreting issues. ("I could support that as long as the cost isn't outrageous, meaning that it is less than $10,000.")
- **Elaborating:** expressing judgments about the relative worth of information or ideas; proposing or applying criteria. ("Here are three problems I see with the production.")
- **Summarizing:** reviewing what has been said previously; reminding the group of items previously mentioned or discussed. ("So by next week, Delores will have the costumes made and Noel will have cast members committed to the play.")
- **Consensus testing:** asking if the group has reached a decision acceptable to all; suggesting that agreement has been reached. ("We seem to all agree that we do not have enough men for the parts and it is OK for me to find women for those parts.")

"Would you please elaborate on 'then something bad happened'?"

Clarifying is an important task function in a group. © The New Yorker Collection; 2004 Leo Cullum from cartoonbank.com. All Rights Reserved.

- **Recording:** keeping group records; preparing reports and minutes; serving as group memory. ("I have a laptop so I can bring it to our meetings to take notes.")
- **Suggesting procedure:** suggesting a method or procedure to follow. ("Why don't we try brainstorming to help us come up with something new and different?")

**Maintenance Roles.**   **Maintenance roles** incorporate those behaviors that help the group maintain harmonious relationships and a cohesive interpersonal climate. One member of the church building committee welcomed another member back from a three-week trip by saying, "It's great to have you back! Here's a summary of everything we did while you were gone. We held off making a decision until you got back because we really wanted to know what you thought." These remarks demonstrate a *gatekeeping* function by allowing the absent member to contribute to the discussion, and they *show solidarity* and *support.* Other helpful maintenance roles are:

- **Establishing norms:** suggesting ways to behave; challenging unproductive ways of behaving; calling attention to violations of norms. ("Let's not call each other names because it does not get us anywhere.")
- **Supporting:** agreeing; expressing support for another's idea or belief; following another's lead. ("I think Noel is right. We should consider putting women into some of the male parts.")

- **Harmonizing:** reducing tension by reconciling disagreement; suggesting a compromise or new alternative acceptable to all; combining proposals into a compromise alternative; calming an angry member. ("Gena and Davida, I think there are areas where you are in agreement. Let me suggest a compromise.")
- **Tension relieving:** joking and otherwise relieving tension; making strangers feel at ease; reducing status differences; encouraging informality. ("We're starting to get on each other's nerves, let's take a break.")
- **Dramatizing:** storytelling and fantasizing in a vivid way; evoking fantasies about other people and places. ("You just reminded me about the time . . .")
- **Showing solidarity:** indicating positive feelings toward one another; reinforcing a sense of group unity; promoting teamwork. ("We've done a great job pulling together. I have no doubt our performance will win rave reviews.")

**Individual Roles.**     **Individual roles** consist of self-centered behaviors. A self-centered member places his or her needs ahead of the group's. These roles do not help the group in any way and may be extremely harmful. Self-centered members may end up reducing their ability to influence other members because they generally are less well liked. Members prefer colleagues whose communication is other- rather than self-centered.[25] Unhelpful individual roles are:

- **Withdrawing:** giving no response to others; avoiding important differences; refusing to cope with conflicts; refusing to take a stand. ("Do whatever you want; I don't care.")
- **Blocking:** preventing progress toward group goals by constantly raising objections, repeatedly bringing up the same topic or issue after the group has considered it and rejected it. ("I know we already voted, but I want to talk about this again.")
- **Status seeking and recognition seeking:** hogging the stage, boasting, and calling attention to one's experience when it is not necessary; playing games to elicit sympathy. ("I think we should do it the way I did it last year. I won Committee Chair of the Year award, you know.")
- **Playing:** refusing to help the group with the task; excessive joking, dramatizing, and horsing around; making fun of others who are serious about the work. ("Don't be such a stick-in-the-mud; we've still got lots of time to finish. One time I remember . . .")
- **Acting helpless:** trying to elicit sympathy by constantly needing help to complete tasks; showing inability for independent thought or action; forcing others to complete or redo work turned in. ("I don't know what you want me to do here. I have never used a computer and I don't think I can do it.")

The task, maintenance, and individual roles are but one system for categorizing roles in a group. Other systems exist, but this one has held up well and has been described as fairly accurate.[26] In addition, recent research suggests the value of having a balance of roles in a group.[27] Different types of behaviors and ways of approaching issues are needed at different points during a group's life cycle; having individuals whose roles complement one another enhances a team's performance.

## THE EMERGENCE OF ROLES IN A GROUP

Through communication with each other, members gradually structure their unique contributions and roles. Think for a moment about the groups you belong to. Do you act exactly the same way in each one of them? Probably not. There are variations in your behavior because each group brings out different combinations of your skills, abilities, and personality characteristics. Normal people want to contribute their unique talents and abilities so they will be valued by the group. When the other group members appreciate and reward those behaviors, they perform them more often. In that way roles and a division of labor develop in the group.

Let's look at an example of how this occurs. Jan had a gift for storytelling. Because Jan felt uncomfortable whenever there was a lull in her seminar's discussion, she generally filled the silences with a story. Stories about her extensive travels easily captured the other members' attention and relieved the uneasiness that silence sometimes caused. The rest of the group encouraged her to relate her stories. Because of both Jan's ability to entertain and the other members' desire to listen, she carved out an informal (behavioral) role as the group's storyteller.

The other members of the group must reinforce a member's behavior if a role is to become stable and strong. If the other members had not been eager to set aside their work momentarily to listen to Jan, they would not have encouraged the development of her storyteller role. Instead, they would have discouraged her by paying little attention or reminding her that she was deflecting the group from its task. In that case Jan would have downplayed her storytelling and searched for another way to contribute. For example, she also was an active listener who clarified and summarized what others said. If she had not won esteem as the group's storyteller, she might have become the group's recorder or historian. From this example you can see how a member's role in a group depends not only on that member's characteristics, but also on how the other members respond.

## Creating a Space for Yourself in the Group

**APPLY NOW**

Everyone needs to feel valued and appreciated by his or her fellow group members. Sometimes, it isn't clear what your contribution—your role—should be. It was especially hard for members of the *Man of La Mancha* extras to know what their contributions should be. Most of them were not actors or dancers; quite a few were not even very good singers! Assume you are Davida, one of the people cast as extras, with limited performing talent. However, you like the idea of the project, you like your fellow cast members, and you really want the project to succeed. What can you personally do to make this project your own?

1. As Davida, do a brainwriting assignment: List your assets and talents. (In addition to the artistic talent we know you have, list at least five other assets.)
2. How could those assets and talents be used for this project?
3. Of the talents/assets listed in step 1, which one or ones would you prefer to use to help this project?
4. What strategies could you use to help ensure that you get to contribute in this way?

The advent of new communication technologies such as net conferences and group decision support systems can produce unanticipated effects on group dynamics, including role emergence.[28] Some types of net conferencing require a facilitator to coordinate their use, which can change the role dynamics of the group. More routine CMC such as e-mail offers those group members experienced in computers opportunities to take over leadership roles they might not otherwise be open to. In addition, the anonymity of some communication technologies and their asynchronous nature can alter who in the group typically dominates, horses around, or fills the leadership functions.

## MANAGING GROUP ROLES

Equally important to understanding the role dynamics of your group is recognizing that effective management of group roles requires that members realize they bring to their groups roles from other groups they participate in. The bona fide group perspective we touched on in Chapter 2 acknowledges that group members are often simultaneously members of other groups. These role demands may conflict with the time and commitment expectations of our roles in other groups. These sometimes conflicting demands brought on by membership in multiple groups affects the role negotiation and emergence of our roles in these groups. Just how might the cast and crew of *Man of La Mancha* have managed their simultaneous roles in their theater group with their professional and family group demands?

Most of us desire to be a part of volunteer "life enrichment groups" such as church and community groups. Anyone who has been a member of one or more of these groups knows they can clash with the demands of work and family. The trick is finding a balance between the multiple group demands on our time and commitments. Michael Kramer, who studied one community theater group extensively, found that members used a variety of strategies to manage these multiple group demands.[29] One strategy people use to balance these demands is to express to the members of the volunteer groups how important both kinds of groups are to them while also showing the sacrifice made to the volunteer group. When conflicts between life enrichment groups and family and work occur, members can either segment or integrate their membership. Had these conflicts arisen for the cast and crew of *Man of La Mancha*, they could have given priority to family and work during the day and then committed evenings to the theater group. They could also have been very clear early as to the limits of their commitment. As more and more of us work at home and the boundaries between work, family, and our volunteer groups blur, negotiating these kinds of multiple group membership may get harder and harder.[30]

Roles emerge from the structuration processes of a group as members seek to balance the demands of the task and their interpersonal relationships. Out of this same trial-and-error interaction, groups will create their rules and norms. We turn our focus to a discussion of how rules and norms form and change over a group's life cycle, as well as how they affect group dynamics.

# Rules and Norms

The premise throughout this text is that communication is *the* essential throughput process within a small group. Structuration theory, introduced in Chapter 4, helps explain how a group's communicative patterns create and sustain the group's norms and

**GLOSSARY**

**Rules**

*Formal, explicit standards of behavior and procedures by which a group operates*

**Norms**

*Informal, implicit standards of behavior and procedures by which members operate*

operating procedures. Recall from this earlier discussion that group members do not come to a group void of any assumptions about how to behave. Instead, they bring to the group complex understandings of how to behave from the general culture and past group experience. These rules and norms do not force members to act in a certain way but act as guides for behavior. Group member behavior can maintain these standards, modify them, or even ignore them and create new ones. Group communication simultaneously reinforces previous standards and creates new ones to be maintained or changed in the future.

The whole process of communication among group members is rule-governed.[31] **Rules** and **norms** are the standards of behavior and procedures by which group members operate. Norms (informal standards) are not written down. In contrast, rules are more formal and usually are written in minutes or bylaws. Norms and rules tell members what they are allowed to do (e.g., "Members may call for a soda break after an hour"), what they are not allowed to do (e.g., "The seat at the head of the table is reserved for the group's chair, and no one else may occupy it"), and what they should do (e.g., "The designated leader is responsible for reserving the meeting place"). Both rules and norms belong to the group as a system rather than to any individual and differ from each other only in their degree of formality. Norms are enforced by peer pressures, whereas rules are usually enforced by the designated leader. Rules must be changed by voting, but members may agree to change norms after an informal discussion.

Rules and norms serve several functions for the group. By letting group members know what is and is not acceptable behavior, rules and norms reduce the uncertainty members feel about how to act. They establish procedures for working as a coordinated team. In the long run, productive rules and norms help the group achieve a high level of efficiency and quality control so that it can accomplish its assigned task well. Can you imagine how hard it would be if, every time you had a meeting, you had to negotiate the procedures by which the group should operate? You would be wasting all your valuable time deciding *how* you should work instead of getting your job done.

Formal rules are constructed in a couple of ways. Sometimes committees and other small groups establish their own formal rules for how they want to operate. Other times the parent organization that created the group also gives it rules by which to operate. For example, many large organizations use the committee procedures in *Robert's Rules of Order Revised* to govern meetings.

Norms usually are not discussed openly, but they still have a strong effect on the behavior of the group members. A friend of ours served on the city council of a small town. The council had developed a norm of meeting until all old business had been cleared, which meant that they sometimes met until midnight. Carla, a new member appointed to fill a vacancy for a council member who had been transferred, started to pack up her materials to leave at 9 o'clock. She explained that she assumed the group would end the meeting by 9 whether members had finished or not, and she had not made child care arrangements past that time. The other members looked at her in surprise. Some were sympathetic, but all continued to meet after she had left. At subsequent meetings Carla, who realized her mistaken assumption about meeting norms, changed her child care arrangements so she could stay until the meeting's end.

## DEVELOPMENT OF GROUP NORMS

How do you suppose the council members established their norm of working until the old business was cleared business? There are a number of ways norms are set in a small group.[32]

1. **Behaviors that occur early in the group's history often establish norms through primacy.**

   When group members first meet, they feel uncertain and uncomfortable. Anything that reduces the uncertainty is welcomed. Thus, what first occurs in a group can easily become habit because it helps reduce the feeling of uncertainty. For example, suppose you serve on a committee that includes faculty and students. Initially, you aren't sure whether to address the faculty members by their first names; if you hear a fellow student member addressing them by titles, chances are you will follow that lead.

2. **Sometimes norms are established by explicit statements that a leader or another member makes.**

   For example, one member might tell a new member, "The boss likes to have proposals in writing. If you want to make a suggestion about work procedures at the staff meeting, you should bring a handout for everyone to use." This statement relays information about the group leader's preferences and also subtly lets the new member know that suggestions are supposed to be well thought out before being presented to the group.

3. **Some norms are established through critical events that occur in a group.**

   For example, one of us once taught a graduate seminar of nine people who came to trust each other, often revealing personal information in class. Two of the students told nonmembers some of what occurred in the class. When the other members discovered this, they felt angry. At the next class meeting, members expressed their feelings of betrayal. Before the critical incident, some members thought it was all right to reveal in-class information to selected outsiders, but after the meeting it was clear to all members that such behavior was a serious violation of a group confidentiality norm.

4. **Many norms are taken from the general culture in which the group members live.**

   For example, you know a lot about how to behave as a student, no matter what the class. True, some professors are more formal than others, but certain standards of behavior (such as raising your hand when you have a question or a comment and not calling the professor or other students rude names) carry over from one class to another. Thus, many carryover behaviors in a group are ones we have learned as members of a particular culture.

This particular origin of small group norms may become troublesome when we interact with members from different cultures. For example, we have observed students from Asian cultures behave very submissively in groups of American students. These international students were following the norms of their native cultures, just as were the American students. Likewise, African Americans and Hispanics tend to use the vocal backchannel

Go to
**www.mhhe.com/
adamsgalanes7**
for additional
weblink activities.

## Norm Enforcement in Internet Groups

**MEDIA AND TECHNOLOGY**

Participants in an Internet chat room sometimes experience *flaming,* or a personal attack (i.e., insults, sarcasm, intense language) on someone for a posting. Flaming has become a distinct characteristic of CMC and has been interpreted by many providers to be unsuitably hostile. These behaviors range from personal attacks to a mild form of teasing, and a number of researchers have found that flaming can serve an unintended purpose in chat rooms. In his examination of Internet mailing lists, Hongiie Wang found that flaming was one of the only tools users had to enforce the informal rules they believed to exist. Flaming was used as a form of policing or a method to "educate the ignorant" about the rules and norms of the Listserv. Additionally, findings indicated that flaming (when handled appropriately) helped to foster effective communication by encouraging participants to write clearly, thereby reducing the potential ambiguity that may produce flaming. Despite the unintended consequences that flaming has to facilitate the norms and rules for Internet groups, most Listservs or chat room providers attempt to hinder this practice by establishing their own explicit norms for the behavior of members. These sites include examples of explicit guidelines developed by chat room providers: **www.ybrt.org/guidelns.html** and **www.fortnet.org/fapg/posting.htm.**

SOURCE: H. Wang, "Flaming: More Than a Necessary Evil for Academic Mailing Lists," *Electronic Journal of Communication* 6 (1996).

(saying things like "mm-hmm" and "OK" while another is speaking) more frequently than European Americans. Lack of understanding of another's cultural norms can cause problems in a group.

## ENFORCEMENT OF GROUP NORMS

If norms are not written down, how do group members learn them? Observant group members pay attention to how other members act. From this information norms can be inferred. In particular, you should pay attention to two types of behaviors: those that occur regularly and those that incur disapproval.

Behaviors that occur consistently from one meeting to the next probably reflect a group norm. For example, if at every meeting each group member sits in the same seat and waits for the leader to start the discussion, you are seeing evidence of two norms.

Behaviors that are punished by peer pressure also indicate norms. The strongest evidence of a group norm is members' negative reaction to a particular behavior. Most peer pressure comes in the form of nonverbal signals, as group members roll their eyes at each other, glare, shake their heads, or turn away from the violator. Sometimes they pointedly ignore the offending member's contributions. Carla, the new council member who left early, received only mild expressions of surprise and even some verbal expressions of sympathy, but there was no doubt that she had violated a norm, and she quickly came into compliance with that norm at the next meeting.

Members who consistently violate important group norms are called **deviants,** and they make the other group members very uncomfortable—even angry. To conscientious group members, deviants seem to thumb their noses at the group by implying that their own needs and wishes are more important than those of the group. The other members try to force the deviants to fall in line by applying increasing pressure to conform (see Table 5.2).[33] This is what the rest of the city council might have done had the new member not corrected her behavior right away.

Just because groups usually pressure a deviant to conform does not mean the deviant should automatically cave in to such pressure. Sometimes groups consider people deviant if they disagree or won't go along with the group's plans. However, such people can actually be helpful to a group if they cause the other members to examine information and ideas more carefully. Even so, the other members may not recognize that such disagreement, or idea deviance, can be helpful, so they try to force agreement. This pressure can be hard to resist, even when the deviant has a good case. We present more information about the effect of idea-deviant disagreement in Chapter 9.

| TABLE 5.2 | **How Groups Deal with Deviant Members** |
| --- | --- |

**FIRST, MEMBERS TRY TO PERSUADE THE DEVIANT MEMBER TO CONFORM TO THE GROUP NORMS:**

- They try reasoning with the deviant: "When you aren't here, Carla, we miss your important input."
- They try to persuade the deviant, first with teasing and then more insistently: "Your husband can survive one evening without you, can't he, Carla?" and "Look, Carla, it really messes up the rest of our schedules when you leave early. Why don't you get a babysitter for one night a week—that wouldn't be so bad, would it?"
- They may attempt to punish or even coerce the deviant: "If you really want to be a part of this council, Carla, you're going to have to put in the same amount of effort as the rest of us. Otherwise, we can't support that ordinance you've been promoting."

**SECOND, SOLIDARITY BUILDS AMONG THE OTHER MEMBERS AGAINST THE DEVIANT:**

- "I don't see why we should go out of our way to help Carla pass that ordinance—she doesn't seem to care about any of our schedules!"

**THIRD, MEMBERS IGNORE AND WILL EVENTUALLY ISOLATE THE DEVIANT:**

- "Carla, we've all agreed that it would be better if you resigned from the council. We need a full-time member."

## When Is It OK to Be Deviant?

In the 1980s Beechnut, the second-largest producer of baby food in the United States, was found knowingly to have sold adulterated apple juice.[34] The company had been losing money, and using concentrate with artificial ingredients saved millions of dollars. Beechnut officials argued that other companies were also selling fake juice, that it was perfectly safe, and that their own research and development laboratories couldn't prove that their suppliers were providing artificial concentrate.

Assume you are a Beechnut executive who strongly disagrees with the action the rest of the Beechnut officials seem determined to take. You've mentioned your disagreement a couple of times and have been getting both subtle and not-so-subtle pressure to keep quiet. Members have said things to you like, "We've been over this and over this. You keep bringing this up after we've decided." You're marketing the juice as "100 percent pure," which isn't accurate. But on the other hand, no one is claiming that the impure juice is unsafe. Is that really so bad, when it's saving money and jobs for the company?

Groups can be vicious to members who are deviant, and you are definitely a deviant in this group.

1. What do you say to the other members?
2. How can you withstand the pressure the others are placing on you? Should you withstand it?
3. For what reasons would you go along with the other members?
4. For what reasons would you resist?
5. What would you do?

## CHANGING A GROUP NORM

We noted earlier that behaviors occurring at the first few meetings may become norms that can cause problems later. For example, recall that when members first meet, they experience primary tension, which makes them so polite and stiff that they do not confront or disagree with each other. This can easily develop into a norm of "no conflict," which stops members from expressing disagreements or doubts. This "no conflict" norm can be detrimental to the group's later decision-making abilities.

Although it isn't always easy, groups recognizing and using their own structuration process can change unproductive norms. One effective approach is to focus the group's attention on the norm and the harm it is creating rather than on the person violating the norm. In addition, do not try to force other members to accept your suggestions for changing the norm. They are likely to become defensive, refuse to change, and resent your attempt to control them. Instead, you want the group to think of ways to change the norm so that all the members participate in establishing a more productive group norm, for only the group can make a lasting change in a norm. The guidelines in Table 5.3 will help you.

| **TABLE 5.3** | **Changing a Group Norm** |
|---|---|

**PREPARATION**

**1.** Make sure you are seen as a responsible, loyal member of the group; others won't appreciate your comments if you have been unreliable or act "holier than thou."

**2.** Ask yourself, "What harm is the norm causing?" Observe the effects of the group norm on the members and the group as a whole; count the offending behaviors and make notes of your observations.

**CONSTRUCTIVE CONFRONTATION**

**1.** Select an appropriate time to share your information with other members.

**2.** Share your observations about the effects of the unproductive norm on the group; explain what you have observed the norm to be and what problems it causes.

**3.** Ask whether others also have observed these effects or share your concerns.

**4.** Express yourself supportively, not defensively:

    ***a.*** Defensive comment: "I'm sick and tired of always being on time while the rest of you wander in any time you please!"

    ***b.*** Supportive comment: "For the past four meetings we have started between 15 and 25 minutes late. We seem to have developed a norm that scheduled starting times do not need to be observed. Two of us have had to leave these meetings before they were finished in order to go to class. As a result we have missed several key decisions, and the rest of you have had to bring us up to date on what happened. Does anyone else see this as a problem?"

The elements we have discussed thus far—how group members manage their tensions, how they work through important tasks in their development and formation, and what roles, rules, and norms they establish—all help create the group's climate. We now examine how the group's climate contributes to the formation of an effective team.

# Development of a Group's Climate

Maintaining a pleasant interpersonal climate was the most frequently mentioned communication skill needed, as reported by managers of work groups.[35] Joseph Folger and Marshall Poole, experts in group conflict, define **group climate** as "the relatively enduring quality of the group situation that (*a*) is experienced in common by group members, and (*b*) arises from and influences their interaction and behavior."[36] A few key ideas are important to keep in mind when you consider your group's climate. This general environment, atmosphere,

**GLOSSARY**

**Group Climate**

*The atmosphere or environment within a group*

## Changing a Norm You Believe Is Harmful

**APPLY NOW**

Carla, our city councilwoman, chose to accept the group norm of meeting as long as it took to complete the group's work. However, there are pros and cons to that norm. Yes, the work was not permitted to pile up, and the group achieved closure at each meeting. But members were visibly fatigued at midnight, and there was a noticeable loss of concentration and productivity after 10 P.M. Assume Carla's position for a moment and address the following questions:

As Carla you genuinely believe the group would be more productive and make better decisions if they had more, but shorter, meetings. List at least three choices you have for dealing with this norm.

1. What are the consequences, both to you and to the group, of each choice?

2. What strategy do you think would be most likely to succeed? Why?

3. If you decide to try to change this group norm, how would you go about doing it? In your answer include any planning you might do for bringing this up to the group. Also, describe exactly what you would say to bring this up.

Select five people, including one to play Carla, to role-play a city council meeting where Carla brings up the question of the meeting length norm. After the role-play, discuss as a class what worked and what did not. Make sure to let the participants in the "meeting" express any feelings they might have experienced during the role-play.

emotional tone, or "air" of a group is pervasive; emerges from and impacts the group's communication; and is experienced by all members of the group. Climates, whether positive or negative, are the ongoing consequences of member communication and relationships.

Members who could disagree without being disagreeable, who could admit mistakes, and who could keep emotions on an even keel were particularly valued by the work group managers mentioned above.[37] You probably have attended group meetings in which you felt the warmth and affection of the members for each other. The climate was empowering, flexible, and participatory. Conversely, you probably also have observed meetings in which you felt tension and distrust. The climate was defensive, rigid, thwarting, hostile, and authoritarian. These are but two examples of types of group climates or atmospheres. There are many dimensions of a group's climate. We explain three we consider most important: trust, cohesiveness, and supportiveness.

### TRUST

**Trust** refers to the general belief that members can rely on each other. When group members trust each other, they do not have to worry that others might be lying to them or may have secret reasons for their behavior. Instead of being suspicious and secretive, members

**GLOSSARY**

**Trust**

*The general belief that members can rely on each other*

## Can You Be Trusted?

Imagine that this is a particularly busy semester for you, and you feel as if you barely have time to breathe. You will graduate at the end of the semester, and you don't know how you'll manage all your coursework, to say nothing of job hunting. One of your courses entails a group project; you have just met with your team members for the first time in class. The others are enthused about the project and have already started to make a schedule of meeting times for the semester. You think they are planning far too many meetings—many more than the project will need. Privately, you think you can get your own work on the project finished and attend perhaps half of the meetings the others have scheduled. But if you say that to your fellow group members, you're afraid that they'll think you don't care about the project. And if you just skip meetings without saying anything now, you're afraid they'll think you're a slacker. But then again, you'll probably never see these people again. Either way, though, it seems like you can't win.

1. What other choices do you think you have besides saying no to the meetings now and just not showing up later?

2. Do you stay silent and make a private decision to make the meetings you can and not worry about the rest?

3. Do you say something to the group? If so, what?

4. For each of the options you came up with, what are the consequences to the group of that action?

5. What action is least likely to undermine the group's trust in you?

who trust one another are more likely to create an open climate in which people share freely. Two kinds of trust are particularly important to groups: task-related and interpersonal.

A member who is trustworthy regarding the task can be counted on to complete assignments and produce top-notch work for the group. The higher the quality of the individual work that members do for the group, the higher will be the quality of the group's outputs. One behavior that can destroy trust quickly is failure to complete assignments for the group. A member who does not come through for the group forces the other members to pick up the slack. This is one of the most common sources of conflict and can poison a group's climate.

*Interpersonal trust* refers to the belief that the members of the group are operating in the group's best interests and that they value their fellow members. Suppose a member you trust says to you, "I think there are lots of problems with your idea." You are likely to ask that member for reasons and to pay careful attention to the reasons given. On the other hand, if the same statement comes from someone you don't trust, you may wonder what's behind the statement, ignore it, get into a shouting match, or try to find subtle ways of sabotaging that member's suggestions. Members who appear to operate from **hidden agenda** motives, or personal and private motives, are seen as untrustworthy by others.

### GLOSSARY

**Hidden Agenda**

*An unstated private goal a member wants to achieve through a group*

**GLOSSARY**

**Cohesiveness**

*The bonds of
attachment
members have
for each other*

**Groupthink**

*The tendency of
highly cohesive
groups not to eval-
uate thoroughly and
critically all aspects
of a decision or
problem*

So are "politicians" who always seem to have a personal angle for their behavior that has nothing to do with the group. In fact, politicians can be so destructive to a group that Carl Larson and Frank LaFasto, who studied "excellent" groups, recommend that the group leader get rid of them as soon as possible.[38]

## COHESIVENESS

**Cohesiveness** refers to the attachment members feel toward each other, the group, and the task—the bonds that hold the group together. In a highly cohesive group, members feel a strong sense of belonging, speak favorably about the group and the other members, and conform to the norms of the group. In a group that is not cohesive, members do not feel much sense of belonging. They may not attend faithfully or may even leave the group because they find other groups more rewarding.

As with trust, there are two types of cohesiveness: task cohesiveness and social (or interpersonal) cohesiveness.[39] In a group that has high task cohesiveness, members understand and accept the task, are committed to completing it, may be excited about working on it, and experience what has been called *group drive,* or motivation to accomplish the task.[40] This describes the *Man of La Mancha* cast very well. Interpersonal, or social, cohesiveness means that members like and are attracted to each other as people. They like to spend time together and enjoy each other's company. These two forms of cohesiveness affect group productivity and decision-making quality in different ways.[41] When a group's cohesiveness is due to interpersonal attraction, the task may take a back seat, which can lower the quality of a group's decisions. In addition, sometimes groups high in interpersonal cohesiveness develop norms that keep productivity low or find themselves getting off track easily. A friend of ours sorted letters for the Postal Service. His co-workers let him know that he was working too fast and that if he wanted to stay in their good graces he would not exceed the informal production norm they had developed. In contrast, groups with high task cohesiveness generally are more productive, and decision making is enhanced. Thus, the presence of task-focused norms in a group moderates the effect of cohesiveness—groups with strong task norms and high cohesiveness outperform cohesive groups without strong task norms.[42]

Highly cohesive groups need to be particularly careful to guard against **groupthink,** the tendency not to examine critically all aspects of a decision or problem.[43] The term was coined by Irving Janis, who conducted an exhaustive study of the disastrous 1961 decision made by President Kennedy and his advisers to invade Cuba at the Bay of Pigs. This now-classic study concluded that although the advisers were well-informed experts, their decision-making procedures were badly flawed. In large part the group's cohesiveness contributed to the problem: Members defined their roles as supporters of a decision the president seemed to favor rather than as critical thinkers determined to make the best decision possible. Members made it difficult for those who disagreed to speak up by implying, both subtly and overtly, that disagreement was tantamount to disloyalty to the group and to the president. The group members' interpersonal cohesiveness got in the way of their evaluating information thoroughly and carefully. This is similar to the situation Beechnut faced, as described in the Ethical Dilemma box on page 128. We discuss groupthink, including its symptoms and how it can be prevented, in detail in Chapter 7.

Highly cohesive groups are also more satisfying to their members. You have no doubt belonged to a cohesive group in which you felt the warmth and closeness among the members. Terry, one of our former students, decided to campaign for office in a campus

| TABLE 5.4 | **Increasing Cohesiveness in a Group** |
|---|---|

1. Develop a strong group identity.

2. Encourage group traditions, such as annual parties, special greetings and handshakes, and rituals.

3. Develop in-group insignias, such as T-shirts and sweatshirts, pins, or hats.

4. Refer to the group members as *we* and *us*.

5. Give credit to the group as a whole when representing the group to outsiders or other groups.

6. Give credit to individuals within the group for contributions they make toward the group's goal achievement.

7. Support both disagreement and agreement by encouraging openness and freedom of expression.

8. Create a climate of supportiveness in which every individual feels appreciated and believes his or her ideas are valued.

9. Set clear and attainable goals for the group.

   *a.* Goals should be difficult enough to provide a challenge and produce group pride when they are met.

   *b.* Goals should not be so hard that they are nearly impossible to attain, because failure will lower cohesiveness.

organization because she had so envied the obvious cohesiveness expressed by the previous year's officers—she wanted the experience of being part of such a group. Table 5.4 provides suggestions you can use to increase the cohesiveness of a group.

## SUPPORTIVENESS

In a supportive climate members encourage each other, care about each other, and treat each other with respect. Supportive members uphold ethical principles about how to treat each other. They believe their opinions are valued by the group, even when other members disagree with their opinions. Because members feel safe from psychological assault, they are free to direct most of their energy toward helping the group accomplish its task. On the other hand, a defensive climate emerges when members try to control, manipulate, and criticize each other.[44] If members are afraid they will be attacked by other members, they hesitate to offer their opinions. They spend so much time defending themselves or being on the alert for psychological assault that they do not pay much attention to the task of the group. Table 5.5 provides a list of supportive and contrasting defensive behaviors with sample statements for each.

| TABLE 5.5 | **Defensive and Supportive Communication Behaviors and Statements** |

| **Defensive Behaviors** | **Supportive Behaviors** |
|---|---|
| **Evaluation** Judging the other person; indicating by words or tone of voice that you disapprove of a person: "That's a pretty dumb idea!" | **Description** Desiring to understand the other's point of view without making the other person wrong: "Tell me more about how your idea would work." |
| **Control** Trying to dominate or change the other person; insisting on having things your way: "I want to do it this way, so that's what we're going to do." | **Problem orientation** Trying to search honestly for the best solution without having a predetermined idea of what the solution should be: "What ideas do you all have about how we might solve this?" |
| **Strategy** Trying to manipulate the other person; using deceit to achieve your own goals: "Don't you really think that it would be better if we did it this way?" | **Spontaneity** Reacting honestly, openly, and freely: "I really like that, and here's something else we could do. . . ." |
| **Neutrality** Not caring about how the other group members feel: "We don't have time to hear about your car accident right now; we have work to do." | **Empathy** Showing by your words and actions that you care about the other group members: "You had a car accident on the way here? Are you OK? Is there anything we can do to help?" |
| **Superiority** Maximizing status differences; pulling rank on other members with title, wealth, expertise, and so on: "Well, I'm chair of the committee, and I believe I make the final decision about how we do this." | **Equality** Minimizing status differences; treating every member of the group as an equally valued contributor: "I know I'm the chair, but the solution belongs to the whole committee, so don't give my ideas any more weight than anyone else's." |
| **Certainty** Being a know-it-all; acting positive that your way or belief is the only correct one: "I know exactly what we ought to do here, so I'll take care of it." | **Provisionalism** Being tentative in expressing your opinions; being open to considering others' suggestions fairly: "I have an idea I think might work. . . ." |

All the defensive behaviors include an element of negative evaluation. These are judgmental behaviors that hurt interpersonal relationships within a group. Instead of critically evaluating ideas, members are critical of each other as persons. Notice, also, the relationship between cohesiveness and supportiveness. It is hard to feel strongly attached to a group if you don't know from one moment to the next when you are going to be attacked. Perhaps you also can see the relationship to open-mindedness—a supportive group consists of members who listen actively to each other and who are egalitarian in their approach to others. Open-minded members do not demand that the group perform in a particular way, the one and only "right" way. Can you begin to see how each element of the group system is related to all the other elements?

All the factors we have discussed in this chapter contribute to the structure that creates a team out of individual members. The way members develop over time and manage their tensions, the roles and norms that develop, and the climate members create—all work together to make each team a unique culture.

# Ethical Behavior during Group Formation

Members need to pay attention to the ethics of their behavior particularly as a group's roles and norms develop. Patterns that form in the early stages of a group's life cycle can become established and difficult to break later. That is why it is critical for those patterns to be productive and to adhere to the highest standards of ethical behavior. The following ethical guidelines emerge from the National Communication Association Credo for Ethical Communication that we introduced in Chapter 1. They speak to those issues, such as the development of norms, that have been the focus of this chapter about how a collection of individuals becomes a group.

1. **Group members should communicate in ways that help establish a supportive climate.**

   As discussed in the chapter, members will not do their best thinking if they feel they have to hold back for fear of being ridiculed or attacked. Ironically, honest disagreement is more likely to occur in a supportive climate of trust. Members must monitor their own and one another's behavior to ensure that their communication encourages others to share freely. Working actively to create a supportive climate is the responsibility of each member.

2. **Communication that degrades other members must not be tolerated.**

   This principle represents the flip side of the previous principle. Behaviors that degrade, ridicule, attempt to intimidate, or coerce others must be stopped immediately. Such behaviors violate the mutual respect that should be present among group members. They also contribute to poor decision making.

3. **Freedom of expression, diversity of perspective, and tolerance of disagreement must be encouraged.**

   If every member of a group has exactly the same perspective (unlikely in any case) and believes exactly the same thing, why bother to assemble the group? The best group work emerges when members share their diverse perspectives and points of view. This means that disagreement will surely occur—and should be welcomed! We discuss group conflict fully in Chapter 9.

4. **Members must be willing to express their genuine personal convictions, even if this requires courage to disagree with other members.**

   Ultimately, members are responsible for their own behavior. Ideally, a group's climate encourages free expression and tolerates disagreement, but even when it does not, individual members must be willing to speak their minds. To say that you agree with a course of action the group plans to take when you privately disagree is unethical and will not support that course of action. Be willing to hear what the other members have to say and to be persuaded, but in the end, if you think the group is about to make a big mistake or engage in unethical behavior, you must be willing to speak out. Doing so could prevent a disaster down the road.

## RESOURCES FOR REVIEW AND DISCUSSION

**SUMMARY**

- As groups form, members must handle both task and socioemotional issues simultaneously, as well as deal with primary, secondary (task-related), and tertiary tension over power struggles.

- Many groups experience predictable phases in their development. Tuckman's model describes five phases of forming, storming, norming, performing, and adjourning; Gersick's model of punctuated equilibrium describes a make-or-break transition occurring at the midpoint of a group's time frame.

- Group socialization of new and/or established members and the group is a complex process of learning how to fit together. Effective communication between all parties is crucial to successful and positive socialization, which in turn influences other group processes such as leadership, roles, norms, and climate. The process can be described in five phases: antecedent, anticipatory, encounter, assimilation, and exit. Group socialization continues throughout the life of the group until the new member leaves or the entire group disbands.

- Task, maintenance, and individual roles are three main categories of roles members perform in the group.

- Rules and norms, the standards of behavior for members of the group, differ only in their degree of formality. Group norms, or informal rules, are established through primacy, explicit statements members make, critical events in the group's history, and carryover behaviors from the culture at large.

- The group's climate is the atmosphere in which members work. Three important aspects of a group's climate are trust, cohesiveness, and supportiveness.

- Four ethical principles are particularly important during group formation: creating a supportive climate, stopping behaviors that degrade others, encouraging freedom of expression, and being willing to speak honestly.

**EXERCISES**

1. Watch a film that shows group formation (classic examples include *The Breakfast Club, The Commitments,* and *Lord of the Flies*), and discuss the following questions:

   *a.* How did the group manage important issues in its formation phase? Were there any unresolved issues that later hurt the group?

   *b.* What instances of primary, secondary, or tertiary tensions did you observe?

   *c.* Who became the emergent leader of the group? Why did this person emerge? What were the sources of this person's power as a leader?

2. Observe an actual group or watch a video of a task-oriented group. (Two videos produced especially for this textbook contain suitable segments for this exercise.) Make a chart based on the task, maintenance, and individual behaviors described in the chapter. List the people's names at the top and the task, maintenance, and individual behaviors along the left side. Whenever each person speaks, categorize his or her remarks by making a note in the appropriate category. For each person in the group you observe:

   *a.* What sort of role profile would you draw for that person?

*b.* How would you label that person's informal role?

*c.* Do you think the person's behaviors were helpful or not? Why?

*d.* How would you change the category system to be more useful for you?

**3.** Think of the most (or least) cohesive group you have ever belonged to, and explain why this group was so cohesive (or uncohesive). Which supportive (or defensive) behaviors were most prevalent in the group? What forms of trust did you observe (or not observe) that made the biggest difference in the group's climate?

Go to **www.mhhe.com/adamsgalanes7** and **www.mhhe.com/groups** for self-quizzes and weblinks.

---

**KEY TERMS • CONCEPTS**

| | | |
|---|---|---|
| Antecedent Stage | Group Climate | Primary Tension |
| Anticipatory Stage | Group Socialization | Punctuated Equilibrium |
| Assimilation Stage | Groupthink | Role |
| Cohesiveness | Hidden Agenda | Rules |
| Deviants | Individual Roles | Secondary Tension |
| Encounter Stage | Life Cycle | Task Roles |
| Equilibrium Problem | Maintenance Roles | Tertiary Tension |
| Exit Stage | Norms | Trust |

**www.mhhe.com/adamsgalanes7**

Use the flashcards and crossword puzzles on the Online Learning Center to further your knowledge of these key terms.

# Working with Diversity in the Small Group

## CHAPTER OUTLINE

What Is Diversity?

Diverse Member Characteristics

Cultural Diversity

Working with Diversity/
Bridging Differences

## CHAPTER OBJECTIVES

**After reading this chapter you should be able to:**

1. Define *diversity* and give several examples of diversity within a group.

2. Explain how diversity benefits a group.

3. Describe the four learning styles identified by Kolb and explain how each can benefit a group.

4. Describe the four dimensions of the Myers-Briggs Type Indicator® personality inventory.

5. Define *culture,* describe three dimensions on which cultures differ, and explain how each can affect group interaction.

6. Explain how racial or ethnic, gender, and generational differences are cultural.

7. Explain why symbolic convergence and fantasy can help group members bridge differences by contributing to a group identity.

8. Explain how SYMLOG methodology can be used to help a group identify and overcome differences.

## The Misfit

Judy, a gregarious and sociable class member, had the gift of making everyone laugh. When the class formed task groups that would stay together for the entire semester to complete a major project, several groups wanted Judy to join them. She chose to join a group with two other women and two men who, from their participation in class discussions, were bright and conscientious students. This group had a good mix of talent—members who could organize a task, members who could write well, members who had many contacts throughout the university to help them find the resources they needed, and members, like Judy, who could make the task enjoyable. The group appeared to be headed for success. All the elements existed to make this a productive and fun experience.

Several weeks later, group animosity ran dangerously high. Three members wanted to fire Judy from the group. The fourth member, Misty, liked Judy well enough but was also frustrated by her behaviors that pulled the group off-task. Her constant joking, socializing, and attempts to ensure that everyone was having a good time had backfired. Instead, the others concluded that Judy was an airhead; they were frustrated by her inability to stay on task and what they perceived as her lack of seriousness. The members wanted an A+ for this major project. They had decided to give the finished project to their instructor a week early for feedback about how to revise and polish it. Judy's constant socializing had slowed them down. The others blamed her for missing their original, self-imposed deadline. By the end of the semester, Misty was the only member who would speak directly to Judy and thus served as the only link between Judy and the others, who ignored Judy whenever they could. The project was turned in on time but not early enough to receive instructor feedback; it received a B, for which everyone (but Judy) blamed Judy.

These students' journals revealed that none of them had much insight into their own or other members' behavior during the semester. Misty and the others held Judy responsible for everything that went wrong. But Judy was the most puzzled and frustrated member of all. She never understood why the others were so "cold." She had looked forward to making some new friends during the project, but her group members didn't seem to be interested in her. The harder she tried to take an interest in them, the more she felt rebuffed.

One of us had the chance to observe a meeting of this group. Judy's sociability and humor could have added quite a bit to the process—if she had only recognized that the others' priorities were not social. But the others, with their extreme task-orientation, were unable to see how Judy's personality could potentially have benefited their group. Instead, group members were locked into a struggle for control over their priorities, and no one won the struggle.

This situation is all too typical. Many groups self-destruct because they mismanage members' diverse perspectives and personalities. Most of us think others should share our goals, priorities, communication patterns, and working styles. When they don't, we often blame them for being wrong. Few of us appreciate others who are quite different from us. Ironically, it is our very differences that contribute to making a group potentially more effective than an individual. After all, if you and I think alike, act alike, and process information alike, one of us is unnecessary to the process! Diversity is central to effective group problem solving. Ineffective management of diversity produces the difficulties so many groups experience, not diversity itself.

This chapter will show you how you can accept and capitalize on diversity to produce a better group outcome. We discuss several types of diversity, including differences in motives for joining a group, in learning styles and personality, and in cultural backgrounds. We conclude by discussing symbolic convergence and fantasy as a way members can bridge their differences, and we present a methodology, SYMLOG (system for the multiple-level observation of groups), designed to help groups identify their differences and develop strategies for capitalizing on them.

## What Is Diversity?

This chapter on diversity marks the midpoint in our discussions of small group communication. We have shown why small groups are the heart of society—because they provide us with a fundamental social unit central to our relationships and the work we do together. Communication, both verbal and nonverbal, is the lifeblood of these social units and is key to creating meaningful small group experiences. Small groups have a life of their own, moving and changing internally and externally in association with other social networks. The issue is not whether small groups are central to our lives but how we can make them work most effectively. Small groups provide a rich and complex means for solving all sorts of conjunctive tasks whose outcomes depend on members pooling their information. Thus, groups must process all kinds of resources—including each other—and this requires coordinating differences. This chapter addresses one of the most fundamental features of effective group work: diversity.

*"In the interest of cultural diversity, we've hired Jason, here, who owns a number of hip-hop CDs."*

Working with diversity is central to an effective group. © The New Yorker Collection; 2000 Alex Gregory from cartoonbank.com. All Rights Reserved.

**Diversity** in a group refers to differences among members. A critical benefit to selecting a group to tackle a problem is the multiple resources members bring to the group, which can be used not only to understand the problem but to find a good solution. There are endless ways in which members can differ, from how members learn, to personality differences, to differences of opinion. For example, Clifton may remember everything told to him, but Tia is better recalling information she has read or seen. Misty may want to get right down to business; for her, chitchat is a waste of time. Judy, on the other hand, is better able to focus on the task once she has connected informally with others.

Working with diversity means finding the "good mix" of member and group characteristics that can facilitate effective group outcomes and not hinder them. From the outset we want to emphasize that simply recognizing that differences are essential to group problem solving and then "mixing up" group member characteristics are not enough. Finding the different pieces and then throwing them together is a recipe for disaster, as our classroom group found out. Successful group members reflect on how those differences can best be applied to solving their task effectively. But the journal entries of our classroom group showed little self- and group-reflection on their differences.

The diversity of group member composition has intrigued small group researchers for years. **Homogeneity** (similarity) and **heterogeneity** (difference) are terms typically used to capture the degree of variance in group composition. Marvin Shaw, an early pioneer in small group research, said, "The general assumption is that most group activities require a variety of skills and knowledge; hence the more heterogeneous the group, the more likely the necessary abilities and information will be available and the more effective the group is likely to be."[1] Sounds simple enough, but as the early group researchers found, getting the "good mix" is not easy. Group members can be different in any number of ways, but those differences have to be tied to the task and must be coordinated. This is no easy undertaking. Research has shown that diversity in group composition entails difficulties early

**GLOSSARY**

**Diversity**

*Differences among group members, from personality and learning style differences to differences of opinion*

**Homogeneity**

*Groups composed of members who are similar or alike in member characteristics*

**Heterogeneity**

*Groups composed of members who are different on one or more dimensions*

on compared to the smoother communication of homogeneous groups; however, given time to find ways to work with their differences, diverse groups perform more effectively.[2]

Today the issue of group diversity and its effect on group processes and outcomes is more relevant than ever. William Johnston and Arnold Packer tell us in their *Workforce 2000* report that the workplace in the twenty-first century will be characterized by unprecedented diversity in terms of gender, age, ability, and minority and immigrant status.[3] Learning to work with diversity is a must and requires identifying those member differences that are most relevant and effectively coordinating the obvious and less obvious diversity in small groups. The best teams have a balance of member abilities, with individual approaches and skills complementing one another.[4] Do not expect your fellow group members to change their basic needs, learning styles, personalities, or cultural backgrounds! Too often we assume that we are doing things right and that someone else needs to conform to our preferences. So working with diversity in your groups is a matter not only of understanding why diversity influences group processes as it does but also being willing to listen to and work with others' explanations for their behaviors. Understanding, sensitivity, and appreciation of the differences are more likely to produce a willingness on everyone's part to adjust behavior so differences can facilitate, not harm, your group's relationships and work.

Years ago Marvin Shaw noted that group members can vary along several dimensions. Early interest in group diversity focused on gender, personality, and race. Today so many different dimensions of group composition have been identified as to warrant several ways of categorizing them.[5] Our task was to select enough areas of diversity to capture its complexity but not overwhelm you. We have divided up our discussion into two broad categories of diversity: those that are not tied to discussions of culture (motives, learning styles, and personality) and those that are (ethnicity, gender, and age).

# Diverse Member Characteristics

### DIFFERENCES IN MOTIVES FOR JOINING A GROUP

One of the most obvious differences to face group members is realizing they haven't all joined a group for the same reasons. People join groups in large part to satisfy psychological needs, among which are the needs for inclusion, affection, and control mentioned in Chapter 1. Robert Bales, the small group pioneer mentioned in Chapter 5, notes that our behavior stems from our values and our psychological needs.[6] Members who join primarily to meet control or achievement needs will be task-oriented, whereas members whose needs for affection and belonging predominate will be socioemotional, focusing on the interpersonal relationships in the group. These two sets of needs, and their corresponding approaches to the group's work, can often compete with each other in a group, as you saw in Case 6.1.

Task-oriented individuals, with their focus on control and achievement needs, believe the group's task is the reason for the group's existence. They perceive any digression from the task as a waste of members' time, so they keep chitchat to a minimum. They are highly frustrated when the group digresses and may give dirty looks to those who pull the group off task; they are likely to be the ones who bring the group back on task when the group has digressed. Task-oriented members, like Misty in Case 6.1, value accomplishment and feel a tremendous sense of achievement and relief when the group's task is completed.

Relationally oriented individuals, like Judy in our opening case, value human relationships more than they do task accomplishment. These individuals want to get to know the others in the group and want to experience each member as a friend. Their needs for affection and inclusion take precedence over their needs for control. Thus, if a member is having a personal problem, socioemotional individuals will usually perceive that member's needs as being more important than the group's task and will willingly sacrifice the group's task accomplishment to help the member.

Investigations by Carolyn Anderson and Matthew Martin suggest that some motives, particularly the needs for control and affection, may be traits that are consistent across situations.[7] This may pose particular challenges for members with control needs, who tend to focus solely on the task and may downplay the importance of camaraderie and chitchat. These authors note that cohesiveness and satisfaction increase when group members help each other meet their needs.[8] Group members may actually do a better job of accomplishing their tasks when their personal needs for affection are met. Thus, it is important for group members to recognize and help *all* members meet their needs in the group. Task-oriented members must recognize the value of social talk.

Both kinds of members are valuable to the group.[9] The most effective and rewarding teams are often those that integrate secondary (task-oriented) and primary (relationship-oriented) elements. In addition, most of us participate in groups for several reasons, of which accomplishing the task is only one. We want to experience the pleasure of each other's company and the fun of interaction.[10] John Oetzel, in his studies of effective group decision making, makes a critical point about the interplay between task and social needs in a group.[11] Do not assume that a task-focused member does not care about the social needs of a group or that a socially focused member does not care about the work to be done. First, members can care about both needs at the same time. Second, their differences become apparent in how they get to the goal. Task-focused members can use work to facilitate good relationships, and socially focused members can use relationships to facilitate work dynamics. The task and social dimensions of a group are interconnected and should not be construed as an either-or proposition. Judy's group failed to see the interrelatedness of these behaviors and failed to understand each others' social realities. Each expected the other to change or to switch focus instead of realizing that they needed both functions in their group and asking how members could all be *both* task and socially focused. Appreciation and open discussion, rather than closed harping in private journals, could have helped them work with these two relevant dimensions of group dynamics.

## DIVERSITY OF LEARNING STYLES

Group members bring different learning styles to their group experience. Although you may wonder why we have chosen an individual characteristic more obviously applied to educational contexts, we believe learning styles are relevant to group problem solving. Working on a problem as a group first entails that members learn new information, integrate this information into commonly shared information, and then coordinate the informational resources of the group and its members.[12] Our learning preferences affect how and what we talk about, whether we understand one another, and what aspects of a group's task we feel most comfortable taking on. Our learning style differences can set us

## Handling Different Motives and Orientations toward Work

Judy and her fellow group members were highly frustrated by each other, in part because their needs and corresponding orientations toward the group's work were so different. However, instead of recognizing this as a potential plus, they responded by blaming each other for not doing things "right."

Assume you are Judy, and you're having a hard time understanding why your group members seem constantly to be rebuffing your attempts at friendship.

1. What is your perception of the group's situation? If you were to describe the situation to a friend, what would you say about it?
2. What effect is your perception of the situation having on your behavior in (and outside) the group?
3. What could you do to make the situation better, from your perspective? List at least five possible things you could do.
4. Which of those actions do you think is most likely to improve the situation, and why?

Assume you are one of the other members of the group, and you don't understand why Judy isn't getting the message.

5. What is your perception of the group's situation? If you were telling a friend about it, what would you say the problem was?
6. What effect is your perception of the situation having on your behavior in (and outside) the group?
7. What could you do to make the situation better, from your perspective? List at least five possible things you could do.
8. Which of those actions do you think is most likely to improve the situation, and why?

up for misunderstandings if we aren't careful. For example, Gloria is a visual learner. In one group meeting a member tried to explain something to her in several different ways, none of which got through. Then a third group member drew a simple diagram and Gloria instantly "saw" what they were talking about. Had the third member not observed that she needed a different type of explanation and been flexible enough to provide it, both Gloria and the rest of the group would have stayed stuck on one point.

Other group members may be kinesthetic, or touch, learners, who process information best if they can physically do something with the information. Group members often reveal these preferences in their talk. For instance, Gloria often says, "I *see* what you mean," when she understands someone. Another member says, "I *hear* you," to indicate understanding, while a third member may say, "I've *got* it!" Each of these metaphors for "I understand" reveals a clue as to the dominant sensory (e.g., sight, hearing, touch) learning style of the speaker. In cohesive groups, members tend to converge on a single dominant

**FIGURE 6.1    The Kolb Learning Cycle**

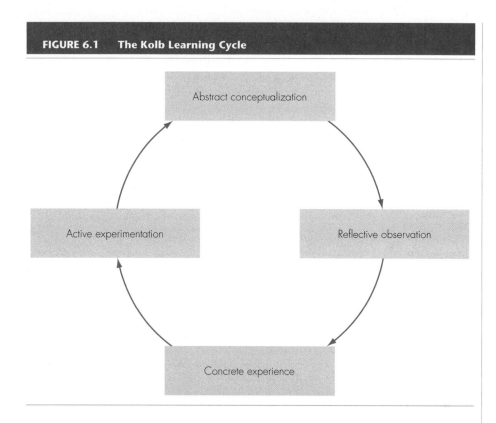

sensory metaphor without even knowing it.[13] For instance, after a while group members will all start to say things like "It *fits,*" "I *grasp* what you're saying," or "There's a hole big enough to *walk through* in that argument" if the kinesthetic or touch metaphor is being used.

There are strengths to having all three preferences included in a group. For example, in a proposal created by the group, Gloria will contribute diagrams and visual displays that communicate well to other visual learners. John may be the member best suited for presenting the proposal orally to the parent organization. Sometimes just talking about these preferences is enough to help members appreciate them and work a little harder to communicate well with members whose preferences are different.

David Kolb has developed another model that demonstrates several key differences in learning styles that can affect how group members work together.[14] He suggests that people have one of four basic preferences for learning new information, and they enter the learning cycle by way of their preferred style (see Figure 6.1). This information can heighten your awareness of the learning style differences among your group members and how they might effectively impact your group's informational environment. Each of the styles has strengths to lend a group, which is best served with an overall balance of the styles.

The **concrete experience learning style** describes those individuals who learn well from events they actually observe or activities in which they actually participate. They are concerned with unique, particular experiences rather than theories and generalizations. They trust their feelings and are intuitive. As group members they are "doers" and may

**GLOSSARY**

**Concrete Experience Learning Style**

*A preference for learning by participating and doing*

become impatient with theoretical discussions or research on background information. For example, if your group is charged with investigating a parking problem on campus, a concrete experience learner may volunteer to count cars illegally parked or observe how many cars leave a lot without finding a parking place. But such a person may be uncomfortable if asked to synthesize three theoretical articles about traffic flow and facility usage.

The **reflective observation learning style** describes individuals who prefer to get perspective on their direct experience by standing back from it, gaining psychological distance from it, and thinking about it reflectively. They emphasize understanding rather than practical application; they are the group "thinkers." They mull information over in their minds, may talk to others about it, and learn particularly well by writing about the experience. As group members they are likely to benefit from group discussion about issues. They may help the group think through a group project or show how theoretical concepts are applied, but they may be less comfortable jumping in to help implement a group project.

The **abstract conceptualization learning style** describes learners who process a considerable amount of information by reading and solitary study. They are comfortable working alone, can perceive broad patterns, readily understand theoretical material, and can pull together information from a variety of sources in a way that makes sense. They are logical and emphasize thinking as opposed to feeling. In a group they are the "synthesizers" and enjoy pulling together available research for the group's project; however, they may be less enthused about conducting observations or implementing the project.

The **active experimentation learning style** describes individuals who learn by trying different things until they find one that works. Such people are comfortable trying something new. They can apply information in a variety of ways. They like to actively influence others and prefer to do rather than observe. As group members they are effective in a crisis because they can think and problem-solve on their feet. Such a member might like to be given responsibility for conducting a pilot test of your group's recommended solution to the parking problem but is likely to have less patience for solitary thinking and writing about the problem.

Generally, our preferences lead us to develop strengths in some styles more than others. In a balanced group, though, all styles are represented; the group has members who can research a problem, extract the important information from the research, develop a plan, test the plan and modify what doesn't work, then finally implement the plan. An effective group needs the benefits of all the learning styles. Like the task and social preferences of members, learning styles do not have to be treated as mutually exclusive or independent of each other. Rather, they are interrelated, complementary to each other. Understanding what each can bring to a group, asking how all three can be used to facilitate your problem solving, and assessing the balance of the styles are important to an effective outcome. Should you discover that your group is missing one or more of these styles, you need to try to bring the missing styles into the group either by expanding the abilities of members or by using trusted outsiders to supply the resources that are lacking. Likewise, should you discover that one or more of these preferences are producing behaviors that clash, you need to talk about how to better use the styles together rather than treat one style as negating another.

## PERSONALITY DIFFERENCES

Mishandled personality differences create as much havoc in groups as any other factor. As mentioned earlier, it isn't the fact that members have different personal styles that causes the problem—it's the fact that many members don't know how to work with others whose personalities are markedly different. They waste their energy trying to get those with dissimilar personalities to change, are simply unwilling to work with people different from themselves, or treat these differences as mutually exclusive with room for only one personality.

Hundreds of personality characteristics have been investigated by social scientists. Instead of making an inventory of characteristics that affect group interaction, we have chosen to look in depth at one popular classification system, the **Myers-Briggs Type Indicator®** **(MBTI).**

The MBTI, based on the work of psychologist Carl Jung, is a personality measure developed by Isabel Briggs Myers and Katherine Briggs.[15] The system looks at four dimensions that relate to how individuals interact with the world. Each dimension is a continuum with opposite characteristics at either pole. Each of us leans, a little or a lot, toward one or the other of the poles. Thus, MBTI assesses our preferences and describes the characteristics we display and the behaviors with which we are most comfortable. However, no one is a "pure" type—we all display some characteristics of all the personality types. In this next section, we will describe the four dimensions that underpin the MBTI (see Table 6.1) as they may relate to group dynamics.

The **extraversion/introversion dimension** bears on whether your energy is directed toward the outer, observable world or your inner, mental landscape. *Extraverts* as group members look a lot like Judy in Case 6.1. They are tuned in to the outer world, are outgoing, and usually like and get along well with other members. They tend to be open to others' ideas yet can be seen as impatient and, as in Judy's case, "not very serious." Extraverts also tend to use group discussion to arrive at their own positions on group work rather than come to a meeting with their minds made up. During group presentations you may want to turn to your extraverts as the primary speaker or moderator. These members may also be the ones you ask to interview key sources for your research because they like to interact with others. *Introverts* may not like working in groups at all; however, they enjoy working on ideas and can contribute effectively to group problem solving. They may prefer, for example, to work independently and then bring their work to the group rather than working on a task together during a meeting. Introverts tend to come to meetings having thought carefully about how they stand on group task issues and can lose patience with the discussion. If extraverts and introverts do not understand the underlying values of one another's work styles, their approaches can appear so different that misunderstandings can easily occur.

The **sensing/intuiting dimension** refers to the type of information you naturally tune in to. Do you prefer to focus on facts in the here and now, or are you more likely to dream of possibilities and imagine new connections? The *sensing* group member is careful and factual and may lose patience with abstract theories. Sensing members can provide a group with specific and concrete examples for reports. In addition, these members can provide concrete examples to enhance other members' sections if a discussion appears too abstract. During group presentations these members can report on the background of the project as well as the details of the solution the group is proposing. The *intuitive* group member can be very creative and imaginative, losing patience with detail but very interested in the novel. Whereas the sensor may be focused on the details of a complicated issue, the intuitive member is focused on the bigger picture that contextualizes the problem. Intuiting

## GLOSSARY

**Myers-Briggs Type Indicator®**

*A personality measure, based on Jung's work, that classifies people into 16 basic personality types according to their scores on four dimensions*

**Extraversion/ Introversion Dimension**

*The Myers-Briggs® dimension that describes whether someone's energy is directed outward toward observable events or toward an inner, mental landscape*

**Sensing/Intuiting Dimension**

*The Myers-Briggs® dimension that describes whether someone focuses on present facts or future possibilities*

| TABLE 6.1 | **Strengths and Weaknesses of the Myers-Briggs® Dimensions** |
| --- | --- |

|  | **Introvert** | **Extravert** |
| --- | --- | --- |
| **STRENGTHS** | • Can work independently | • Interacts well with others |
|  | • Likes working with ideas | • Is open |
|  | • Is careful before acting | • Is an active doer |
| **WEAKNESSES** | • Dislikes being interrupted | • Is impulsive and impatient |
|  | • Misses opportunities to act | • Needs change and variety |
|  | • Can be secretive or appear unsociable | • Needs others to work best |
|  | **Sensor** | **Intuitor** |
| **STRENGTHS** | • Pays attention to details and facts | • Sees possibilities |
|  | • Is patient and systematic | • Likes complicated issues/problems |
|  | • Is practical | • Likes working on novel problems |
| **WEAKNESSES** | • Can't see the forest for the trees | • Lacks patience with tedious work |
|  | • Cannot see possibilities or imagine the future | • Is inattentive to detail or practical considerations |
|  | • Is frustrated by complexity | • Jumps to conclusions |
|  | **Thinker** | **Feeler** |
| **STRENGTHS** | • Is logical, analytical, organized | • Is considerate of others' feelings |
|  | • Has good critical ability | • Understands others' needs/feelings |
|  | • Is fair but firm | • Is interested in maintaining harmony |
| **WEAKNESSES** | • Doesn't notice others' feelings | • Can be disorganized |
|  | • Is uninterested in harmony; shows less mercy | • Is overly accepting (of others, of information) |
|  | • Misunderstands others' values | • Is not logical or objective |
|  | **Perceiver** | **Judger** |
| **STRENGTHS** | • Sees all sides of an issue | • Is decisive |
|  | • Is flexible, spontaneous | • Persists in staying with a task |
|  | • Is nonjudgmental, accepting | • Makes plans and sticks to them |
| **WEAKNESSES** | • Is indecisive | • Is stubborn and inflexible |
|  | • Is easily distracted; does not finish tasks | • Is controlled by the plan/tasks rather than in charge of the plan |
|  | • Does not plan | • Decides with insufficient data |

SOURCE: Adapted from John N. Gardner and A. Jerome Jewler, *Your College Experience: Strategies for Success,* 2nd ed. (Belmont, CA: Wadsworth, 1995), pp. 83–89.

members can be invaluable when brainstorming possible solutions to problems; they are very good at arriving at innovative plans or novel ways to present a project for class presentations.

The **thinking/feeling dimension** concerns how individuals make decisions, whether by analysis and objective evidence or through empathy for others and subjective feelings. The *thinkers* in groups are those who enjoy evaluating information critically, spotting flaws in arguments, and producing logical plans. They do not jump to conclusions; rather, they use evidence and careful analysis, essential to critical thinking in a group. The *feelers* in a group use empathy for others as their standard for making decisions and are more willing to adjust standards to meet individual circumstances, with a focus on group harmony. You will see feelers making efforts to take members' feelings into account and helping to ensure that a decision is acceptable to those most affected by the decision.

The **perceiving/judging dimension** refers to the way people organize the world around them, whether they are spontaneous and flexible or planned and orderly. The *perceivers* in your group are like sponges, gathering as much information as they can and putting off a decision for as long as they can. They are open to new perspectives and multiple sides to issues. Perceivers roll with the circumstances and are not freaked out if the group's work plan is disrupted. These members can have difficulty reaching closure, and when the task is finished, they can second-guess by wondering aloud whether there was a different or better way to have solved the problem. Group members who are *judgers* set plans and stick to them. They finish tasks and are ready to move on, much like Misty in Case 6.1. They are less willing to roll with changing circumstances. These group members can help the group get their work done by establishing a work plan and encouraging members to follow the plan. Perceivers and judgers can drive each other crazy, yet group dynamics requires both stability and change, not one or the other process.

If you noticed some common themes between individual motives, learning styles, and personality types, you have been paying attention! For example, introversion and reflective observation exhibit similarities, as do extraversion and active experimentation. Concrete experience preferences are related to both sensing and feeling; abstract preferences are related to both intuiting and thinking. Thinkers, introverts, and judgers may exhibit behavior indicating strong task motives. Likewise, feelers, extraverts, and perceivers may be seen as strongly motivated by social needs. How we attend to the world around us and the people we come into contact with is a general orientation that can be manifested as motives, learning styles, and personality types. While similar, these broad categories give us more in-depth knowledge about individual preferences and the values behind those preferences, which influence the meaning we assign to others' behaviors, our group tasks, the measures we take to accomplish the task, how we judge success, and so on. As stated earlier, no one person is "purely" one or the other style or is capable of only one motive. We learn these preferences and use those that make the most sense to us. As group members we need to be sensitive to the benefits and drawbacks of each one and recognize that we are often a mix of these apparently contradictory preferences, which do not have to be mutually exclusive. Each group together needs to find their balance. In the next section we will discuss differences that have come to be most associated with diversity: cultural differences.

### Balancing the Church Board

A friend of ours served on the board of directors of a Unity church. The board and congregation were having problems getting things done. The board made decisions and set policies, but no action resulted. For example, the board noticed that, although many new members had joined the church, they often drifted away after a few months. Board members decided to create a program that would help new members integrate themselves quickly into the church community so that they would feel part of the congregation and be motivated to stay. They instituted a volunteer program to help members, especially new ones, identify their talents and find places where they could make their talents available to the church. However, this program never got off the ground, and although new members continued to join, they also continued to leave.

About this time, a representative from the Association of Unity Churches came to conduct a board/congregation seminar based on the Myers-Briggs® classifications. Of the seven board members, six were identified as intuitive feelers and one as an intuitive thinker.

1. What relationship do you see between the classification of board members and the kinds of problems the church was experiencing?

2. What classifications do you think would be most helpful in supplying balance to this board?

3. If you were the board president, what would you do with this information? For instance, would you ask potential board members to construct their profile before endorsing them to run for the board? What ethical problems might this create?

**MHHE.com/ groups**
For more information on exploring cultural diversity, go to the Online Learning Center at **www.mhhe.com/ adamsgalanes7**

---

**GLOSSARY**

**Culture**

*The system of beliefs, values, and symbols shared by an identifiable group of people*

---

# Cultural Diversity

Cultural differences represent a major form of diversity in a group, and as we indicated previously, groups in the twenty-first century will be increasingly diverse. Some small group research today is dedicated to exploring *why* culturally heterogeneous groups experience difficulty.[16] If we can explain the complex interplay between cultural factors, individual factors, and group composition on group problem-solving processes and the quality of a group's output, then we are in a better position to know how best to work with, not against, cultural diversity.

## DIMENSIONS OF CULTURE

**Culture** is the system of beliefs, values, symbols, and rules that underlie communication patterns within a discernible grouping of people. It doesn't necessarily refer to people from another country. A co-culture is a smaller identifiable group contained within a larger cultural grouping. For example, you belong to the co-culture of "college students." In this text we use the word *culture* to refer also to race, gender, and generational differences, which we'll discuss later.

Unless someone calls our attention to a feature of our culture, we don't think too much about the significant role it plays in shaping our behavior. In addition, we tend to assume that individuals from other cultures share our values, behaviors, and communication patterns, but they don't! Cultures differ along a number of dimensions that affect communication rules and preferences; we discuss three of them here (see Table 6.2).[17] Knowing something about them will help you communicate better in groups made up of individuals from diverse cultures so that you can capitalize on the strengths of these cultures. Moreover, because American business is increasingly becoming global in scope, at some point you likely will belong to a group composed of members from more than one country. In that case it will be especially important for you to be sensitive to cultural differences, not only so you don't offend others but also so you can participate profitably in a global economy.

The first important dimension along which cultures vary is the individualist/collectivist dimension. An **individualistic culture,** such as the predominant culture of the United States, values individual goals more than collective, or group, goals. In a **collectivist culture** the needs of the group take precedence over the needs of the individual, and conformity to the group is valued. So, for example, a group member from a collectivist culture will willingly abandon personal plans to attend a group meeting, but a member from an individualistic culture will say something like, "I've already got plans, so you'll either have to meet without me or reschedule the meeting at a time that I can make." The underlying value—what's most important—differs. It is easy for group members who value collectivism to become frustrated with a highly individualistic member, whom they will perceive as selfish and uncaring. However, it is also easy for individualistic members to perceive collectivist ones as caring too much about what others think.

Asian, Native American, and Latin American cultures (including the Mexican American co-culture within the United States) tend to be more collectivist than the cultures of the United States or Western Europe.[18] For instance, in Asian cultures relationships are crucial. If your company sends you to negotiate a contract with a group of executives in Taiwan, you must plan on a perhaps lengthy social engagement before business can be discussed. Americans who rush the process have inadvertently insulted their Taiwanese hosts. Individualistic Americans also tend to be competitive and argumentative, particularly in comparison with collectivist cultures, where allowing group members to "save face" is necessary to preserving group harmony. In conflict situations they are comfortable forcing their opponents to capitulate. But instead of assuming that someone must win and someone must lose, it may be more productive to find the common ground instead.

Individuals from collectivist and individualistic cultures have developed different communication preferences. For instance, individualistic members value clear and direct communication that is unambiguous.[19] In contrast, members from collectivist cultures, which value harmony, prefer ambiguous communication that is more subtle and tentative. For example, suppose both Nguyen and Sam disagree with something contained in a group report being prepared. Nguyen, the collectivist member, says, "I wonder if we should look more closely at Part 2 of the report? Was anyone else confused in that section?" But Sam, the individualist member, says, "I think Part 2 is terrible and has to be done over." Nguyen likely thinks Sam is selfish and rude, whereas Sam sees Nguyen as wishy-washy and spineless.

**GLOSSARY**

**Individualistic Culture**

*A culture that values individual needs and goals more than group needs and goals*

**Collectivist Culture**

*A culture that values group needs and goals more than individual needs and goals*

| TABLE 6.2 | **Three Important Dimensions of Culture** |
|---|---|

**Individualism/Collectivism**

**HIGH INDIVIDUALISM**

Values independence, autonomy, and privacy; encourages dissent; encourages people to "do their own thing."

- "I won't be at the meeting tomorrow. I've got a chance to go skiing with a friend and I really need some time off from school."

- "I know you all agree, but I don't, and I won't support that decision."

**HIGH COLLECTIVISM**

Values harmony, conformity, and loyalty to the group; discourages dissent.

- "I'm taking my mother to the hospital for surgery in the morning, but I'll be at our meeting for sure at noon. I can call from there to see how she's doing."

- "I'll go along with whatever you all want to do."

**Power Distance**

**HIGH POWER DISTANCE**

Maximizes status differences between members; values hierarchical structure and strong authoritarian leadership.

- Leader says, "I've decided that we're going to do it this way."

**LOW POWER DISTANCE**

Minimizes status differences between members; values sharing power, participatory decision making, and democratic leadership.

- Leader says, "We've all got to live with the decision we make, so we should all have a say in it. Tell me what you think?"

**Context**

**LOW CONTEXT**

Lets the words themselves carry most of the meaning; values direct, unambiguous communication.

- "Your idea is intriguing. Maybe we should explore it in more detail" (said with a smile) means, "I'm interested and I want to explore it in more detail."

- "I love that idea" means "I love that idea."

**HIGH CONTEXT**

Lets the situation, or context, carry most of the meaning; communication is indirect; nonverbal signals are crucial to understanding a message.

- "Your idea is intriguing. Maybe we should explore it in more detail" (said with a smile) may mean, "I hate it" or "I really like it" or "It might have some possibilities but I can't commit yet."

Each way of stating the same opinion has advantages and disadvantages. Nguyen's way is polite and allows the writer of Part 2 to save face; however, we can't tell how strongly Nguyen feels about it, so Part 2's writer can easily misinterpret Nguyen. In contrast, there's no mistaking how Sam feels, but his statement may make the author so angry that nothing in Part 2 gets changed.

Degrees of individualism and collectivism also influence patterns of turn taking in heterogeneous groups.[20] Turn taking was much more unequal in mixed groups of Japanese and European American students than in homogeneous groups of either all-Japanese or all–European American students. This shows how hard communication can be in heterogeneous groups, especially early in their development. The mix of individualistic and collectivist values influenced the equitable distribution of turns, with the European American students taking more turns. Groups should work toward an equitable balance of turn taking because this kind of member contribution is important to effective decision making in groups.

The second dimension of culture we discuss is **power distance,** or the extent to which a culture maximizes or minimizes status and power differences among individuals. In a low-power-distance culture (the United States has relatively low power distance), status and power differences among individuals are downplayed. Individuals believe that power should be distributed evenly, that just because someone has a title or money does not entitle them to privileges under the law that others don't have, and so forth. In a group, members from a low-power-distance culture believe that they have as much right to speak up and participate in decisions as the group's leader. In high-power-distance cultures such as Mexico and the Philippines, status differences are magnified and a rigid hierarchy exists. Members of such cultures believe that each person has a preassigned place in the society and should not seek to step out of that niche. In a group, members from high-power-distance cultures expect the leader to control and direct the group and may become frustrated with participatory leadership.

Members from low-power-distance cultures expect to participate in decision making, prefer a democratic leadership style, and assume that everyone else wants to participate in decision making as well. For instance, group leader Sarah says to her group, "What ideas do you all have for solving the parking problem?" Members from high-power-distance cultures value authoritarian leadership and may see a democratic leader as weak and incompetent. They expect low-status members to conform to high-status members. They assume others will accept the leader's control and direction. For example, group leader José says to his group, "I believe the parking problem is due to bad class scheduling. Here's what I want you to do. . . ." You can see the possibility for misunderstanding and hurt feelings here!

The third dimension is that of context. In a **low-context culture,** such as that of the United States, the verbal part of the message carries the meaning—what you say is exactly what you mean. If you say that you like my proposal, I can trust the fact that you really *do* like it. In a **high-context culture,** such as most Asian and Native American cultures, features of a situation or context are more important than the words themselves. So if you tell me you like my proposal, I'd have to take into account the setting, the people, the purpose of our conversation, and other factors to know for sure whether you *really* liked it or you were just being polite to avoid hurting my feelings. High-context cultures tend to be collectivist, with group harmony an important value. Ambiguity and indirectness may help preserve this harmony by allowing disagreement to happen gently, in a way that doesn't upset the balance of the group.

## GLOSSARY

**Power Distance**

*Whether a culture maximizes or minimizes status and power differences*

**Low-Context Culture**

*A culture in which the words used convey more meaning than the situation or context*

**High-Context Culture**

*A culture in which features of the situation or context convey more meaning than the words people use*

For example, context differences have produced problems between U.S. managers and their Mexican counterparts at the *maquiladoras,* the assembly plants in Mexico near the U.S. border.[21] Expectations about how managers should express disagreement differ. Mexican managers use an indirect communication style in conflict situations, but U.S. managers expect disagreements to be expressed openly and unambiguously. These differences in expectations can cause problems and misunderstandings.

Group members from low-context cultures sometimes try to force others to be direct and clear. They may perceive members who are not straightforward as manipulative or insincere. On the other hand, members from high-context cultures perceive members who are verbally blunt as rude and aggressive. As the earlier example demonstrates, the advantage of being clear, like Sam, is that your meaning is unmistakable. However, the advantage of being tentative, like Nguyen, is that you allow discussion to occur without polarizing members' opinions or making them lose face.

## Euro-Disney Stumbles

**APPLY NOW**

According to Carl Hiaasen in *Team Rodent: How Disney Devours the World,*\* Disney's venture in France, Euro-Disney, got off to a slow start when it opened in 1992. Disney executives decided to import the Disney concept intact when they created their European theme park. The Disney parks in the United States have a clean-cut image—at least, as Americans define *clean-cut.* Those who work in the park, mostly young people, abide by strict rules of dress and demeanor. For example, they must not wear bright nail polish, heavy makeup, or facial hair. In addition, the parks do not serve wine or other alcoholic beverages, which contributes to the clean-cut image in the United States.

However, these rules seemed offensive and ridiculous to Europeans, particularly the French. Not serve wine in France? Unthinkable! These factors contributed to Euro-Disney's dismal early performance. However, Disney rethought its rules and relaxed several, in particular the makeup, facial hair, and wine rules. Euro-Disney is beginning to catch on in Europe, the way it has in the United States.

1. Are there any other "rules" or communication patterns observed by North Americans that Europeans might consider silly?

2. Are there any "rules" or communication patterns observed by Europeans that North Americans might consider silly?

3. What does the above story suggest to you about cultural practices, particularly applying in one culture practices that are normal in another?

4. Disney executives are intelligent and experienced. What factors do you think might have contributed to this not-well-thought-out decision by Disney?

\*Carl Hiaasen, *Team Rodent: How Disney Devours the World* (New York: Ballantine Books, 1998).

Appreciation of cultural differences in a group is very important. The United States is a pluralistic culture to which many different cultures have contributed and continue to contribute. This means that little can be assumed or taken for granted, including assuming that a person's cultural identity predicts everything said and done in a group. The individualism/collectivism dimension of culture is arguably the most used dimension to help explain various cultural values that affect group dynamics. Most broadly, individualism is tied to having interest in the task and getting down to business, and collectivism is tied to having respect for harmony and building the social climate of the group as a context for work. Small group researchers like John Oetzel have recently argued that using *only* this dimension, without considering the fact that individuals *within* a culture vary, renders any cultural theory of group behavior weak.[22] As Oetzel points out, we are individuals acting in cultures; thus, we often find ourselves acting contrary to our claimed cultural identity—we cannot use *only* culture to predict individual behavior. Oetzel's effective decision-making theory (EDMT) explains that both cultural and individual preferences, called *self-construals,* affect group member behaviors. How cultural and individual preferences interrelate helps explain why culturally heterogeneous groups have problems functioning initially and why members from the same culture can vary in when and how much they contribute, how they solve problems, and how they approach conflict.

There are two types of self-construals, or ways we define ourselves to the world and to others: independent and interdependent. Those group members who invoke an independent image of themselves see themselves as unique, with their thoughts and feelings as their own. They are goal-driven, seek clarity, and attend less to nuances of context. Those who invoke interdependent images of themselves define who they are in connection to others. They value helping others meet their goals. They value fitting in, work to uphold the self-image of the other, and also try to avoid negative assessments of themselves. The two types of self-construals are correlated with individualistic cultures and collectivist cultures, respectively. In addition, these two types of self-image are found in everyone, regardless of their cultural identity.

When cultural heterogeneity, individualism/collectivism, and self-construal are examined together, a rather complex relationship emerges in which culture sometimes directly affects group behaviors (e.g., starting conflict episodes) and sometimes indirectly affects them, as when self-construals better predict a person's behavior (e.g., the choice of conflict tactics and number of turns taken). What is important to note is that Oetzel has found that *both* the cultural input variable of individualism/collectivism *and* the personal input variable of independence/interdependence influence the contributions of members and conflict.

## RACIAL AND ETHNIC DIFFERENCES

We began our discussion of cultural diversity with a global emphasis, talking broadly about differences group members from different countries may bring to a group. In this section we focus more on those same cultural and co-cultural dimensions within the boundaries of the United States. Discussions of racial and ethnic differences are complicated and often very difficult in the United States. We seem to shout at each other, producing more heat than light, or pretend there are no differences or problems anymore. However, if we do not find ways to effectively negotiate one another's relevant ethnic and racial differences within a climate of mutual respect while solving problems impacting all of us, we will not find the benefits in cultural diversity. In the twenty-first century multiracial and multiethnic groups are the norm, so we have to do better than we have in the past.

Major ethnic and racial groups in our country include African Americans, Asian Americans, European Americans, and Hispanic Americans. We know quite a bit about the communication within many cultures, but we don't know very much about interaction between individuals from a variety of cultures. In this section we provide information about some of the major differences in communication styles and patterns in these groups, but we focus on differences between African Americans and European Americans because relationships between these two groups are among the most discussed and debated in this country. We offer a very important caution. We discuss each culture as if members from that culture display a single consistent pattern of communication, but this is not the case. There are as many communication style differences *within* these co-cultures as there are between them. Although we know we are overgeneralizing, if you aren't aware of differing cultural practices, your lack of knowledge may interfere with effective group discussion. If you find yourself uncomfortable in an encounter with someone whose race or ethnicity is different from your own, and your impulse is to blame the other person for your discomfort, stop! Your discomfort may be due to unexamined differences between two cultures; the other person may be just as uncomfortable as you are.

Earlier we presented information about collectivist and high-context cultures. Asian cultures tend to be both. Asian Americans who are close to their original family cultures may communicate indirectly. Group harmony takes priority, so conflict will be expressed indirectly and ambiguously. Non–Asian Americans may have to pay careful attention to recognize they've been disagreed with, because actions in context are trusted more than words.

Most Hispanic cultures are collectivist and have a high power distance. This means that individuals are expected to subordinate their wishes to the group, and strong, authoritarian leadership is expected. These expectations and values may clash with the individualism and relatively low power distance in the predominant European American culture in the United States.

The relationship between African Americans and European Americans can be particularly complicated. These two cultural groups have traditionally misunderstood each other, often with serious consequences to both. We hope the information we provide about communication differences between these groups will prevent you from saying or doing something insensitive that contributes to group self-destruction.

The African American culture values sharing, emotionality, verbal expression, and interactivity.[23] These values express themselves in a variety of ways. African Americans appreciate verbal inventiveness and expression. Verbal play as a type of performance is particularly valued. However, what African Americans intend as a playful display is often interpreted by European Americans as bragging or strutting. African Americans are generally more expressive and interactive. Open expression of feelings is encouraged as an important way to share and connect. However, this too can be misinterpreted. African Americans think European Americans are cold and underreactive because they don't share feelings as readily and are not as expressive. Similarly, European Americans think African Americans are overly emotional and overreactive.

## Different Voices for Making Ethical Decisions

**ETHICAL DILEMMA**

Assume you are on a student judicial committee charged with deciding the punishment of students who have violated your institution's rules and policies. Rob, the student before you, is charged with plagiarism. He submitted a paper very similar to one that another student had turned in the previous semester to another teacher for the same course. Sections of Rob's paper are identical to the earlier paper, but some parts of the paper contain new research and appear to be Rob's own work. Rob has admitted that he plagiarized portions of the paper but pleads extenuating circumstances and asks for your committee's mercy. Soon after he started his research for the paper, he learned that his younger sister, still in high school, had been diagnosed with leukemia. She is being treated, so far successfully, but for the last few weeks Rob has driven home on weekends to be with her. He and his sister are close; she relies on him for emotional support, which he has been happy to provide. But helping her has drained him of the ability to concentrate and consumed all his time. He took the easy way out but made sure that he incorporated his original research into the paper he "borrowed." Rob asks you to let him drop the course with no penalty so he can take it again the next semester. However, your institution has an honor code all students sign as freshmen; the code specifies a *minimum* of one semester's suspension for all honor violations, including plagiarism. In practice, though, the student judicial committee's recommendations are accepted. Here are your choices:

- Let him drop the course with no penalty.
- Give him an F in the course.
- Give him an F in the course with a notation that the F is due to plagiarism; this remains on his permanent record.
- Give him an F in the course and suspend him for one semester.
- Give him an F in the course and expel him from school permanently.

   **1.** Before you form groups of five or six, what would you personally recommend for Rob? What is your reasoning for your recommendation?

   **2.** Get together in groups, as if you were the student judicial committee, and come to consensus about what you would recommend. Then discuss what your reasons were for your ultimate recommendation. What considerations were most important to you?

   **3.** How did you balance being fair to Rob, being fair to other students, and upholding your honor code?

(*continued*)

*Continued*

This example allows for a number of individual differences in ethical reasoning to emerge. Educator Carol Gilligan, in her book *In a Different Voice,*\* suggests that men and women use different ethical logic systems when making decisions like this. Men are believed to make ethical decisions from so-called objective positions that focus on abstract concepts such as justice, freedom, and truth. Women, Gilligan believes, make ethical decisions based on concerns for people, taking compassion, desire to alleviate suffering, and loyalty into account.

4. Did you observe either of these ethical systems during your discussion? Did any other ethical systems emerge during your discussion?

5. To what extent do you agree with Gilligan's assessment of men's and women's reasoning during ethical dilemmas like this?

6. What implications might the conflict of different ethical systems have for small groups?

\*Carol Gilligan, *In a Different Voice: Psychological Theory and Women's Development* (Cambridge, MA: Harvard University Press, 1982).

Each group perceives the other negatively.[24] A number of communication patterns may contribute to this. For instance, African Americans stand closer to each other than European Americans, who may interpret that nonverbal behavior as threatening. European Americans make more direct eye contact when they listen than when they talk. For African Americans the pattern is reversed; they make more direct eye contact when they talk than when they listen. This can seriously affect perceptions of trust, interest, and acceptance.

The African American communication style is much more interactive than the typical European American style. For instance, traditional African American church services often display the call-response style, whereby congregation members shout "Amen!" and "Tell it like it is, brother!" while the preacher is talking. They also use the backchannel more than European Americans. This means that they say things like "Uh-huh" and "Mm-hmm" in everyday conversation to signify interest and attention. However, European Americans can easily interpret someone talking during another's talk as rudeness. On the other hand, African Americans, who are used to getting such verbal signs of attention, may interpret that lack of backchannel responses from European Americans as lack of interest. African American conversational style is a narrative, storytelling style. European Americans may interpret it as disorganized, rambling, or off-task. To European American teachers a paper written in traditional African American narrative style can appear disorganized and rambling.

Most African Americans have had more practice in understanding European American culture than vice versa because they have been forced to.[25] Many African Americans consider themselves bicultural because they can negotiate "typical" African American conversational contexts as well as the European American contexts that currently predominate in the business and education arenas. However, it is difficult for minority group members to express themselves fully in groups composed primarily of individuals from other cultures.[26] Unfortunately, this suggests that multicultural groups are not realizing their full potential as groups because they aren't incorporating fully the ideas of the minority group members.

## GENDER DIFFERENCES

You will never be able to escape one of the most important influences of culture: the effect of gender roles in a group. The masculine-feminine continuum is often listed as another dimension of culture, along with individualism/collectivism, high or low context, and power distance.[27] Broadly speaking, more feminine cultures (e.g., Norway, Costa Rica, Sweden) prefer an overlap of roles such that both males and females are expected to be modest, nurturing, and generally other-oriented. In more masculine cultures (e.g., Australia, Mexico, the United States, Japan), gender roles that complement each other are reinforced, with men acting assertive and women acting modest. The gendered communication rules we all use have been taught and reinforced by our cultures. Culture, and our own construction of gender, influences how we experience behaviors in groups and what choices we make. Nina Reich and Julia Wood examined research studies about male-female behavior in small groups. Four areas emerged in which women and men show different tendencies; these are not absolute differences but rather are matters of degree.[28]

The first area of difference is between *expressive* and *instrumental* behaviors. Expressive behaviors focus on feelings and relationships. For instance, before the meeting gets under way, Susan may ask Allen how he did on the calculus test he was worried about. Instrumental behaviors focus on accomplishing the group's tasks. Allen may tell Susan he'll talk to her about it after the meeting, but first they have to assess where they are on their group project.

A second, related difference is *task* versus *relationship* focus. Women generally place more emphasis on relationships and are more likely to show, by their communication behavior, that they care and want to help. One woman we know, a particularly effective leader, touches base with members between meetings, especially if there has been a disagreement, to make sure everyone is OK and no one's feelings are hurt. She believes that things go better when relationships are harmonious. As with expressive and instrumental behavior, men and women both communicate caring as well as interest in the group's task.

Third, there are differences in *forcefulness,* which involves how much someone talks, interrupts others, claims personal space, or otherwise calls attention to him- or herself in the conversation. It also refers to how directly and assertively someone communicates. Men tend to be more forceful than women. They talk more than women, interrupt more, engage in more self-promotion, claim more space, and are more assertive. A man is more likely to say, "OK, here's what I think we should do," but a woman is more likely to say, "This seems like a good idea, but what do the rest of you think?" The first statement is more direct and powerful, but the second is more polite and inviting.

Finally, male-female differences have been observed between *individual* and *group* orientation. Men exhibit more individualistic behavior that calls attention to their own personal status. They tend to seek the spotlight more often and to highlight their own individual accomplishments: "I think I did a great job of researching our topic." In contrast, women show more collectivist behavior that emphasizes the group as a whole: "We have done a wonderful job of gathering all the information we need." They stress building the team rather than increasing their own individual status.

Interestingly, sex itself seems to function as a status characteristic in small groups, with men having higher status. In one study in which group members interacted anonymously via computer-mediated communication, men were more likely than women to reveal that they were men.[29] Women hid identifying information or even represented themselves as men. Women believed that their contributions were more readily accepted when they were anonymous than when they engaged in face-to-face interaction and could clearly be identified as women. They preferred to remain anonymous during computer-mediated interactions because they believed they had more influence that way.

Generalizing about male and female behavior is misleading for all sorts of reasons. Multiple factors—such as the nature of the task, group composition, member roles, the behaviors used to cue status, and individual identity preferences—can mediate the influence

### Diminishing Implicit Assumptions of Group Diversity

Go to
**www.mhhe.com/ adamsgalanes7** for additional weblink activities.

**MEDIA AND TECHNOLOGY**

Diversity in experience, expertise, and perspective is encouraged in group interaction because of the potential it adds to the quality of group decisions. However, a number of implicit assumptions about diversity (personality, culture, gender, etc.) can sometimes diminish the rewards that would otherwise be gained by having a group composed of a mixture of personalities and experiences. Think how your group interactions might differ if you had no preconceived assumptions about the members you were about to work with. How would that change the way your group started its meetings? What things would you talk about to develop relationships?

One feature of group support systems is anonymity, a feature that can be used to help circumvent many assumptions members bring to the group (e.g., males are better at working on task, or younger group members know more about technology). Consider some of the stereotypes you have about male and female group members. Do you have different expectations for male group members compared to females? Are there tasks that you feel certain genders are better at? In her examination of gender masking on the Internet, Brenda Danet found that, when given the opportunity, individuals (both male and female) enjoyed experimenting with altering their identity because of the freedom that came from gender-free interaction. The anonymous interaction of a CMC environment gives people a chance to understand how social and cultural information about others is used to guide interaction. To learn more about the potential for gender masking, go to **www.newcastle.edu.au/discipline/social-anthrop/staff/ kibbymarj/gender.html** for a comprehensive list of available resources on the subject.

SOURCE: Based on Brenda Danet, "Text as Mask: Gender, Play, and Performance on the Internet," in *Cybersociety 2.0* ed. S. Jones (Thousand Oaks, CA: Sage, 1998).

of gender. As with any cultural variable, we should stay away from either-or thinking—that is, thinking that men are only *this* way and women are only *that* way, and one way is better. Lindsey Grob and colleagues, in studying gender differences in small group communication contexts, make the case that too much scholarship in this area focuses on the differences between men and women and not the similarities.[30] When men and women are treated as being socialized in two different cultures, we tend to stereotype men as instrumental/powerful and women as affiliative/powerless. You see this dichotomy in the previous expressive/instrumental, task/relationship, and individual/group tendencies.

Typically, powerful speech has been defined as speech heavy in interruptions (seen as assertive) with minimal use of speech that can be seen to soften discourse, such as disclaimers (e.g., "*This could be wrong,* but don't we need more cash?") and tag questions (e.g., "Increasing tuition will lead to higher dropout rates, *won't it?*"). Women are stereotyped as using more disclaimers and tag questions, and men are stereotyped as using more interruption and being interrupted less. When we change our theoretical approach to one of emphasizing the similarities between men and women, we are not as apt to dichotomize male and female behavior. Grob and colleagues found that males and females interrupted others with similar frequency and used disclaimers and tag questions similarly. In fact, they found that it was the *males* in the groups who were interrupted more. However, they also found that when males interrupt others, they are more successful than females.

What are we to make of all this? Once again, it's important not to lose sight of the fact that there are many similarities between cultures, and cultural groups have a lot more differences *within* groups than *between* them. Also, when we approach difference from an either-or perspective, we tend to draw destructive value judgments about behaviors—we have to behave *this* way or *that* way, but not both ways. Chapters 3 and 4 on communication emphasize that our communicative choices are not limited or mutually exclusive. In addition, any communicative choice can serve multiple functions rather than just one, no matter who the messenger may be. For instance, interruptions can show support for another individual's arguments, disclaimers can be used to help the other person save face or maintain positive face, and tag questions may be important as group members begin to converge on issues. Finally, remember that we are studying male and female behavior in groups not dyads. In mixed groups we see less stereotypical behavior, with members showing different patterns of mutual influence as groups develop over time.[31]

## GENERATIONAL DIFFERENCES

A few years ago, Gloria served on the board of directors at her church. Gloria is a baby boomer and was the youngest member of the board. As a boomer she believes all people—women included—have the right to express opinions; she also values frank and open discussion in the course of making decisions. It simply never would occur to her that she *shouldn't* say what she thought. Most of the other members of the seven-member board were a generation older. During their board meetings they signaled—primarily through their nonverbal behavior—that they were uncomfortable with her high level of participation. It seemed to her that she was violating an unspoken rule of "be seen and not heard until you've paid your dues." Her values and beliefs seemed to clash with the others' values, and she interpreted the clash as stemming from generational differences. These kinds of generational differences can negatively influence feelings of trust, for instance, among group members of different generations. When age differences are not apparent, such as in virtual work teams in which members interact via computer, the impact of age on trust is not as readily apparent.[32] Understanding the potential effect of generational differences on group processes at school or at work is important.

Think, for a moment, about your parents' and their friends' generation. Do you have the same values? Do you live your life in the same way as your parents? What differences do you observe? If you are old enough to have children, what differences do you observe between your own beliefs, behaviors, and values and those of your children?

A number of writers have characterized major generational differences that appear in the U.S. workplace today. Much of this information has been synthesized by Rick and Kathy Hicks, whose work provides the basis for this section.[33] Although the Hickses do not use the term *co-culture,* that is in fact what they describe. Their key assumption is that each generation forms a particular co-culture, with similar values, goals, and outlook, on life. The members of each generational co-culture are highly influenced by the major events, people, and activities prominent during their formative years, particularly when they were about 10 years old. At 10 years old, forces outside the family—friends, teachers, the media—begin to assume increased and lasting importance in our lives. To really understand the core values of a particular generational co-culture, it is necessary to take a look at those influential events.

The Hickses describe four broad generations that are found in today's workplace: builders, boomers, generation X, and the net generation. Table 6.3 summarizes this information. As we describe these generations, we recognize that we are again overgeneralizing and oversimplifying. However, you are bound to experience generational clashes in every arena of life—including in small groups you join. Appreciating some of the differences—and perhaps the reasons for them—will help you draw from the strengths of these generational differences instead of being mired in resentment.

The **builders,** born between 1901 and 1945, lived through two world wars and the bust of the Great Depression. They learned to work very hard, to save money, and to postpone gratification, preferring to save money for the things they need rather than use credit cards. Many of this generation are retired but remain active in American governmental and civic life. They are comfortable with hierarchy, willingly climbed the corporate ladder by placing their personal interests aside to complete tasks. Personal discipline and self-sacrifice are central to their outlooks on life and work. These values may appear old-fashioned, but builders can provide loyalty and stability to groups. Builders, like sensors, are very thorough and do not ignore detail. They like completing a job, knowing it was done well, and appreciate being respected for their hard work. Although they can resist change and may act very reserved during conflict, their perseverance in seeing a job through is tremendously beneficial to a group.

The **boomers,** born between 1946 and 1964, are the children of the builders, who, because they tried to make the world easier for their kids, created a generation of people who believe in their own importance! Television and the social unrest of the 1960s produced individuals who are impatient for answers and want immediate solutions. They resist authority and value education as a means of addressing societal ills. They value hard work for the personal gratification they get from it, and not so much for the product. They can appear idealistic and self-centered, but they do bring valuable resources to the group. Boomers are responsible for the team concept in business and the continuing focus on

| TABLE 6.3 | Characteristics, Strengths, and Weaknesses of Four Dominant Generations | | |
|---|---|---|---|
| | **Characteristics** | **Strengths** | **Weaknesses** |
| **BUILDERS (1901–1945)** | • Major influences: Depression and WWII<br>• Are cautious about spending money<br>• Will work hard at single task until completed<br>• Put own interests aside for common good | • Are careful with resources (e.g., money)<br>• Plan ahead<br>• Are reliable, dependable<br>• Are disciplined | • Are too cautious with resources<br>• May lack spontaneity and flexibility |
| **BOOMERS (1946–1964)** | • Major influences: TV, Vietnam War, the Pill, assassinations, civil rights movement, size of generation<br>• Major consumers; value "good life"<br>• Are self-absorbed; believe they're special<br>• Work as end in itself; expect to be fulfilled at work<br>• Value education | • Are confident<br>• Will put in whatever time task takes<br>• Will challenge "old ways" of doing things<br>• Will take on big causes | • Think they're right all the time<br>• Expect others to hold similar beliefs/values<br>• May break rules of ethics if they think it's best for them |
| **GEN-XERS (1965–1976)** | • Major influences: rising divorce rate, Watergate, Pentagon Papers, MTV<br>• Distrust institutions, particularly government<br>• Are comfortable with diversity<br>• Work as means to an end<br>• Value family (broadly defined)<br>• Are comfortable with technology<br>• Endure education | • Are independent thinkers<br>• Are sensitive to people; value relationships<br>• Are tolerant; accept competing points of view<br>• Are comfortable with change<br>• Are highly computer literate | • Appear pessimistic and negative<br>• Are unwilling to put personal life/concerns aside to complete task<br>• May seem alienated and unmotivated |

*(continued)*

| **TABLE 6.3** | *Continued* | | |
|---|---|---|---|
| | **Characteristics** | **Strengths** | **Weaknesses** |
| **N-GENERS**<br>**(1977–1997)** | • Major influences: AIDS, technology and Internet, death of Princess Diana<br><br>• Are still young and in process of being formed<br><br>• Value diversity; highly tolerant<br><br>• Are major consumers<br><br>• Are nonlinear thinkers<br><br>• Value family | • Are open-minded and tolerant; welcome different viewpoints<br><br>• Are completely technology and media savvy<br><br>• Are optimistic<br><br>• Are innovative<br><br>• Are comfortable with and like collaborative work, networking | • Seem to lack initiative; seem unmotivated<br><br>• Are unlikely to conform to bureaucracy, hierarchy, organizational "rules" |

*"Take a load off, Leonard—we're watching Generation X and Y duke it out."*

Generational diversity in groups can be as significant an influence as culture. © The New Yorker Collection; 2001 Lee Lorenz from cartoonbank.com. All Rights Reserved.

service. Their confidence and ease with alternative views that may be contrary to those of the establishment can help in projects. Boomers value being noticed for their contributions and can help group members show gratitude to other members. Boomers are still in many leadership positions in industry, education, and government—holding those places the gen-Xers would like to have!

**Gen-Xers** were born between 1965 and 1976. They are commonly referred to as the *latchkey generation* and often emotionally neglected by their boomer parents, with their high divorce rates. Living through Watergate and President Nixon's resignation, they do not so much resist authority as mistrust it. Seen by boomers and traditionalists as lacking in job skills and self-confidence, as well as being pessimistic in their outlooks, they have the ability to balance work and their personal lives. They are not willing to sacrifice their personal relationships for work and thus bring multitasking to group work. This generation has grown very adaptable; gen-Xers build careers not in one place or with one company but around themselves. They were the first generation to experience Atari as children. Although they may not appear to be team players or interested in long-term commitments, they are flexible and are much more at ease with diversity than previous generations. They speak their minds more than boomers or traditionalists might and are motivated best when they perceive that they have control over their tasks and can still value aspects of their personal lives. They have a broad concept of family, which encompasses people they feel emotionally connected to, whether related by blood or not.

The **net generation** (or N-gen) was born between 1977 and 1997. They are sometimes referred to as the *echo boom, millennial generation,* and *generation Y.* This group is particularly large and the first truly wired generation. Gen-Xers grew up with the computer as entertainment; this generation uses computers for *everything.* In fact, they are the most receptive to the use of emoticons in e-mail correspondence (the builders are the most uncomfortable with emoticons and prefer instead more personal correspondence, such as handwritten letters).[34] More hopeful than the Xers, N-geners are even more comfortable with diversity and more confident in their skills (especially computer skills), and they have better relationships with their parents. They are accustomed to collaborative work in school and via the net, which makes them value peer relationships rather than hierarchical relationships. In groups they value others based on their contributions not their ascribed status. They have a strong live-and-let-live philosophy tempered by the stress of relying on their day planners. They are part of a generation that has come to value mentoring relationships, and they look to others to provide that kind of help. They, too, are multitaskers who can be in more than one place at one time, accomplishing several different things at once. We see this more and more in our classroom groups, with several members doing group work via the Internet and personal computer devices.

The builders are gradually fading from the scene as the boomers assume and hang onto power. The gen-Xers, small in numbers and impaired in terms of job skills and self-esteem, are not a powerful force in the workplace. The N-geners, however, because of their mastery of technology and their numbers, will be a huge force in the workplace, and some foresee a major values clash between them and the boomers. In many ways, because the N-geners have used collaborative learning in schools and are used to interacting with people from all over the world, they are well suited to small group collaboration. But they won't sit quietly and wait to be called on. They want to be respected for

## GLOSSARY

**Gen-Xers**

*Individuals born from 1965 to 1976; influenced by Watergate and general mistrust*

**Net Generation**

*Individuals born from 1977 to 1997; influenced by computers and the information/digital revolution*

their competence and contributions, regardless of their age or position in the company. If you're a boomer, with the expectation that you will command and lead, expect to be challenged!

The previous discussion, as we mentioned earlier, represents overgeneralization and oversimplification. We all can see characteristics of each generation in ourselves. We also know people who display few or none of the characteristics that are supposed to exemplify their generation. However, the point to remember is this: Our early influences from family, friends, and institutions such as the media affect the way we perceive the world around us and the way we communicate, which in turn affects our behavior in small groups. Understanding something about members of generations different from yours—what their hopes and fears are, what pressures operate on them, what the formative events were in their lives—will help you make the most of your differences in small groups instead of bogging you down.

It is easy for a group to get off track or make negative attributions about others whose communication styles and practices differ from ours. We have to learn not to interpret others' actions through the lens of our own culture but to appreciate what other cultures

### Mom's in My Group!

**APPLY NOW**

In the early 1990s one of us observed a classroom group of five members who included two men and two women in their early 20s and one woman in her mid-40s. This group had made some progress on its assignment, but tensions were beginning to build between one of the young women, Mindy, and the older woman, Sarah. A single mother with teenagers at home, Sarah had a very full schedule. She tried hard to keep the group task-focused so the project could be completed early, in time for feedback from the instructor. The more she made suggestions about the content of the project, about meeting more often, or about establishing deadlines for the members' individual assignments, the more Mindy resisted: "I can't meet then, I've paid for tickets to a concert and I'm not going to give them up," and "Chill, Sarah, it'll get done" were typical remarks. Mindy, exasperated with Sarah's task focus, complained to one of the other members that Sarah reminded her of her mom—"Always hassling me about something!" This conflict threatened to derail the group's progress.

1. What generations do Mindy and Sarah represent?
2. In what ways does each seem typical of her generation? What communication behaviors seem rooted in generational differences?
3. With whom do you personally have more sympathy? Why?
4. Assume that you are one of the other students in the group. How might you use what you know about generational differences to help the group resolve this problem?

have to offer. If we take the time to do that, our group processes and outputs will benefit. Evidence suggests that, although groups composed of culturally diverse individuals experience more process problems and perhaps lower cohesion initially, over time they can overcome these problems to experience improved performance in certain areas.[35] In one study groups composed of members from the same nationality and ethnic background demonstrated more effective decision-making processes at first, but over time the culturally diverse groups caught up. At the conclusion of this study, the diverse groups were outperforming the homogeneous groups in the range of perspectives considered and the number of alternatives generated. Clearly, working in a culturally diverse group is more challenging and requires members to pay greater attention to their communication behaviors, but the payoff can be significant!

We have not intended to teach you everything there is to know about cultural differences. Rather, we have tried to alert you to some common causes of misinterpretations in the listening process. Remember that cultural rules are not automatic; they are taught and constantly evolving. Remember also that cultural differences are not a matter of right or wrong and that you have absorbed the rules of your culture so completely that they are invisible to you until you start to examine them or to interact with people from a very different culture.

# Working with Diversity/Bridging Differences

So far in this chapter we have stressed the value of diversity and provided information and examples to illustrate how member and cultural diversity can make small group communication more complex. We emphasized that the value of diversity does not just happen by mixing together people with differences. Those differences have to be recognized and deemed relevant to the effectiveness of the group. This takes work, and the National Communication Association Credo for Ethical Communication reminds us that ethical communication transcends cultures and enhances human worth and dignity (see Figure 1.2). The credo's principles give us ideas for good practice: listening actively to understand before passing judgment, building communicative climates that foster respect for the unique needs of members, and avoiding communication that is harmful to the humanity of another.

Stella Ting-Toomey, a respected scholar of intercultural communication, has written extensively on the complexities of difference in our communicative lives. Working with diversity does not happen without **mindful communication.**[36] We have to be alert, open, willing, and reflective if we are to bridge differences. No practice or helpful tips will work unless group members are the reflective participant-observers we discussed in Chapter 1. You simply cannot stay stuck in your routine ways of doing things, unwilling to experiment, listen, learn about others, or be open to new possibilities. Our goal is to help group members blend into a well-functioning team that capitalizes on member diversity. The key to mindful communication is obtaining knowledge of the values behind those differences and being flexible enough to create new possibilities. Symbolic convergence is one way groups merge into a cohesive, productive team through fantasy chains (see below) that promote a team identity out of individual cultural and personal identities. The system for the multiple-level observation of groups (SYMLOG) is a tool groups can use to actually picture particular group differences in an effort to be mindful of them and proactively capitalize upon them.

**GLOSSARY**

**Mindful Communication**

*Communication that is open to multiple perspectives, shows a willingness to see the world from another's standpoint, and shifts perspective if necessary*

**GLOSSARY**

**Fantasy**

*Group discussion not focused on the present task of the group*

**Symbolic Convergence**

*The idea that humans create shared meaning through their talk; the basis of group fantasy*

## CREATING A GROUP IDENTITY THROUGH FANTASY

Diversity is potentially useful, and somehow group members must find common ground if they are to transcend their diverse styles, talents, and perspectives and operate as a team. Developing a symbolic life meaningful to all members can help accomplish this.

Even in the most hardworking, task-oriented groups, members do not stick to business all the time. They often get sidetracked, as if they have made a tacit agreement to "take a work break." Whenever a group is not talking about the here and now of the group, it is engaged in **fantasy.** This technical definition of fantasy does not mean "unreal" or "untrue." It simply means that group members are not discussing the present task of the group but are discussing an apparently unrelated topic.

The study of fantasy stems from the theory of **symbolic convergence.**[37] This theory recognizes that human beings create and share meaning through their talk. For a group to exist, there has to be some shared meaning among the members; otherwise, there would be no group. *Convergence* signifies that members have "come together" on what certain events, ideas, words, and so forth will mean. Members have developed similar feelings and beliefs about certain things (e.g., "We hate the boss's pep talks because she has no clue whatsoever about our work"). They may have in-jokes, a shared identity, or special meanings for words that only they understand (e.g., "We use 'fish face' as a term of affection because everybody in our group loves to go trout fishing"). They may also have developed rituals that are meaningful to them (e.g., "We always go out for a pizza on Friday afternoon before everybody goes their separate ways on the weekends"). These shared symbols help establish common ground and common bonds and help groups overcome differences among members.

Fantasy helps such shared symbols become a reality to a group. The process works like this. One member introduces a fantasy, and other members pick up on it and add to it. This group storytelling, called a *fantasy chain,* is similar to a party game most of us played as children. One person starts a story, the person to the left adds something, and this continues around the room until each person has contributed to the final story. Group fantasy chains are created in a similar way, and like the party game they have a central idea, or *fantasy theme,* that suggests what the fantasy is about.

The following is an example of a fantasy theme that occurred at a student government association executive committee meeting, in which members were bemoaning the lack of a day care facility on campus and were trying to figure out what to do about it. This group includes three men and two women, one of whom (Nan) was a nontraditional student with children.

| | |
|---|---|
| **Char:** | I'm not surprised that we don't have a center! We have such a retro-administration. [Char introduces the fantasy, which contains the retro idea.] |
| **Rob:** | I know; they're stuck in the 1970s. Next they'll probably let their sideburns grow! [Rob picks up the fantasy and starts the chain.] |
| **Bill:** | Can't you just see President Kramer coming to school in a tie-dyed suit? [Bill adds his part in a vivid, colorful way.] |
| **Nan:** | Better yet—a tie-dyed leisure suit! That would be about his speed. |
| **Joel:** | I can just see a big, tie-dyed sunspot on his chest and peace-sign earrings in his ears! And they ought to change the sign on the administration building to Retro-Administration Building! [Joel joins in, embellishing Nan's and Bill's comments.] |

| | |
|---|---|
| **Rob:** | I feel like we're trying to drag all of them into the twenty-first century. [Rob's comment hints at what this fantasy might mean to this group.] |
| **Char:** | I know they're really behind the times, but we really need to get back to the day care center. How can we get our retro-administration to listen to our ideas about that? [Char ends the fantasy and gets the group back on track.] |

What do you think this fantasy is about? Fantasies actually have two themes—the manifest, or obvious, theme and the latent, or underlying, theme. The *manifest theme* is what the fantasy chain is about at the surface level. The student government committee members were imagining the 70s attire of their retro-administration. The manifest theme was "Wouldn't that kind of clothing be funny?" The *latent theme*, which was actually not very far below the surface, was hinted at by Rob: "I feel like we're trying to drag all of them into the twenty-first century." In other words, "We, the students, are very forward thinking, but our retro-administration has to be forced to move forward, and we're the ones who have to drag them forward." It's an "Aren't we wonderful, but aren't they a mess" type of self-identity. The operative word here is *we*—these students, different though they may be, have defined themselves as "we" and the retro-administration as "they."

Fantasies—digressions apparently unrelated to the group's task—are introduced by members all the time, but not all fantasies are picked up on by the rest of the members or are meaningful to the group. When a fantasy captures the group's imagination, it usually means that it has some deeper relevance to the members. Thus, although it may appear during a fantasy chain that a group is goofing off, the group may be accomplishing something quite important. First, fantasies can help the group define itself by creating symbols that are meaningful and that help determine its values.[38] For example, the student government committee members who sidetracked into a discussion of tie-dyed clothing were actually using fantasy to help define themselves as forward-thinking representatives of the student body.

Second, fantasies enable a group to discuss indirectly matters that might be too painful, emotionally "weighty," or difficult to bring out into the open.[39] For example, Cassie, one of our students, managed a social service agency. A particular client had become adept at getting what she wanted by manipulating the social workers against one another. The social workers were pointing fingers at each other for the client's problems. Cassie, as the person in charge, dreaded chairing the meeting in which the social workers had to come to a decision about what to do with the client. Before the meeting started, one social worker started to talk about the movie *Erin Brockovich* (clearly an off-the-topic fantasy). In particular, she thought the main character exhibited "borderline personality disorder." Others picked up on this idea and added examples from the movie to support the "diagnosis." Soon, one social worker mentioned how Erin Brockovich reminded her of the client they were gathered to discuss. The rest of the social workers started laughing. They had an "aha" reaction when they realized how the client had been able to jerk them around. Cassie reported that they were able to come to a quick, cordial consensus about what to do. Their shared fantasy had allowed them to talk about this potentially difficult topic.

## USING SYMLOG TO "PICTURE" DIVERSITY

We have said that diversity in a group is a desirable feature, but we also know that diversity makes group discussion more challenging. Sometimes the very diversity that enhances group problem solving may become difficult or impossible to manage. Something is needed

**GLOSSARY**

**SYMLOG**

*The System for the Multiple-Level Observation of Groups, a theory and methodology that produces a diagram of relationships among group members*

to help members diagnose their differences and plan how to reconcile those differences so that the group's diversity can help rather than hurt the group. SYMLOG provides a methodology that can "show" a group where its most acute differences are and in what directions members should move to get the group on track.

**SYMLOG** is an acronym for System for the Multiple-Level Observation of Groups; it is both a comprehensive theory and a methodology that produces a diagram of relationships among group members.[40] We present a simplified explanation here so you can understand how SYMLOG can be used to describe and help a group.

SYMLOG theory assumes that behaviors in a group can be classified along three dimensions: dominant versus submissive, friendly versus unfriendly, and task-oriented versus emotionally expressive. An observer uses a 26-item rating scale to categorize each member's behavior; the rating scale is then tallied in a special way so that each member can be placed on the SYMLOG diagram. An example of a SYMLOG diagram, or map, is shown in Figure 6.2. The more a member is task-oriented, the closer he or she is to the top of the diagram; the more emotionally expressive, the closer to the bottom. (The F stands for forward, or task-oriented behavior, and the B stands for backward, or emotionally expressive

**FIGURE 6.2    SYMLOG Diagram of a Noncohesive Group**

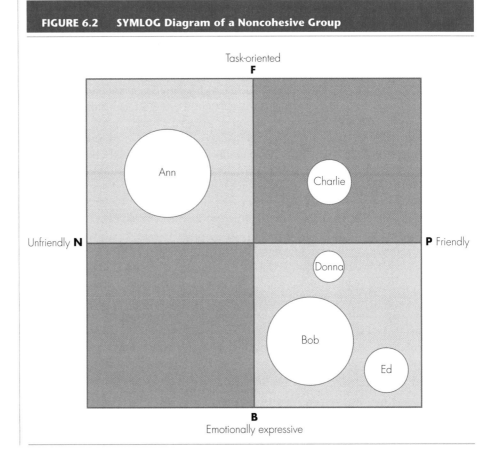

behavior.) The friendlier a member is toward the other members of the group, the closer he or she is to the right; the more unfriendly, the closer to the left. (The P stands for positive or friendly behavior, the N for negative or unfriendly behavior.) The third dimension, dominance or submissiveness, is shown by the size of the circle; a dominant member has a large circle, while a submissive one has a small one.

In the SYMLOG diagram in Figure 6.2, Ann is very dominant, task-oriented, and negative toward other members of the group. In contrast, Bob is friendly and emotionally expressive, although he also is dominant. A group with two such strong, but opposite, individuals is likely to experience conflict during meetings. Charlie is moderately dominant, positive, and task-oriented. (This is how democratic leaders and members of productive, democratic groups often appear in SYMLOG diagrams.) If you were asked to describe this group, you would probably say that it is unproductive, lacks cohesiveness, and appears to waste a lot of time during meetings because there's a struggle between the most task-oriented and most emotionally expressive members.

The SYMLOG diagram in Figure 6.3 shows a unified, cohesive group. All the members are in or near the upper right-hand quadrant (the decision-making quadrant), which shows

**FIGURE 6.3    SYMLOG Diagram of a Cohesive Group**

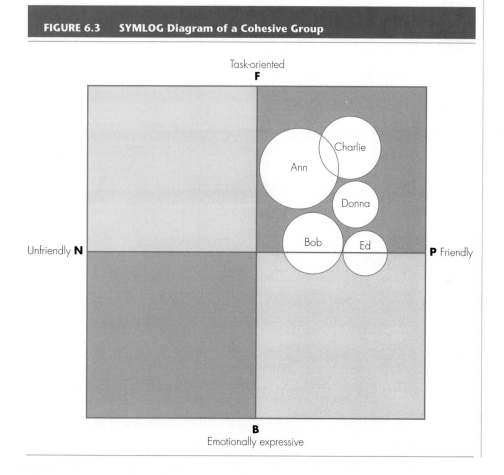

that they are task-oriented enough to make progress toward the group's goal but friendly enough toward each other that interpersonal relationships are probably harmonious. This group is likely to be productive and efficient.

Thinking in SYMLOG terminology helps you manage the complexity of group interaction as you create a snapshot capturing the texture of a group. Because SYMLOG gives you that visual representation, it is easy to grasp several complex relationships at once. That makes this tool particularly effective in helping you and your fellow group members analyze and diagnose yourselves. It also gives you an idea of what you might do if problems are revealed. A SYMLOG diagram represents the perceptions of the person who constructed it; this provides potentially valuable information to help group members begin discussing their perceptions and preferences. For instance, those members whose SYMLOG diagrams show that they perceive Ann to be unfriendly may be asked to share

## Using SYMLOG to Help a Group

**APPLY NOW**

Assume you are a consultant who has been brought in to help Judy and her group, described in the opening case. In preparation for meeting with the group, you have asked all the members to rate their own and the others' behaviors with the SYMLOG rating scales, and you've constructed five SYMLOG diagrams, one for each member of the group. Judy's diagram is shown on the left below. The other four members' diagrams are almost identical; the diagram on the right is an average of those four diagrams.

Judy's diagram

Average of other members' diagrams

1. Interpret the group from Judy's perspective.
2. Interpret the group from the other members' perspectives.
3. As a consultant, how would you use this information to help the group? What would be the focus of your work with this group?
4. In what ways do you perceive SYMLOG to be helpful to groups such as this?

specific examples that led them to that conclusion. Likewise, those whose diagrams place Bob in the emotionally expressive area can explain why they see him that way and what they feel about it.

If it is too threatening or frightening for group members to conduct such discussions on their own, a trusted facilitator can help manage the discussion. Consultants who use SYMLOG often ask members of the group being observed to complete the SYMLOG forms in advance. From these they create SYMLOG diagrams to distribute to the group. Having the SYMLOG "pictures" prompts members to talk about themselves and their relationships with each other in a relatively nonthreatening way. This can set the stage for tremendous growth and development in the group.

There are a variety of ways to use SYMLOG, and several computer programs have been created to make its use easier.[41] However, it is possible to construct a SYMLOG diagram by hand. If this analysis appeals to you, we recommend that you purchase the *SYMLOG Case Study Kit,* which contains all the instructions and forms you need to produce a diagram by hand.

We have presented two ways in which group members can bridge their differences by becoming more mindful in their communication. Once again, the most important thing members can do to transcend differences is to *want* to do so. Along with willingness, Ting-Toomey argues that attempts to bridge differences begin with the offer of basic human respect.[42] Assuming you want to work together productively and mindfully to find the potential in your relevant differences, we offer in Table 6.4 tips for doing just that.

| | **Tips for Appreciating Diversity and Bridging Differences** |
|---|---|
| **TABLE 6.4** | |

1. Decide that you want to appreciate the differences among you. Making understanding and appreciating your diverse talents, approaches, and styles a priority for your group is the single best thing you can do.

2. Schedule plenty of "get to know you" time. This can be a purely social gathering with no business conducted, or you can set aside a brief "check-in" time before you get started on your business. However, don't rush this process. You will need time to learn about each other.

3. Be willing to talk about and praise the differences among you. When people believe their unique approaches or contributions are valued, they relax and are willing to contribute more to the group process.

4. Be open to new ways of doing things. Nothing dampens the positive potential of diversity more than rigid adherence to doing things the same way they've always been done. Be willing to listen and to try new ideas.

5. Avoid seeing difference as a zero-sum game. Think of ways to integrate differences. For example, consider how you can both work on the task and build relationships.

*(continued)*

| **TABLE 6.4** | *Continued* |
| --- | --- |

6. Find ways you can create common experiences for group members. For instance, you may want to schedule a retreat, an outdoor activity, or a baseball game—anything that gets all members participating in the same experience.

7. Create rituals for the group. Meaningful rituals can go a long way toward reminding members that their purpose in coming together is greater than any individual differences they may possess. For example, one church board always begins its routine meetings with a prayer and its annual retreat with a communion service. However, rituals don't have to be serious. Some work groups pass out cookies or bagels at the beginning of the meeting, with members taking turns bringing the snacks.

8. Encourage members to create symbols that represent the group. Many groups have T-shirts with a meaningful saying or symbol. Sometimes members participate in creating symbols or logos for the group.

9. Use methods, such as SYMLOG, that provide a vehicle for members to talk about their differences and how they can surmount them. SYMLOG and other methods provide a relatively safe way and a nonjudgmental vocabulary for members to depict and discuss their perceptions of their own and others' behaviors. SYMLOG also gives members a handle on how to establish direction for the future to help the group capitalize on its diversity.

## RESOURCES FOR REVIEW AND DISCUSSION

**SUMMARY**

- Diversity is the essence of group problem solving. The differences by themselves are not a problem, but members often don't know how to or don't want to manage their diversity so the group can benefit.

- Diversity comes in many forms. Members may have different motives for joining a group; they may differ in their learning and personality styles.

- Another major way group members differ is in their culture or co-culture. Three main dimensions along which cultures differ are collectivist/individualistic, power distance, and context.

- Gender and racial or ethnic differences are, at heart, cultural differences. Men and women consistently differ in four ways; similarly, African, Asian, European, and Hispanic American cultures have developed different communication patterns that can be misunderstood by outsiders.

- Diversity is valuable, and group members can bridge their differences through fantasy and the SYMLOG methodology.

1. Look at the descriptions of four different work styles below:

   ■ Task-oriented people, who believe a group's main job is to get down to business as soon as possible

   ■ Relational people, who believe that group work can be fun and that getting to know each other is part of the fun

   ■ Systematic decision makers, who believe in gathering all the facts and weighing them before deciding

   ■ Intuitive decision makers, who assess a situation instantly and leap to a conclusion

   *a.* Each of the four work styles should be assigned to a different corner of the room. Then, without thinking about it too long or too hard, go to the corner of the room that represents the work style most like yours.

   *b.* Elect a reporter to record your group's responses and report to the class at the end of the session.

   *c.* In five to six minutes, write down all the advantages people like you have to offer a group.

   *d.* In five to six minutes, write down all the disadvantages people like you bring to a group.

   *e.* Reconvene the class as a whole, and have each group report, first the advantages and then the disadvantages, while a class member or your teacher writes each one on the board for all to see.

   *f.* After each group has presented its list, the other groups may add advantages or disadvantages to the list.

   *g.* Talk as a class about what you learned from this exercise and what you perceive can be the advantages such diversity of approach represented in the group.

2. Your family represents one example of a co-cultural grouping. Form into groups of four to six, and ask each person to assume that he or she has invited the rest of your group members home for Thanksgiving dinner with the family. Each person should describe what the "rules" are for Thanksgiving dinner. For example, where does everyone sit? When do you know you may start to eat? Does the food get passed around, or does someone put food on each person's plate and pass the plate down? What are acceptable topics of conversation? Is conversation lively or muted? How did the "rules" become established in the family, and so forth?

   When everyone has finished, discuss the differences you discovered among each other's "cultures." What dimensions of culture seem to be most important in each family grouping? Were there any surprises? What does each family do when it encounters a violation of the rules? Are the rules ever discussed openly among family members? Are there rules that prohibit what you can talk about?

3. Class members should divide themselves into groups of four to six along gender, race/ethnicity, or age lines. For example, the class might form several single-sex groups. Each group should first appoint a recorder/spokesperson to take notes. Then each group should discuss the following two questions:

   *a.* How do you see yourselves as group members? What characteristics do you believe you have?

   *b.* How do you see the other group as group members? What characteristics do you believe they have?

   Finally, when each group is finished, all should share their results with the class and the class should take this opportunity to talk about the stereotypes they hold and how accurate those stereotypes are (or are not).

 Go to **www.mhhe.com/adamsgalanes7** and **www.mhhe.com/groups** for self-quizzes and weblinks.

**KEY TERMS • CONCEPTS**

Abstract Conceptualization
   Learning Style
Active Experimentation
   Learning Style
Boomers
Builders
Collectivist Culture
Concrete Experience
   Learning Style
Culture
Diversity

Extraversion/Introversion
   Dimension
Fantasy
Gen-Xers
Heterogeneity
High-Context Culture
Homogeneity
Individualistic Culture
Low-Context Culture
Mindful Communication

Myers-Briggs Type Indicator®
Net Generation
Perceiving/Judging Dimension
Power Distance
Reflective Observation
   Learning Style
Sensing/Intuiting Dimension
Symbolic Convergence
SYMLOG
Thinking/Feeling Dimension

**www.mhhe.com/adamsgalanes7**

Use the flashcards and crossword puzzles on the Online Learning Center to further your knowledge of these key terms.

## PART FOUR

# Understanding and Improving Group Throughput Processes

In Part Four we continue the discussion of throughput processes we began in Part Three. As members form into a productive team and learn to manage their differences, they are simultaneously engaging in several important throughput processes. Chapter 7 explains why both creative and critical thinking are important and shows how group members can enhance both processes. Chapter 8 discusses group problem-solving procedures and describes what members can do to help ensure effective problem solving. Chapter 9 describes why conflict occurs in a group and how it can be managed to improve the group's problem solving. Finally, Chapter 10 explores important leadership principles and provides suggestions for applying them.

# Creative and Critical Thinking in the Small Group

## CHAPTER OUTLINE

What Is Creative Thinking?

Enhancing Group Creativity

What Makes Thinking "Critical"?

Enhancing Critical Thinking
in a Group

## CHAPTER OBJECTIVES

**After reading this chapter you should be able to:**

1. Define creative thinking and explain why it is important to small group problem solving.

2. Describe brainstorming, synectics, and mind mapping, and explain how they can be used to help enhance group creativity.

3. Define critical thinking and explain why it is important to small group problem solving.

4. List and describe the attitudes most conducive to critical thinking in a group.

5. Explain how group members should use critical thinking during the information-gathering stage of problem solving.

6. Describe and give examples of each of the five steps crucial to evaluating information.

7. Define and give examples of each of the five reasoning errors described in the text: overgeneralizations, attacks on a person instead of the argument, confusing causal relationships, either-or thinking, and incomplete comparisons.

## Ozarks Greenways, Inc.

The "Rails to Trails" movement in the United States is committed to converting unused railroad tracks to biking and hiking trails and establishing usable greenways for citizens to enjoy. Several years ago, a group of committed citizens in Springfield, Missouri, formed Ozarks Greenways, Inc. (OGI), whose mission is to preserve green space through the creation of linear parks. This long-term project requires the members to raise funds to buy and acquire access rights for the greenway. One proposed spur of the Ozarks greenway system would connect a park near the center of Springfield to Wilson's Creek Battlefield, a national Civil War battlefield 10 miles to the southwest.

Bikers and hikers prefer trails that allow them to proceed at a steady pace without worrying about traffic and traffic lights. That presented a major challenge for OGI because to connect the park and the battlefield, the greenway would have to cross Kansas Expressway, a busy highway dangerous for bikers and hikers. The most obvious solution was to reroute the greenway to have it cross Kansas Expressway at a traffic light. But this would have meant rerouting the trail to run parallel to two major highways—a major hazard for bikers, who travel not on sidewalks but on highways next to speeding cars. In addition, rerouting the greenway would have forced OGI to acquire additional access rights along commercially developed areas. Even if that could have been done, it would have been prohibitively expensive and would have delayed completion of the greenway for years, perhaps decades. OGI's goal was to establish a route that was relatively safe and would allow steady biker and hiker movement by avoiding travel on major highways and stoplights that would entail long waits. The OGI committee decided to stick with the original route.

The problem OGI faced could be stated thus: How can the greenway path cross Kansas Expressway safely and without forcing long waits at traffic lights? OGI needed (and eventually found) a creative solution that met all its main criteria: safety, cost, and ease of use. Read the chapter to find out what OGI did.

This chapter examines two processes essential for problem solving in small groups: creative and critical thinking. Both creativity and critical thinking are necessary for effective discussion groups; neither one alone is sufficient to ensure effective solutions. Also, creative and critical thinking cannot be done simultaneously; that would be like trying to drive a car with one foot on the accelerator and one foot on the brake! Group members must learn when to be creative, when to be critical, and what kinds of procedures help the group do both.

# What Is Creative Thinking?

Typically, when we think about the dynamics of problem solving in groups, we focus only on work that is rational, logical, and critical to the process; we neglect creativity. In Chapter 6 we showed that creativity is an important component of working with diversity. We saw it as members converged symbolically on central, unifying fantasy themes and as a necessary part of mindful communication. Members have to be open to the innovative possibilities difference can bring to a group. A group can overcome an impasse by coming up with an unusual or novel solution to any number of task or social issues in the group. Creativity "involves the generation, application, combination, and extension of new ideas."[1] In small groups **creative thinking** is fostered when members use imagination, intuition, hunches, insight, and fantasy to devise unusual or innovative solutions that probably would not emerge from ordinary group discussion. Contrary to the popular myth of the solitary genius working alone, groups produce many of today's creative ideas and innovations.[2]

American business and industry, in particular, recognize how important creativity and innovation are to their success and have focused on how to enhance creative processes. A recent investigation of more than 2,000 senior managers from around the world found four factors related to an organization's ability to innovate: how much support there is for risk taking, how much tolerance there is for making mistakes, how effectively members can work together as a team, and how quickly decisions can be implemented.[3] A team's climate is especially important, particularly support for innovation and task orientation, or the ability to get things done.[4] Creative thinking in groups helps us invent better, less expensive products or services that improve our lives. How to enhance that creativity is important for you to understand.

Group creativity involves both *divergent* and *convergent* thinking; each thinking process requires slightly different communication behaviors to succeed.[5] During divergent thinking, ideas should vary—members must think as differently as possible from one another so the team will have a wide array of options from which to choose. Quantity of ideas and breadth of thinking are important. As you can imagine, members must feel safe in the team to be willing to share new and perhaps crazy ideas. Being overly critical at this point stifles creativity. For example, in one study of an electronic problem-solving group, the group's leader gave members feedback privately via computer; even this feedback, designed to motivate, was interpreted as critical and choked group creativity.[6] However, at some point members must select the best ideas or converge them in ways that will actually work. During this phase "constructive debate" among members helps them identify the best ideas and eliminate the less useful ones.[7] Too much emphasis on harmony prevents the group from weeding out unworkable ideas.

For a group to be creative, both *individual* and *group* creativity are needed. Creative individuals tolerate ambiguity, have low levels of communication apprehension, and aren't afraid to violate societal norms and rules (think of the student whose hair is dyed purple).[8] They don't fear rejection by others, are open to new ideas, and like to play and have fun.

As important as individual creativity is, however, *group* processes are just as important. That is the reason Pat, a friend of ours, structures her group meetings so that they will feel like parties—she reasons that people are more creative when they are relaxed and having a good time. She makes sure food is served, people are introduced, and no one feels left out. Ironically, she works hard to help others have fun so that members' potential for creativity isn't derailed by the group's own norms and processes.

Bernard Nijstad and Paul Paulus synthesized considerable research on group creativity and grouped the factors influencing group creativity into four areas.[9] First, creative groups are diverse. Members bring a variety of skills, knowledge, problem-solving approaches, and perspectives to the table. Group diversity doesn't guarantee creative thinking—some groups cannot overcome the challenges that diversity brings (we discuss some of these in Chapter 6). But in general, heterogeneous groups produce more diverse ideas. Second, creative groups structure their discussions so that their creative potential is realized, not lost. Both individuals and groups prefer closure, or completing discussion, because they fear being judged, grow tired during and after intense discussions, or feel pushed to make a decision.[10] Be alert

*"Never, ever, think outside the box."*

Despite any hesitations we may have about being creative in groups, creative thinking is essential. © The New Yorker Collection; 1998 Leo Cullum from cartoonbank.com. All Rights Reserved.

to premature closure tendencies by avoiding early consensus and refraining from pressuring others to conform. Allow the group time to develop; we saw in Chapter 6 that in heterogeneous groups it takes time for members to understand and appreciate one another's special contributions. Alert, mindful groups encourage others to share their unique information and perspectives. Third, the importance of a group's climate cannot be overemphasized. Human communication is about both content and relationship. Both in what they do and how they do it, members can facilitate a climate of openness to new ideas, high levels of trust, and a willingness to disagree with respect. However, balance is important, because developing extreme levels of cohesiveness increases the potential for groupthink, introduced in Chapter 5. During periods of divergent thinking is the best time to uncritically encourage unusual ideas; during convergent thinking, members should encourage constructive debate. Finally, a group's creativity is affected by the environment in which it operates. If a group's parent organization doesn't value creativity or won't allow the group to operate with some autonomy, group creativity will be hurt. Table 7.1 summarizes the individual, group, and environmental characteristics that promote creativity. We cannot emphasize enough that creativity is a characteristic not only of individuals but also of groups; groups need to encourage and support group norms that promote creativity.

| TABLE 7.1 | Individual, Group, and Environmental Factors That Promote Creative Thinking |
| --- | --- |

**MEMBERS**
Are willing to communicate

Are willing to be unconventional and violate societal norms

Tolerate ambiguity

Are not afraid of rejection

Are open to new ideas

Are playful and like to have fun

**GROUPS**
Have diverse knowledge, skills, perspectives, approaches

Work to overcome norms that interfere with creativity (premature consensus, pressures to conform, groupthink) and promote norms that foster creativity (take time to learn each other's unique contributions, encourage sharing of diverse ideas)

Develop an appropriate group climate (foster trust, encourage constructive debate)

**ENVIRONMENT**
Place high value on creativity

Give the group autonomy and room to breathe

Creative thinking is always appropriate, but it is especially useful at the beginning of a group's problem-solving process. An ideal time to use creativity-enhancing procedures is after members have learned something about a problem but before they have gotten bogged down in details. Members can create a number of innovative ideas that they later can examine carefully and critically. However, creativity may take extra time, which may not be worthwhile for relatively unimportant decisions.

# Enhancing Group Creativity

At some point groups will be faced with the task of discovering a creative solution to a problem—an idea for a new product, an eye-catching print advertising campaign, a way to bridge two very different perspectives on the problem, a novel group presentation that will earn an A, or an innovative way to build a safe greenway across a busy expressway. The group may need to be shocked out of its habitual ways of thinking to find a creative idea. You can use brainstorming, synectics, or mind mapping to help a group tap its creative potential.

## Creative Fund-Raising for the College

**APPLY NOW**

Several years ago, members of the Advisory Council of the College of Arts and Letters where one of us works met to discuss creative fund-raising ideas to enhance the college's endowment for student scholarships. One council member mentioned a combination lecture/dinner fund-raiser a museum in New York City had initiated, which had become a highly successful event. Members began to talk about ways that event could be modified to work in Springfield, Missouri. They decided to have faculty give presentations or performances based on their expertise, combined with a dinner at one of the council member's homes. For instance, a film professor followed his lecture about a particular film director with a special showing of one of the director's lesser-known films, followed by dinner. Another professor gave a brief piano concert followed by an elaborate dessert. These events, known as the A La Carte Series, have become so successful that the college has a long list of volunteers wanting to host one of the dinners. In addition, the events sell out quickly, sometimes the first day that tickets become available. This is an example of how a group can modify an existing idea to arrive at something unique. Before you read further in this chapter, address the following questions:

1. What communication behaviors and skills would group members have to demonstrate to encourage the kind of creativity demonstrated by the advisory council?

2. What member behaviors would interfere with this kind of creativity?

3. What group rules, norms, and procedures would support this type of creativity?

4. What group norms would interfere?

---

**FIGURE 7.1    Guidelines for Brainstorming**

| 1. Group previews the rules for brainstorming. | → | 2. Group is presented with a problem to solve. | → | 3. Members generate as many solutions as possible, without any criticism. | → | 4. All suggestions are recorded for group to see. | → | 5. Ideas are evaluated at another session. |

---

**For more information on using the Internet to brainstorm, go to the Online Learning Center at www.mhhe.com/ adamsgalanes7**

## BRAINSTORMING

Many groups use **brainstorming,** a procedure designed especially to release a group's creativity.[11] Brainstorming is used most often when groups are generating ideas. Brainstorming consciously separates idea creation from idea evaluation by not allowing any criticism to occur while the group is generating ideas. Later, the group evaluates the ideas, combines or modifies them, and selects the best ones. The basic procedure is described below. Figure 7.1 summarizes these brainstorming guidelines.

1. Any technique used to promote creative thinking simply does not just happen. You need to describe the spirit of the procedure prior to actually beginning the process. Remember, your primary goal is to prevent both individual and group tendencies toward premature closure by using a process that encourages openness and holds criticism back until it is needed. The best way to do this is to set the scene by calling for alert, conscious participation and reviewing the stages of brainstorming and the rules members will be expected to follow and monitor.

2. The group is presented with a problem to solve. The problem can range from something specific and concrete ("How can we raise more money for student scholarships?") to something abstract and intangible ("How can we improve the quality of work life for employees?").

3. Members are encouraged to come up with as many solutions as possible to the problem. Quantity is the goal here, and several rules must be followed. The first and most important is that no evaluation is permitted during brainstorming. With judgment temporarily suspended, members are encouraged to turn their imaginations loose, to let wild and crazy ideas surface, to build on each other's ideas, to combine ideas, and to strive for more and more suggestions. Second, you do not want to stop generating ideas too soon. Often, the best ideas—the ones a group eventually selects—are listed during the latter part of the brainstorming session.[12]

4. All ideas are recorded so that the whole group can see them. Usually, the group's recorder will write ideas on a large pad of paper. As the top sheet is filled, it is posted on the wall so that all ideas are clearly visible at all times. Seeing the previous ideas often triggers new ideas. Keeping the generated ideas visible for everyone to see throughout the process is more important than you might think. Premature closure of the discussion may sometimes happen when members forget what has been said earlier.[13]

5. The ideas are evaluated at another session. Just because brainstorming requires temporarily suspending critical evaluation does not mean the critical thinking function

is unimportant. Also, incubation is an important feature of creative thinking. After brainstorming has generated a lot of ideas and the group has had a chance to let the ideas sit for a while, critical thinking is used to evaluate each idea and to modify or combine ideas into workable solutions to the problem.

The basic brainstorming technique has several variations. Often groups have one or two vocal people who are highly creative, share many innovative ideas, and intimidate others into not participating. In this case it may be more productive for each person to brainstorm silently rather than openly in a group. In this form of brainstorming, called *brainwriting,* each person quietly writes as many new and different solutions as possible on a notepad. Then each person shares one new idea, round-robin fashion, as the facilitator posts it on a chart for all to see. The sharing continues until all ideas have been posted. Members are encouraged to add to the list as new ideas occur to them.

Both brainwriting and brainstorming is work, and members can become tired. When this happens their ideas decrease and they tend to get stuck on similar ideas and idea categories.[14] Hamit Coskun suggests that when your group begins to show signs of fatigue or convergence, take a break from the task and complete a divergent thinking activity unrelated to the problem at hand. This can be as simple as throwing a list of fun terms on the board and asking members to generate opposite terms. The key is to take a mental break so members can get back to divergent thinking mode. After the activity is completed, move back into the brainstorming or brainwriting task.

*Electronic brainstorming,* another variation, has proven useful in addressing the factors that can lead face-to-face groups into early convergence or premature closure. The anonymity can help prevent individuals from censoring themselves. In this variation each group member sits at an individual computer terminal (all of which may be in the same room) and types out her or his ideas. The ideas are posted onto a large screen visible to everyone, so the group can keep track of previous remarks. In addition, members who may tend to remain quiet in face-to-face group interaction find it harder not to contribute online, and members do not have to deal with the fatigue or frustrations that can come from people talking all at once.[15] Because no one knows who contributed what, electronic brainstorming, especially with 8- to 10-member groups, often generates more and better ideas than traditional brainstorming.[16]

## SYNECTICS

**Synectics** is a technique that stimulates thinking in metaphors and analogies.[17] Why is that important to creativity? Consider the example of how Velcro was created. One day after a walk, Swiss engineer George de Mestral noticed cockleburs stuck to his jacket.[18] Examining one under a microscope, he observed how the hooks latched onto the fabric, and saw its potential as a hook-and-loop fastener. It took him eight years to develop and perfect, but today Velcro turns up everywhere, from shoes to children's clothing to camping equipment. The cockleburs served as the nature-based analogy, or metaphor, for the manufactured fastener.

Serendipity helped de Mestral link burrs from the natural world to this new kind of manufactured fastener. The synectics technique tries to stimulate such chance connections between apparently unrelated elements. First, the group identifies the essence of the problem. For instance, "sticking together" could have been the metaphor that led to Velcro: "How can I create a fastener that sticks together like burrs do to clothing?" Second, the

**GLOSSARY**

**Synectics**

*A procedure designed to stimulate creative thinking by using metaphors and looking for similarities in different things*

### Creating Suggestions for Crossing Kansas Expressway

Ozarks Greenways, Inc., had to come up with a solution to the following problem. Land had been acquired on either side of busy Kansas Expressway for a greenway, a bicycle and hiking path to link Springfield with Wilson's Creek Battlefield. However, there was no traffic light where the land reached the expressway, and the city had no plans to put a light there. Your task is to come up with a solution for the greenway that will keep bikers and hikers moving and that will be safe and inexpensive.

Divide the class into groups of five or six. Appoint a facilitator to record suggestions and make sure the group follows the "no criticism" rule. Ask each group to brainstorm a list of suggestions for the greenway problem. The groups should brainstorm for 10 minutes and think of as many suggestions as possible. At the end of the period, all the suggestions should be posted at the front of the class so that all can see. The class should then address the following questions:

1. Was it easy or difficult to follow the brainstorming rules? What was the hardest to do?

2. How did members feel during the process?

3. What do members remember thinking during the process?

4. Did anything stand in the way of being imaginative and having fun? If so, how might the process be modified to encourage more imagination and fun?

As an alternative to this exercise, some groups can brainstorm in the traditional way while others use brainwriting. If this is done, class members can compare the efficacy of each technique. Groups can also use a facilitator to help members stick to the brainstorming rules.

group is asked to create analogies that capture that essence. For instance, group members might ask, "Where in everyday life do we find things that stick together?" Answers could include things like burrs, gooey stuff from plants, white glue, and zippers. Finally, group members look for metaphors or analogies that use a different sensory perception than the one being observed. For example, if the analogy relates to touch, such as the cocklebur example, members might be asked to think of a visual or hearing metaphor. A visual metaphor could include a fishhook; an auditory metaphor might include the sound of a zipper closing and opening. A different kind of metaphor could be just the thing producing the "aha" insight that leads to a solution. Asking the group to consider the following questions helps trigger such insights.

1. Change your perspective. Sometimes, changing the angle from which you view a problem gives you a different insight. For example, if you are an Ozarks Greenways member, imagine that you are Superman and can view the city's streets from above.

2. Look for a direct comparison, something from another field that is similar to your problem. This is exactly what happened in the Velcro example—the physical attachment of the burrs provided the idea for this new type of fastener.

3. Temporarily suspend reality to use fantasy and imagination. Ignore objective reality for a moment to learn what you can discover. Imagine that your bicycle has wings and can fly over Kansas Expressway to solve the greenway problem.

Synectics may seem strange at first because it forces group members to jump out of their self-imposed conceptual boxes and stimulate rather than reduce ambiguity, but that's exactly why it works. Some corporations, such as General Electric, deliberately send groups of employees away from their normal work settings to jolt them out of possible ruts so they can come up with new ideas.[19] In one such group meeting between GE middle managers and colonels from the Army War College, GE's long-standing rule about having to be number one or two in every business it entered or product it produced was challenged. One of the colonels asked whether that rule caused the company to miss profitable opportunities. His statement produced an instant "aha" reaction from the GE managers, who recognized that they dismissed good ideas if those ideas wouldn't lead to the top market share. The managers were able to persuade CEO Jack Welch (now retired) to rethink the "GE must be Number 1 or 2" rule. The limitations of this rule would never have been questioned from the safety of the GE home base—the executives needed to be in a new setting to see things from a different perspective. This is exactly what synectics promotes.

## MIND MAPPING

**Mind mapping** is a technique that tries to jolt a group out of linear ways of thinking by encouraging the radiant thinking produced by free association.[20] Radiant thinking can lead to insights that linear thinking misses. Developed as a technique to foster individual creativity, the technique has also been adapted for small groups.[21] In mind mapping a facilitator places a word or phrase that is the essence of the problem in the center of a large sheet of paper or a white board for all group members to see. That central concept forms the nucleus for the spin-offs that group members will add. Sometimes a facilitator adds the connections as instructed by group members, but often group members themselves use colored markers to print or draw the phrases, ideas, or concepts they associate with the central concept. The final mind map looks like colorful multiple branches of a tree shooting off from the central idea. Because the branches are more like a web than a line, group members often see connections they might otherwise miss.

For instance, assume you belong to the Ozarks Greenways group trying to find a safe way to cross Kansas Expressway without asking bikers to stop for traffic. The facilitator prints the phrase "Crossing Kansas Expressway" in the center of the sheet and draws a circle around it. (As an alternative, a line drawing of a busy highway could be placed in the center.) Each member then adds his or her mental associations to this central idea. One member connects a bicycle with wings to the central concept. Another draws an arch spanning the busy highway. A third member connects "stop light" to the central idea. Someone else connects the words "annoying" and "interfering with the flow" to the "stop light." The picture of the winged bicycle next to the arch suggests to yet another member the idea of constructing an overpass that would allow bikers to cross without stopping. In fact, construction of an overpass was the solution chosen by Ozarks Greenways, Inc. (see Figure 7.2).

**FIGURE 7.2     Model of Mind Mapping Crossing Kansas Expressway**

"Annoying"

"Interfering with the flow"

"What about an overpass?"

Mind mapping can be a lot of fun, particularly if members draw their associations using colored markers. The process taps into members' creativity by encouraging them to make visual connections they otherwise would miss. In addition, drawing is different enough from what groups usually do that members enjoy the process.

As with brainstorming, members should not criticize the associations that appear on the mind map. As the group mind map is being developed, members need to feel mentally and emotionally uninhibited so they can make unusual connections. Fear of being ridiculed or criticized could make them feel self-conscious. However, *after* the mind map has been developed, members should begin to evaluate the ideas on the map.

Creative thinking plays a significant role in group problem solving. Groups trained in creative thinking have been found to show more humor and to have higher rates of participation than those not trained to think creatively. Members of such groups support more ideas and criticize less, both of which are important to creative thinking.[22]

Creativity in group members and group processes is essential to productivity and effective problem solving, but it must work alongside critical thinking. Critical thinking, like creative thinking, is found both within individuals and in a group's norms. Critical thinking involves careful and systematic examination of the information used by the group. Informational resources have to be critically assessed, as do the potential solutions the group derives. Surprisingly, groups have more problems being critical than being creative, which can have dire consequences. Failure to be critical is more dangerous than failure to be creative, because it can lead to groupthink, discussed in Chapter 5. Group problem solving can be effective because several heads are potentially better than one.

However, simply placing divergent talents and perspectives in a group does not make critical thinking happen! Groups are notorious for not being vigilant or critical in their discussions because members tend to avoid challenging each other and also develop their own arguments.[23]

We now turn our discussion to how groups can help ensure good decision making and problem solving to complement their creativity. We will use a case study (Case 7.2) to help show the implications and consequences of poor critical thinking.

# What Makes Thinking "Critical"?

We have seen that creative thinking is intuitive, unsystematic, and spontaneous. In contrast, **critical thinking** involves using information that is supported by evidence and reasoning and examining both the evidence and the reasoning systematically to ensure that they are sound.

Two principles differentiate critical from creative thinking: (1) the use of **evidence** (facts, data, opinions, and other information backing a claim or conclusion) and (2) the logical **arguments** speakers and writers make with that evidence to support what they believe are valid reasons to accept their claims and assertions. Critical thinking occurs when a problem is analyzed thoroughly, using as much relevant information as possible. Then the solution is developed on the basis of all that information and the best reasoning and logic you can use.

Critical thinking, like creative thinking, is both necessary and time consuming. You should be able to determine when you need to take the extra time that critical thinking demands and when you can make a decision that is just "good enough" without analyzing all your choices. For example, suppose your committee is charged with deciding whether to give coffee mugs or comparably priced pens with your organization's logo as souvenirs at your annual banquet. Does it really matter which favor is selected? Will anyone be hurt by your choice? Such a decision probably does not warrant taking the time to agonize over every aspect of the choice. However, with decisions for which human lives are at stake, such as whether to launch a space shuttle, critical thinking is essential.

# Enhancing Critical Thinking in a Group

Looking for ways to enhance critical thinking in groups is not only necessary—it is also a central principle of ethical communication. In the world of business, critical thinking has been the focus of organizational training workshops for managers and staff. Treated as an important skill for meeting the complex demands of rapidly changing and diverse organizational environments, it is often placed front and center in models of ethical decision making in organizations.[24] No matter what the setting of your group—work, school, church, or something else—critical thinking, as ethical communication, is so important that it is the first principle in the National Communication Association's Credo for Ethical Communication, introduced in Chapter 1: "We advocate truthfulness, accuracy, honesty, and reason as essential to the integrity of communication."

## Problems at NASA

On February 1, 2003, many of us watched in horror as the space shuttle *Columbia* disintegrated upon reentry after what had been a successful mission in space. The National Aeronautics and Space Administration's (NASA) investigation into the causes zeroed in on pieces of foam insulation that detached at liftoff, damaging or knocking off some insulation tiles designed to protect the shuttle from the extreme heat of reentry.[25] No longer shielded from the heat, the fuel tank exploded. NASA records disclosed that foam insulation had caused damage to the tiles since the very first shuttle launch! One NASA official lamented, "How were the signals missed?" In early 2004, NASA released the results of an internal survey of its employees, which showed that the culture of NASA contributed to why these signals were missed.[26] The survey, completed by only 45 percent of employees, revealed that many employees are afraid to speak out about safety concerns and are reluctant to "express dissenting views in a large group." One NASA administrator pointed out that in NASA's culture, both managers and peers pressure dissenters to conform, even when they have safety concerns: "We don't have time to listen to everybody moan and groan about every issue out there." NASA concluded that this mind-set contributed to the *Columbia* disaster.

This isn't the first time NASA's culture has been implicated in a disaster. The 1986 explosion of the shuttle *Challenger* shortly after takeoff was caused by malfunctions of the O-ring seals on one of the solid rocket boosters—a particularly distressing event because, like the problems with the foam insulation, NASA knew about potential problems with the O-rings failing to seal in cold weather. In other words, the *Challenger* disaster was predictable. The decision-making procedures *should* have revealed the O-ring safety concern—but did not.

Communication scholars have had time to analyze the decision-making procedures leading to the *Challenger* disaster and have concluded that the procedure was flawed in several ways.[27] NASA officials were biased in favor of the launch because of several previous postponements. The engineers, who showed the most concern about the O-rings, were reluctant to bypass their chain of command to demand that superiors pay attention to their concerns. But the engineers also failed to make their objections clear—they used ambiguous language that minimized the significance of their concerns. Several decision makers discounted the relevance of pertinent technical information that, had it been seriously considered, would have led to postponement of the launch. So even a group of highly trained experts can arrive at a fatally flawed decision that ignores relevant information—in other words, the group doesn't think critically.

Critical thinking in groups is not just one activity that members and the group do all at once. It involves many factors, including how members view information, how they gather information, how careful they are in evaluating the pooled information, how skilled they are in making reasoned judgments on the basis of that information, and how alert they are to facilitating group processes that foster critical thinking.

## HAVING THE RIGHT ATTITUDE

The most important "technique" to help groups do a good job of critical thinking is not a technique at all—it is the attitude of the members. Ideally, critical thinkers *want* to make the best possible decision, are skeptical when they receive information, are active in the information gathering and evaluation process, and support group processes that facilitate a constructive, critical climate.

The most important attitude necessary for critical thinking in groups is the desire to make the best possible decision. You have to *want* to make a good decision, because doing so takes a great deal of time and effort. Your desire is what gives you the energy to engage fully in the critical thinking process. Critical thinkers are **open-minded,** which means they are willing and eager to consider new information and ideas, even if that information contradicts what they previously believed. They go out of their way to look for relevant information and tap a wide variety of sources in their attempt to gather information that supports all sides of an issue. Finally, they pride themselves on being objective and fair about evaluating information. Being open-minded and fostering a climate of openness helps to counter the group tendency to move to closure too soon. Groups easily "seize and freeze" onto early positions, especially ones that appear to be shared by others.[28] The NASA officials involved in making the original *Challenger* launch decision were apparently prejudiced in favor of the launch (Case 7.2). This lack of objectivity limited their search for information, so they did not work as hard to find information that opposed the launch as they did to get information that supported it. They evaluated that information in a biased way—they uncritically accepted prolaunch information but were hypercritical of antilaunch data.

A second important attitude is a "show me" skepticism that indicates members want to think for themselves rather than being told what to think by others. Critical thinkers do not assume that anything they read or hear is true or accept something as true just because a parent, friend, or teacher "said so." They are willing to challenge any information, even information presented to them by experts, high-status individuals, or the group's majority, by raising questions about it.[29] This also means they are willing to hold off making a decision until the facts are in, which suggests they can tolerate ambiguity, at least for a while. They don't latch onto a premature conclusion just to get a tough decision-making process over with. They know that better decisions result from applying the same skeptical approach to all claims, including their own.

Skeptical decision makers try to test information and opinions as well as the sources of such information. They do not accept information just because it sounds good, supports what they already believe, upholds the majority stance in the group, comes from someone in authority, or is presented in an entertaining way. A significant way members can test the adequacy and quality of information, reasoning, and sources is by asking each other **probing questions** like the ones in Table 7.2. These questions take a closer look at information and reasoning.

---

**GLOSSARY**

**Open-Minded**

*Willing to consider new information and ideas, even if they contradict previous beliefs*

**Probing Questions**

*Questions designed to help critical thinking by examining information and reasoning in more depth*

| TABLE 7.2 | Probing Questions to Evaluate Evidence and Reasoning |
|---|---|

- What evidence do you have to suggest that the statement is true?
- Where did that evidence come from?
- Does anyone have any evidence to contradict the statement we just heard?
- If we make that decision, what will it lead to?
- What might the consequences be if we are wrong?
- How much danger is there that we have reached the wrong conclusion?
- How did you arrive at that conclusion?

According to Dennis Gouran and colleagues, failures to ask probing questions at several stages of the decision-making process were prime contributions to the *Challenger* disaster. The problem with the O-ring seals in cold temperatures had been observed for years before the launch, but no one asked the tough questions about what was being done to correct the flaw. One engineer who opposed the launch assumed that his objections had been passed on to superiors, without asking whether this was actually the case. When representatives from North American Rockwell, the manufacturer of the shuttle, relayed their concerns about the launch in vague terms, no one asked whether they were trying to tell NASA to postpone the launch. All these isolated incidents, in which no one asked the right questions, contributed to the disaster that followed.

The "show me" skepticism of a good critical thinker needs to be expressed by group members and facilitated as a group norm. Probing questions, when asked and asked right, reflect a willingness to inquire into the accuracy of the information and the appropriateness of the reasoning group members are being asked to accept either by outside sources or by each other. This is tough work, because if this kind of skepticism is not communicated with respect for other group members, it can be seen as threatening and could backfire—by shutting down critical thinking. No one likes to be threatened or judged; probing questions asked in a way that communicates disrespect can get in the way of critical thinking. Questions, like any of our messages, have both content and relationship dimensions (see Chapter 3).[30] We often focus only on their content and forget that *how* they are asked can mean the difference between respectful critical thinking and harmful badgering of group members. One way members can do this is to explain the purpose of the question—for example, "I am asking this because I want to make sure that I completely understand what your main point is about this issue." In addition, remember that your questions can be asked of a group member and/or the entire group. Sometimes directing a probing question to the group deflects it from any one member and reinforces the notion that the group itself engages in critical thinking.

Finally, critical thinking is an active (rather than passive) process of testing information. It demands hard work to find the information necessary to understand the problem and subject solutions to the most rigorous tests possible. Mentally lazy group members object to this hard work, but critical thinkers look forward to it.

The information just presented describes attitudes essential to critical thinking in a small group. Several attitudes and behaviors make it difficult for group members to engage

| TABLE 7.3 | **Attitudes and Behaviors Counterproductive to Critical Thinking** |
|---|---|

- Oversimplification of the thinking process; evaluation of information and ideas in either-or, black-and-white terms
- Impulsiveness; jumping to premature conclusions
- Overdependence on authority figures; waiting for someone else to tell you how to think, what to conclude, or what to do
- Lack of confidence; withdrawing if someone challenges your ideas
- Dogmatic, inflexible behavior; closing your mind and being afraid of change
- Unwillingness to make the effort to think critically; taking the easy way out

in critical thinking, and these are worth looking at briefly. It is just as important for you to know what *not* to do as to know what to do, so Table 7.3 summarizes these counterproductive behaviors.

## GATHERING INFORMATION

One skill essential to critical thinking is the ability to organize ideas.[31] Groups create complicated informational environments; members not only process the information members bring to the group but also must assess information from multiple sources outside of the group.[32] In addition, group members cannot assume that members will willingly share either common or new information during discussion and debate. The first step to organizing your ideas is to assess the information you already have, identify gaps in that information, and then establish and carry through with a plan for plugging those gaps. In the information gathering stage, you cannot tell what is important and what is not, so you should act like sponges—absorbing as much information as you can about your topic or issue and watching for that "seize and freeze" habit of groups mentioned earlier.[33] Information gathering activities are just as essential to critical thinking in groups as evaluation of that information in later stages.

**Assessing Information Needs.**   Before group members begin their research, they need to take stock of the information they possess (see Table 7.4). The quality of an output, such as a plan or policy, cannot be better than the information members have or the way they share and process it. The first step is to make an outline or list of the information you have to help you assess what you need. For example, a university committee was charged with revising the curriculum for communication majors. Members first pooled all the information they had, such as the current major requirements, the problems and issues they had observed, and information about what nearby colleges and universities required of communication majors. Committee members soon realized that they needed to fill several important information gaps before they could begin any adequate discussion of the problem. For instance, the committee members hadn't assessed the perceptions of current students and alumni about the strengths and weaknesses of the existing program—a major oversight! In addition, prospective employers could provide information about the skills and deficiencies of recent graduates and current student interns. Finally, committee members knew they must have information about current practices in the field of

| | **Gathering Information in the Critical Thinking** |
|---|---|
| **TABLE 7.4** | **Process: Assessing Information** |

1. Take stock of existing information.

2. Identify holes and weaknesses.

3. Make a master list of what information is needed and where it can be found.

4. Collect needed resources by assigning members specific responsibilities for items in the master list.

5. Use all appropriate information gathering techniques:
   - Direct observation
   - Reading
   - Interviews (individual or group)
   - Other sources (radio, television, casual conversation)

communication, including what communication professionals were saying about the direction of the field.

Information lists help determine not only what information is missing but also where it can be found. The next step in the critical thinking process is the careful gathering of information to fill the gaps.

**Collecting Needed Resources.**   Group members should organize their information gathering procedures before proceeding. First, from your master list, list all the information you still need. Then you should assign themselves research responsibilities on the basis of their preferences, strengths, and time schedules. Play to group member strengths, which you should know if you have mindfully worked with the diversity in your group and become familiar with member learning styles, motivations, personality characteristics, cultural preferences, and so on (see Chapter 6). Finally, as you proceed with your research, you will discover additional information you need that should be added to the list and assigned to the appropriate group members.

The information a group needs is rarely found in one location. Usually, a variety of information is needed and will have to be gathered in various ways. Some of these are described briefly.

*Direct Observation.*   Sometimes information you need will come from firsthand observation. Recently, at California State University, Fresno, the demolition and renovation of the library meant that student study areas had to be created across campus. A group from a senior small group communication course took it upon themselves to advocate for a study area in their Speech Arts building. Their primary means of information gathering was to visit the different areas of campus and note the study area architecture. From those field notes they designed a study area for their own building. One campus administrator, who had been sent the proposal, remarked at how impressed he was that these students had visited each site and then used that information as the basis for their proposal.

***Reading.*** A wealth of information can be found in many kinds of printed sources, such as newspapers, books, magazines, scholarly and professional journals, technical and trade publications, and government documents. The sheer number of sources available can be intimidating. A reference librarian can help save hours of wasted effort by pointing you in helpful directions and steering you away from likely dead ends. Gloria and Kathy have learned over the years that reference librarians are most appreciative of students who come to the library prepared with their topics and assignment instructions. This kind of preparedness will also increase your chance of a successful trip to the library!

In addition, a number of publications can save you time and effort in locating printed information. Annotated bibliographies and abstracts provide a preview of the type of information in a publication so that you can decide whether it will be worth the search. Encyclopedias summarize vast amounts of information. Specialized indexes and abstracts frequently can help you save time in locating relevant information. For example, the *Business Periodicals Index* summarizes articles from numerous business and trade journals.

***The Internet.*** An easy and convenient way to access information is through the Internet. Use a browser, such as Netscape, Explorer, or Mozilla Firefox, to connect to your favorite search engine. (You may want to try more than one search engine, since no one search engine covers the entire Internet.) Use keywords for your search, following the rules of the particular search engine you're using. Although you may have thousands of hits, most search engines give you the most likely hits first, so search those carefully. You may have to try various keyword combinations. For example, if you are seeking information about the effect of college-age gambling on academic success, you may have to try "college sports gambling," "gambling," "academic success," and so forth.

Be particularly careful to evaluate information you derive from the Internet. *Anyone* can put *anything* on the Internet; no review procedure evaluates the information for accuracy or truth. *Wikipedia* is an online encyclopedia that can be edited by anyone with access to the Internet. Our experience is that it is extremely popular with students. However, neither of us allows it as a main source of information for group projects or presentations because it can be edited by anyone; thus, its accuracy is harder to establish.

Any claim—no matter how outrageous—can be made on the Internet, and websites have been created that contain lies and misinformation. We found a website that advertised manbeef, or human meat, for consumption; it was a spoof, but some people had accepted it as true. To help you use your best critical thinking skills to evaluate online information, we have provided some criteria in Table 7.5.[34] In addition, you can go to the following websites to learn more about evaluating Internet information:

> www.virtualsalt.com/evalu8it.htm
> www.library.cornell.edu/olinuris/ref/research/webeval.html

After all, on the Internet no one knows you are a dog!

***Electronic Databases.*** Electronic databases available at most academic and public libraries provide a very efficient way to find printed information. Many sources formerly available only to those who had physical access to a library can now be accessed at home via the Internet. Electronic databases contain titles, abstracts, and sometimes

| TABLE 7.5 | **Criteria for Evaluating Web-Based Sources** |
|---|---|

**AUTHORITY**

Can you find the source of the information? If not, how can you trust the information? If you can, ask whether you would trust that authority and whether the authority is held to any standards for information, like the American Medical Association.

**AUDIENCE**

Could the audience slant the information, and if so, in which way? Web designers do not just design for the fun of it; they have an audience in mind and tailor the information for that audience. In addition, determine if the information is too technical, simplistic, or jargon-filled for your purposes.

**PURPOSE**

Why is the information being offered? Is it offered to inform, persuade, entertain, or advocate? You can get some clue to its purpose by noting what comes after the dot. The ".gov" government notation is probably intended to inform whereas the ".com" or commercial notation may bring with it something to sell. The ".edu" or education notation will identify faculty and sources at colleges and universities that inform and persuade.

**RECENCY**

Can you determine how current the site is? The Internet allows for instant posting, but often sites are not updated regularly. Be careful with information from a site in which you cannot find when or how often it is updated. Many sites have e-mail contact information for the authors of the site. Use that information to ask questions about updating.

**COVERAGE**

Does the site provide the depth you need on your topic or issue? Sites will often have links to other sites; use these because the use of a variety of sources is preferred.

the full text of magazine and journal articles, newspaper articles, and books on thousands of topics. Commonly used databases include InfoTrac, a general-purpose database that accesses nearly 1,000 business and trade journals; ERIC, which holds education-related materials gathered by the U.S. Department of Education; LexisNexis, which accesses legal and business resources; ComAbstracts, which contains information from all communication-related journals; and EBSCOhost, another general-purpose database of nearly 3,000 periodicals, with full text for nearly 1,500. In addition, many newspapers, such as *The New York Times,* can be accessed electronically. As with Internet search engines, electronic databases typically operate using keywords or author names.

*"On the Internet, nobody knows you're a dog."*

***Interviews.*** Members of your group may need to conduct several interviews. These may be face-to-face individual interviews, group interviews, or those conducted over the phone or via electronic mail. For example, the curriculum committee members interviewed their colleagues in person, phoned or e-mailed colleagues at other schools, and called a sample of alumni to ask for their perceptions and opinions. Examples of the kinds of closed-ended and open-ended questions typically used in interviews are shown in Table 7.6.

***Other Sources.*** Useful information may come when you least expect it. Listening to the radio, watching television, conversing with family or friends, browsing through electronic bulletin boards, stumbling onto relevant information in a magazine while waiting to get your hair cut—all are potential sources. Be prepared to take advantage of these sources by recording the information as soon as possible so you don't forget it. Once you have gathered the information you need, you must decide how useful it is to you.

## EVALUATING INFORMATION

The next step in the critical thinking process is to evaluate the information you have gathered. Like a sponge you've absorbed all the information you think you'll need. Now you must "pan for gold" by trying to find the nuggets of information that are valuable to you.[35] If a group bases its decision on inaccurate or outdated information, its decision will be flawed, no matter how systematic the gathering process has been. For example, the curriculum committee described earlier recommended that communication majors take

| TABLE 7.6 | **Open- and Closed-Ended Questions** |
| --- | --- |

| **Open-Ended Questions** | **Closed-Ended Questions** |
| --- | --- |
| What do you think about the proposal to raise taxes? | Do you agree or disagree that taxes should be raised? |
| What is your opinion of the performance of the committee chair? | Has the committee chair done a good job? |
| How might we enhance our presentation audiovisually? | Should we use a skit or a videotape in our presentation? |
| How can we solve the parking problem on campus? | Where should we put the new parking garage? |
| How effective are your group's critical thinking skills? | Are your group's critical thinking skills: <br> \_\_\_\_ Very effective? <br> \_\_\_\_ Somewhat effective? <br> \_\_\_\_ Average? <br> \_\_\_\_ Somewhat ineffective? <br> \_\_\_\_ Very ineffective? |

several writing courses offered by the English department. However, even though the recommended courses were listed in the school's current catalogue, the English department had revised its curriculum, eliminating several courses and changing several others. This mistake was not a disaster, but it would not have occurred if curriculum committee members had checked with the English department to determine whether any course changes were anticipated.

How can you tell whether a piece of information is accurate and up-to-date and whether a source is credible? Evaluation of available information is perhaps the most crucial step in the critical thinking process. Several factors play a role in evaluating information: determining what someone means, distinguishing fact from opinion, clarifying ambiguous terms, assessing the source's credibility, and assessing the information's accuracy and worth. M. Neil Browne and Stuart Keeley's eighth edition of *Asking the Right Questions: A Guide to Critical Thinking* is an excellent summary of how you can assess the value of information.

**Determining the Meaning of What Is Being Said.**   The first thing you must do is decide exactly what the speaker or writer means. This is not as easy as it may sound. Frequently, people bury the meaning of what they are saying among a jumble of opinions and irrelevant statements. You should identify the author's conclusion, reasons for the conclusion, and evidence to support the reasons. First, ask yourself what conclusion the author is drawing. What does he or she want you to do, think, or believe? Is there an action (such as voting for a particular candidate, writing letters to a television producer, or buying a particular product) that the author wants you to take? Next, determine what main arguments the author provides to support the conclusion or recommended action. For instance, look at the sample letter provided in the Apply Now box on page 201. What conclusion does the author want you to reach, and why?

Often, keeping track of the arguments and evidence that support them is easier if you outline the argument on paper. Write the main conclusion at the top; then list each argument beneath it with space after each one. In this space list every piece of evidence the author or speaker offers in support of the claims. This will simplify your later task of evaluating how good the author's evidence and reasoning are and how valid the conclusions are.

Taking the time to translate the information from original sources into your own material for group projects is crucial if you are to ethically represent the information correctly. This involves not only citing the sources of your information but also paraphrasing that information in your own words. Good paraphrasing does not mean simply changing a word or two or creatively "cutting and pasting" material; it is a skill that takes time and effort. The misuse of another's information, or plagiarism, is a common occurrence. You must familiarize yourself with your own school's plagiarism policies and their examples of plagiarism. In addition, visit the following websites:

> http://www.plagiarism.org/index.html
> http://owl.english.purdue.edu/owl/resource/560/01/

These sites provide detailed examples and concrete tips on how to avoid plagiarism in your group oral as well as written work.

***Distinguishing Fact from Opinion and Inference.*** You must be able to recognize the difference between a statement of fact and statements of opinion or inference based on that fact. **Facts** are descriptions that can be verified by observations and are not arguable. For example, we can verify that the population of Greene County, Missouri, in 2000 was 240,391 by looking in any of several government publications that record population data. Be careful, though—some statements presented as facts are not facts at all but false statements. For example, the statement "Greene County, Missouri, has 500,000 residents" is not true; therefore, it is not a fact. You need to determine whether statements presented as facts are actually true and up-to-date.

Opinions and inferences go beyond what was observed directly and imply some degree of probability or uncertainty. **Opinions,** unlike facts, are not all equal, although everyone has an equal right to express an opinion. Some opinions are more valid than others. Einstein's opinion about the way the universe operates should carry more weight than the opinions of the authors of this book because we are not theoretical physicists. The value of an opinion depends on the evidence supporting the opinion and the quality of the reasoning that ties the evidence and opinion together. Determining an opinion's value is part of your job as a critical thinker. For example, someone might say, "Greene County, Missouri, is growing rapidly." That is not a fact; that is an opinion. It is your responsibility to determine the validity of the opinion by asking questions such as the following: What was Greene County's population 10 years ago? What is the average annual rate of growth in the United States? In Missouri? How does Greene County's rate compare with that of other cities in Missouri? If you learn that Greene County's annual rate of growth for the last 10 years has been 2.4 percent, compared to Missouri's 0.9 percent, you can reasonably conclude that "Greene County is growing quickly."

## GLOSSARY

**Facts**

*Something that can be verified by observation and is not arguable*

**Opinions**

*Inferences that go beyond facts and contain some degree of probability*

**GLOSSARY**

**Ambiguous**

*Refers to a term
that has more
than one possible
meaning*

Thus, opinions are arguable and should be evaluated systematically during a group's deliberations. Groups that make poor decisions do so in part because inferential errors impair their critical thinking.[36]

***Identifying and Clarifying Ambiguous Terms.***     Authors and speakers often make it hard to evaluate information because they use terminology that is **ambiguous,** or unclear. For example, candidate Beasley in the Apply Now box is termed "experienced." What does that mean? What kinds of experiences has she had? Is she experienced as a teacher, a parent, or an administrator? Is she experienced at working in a small group? Each of these experiences is different and paints a slightly different picture of the candidate. Clarification of vague terms is very important in evaluating the worth of your group's information.

Earlier in the chapter, we mentioned the decision made by NASA officials to launch the *Challenger.* In their analysis of the decision-making process, Gouran and his associates discovered that failure to clarify ambiguous terms contributed to that terrible decision. They explain:

> *No one went so far as to say, "We recommend that you do not launch." Instead, they claimed making such statements as, "We do not have the data base from which to draw any conclusions for this particular situation"; "We did not have a sufficient data base to absolutely assure that nothing would strike the vehicle."*[37]

What do those statements mean? This kind of doublespeak confuses issues because it leaves room for a variety of interpretations by permitting others to read their own favorite interpretations into the message. At NASA no one asked explicitly for clarification of the ambiguous terms.

***Evaluating Opinions by Determining the Credibility of the Source.***     We noted earlier that not all opinions are equal. How can you tell whether an author or a speaker is someone whose opinions are worth your attention? Ask yourself several key questions to help you decide how much trust to place in an opinion.

- Is there any reason to suspect the person(s) supplying the opinion of bias? For example, if you find a source that debunks the idea that smoking causes lung cancer, you should treat that information with suspicion, especially if it comes from the American Tobacco Institute. On the other hand, if that statement appears in the scientifically respected *New England Journal of Medicine,* you would have greater reason to expect objectivity.

- Is the source a recognized expert on the subject? Is this someone whom other experts respect? Would you feel proud or silly quoting this person? We may feel comfortable citing Kobe Bryant's opinions about basketball but very uncomfortable citing Aunt Tilly's.

- Is the opinion consistent with other opinions expressed by the same source? Media sometimes misquote people. Are you reasonably sure the opinion stated is accurate? Is there a later interview or quote that reverses the inconsistent opinion? Sometimes people do change their minds for good reasons. What is the reason given for the change of opinion? Does the evidence offered to explain the change seem reasonable to you? If not, suspect inaccuracy or some unknown bias.

***Assessing the Accuracy and Worth of the Information.***     Now that you have established a context for evaluating the information by determining exactly what is being said

## Should You Support Mary Alice Beasley for School Board?

Your local parent-teacher organization has received the following letter from one school's site council. The executive committee, of which you are a member, is meeting to decide what to recommend to the entire PTO. Practice evaluating the information and arguments in the letter.

*Dear Parent-Teacher Organization Member,*

*As you know, the vote to elect a new member to the school board will occur on April 5. We want you to know that the Parents' Excellence in Schools Committee supports candidate Mary Alice Beasley for our school board.*

*Mary Alice Beasley is the best candidate we have running for the Central City school board. We need people like her who care about our kids. She has lived in Central City all her life and now has three children of her own in the school system. She has been an active member of the P.T.O. for the past six years and was chair of the fund-raising committee for Westwood School. Her experience will be invaluable.*

*In her second term as city councilwoman, she was the chief author of the plan to desegregate the city schools; as we all know, other cities have used this plan as the model for their own desegregation efforts. Mary Alice can represent the entire community well—she taught for nine years before she ran for city council, and she has a master's degree in education. Hers is exactly the kind of caring, experienced leadership we need on the school board. Mary Beasley deserves your endorsement. Remember to vote on April 5.*

Either individually or in groups of four to six, answer the following questions and then discuss them as a class:

1. What conclusion are you being asked to reach? Is there an action you are being asked to take in this letter?

2. Like most letters of this type, this letter interchanges fact and inference, or opinion. Make a list of all the facts presented in the letter and a list of all the inferences presented.

3. Ambiguous terms are sometimes difficult to spot because we each think we know what words such as *experienced* mean. Make a list of all the ambiguous terms (terms that can reasonably be understood in more than one way) presented in the letter. Before you assess how the letter's writer interprets each of these terms, what do you mean by each of them? For instance, what does *experienced* mean to you?

4. For each of these terms, what evidence is presented in the letter that supports the author's opinion about Beasley? For example, what facts are presented to support the author's view that Beasley is "experienced"?

5. Would you vote for Beasley on the basis of this letter? Why or why not? What other information about this candidate would you like to have to help you make your decision? Where would you go for the information you need?

| | **Evaluating Information in the Critical Thinking Process** |
|---|---|
| **TABLE 7.7** | |

**DETERMINE WHAT THE SPEAKER OR WRITER IS SAYING**
- What is the conclusion?
- What does the author want you to do?
- What are the main arguments in support of the conclusion?

**DISTINGUISH FACT FROM OPINION AND INFERENCE**
- What are the facts?
- What are the opinions?

**IDENTIFY AND CLARIFY AMBIGUOUS TERMS**
- What are the ambiguous terms?
- What do you think the author means by each term?
- If you can't decide with confidence, what problems does this create?

**DETERMINE THE CREDIBILITY OF THE SOURCE**
- Who is the author or speaker? What are his or her credentials on this issue?
- Is this a recognized expert?
- Is this a biased source or one with something to gain by expressing this opinion?
- Is the information consistent with other credible sources?

**ASSESS THE ACCURACY AND WORTH OF THE INFORMATION**
- What type of evidence (e.g., personal experience, statistical support, opinions of experts) is being offered in support of the author's arguments?
- Is the evidence supported by other experts or authorities, or just this author?
- Is the information based on the scientific method?
- If the information is based on interviews or questionnaires, was the sample large enough and representative enough? Were the questions clear and not biased or loaded?

and how credible the source is, you are in a position to evaluate how good that information is (see Table 7.7). After all, it could be misinformation. You should ask yourself a number of questions about the information before using it during group decision making.

■   What types of evidence are offered to support the argument? Is it a personal experience? Statistical support? The combined opinions of a number of recognized experts? Although many people do so, it is unsafe to accept personal experience as the sole basis for supporting an opinion. For example, assume you were once in a successful and productive group led by a dominant leader who decided everything and delegated these tasks to other members. Thus, your personal experience may lead you to believe that groups work best under strong, controlling leaders. But someone else's experience may differ. Assume a fellow group member worked in a democratic group, in which there was no one leader but all members contributed to leadership based on their areas of expertise. This member thinks that the only good group is a democratic one. Which of you is right? Each of you is right, for the particular circumstances of your experience, but neither of you is right to try to apply your experience to everyone else.

■ Is the information based on the testimony of a number of experts in the field? If so, you can place greater trust in it, especially if these experts are widely recognized and accepted by their peers. Be sure to determine if other experts disagree and why. Be especially careful about accepting information from an expert in one field about another field. For example, movie stars frequently express strong opinions about the American political scene. While some may be well informed, others are not.

■ Is the information based on valid scientific or statistical reasoning? You should ask how the information was gathered, how the questions were worded, whether the data came from a properly designed survey, and so forth. Information must follow strict guidelines before it can legitimately be termed *scientific.* First, such information must be verifiable by others. Thus, although an experience that happens to someone may be true, it is not scientific unless the event is observed or can be re-created by other people. Second, scientific information must be obtained under controlled conditions by controlled observations. Having an informal conversation with your classmates about the death penalty and concluding that "American college students have the following attitudes toward capital punishment . . ." may be interesting, but it is not scientific. But if you surveyed a representative sample of students, asked each of them the same questions, and systematically analyzed their answers, you could reasonably conclude: "Students at my college believe the following about capital punishment . . ." Finally, scientific information must be expressed precisely. Another researcher, after reading an account of a scientifically controlled research study, should be able to carry out a study in exactly the same way, using the same procedures, equipment, and statistical tests.

Information gathered by questionnaires or interviews poses additional questions regarding the individuals who were queried. Were there enough of them, and were they representative of a larger population? In most cases random sampling is most likely to ensure a representative response. For example, assume your committee is charged with making recommendations regarding parking on your campus, and you decide to poll students who drive to campus. If you survey only students who park in one particular lot between 7 and 8 A.M., your results are not likely to reflect the views of the entire student population. Making parking recommendations that will affect thousands of students on the basis of responses from a few students is irresponsible. On the other hand, if you systematically survey students from all campus lots at varying times during the day and evening, your responses will be more representative and your conclusions more valid.

## CHECKING FOR ERRORS IN REASONING

The final element in the critical thinking process is assessing the quality of the reasoning people provide for their opinions or for supporting one conclusion over another. Unfortunately, most speakers and writers often make a variety of common reasoning errors, called **fallacies,** that makes assessing reasoning challenging. Fallacies tend to divert a listener's attention from the issue or sidetrack the discussion so that members of a group begin to debate something other than evidence and claims. However, critical thinkers

**GLOSSARY**

**Fallacies**

*Mistakes in reasoning and faulty reasoning*

## What Would You Do?

You and your group have been working on your panel presentation about the death penalty for several weeks, with one week to go before you are responsible for conducting the panel discussion in your class. This project represents a major portion of your grade in the small group class, and you are required to conclude your presentation by taking a position—your group must come out either in favor of or against the death penalty. After hashing this out for weeks, you have sorted through all your evidence and have almost reached consensus that you will come out in favor of the death penalty. This week, while doing library research for another class, you happen upon a new study, based on systematic examination of states with the death penalty, that strongly suggests the death penalty does *not* deter crime. The study seems well done; you don't think you can dismiss it as a piece of biased or poorly done research. But you know if you present it to your group, you'll push your emerging consensus further away, and you hate to do that! You are so close now to agreement, and you know this study will set you back. What do you do?

**1.** For what reasons would you *present* the article to your group?

**2.** For what reasons would you *withhold* the article?

**3.** What would you actually do?

working together in a small group should be able to spot each other's fallacies (see Table 7.8). The differing but complementary bases of information that individual members bring to a group discussion can help them compensate for each other's weaknesses to produce, on the whole, a superior group result.[38] There is no end to the kind of fallacies you can find in a group discussion. The following ones are common ones and are offered as examples. For a more detailed list of fallacies and ways to correct them, see Richard Paul and Linda Elder's *The Thinker's Guide to Fallacies: The Art of Mental Trickery and Manipulation,* a useful resource.[39]

| TABLE 7.8 | Checking for Errors in Reasoning |
|---|---|

- Does the author overgeneralize?
- Does the author attack a person instead of the issue?
- Does the author argue that because two events are related, one caused the other?
- Does the author present you with an either-or choice when other alternatives are possible?
- Does the author present you with a comparison that is incomplete or invalid?

**Overgeneralizing.**    Generalizations are made when information about one or more instances is said to apply to many or all instances of the same type. For example, someone may read in the newspaper that a certain number of college students have defaulted on their government-guaranteed student loans. If that person concludes from this that "college students are irresponsible borrowers," he or she has made a generalization and implied that *all* college students are irresponsible borrowers. An **overgeneralization,** like the loan default example, is a conclusion that is not supported by enough data.

Generalizations by themselves are not automatically wrong. Conclusions based on carefully gathered data that were analyzed with appropriate statistical procedures are often very accurate and the goal of good scientific theory. Usually, such generalizations are qualified and not stated as applying to all cases. Remember, for a generalization to be factual for all cases, someone would have to observe all of these cases.

To decide whether a generalization is a valid conclusion or an overgeneralization, ask yourself a few questions:

- How many cases is the conclusion based on?
- Are there any exceptions to the conclusion?
- What form of evidence is the source asking us to accept: personal or other forms?
- Is the generalization expressed as probability or in "allness" terms?

**Attacking a Person Instead of the Argument.**    Attacking a person instead of the argument, even if subtly done, is a form of name-calling used to direct attention away from someone's evidence and logic (or lack thereof). Sometimes called ad hominem attacks, such arguments take this form: "Because So-and-So is a _____ (woman, Catholic, foreigner, intellectual snob, atheist, liberal, etc.), you can't believe his/her opinions about the topic." Such an argument sidetracks the discussion of the opinion into a discussion of the merits of So-and-So. So-and-So may indeed be a crackpot about some things, but his or her views about the topic might be quite accurate. More information is needed before a critical thinker would make that judgment.

**Confusing Causal Relationships.**    Another common reasoning error occurs when the speaker or writer mistakenly states what caused an event. Two forms of this error are observed frequently. Sometimes people oversimplify by implying or stating that only one cause exists for an event. In other instances they imply that, because two events are related by subject matter or in sequence, one causes the other. For example, we have heard students say that if a manager implements quality control circles in a company, the company's profits will increase, implying that quality circles cause higher profits. In actuality, better employee training, lower costs of raw materials, increased prices for a company's products, improvements in technology, and improved upward communication and morale produced by the quality circle may contribute to the increased profits.

Neither can we assume that, just because one event preceded another in time, the first caused the second. It may be that both are caused by a third event or condition. For example, one of us overheard someone mention statistics indicating that graduates of all-women's colleges are more likely to become members of the U.S. Congress and serve on the boards of Fortune 500 companies than are female graduates of coed schools. The person speaking was arguing that attendance at women's colleges *caused* this type of career achievement. However, many women's colleges are academically selective as well as expensive.

Women attending such schools are often both exceptionally bright and from families who own or are connected to Fortune 500 companies. It is plausible that these additional factors—ability and family connections—"cause" both the attendance at women's colleges and the career achievement. The relationship between college attendance and later achievement is likely to be a complex one that does not lend itself well to simple causal descriptions.

**Either-Or Thinking.**    **Either-or thinking** (sometimes called a false dilemma) says that you must choose one thing or another, and no other choices are possible. Seldom is this the case. We talked about this kind of thinking and its consequences in Chapter 6 on diversity. In another example, assume your group is preparing a panel discussion about sex education in the schools, and you encounter the following statement: "Sex education is an important element of a young person's education. If the parents won't teach their children about sex, the schools have to." Most people would readily agree with the first sentence. The second, however, reveals either-or thinking. The author is forcing the reader to accept the premise that either the parents will teach the child about sex or the school will. In fact, other alternatives are possible. Perhaps churches, synagogues, or Camp Fire USA leaders could take on the job; or parents and school officials together could design a cooperative program. Just because a writer does not mention other alternatives should not blind you to their existence.

**Incomplete Comparisons.**    Comparisons, especially **analogies,** help us understand issues more vividly. These play an important role in symbolic convergence (Chapter 6) and when the group is being creative. However, there are limitations to such comparisons when the group has moved into critical thinking. Because one thing bears a resemblance to another does not mean they are identical. At some point the resemblance will break down because no two situations are identical in all characteristics. An incomplete analogy (sometimes called a faulty analogy) asks us to stretch a similarity too far. For example, assume you and other students are discussing how well the public relations major at your school prepares students to be public relations professionals. One student says, "You really can't learn much about public relations from school anyway. It's like trying to ride a bicycle by reading books about it but never getting on an actual bicycle."

At first glance, this remark hits home with many of us who complain that school can't prepare us for the "real world." However, let's look more closely. Yes, there are public relations experiences that cannot be duplicated in school. But there are many activities that *do* prepare students for professional practice. Designing flyers and brochures, writing news releases, taking photographs, planning a mock public relations campaign, and designing a survey are all examples of typical activities that public relations students perform in school that are also necessary on the job. Thus, whenever you see or hear someone make a comparison, first determine in what ways the two things being compared are similar, but especially look for ways they are different. Ask yourself if the analogy breaks down at any point. If so, where? How does this affect the reasoning you are being asked to accept?

The fallacies previously described, as we noted earlier, are some of the most common ones. Be alert for fallacies by asking the right probing questions about the ideas, opinions, interpretations, and conclusions someone is asking you to accept. Then pay careful attention to the answers you receive (or don't receive).

## Gun Control

The shooting rampage on the Virginia Tech campus April 16, 2007, turned out to be the largest mass shooting in our country's history. In a dorm and classroom building, 33 people lost their lives. This school shooting revived the ongoing debate over gun control.[40] While news of the tragedy was still fresh, many news programs featured reports about the national debate over how to solve the problem of gun-related violence on college campuses. A heated debate occurred in Virginia's own state legislature as representatives fought over whether concealed weapons should be allowed on their campuses. Virginia and 48 other states do issue gun permits allowing state residents to carry concealed weapons. The issue was whether to lift gun restrictions on college campuses: Virginia voted not to, but Utah voted to allow students to carry concealed weapons on the University of Utah campus. Advocates for allowing firearms on college campuses argued that Virginia already has gun control laws that obviously do not work. If someone plans to kill a bunch of people and then themselves, regulations will not help, but coming face-to-face with another gun will. A concealed weapon is there for self-defense, and had faculty or students been armed, they could have used those weapons to stop the Virginia Tech killer. Opponents argued that allowing guns on college campuses is not going to solve the real problem, which is the *reason* for the violence; thus, we have to find ways to prevent people from using guns to express how disturbed they are. Opponents suggest attending to and treating the reasons for violence, not issuing gun permits to college students and faculty.

Try the following exercise. In a small group or as a whole class, to get a more vivid idea of the types of arguments made in this case, briefly research the issue of gun violence on college campuses and then simulate the point-counterpoint discussion, either between two class members or two large groups role-playing each position.

1. How many arguments can you create to support each position? Put them on the board for all to see.

2. What fallacies can you identify in the arguments presented?

3. Assume the two "debaters" are members of a small discussion group charged with identifying a policy to prevent college shootings. What would you say and do if you heard the kinds of fallacies being expressed during the discussion?

A number of group systems support (GSS) tools can help members probe and evaluate information (see Chapter 8). GSS tools include electronic brainstorming, electronic outliners, idea organizers, and topic commentators. Working with neutral facilitators, groups can lessen the influence of biased information and can be guided in their attempts to track arguments, confront each other's claims, and develop their own lines of reasoning.[41]

## AVOIDING GROUPTHINK

We introduced groupthink in Chapter 5 when we discussed the consequences of excessively high cohesiveness in which disagreement is seen as disloyalty or as "making waves." Coined by Irving Janis and initially applied to the disastrous Bay of Pigs decision by the John F. Kennedy administration, *groupthink* commonly refers to bad decision making due to poor information processing in groups. Groupthink is a hard price to pay for lazy critical thinking and cohesiveness taken to its extremes. We examine this group phenomenon further to help us summarize our discussion of critical thinking in groups and to reinforce its importance to effective decision making. We will use primarily Case 7.3.

### The Class Project

**CASE 7.3**

A group of students in a communication course was given two major assignments: a class presentation of material from one of the book chapters and a research project to be presented to the class. As they prepared to present the book chapter, Cary emerged as the group's informal leader. A theater major, he was charismatic, fun, and creative. At his suggestion the group created a short play dramatizing the chapter content. The members had a blast preparing the presentation. They bonded tightly to become close friends. The presentation received an A, with high praise from the professor. This made them even more cohesive. When time came to plan the research project, they decided, at Cary's urging, to follow the same creative format. They skimmed over the instructions for the research project and concluded that they could rely mostly on material from the text. They focused all their energies on creating a lively, dramatic presentation. But Soshanna, another member, had doubts about their approach. Afraid they were ignoring several criteria their professor required, she timidly expressed her reservation about the direction they were headed. Cary and the rest of the members teased her for being a worrywart: "We got the highest grade in the class last time, and everybody else was envious! The professor loved it! We are the golden group—there's no way we can fail here. Chill, Soshanna— you are *way* too compulsive." Soshanna stifled her doubts and climbed on the bandwagon.

But things didn't turn out so well this time. The group had ignored several key criteria, including the number of outside references they were required to include, the types of references, the length of the research paper, and the format. Their efforts—as much fun as they had been— earned them a low C. This highly cohesive group suffered from groupthink. The members ignored information available to them that would have helped them earn an A, such as the professor's written description of the assignment and her invitation for students to consult with her about the project. Members with reservations, such as Soshanna, kept quiet. The group got overconfident and stumbled badly.

Groupthink represents a failure of the group's critical thinking process—the failure to express doubts, disagreements, and conflict within the group. Consequently, the group's decision is flawed because it is made with partial information that has not been examined carefully. This is exactly what happened with our class project group—members simply ignored the professor's stated criteria for the project. During groupthink behavior some members may privately have doubts about the group's direction. Soshanna had reservations about the project group, but she didn't want the other members to think of her as a "compulsive." Thus, the group was deprived of the full benefit of *all* members' opinions and reasoning.

Soshanna's behavior is not unusual—few people want to be perceived as nuisances. A study of upper-management teams in 26 American corporations found that 19 percent of members said they best went about company business by not making waves.[42] Nine percent prefer to maintain good relationships with their co-workers at the expense of getting the job done. That suggests a lot of flawed decision making happening at all levels! Let's look at how this kind of group dynamic can happen.

**Symptoms of Groupthink.**  We have emphasized that group members, perhaps counterintuitively, do not automatically share information that runs counter to what appear to be group preferences.[43] They "seize and freeze" on early positions expressed by members and on those they think most members prefer, as well as resist positions that may be different from those earlier positions. One reason groupthink is most likely to occur in highly cohesive groups is the pressure to achieve consensus. In particular, cohesiveness based on interpersonal attraction is related to groupthink, but task-related cohesiveness is not.[44] Members of groups that exhibit high degrees of cohesiveness based on their interpersonal attraction to each other tend to be more psychologically connected to each other, and so they resist challenging each other.[45] This is a problem because groups *in general* tend to favor discussing what they already know as opposed to discussing new information.[46] Under conditions of groupthink, this tendency is even harder to monitor. In addition, groupthink is more likely to occur in groups with a long history, groups strongly embedded in their larger organizations, and groups that insulate themselves from their outside environments.[47] Spotting groupthink thus becomes crucial if your decision-making groups are to be effective as they critically analyze problems and draw conclusions. Here are three important symptoms to help you spot groupthink.

1.  **The group overestimates its power and morality.**

    Group members believe their cause is so right that nothing can go wrong with their plans. The student group in Case 7.3 became so excited about the creative aspect of their project that members ignored the requirements for the rest of the project. They prepared a dynamic presentation but left out important information relevant to the topic. However, they had managed to convince themselves that they were giving the professor what she wanted: "She'll love it. No one else has tried anything like it. I just *know* we'll get an A."

2.  **The group becomes closed-minded.**

    Closed-minded people are biased when they evaluate information. Instead of looking open-mindedly at all relevant information, members consider only information that supports their beliefs. Group members may also have a preferred course of action and ignore any information that contradicts their preference. In the class project group,

Soshanna's fears about ignoring certain criteria were downplayed: "Oh, that won't be a major problem. Even if we do leave something out, the presentation will be so creative it will more than make up for it." Members talked each other into believing that some criteria didn't matter by ignoring information to the contrary.

3. **Group members experience pressure to conform.**

Group members experience both internal and external pressures to go along with the group, which show up in several ways. First, members censor their own remarks without apparent pressure from other members. When all the other members of a group favor a certain action, most people are hesitant to express their doubts. This is natural—you want the people in your group to like and respect you, and you don't want to be seen as "popping others' balloons." Thus, self-censorship often prevents conflicting opinions from reaching the group, to the detriment of the group's problem-solving process.

Second, a member who does voice a contradictory opinion can be seen as a deviant, as "making waves," and receive overt pressure from the group. Groups are uncomfortable with deviants (even idea deviants) and pressure them to go along with the group. The initial teasing Soshanna received about being a worrywart served as a subtle form of pressure to conform. It worked—she quit openly disagreeing. If she hadn't, the pressure would have intensified. The teasing and jokes would probably have turned to persuasion and ultimately coercion to force her compliance.

Finally, because self-censorship and group pressure suppress disagreement and doubt, the group experiences the illusion that members unanimously support the decision or proposal. For instance, Soshanna's decision to keep silent made it seem to the rest of the group members that they had a consensus about the project. Assuming that the group is in accord, members carry out the decision without testing to see whether the consensus is genuine. What appears to be an agreement may actually have little support from some members, as was the case with the class project group.

**Preventing Groupthink.** You can take a number of steps to prevent groupthink from occurring. Following are suggestions for both group leaders and members, also summarized in Table 7.9.

1. **Encourage members to "kick the problem around" before they start focusing on a solution.**

One group behavior that fosters groupthink is arriving at premature consensus.[48] The group has shortchanged the recommended first step of most structured problem-solving procedures, which is exploring the problem before trying to solve it. In addition, encouraging disagreement at this stage can help group members understand the problem better. Active disagreement at an early stage of problem exploration promotes increased knowledge and understanding.

2. **Establish a norm of critical evaluation.**

The most important thing a group leader and other members can do to prevent groupthink is to establish a group norm to evaluate carefully and critically all information and reasoning. Such a norm can offset the proven human tendency to ignore or reject information that contradicts one's existing beliefs and values.

| **TABLE 7.9** | **Preventing Groupthink** |
|---|---|

**ENCOURAGE MEMBERS TO "KICK THE PROBLEM AROUND"**

**1.** Be alert to prevent premature consensus.

**2.** Explore the problem thoroughly before attempting to develop a solution.

**3.** Encourage freewheeling argument before settling on a solution.

**ESTABLISH A NORM OF CRITICAL EVALUATION**

**1.** Encourage members to express disagreement.

**2.** Encourage critical thinking rather than the appearance of harmony.

**3.** Assign a devil's advocate to argue against popular proposals.

**4.** Be sure the leader accepts criticisms of his or her ideas open-mindedly.

**PREVENT LEADERS FROM STATING PREFERENCES AT THE BEGINNING OF A GROUP'S SESSION**

**1.** Let other members express opinions first.

**2.** Offer an opinion only as another alternative (not the alternative) to be considered.

**3.** Encourage the group to meet without the designated leader present.

**PREVENT INSULATION OF THE GROUP**

**1.** Invite outside experts to present information.

**2.** Discuss tentative solutions with trusted outsiders to get an unbiased reaction.

**3.** Be alert to information that contradicts the prevailing opinion of the group.

Especially helpful is a norm promoting members' expressions of all disagreements. If a group emphasizes getting along instead of critical thinking, members will hesitate to disagree. A norm supporting open expression of doubts and disagreements makes it OK for members to be in conflict with each other. One study found that, in a group in which everyone seems to hold the same viewpoint, even one member who is willing to share an opposing view can redirect the group's attention so that members examine their decision more thoughtfully.[49] Had Soshanna stuck to her guns, she might have saved the group's grade!

Another way of encouraging honest disagreements is to assign the role of devil's advocate to one or more members of the group. A **devil's advocate** is a person who has been assigned the task of arguing against a popular proposal. Thus, this person serves as an "official" idea deviant because the devil's advocate helps spot

**GLOSSARY**

**Devil's Advocate**

*A group member who formally is expected to challenge ideas to foster critical thinking*

potential flaws in a plan or holes in arguments. If Josie agrees to be the devil's advocate for a particular meeting, it is unlikely the other members will take her criticisms personally.

Groups have also used group support systems and computer-mediated communication (CMC) to encourage honest opinions. We have mentioned that computer use in group problem solving is valued for its anonymity. Users believe that this produces less pressure to conform and thus encourages more honesty. However, a member operating from behind a computer is still aware of expectations from others. Thus, CMC can both enhance and limit the impact of individual members' influence and power.[50] Sometimes the effect of perceived status differences is actually stronger in CMC.

The norm of critical evaluation must also be supported by the leader's behavior. One of us worked with a boss who asked staff members to identify any problems we saw with a plan he had devised to improve the working environment. Taking the boss at his word, a couple of staff members began to question various elements of the plan. As they spoke, the boss became defensive, minimized their concerns, defended his proposal, and appeared to view the questioning members as disloyal. The rest of the members remained silent without voicing their objections to the plan. The meeting concluded with the boss thinking the staff supported the plan, although it did not. In the future, whenever the boss asked for honest reactions to proposals he favored, no one was willing to go on the "hot seat" by expressing a criticism.

3. **Prevent leaders from stating their preferences at the beginning of a group's decision-making or problem-solving session.**

One important source of groupthink is a strong or charismatic leader's preference. Cary's fellow group members really liked him—he had a way of making group work fun. They would have done almost anything *not* to dampen his enthusiasm.

As group leader, in addition to not stating your preferences early in a group's discussion, ask the group to meet without you, especially if you are the supervisor rather than an elected chair. If you suspect that your presence or personality inhibits the group members from saying what they really feel and think, schedule one or two meetings that you do not attend. This will make it easier for other members to express their opinions freely.

4. **Prevent insulation of the group.**

Groupthink often occurs when group members become so cohesive and so caught up in their own ideas that they are insulated from external opinion and expertise. Cary and Soshanna's professor encouraged her students to consult with her as they formulated their research projects. She even offered to pregrade the projects in advance, so students could take her feedback into account to improve their final projects. But Cary convinced his group members that they didn't need outside help—after all, their first project, completed without outside advice, was wildly successful.

Leaders and members of the group can offset this tendency. They can encourage members to present tentative decisions to trusted associates outside the

## Terrorism, TV, and Groupthink

MEDIA AND TECHNOLOGY

On September 11, 2001, people around the world watched images of violence on their televisions. In the wake of terrorist attacks on the World Trade Center and the Pentagon, TV news organizations documented the new focus on the war on terrorism. Nonstop coverage of the attacks transitioned into the war with Iraq, which presumed to be connected with 9/11 terrorists and weapons of mass destruction (WMD). However, the lack of WMD and concrete evidence connecting terrorists to Saddam Hussein has caused many to question the decision to go to war. Consider your own experiences watching TV reports of the terrorist actions and the subsequent war on terrorism. To what extent do you think mediated reports of these events made the public susceptible to groupthink? Are there ways that our culture can reduce the effects of groupthink on the way we assign meaning to mediated messages?

In the summer of 2004, the U.S. Senate Intelligence Committee report on pre–Iraq war intelligence emphasized that many mistakes were made because of "groupthink." Committee members said their findings were based on a presumption that misled the intelligence community. That presumption was that over the years Iraq both had and used WMD. Over time that knowledge led to a belief that Iraq would continue to try to build and obtain WMD. This belief led to groupthink in which the intelligence community interpreted all new data as consistent with that basic presumption, although, the report concluded, that presumption was flawed. Copies of this report and information reflecting the committee's conclusions can be found at the following addresses:

**http://a.rocket-city.us/intelligence.gov.html**
**http://intelligence.senate.gov/conclusions.pdf**

Go to
**www.mhhe.com/
adamsgalanes7**
for additional
weblink activities.

group, then report back to the group with the feedback. They can hold public hearings, at which any interested person can speak on the issues facing the group, as zoning commissions do regularly. They can also arrange for outside experts to talk to the group. Most importantly, they can be alert themselves for any relevant information from outside the group, rather than protecting the group from outside influence.

Groups get caught in groupthink because they do not promote a constructive "show me" skepticism, which thwarts openness to new information, damages the evaluation of gathered information, and limits questioning of the reasoning behind arguments. Additional pressure to conform by ineffective leaders and by members not listening to outside sources of support can inhibit both creative and critical thinking in groups. Getting caught in groupthink leaves groups open to paying a heavy price, sometimes one paid in human life as we saw in the *Challenger* disaster and other national tragedies.

**RESOURCES FOR REVIEW AND DISCUSSION**

- To be effective problem solvers, group members must do a good job with both creative and critical thinking. Creative individuals are willing to communicate, to be unconventional, and to play in the group. Creative groups are willing to examine their norms and change those that interfere with creativity.

- Creativity requires freedom from judgment and can be enhanced through the use of three techniques: brainstorming, synectics, and mind mapping. Brainstorming explicitly suspends criticism, and synectics works by attempting to make the familiar unfamiliar. Mind mapping seeks to avoid linear thinking.

- Critical thinking involves a concentrated effort to assess the value of ideas and conclusions by gathering relevant information, examining that information carefully, and judging the reasoning that supports the conclusions and decisions. Critical thinking in small groups involves knowing when to use critical thinking and requires certain attitudes of group members, a methodical search for information, thorough evaluation of the information, and careful assessment of the reasoning behind opinions and beliefs based on that information.

- In gathering information, group members first should pool their knowledge and identify any gaps that are apparent. Then they should fill those gaps by using appropriate research methods, including direct observation, reading, using electronic databases, interviewing individuals or groups, and consulting other sources such as television, the Internet, and radio.

- When members evaluate information, they first should determine what is being said, which statements are facts and which are inferences or opinions, what terms are ambiguous, how believable the source is, and how accurate and valuable the information is.

- When they check for errors in reasoning, group members should be especially alert to the common fallacies. Critical thinking consists primarily of asking the right probing questions, which can prevent harmful throughput processes such as groupthink.

- Groupthink is the tendency of highly cohesive groups not to examine critically all aspects of a decision. Groups experiencing groupthink overestimate their power, evaluate information in a closed-minded and biased way, and experience pressures to conform.

1. Form groups of four to six students. Each of you should be given some ordinary, tangible object, such as a clothespin, an alarm clock, or a ballpoint pen. Find a new use for the item that has nothing to do with the item's ordinary use. To do this, you must perceive the item in entirely new ways. To help you do this, your instructor can lead you in a guided meditation. For instance, imagine that the clothespins are alive and are sending you messages about what they would like to be used for. After you have discussed the problem in your groups for 15–20 minutes, present your favorite solution to the class. Then all of you should vote to select the most creative idea. (Perhaps your instructor will award prizes to the winning group.)

2. The following exercise helps clarify the difference between statements of fact and statements of inference. Place a familiar item (such as a coffee cup, a chair, or a ballpoint pen) in front of the class so everyone can see it easily. Make

statements of fact about it. Each statement should be written on the board. After about 15 statements, identify as a class those statements that go beyond what was actually observed. Discuss why these statements are inferences rather than facts.

**3.** Videotape one of the many television programs that feature panel interviews with public figures (such as *Meet the Press*). Look for errors in reasoning, places where the interviewee seemed to camouflage what she or he was saying, or places where the interviewee was evasive. Discuss the program in class. It will be particularly helpful if you can show your tape in class.

 Go to **www.mhhe.com/adamsgalanes7** and **www.mhhe.com/groups** for self-quizzes and weblinks.

**KEY TERMS • CONCEPTS**

Ambiguous
Analogies
Arguments
Brainstorming
Creative Thinking
Critical Thinking

Devil's Advocate
Either-Or Thinking
Evidence
Facts
Fallacies
Mind Mapping

Open-minded
Opinions
Overgeneralization
Probing questions
Synectics

 **www.mhhe.com/adamsgalanes7**

Use the flashcards and crossword puzzles on the Online Learning Center to further your knowledge of these key terms.

# 8

# Group Problem-Solving Procedures

## CHAPTER OUTLINE

A Systematic Procedure as the Basis for Problem Solving

Capturing the Problem in Problem Solving

Effective Problem Solving and Decision Making

Applications of P-MOPS

## CHAPTER OBJECTIVES

**After reading this chapter you should be able to:**

*1.* Explain why using a systematic procedure for group problem solving usually produces better solutions than random or haphazard problem solving.

*2.* Define key terms such as *problem solving, decision making,* and *area of freedom* with examples.

*3.* Describe five characteristics of problems.

*4.* Explain why and how you would adjust the problem-solving process to accommodate any of the characteristics of problems.

*5.* Describe the functional theory of problem solving and decision making.

*6.* Describe each step of P-MOPS.

*7.* Explain how you could use techniques such as the *problem census, focus groups, group support systems, RISK,* and *PERT* to help at various stages of P-MOPS.

*8.* Apply P-MOPS to fit a simple or complex problem.

## The Merger

In 2000 a crisis loomed for Ozarks Public Television. OPT had operated in Springfield and Joplin, Missouri, for nearly 25 years with a community-owned broadcasting license, using studios rented from a small, private college in Springfield. But in the 1990s, the U.S. government mandated that all public TV stations switch to digital broadcasting equipment by 2003, a very expensive proposition for OPT. After assessing all their options with the help of a consultant, OPT board members decided to seek an educational partner. Eventually, the board approached Missouri State University with a proposal for MSU to take over the broadcasting license and allow OPT to merge with the university. The MSU board accepted the proposal at its December meeting, and work toward the merger began immediately.

Ideally, the physical move would occur in the summer, when fewer students and faculty would be on campus, but before that could happen, a number of legal and physical changes had to occur. Most importantly, the Federal Communications Commission (FCC) had to approve the license transfer. Space had to be found on campus to accommodate the public television staff, equipment, and control room; the decision had to be made about how to finance and when to make the digital conversion; the merger and its benefits to MSU had to be presented to the faculty, staff, and students; and program planning at a variety of levels had to occur.

Involving every public television and university employee in each decision would have created chaos! Instead, several groups—each composed of different combinations of university and public television personnel—were established to bring about the merger. For example, a facilities subcommittee was charged with assessing university space and determining how it needed to be modified. A public relations subcommittee handled the delicate process of explaining the merger to the university community and to the many volunteers who had worked for OPT over the years. Several similar groups were established, with their work overseen by the steering committee we introduced to you in Chapter 1. The steering committee established the timeline and kept track of the progress of each of the other groups to ensure that the merger would occur on time, with every detail accounted for.

The merger in our opening case is a typical group problem-solving situation. In this case two parent organizations—OPT and MSU—appointed a number of groups to help the larger organizations manage information, make decisions, and complete tasks. A lone individual trying to solve the merger problem would have become overwhelmed at the volume of information and the amount of work! Not only that, a lone individual would have been unable to think of everything that needed to happen for this merger to succeed. Some important piece likely would have fallen through the cracks. On the other hand, involving the entire university community and public television staff in participating equally to identify and evaluate solutions would have created a chaotic and unmanageable process. In this case, using several smaller groups, with the steering committee in charge, enabled the work to be done on behalf of the two larger organizations.

In Chapters 1 and 6 we maintained that groups can produce solutions to complex problems that are better than solutions produced by individuals; they also produce greater member understanding and more satisfaction.[1] The *assembly effect* is achieved when the group solution is superior both to the choice of the group's most expert member and to an averaging of opinions of all members—an exceptional example of the whole becoming greater than the sum of the parts. That is because group discussion can help members collectively recall information some may have forgotten, correct flawed information, help members understand information so that it is more useful, identify gaps in the information base, and help each other appropriately evaluate and weigh the importance of information.[2] However, this kind of synergy and its benefits does not happen if group members work independently.[3] They must work *inter*dependently with each other on their project. Working on individual assignments is OK, but those solo assignments must be consistently talked about as a group (see Table 8.1). Thinking you can simply string together a bunch of smaller assignments into a final project without discussion by the entire group and get the benefits of the assembly effect is naïve and will produce a poorer product. The synergy of the assembly effect is possible only when members communicate with each other throughout the entire process.[4]

| **TABLE 8.1** | **Advantages and Disadvantages of Solving Problems in Groups versus as Individuals** |
|---|---|

| Advantages | Disadvantages |
|---|---|
| • Solutions for complex problems are usually superior. | • Groups take more time. |
| • Groups have more resources, including information and methods. | • Participation may be uneven; some members may dominate, and others withdraw. |
| • Members accept the solutions more readily; satisfaction is higher. | • Interpersonal tension, disagreements about the task, and conformity pressures may interfere with critical thinking. |
| • Members understand the solution more completely. | |

The benefits of group problem solving are not automatic; just because a group is charged with solving a problem does not mean the outcome will be better or that the process will be easy. The good news is that a lot can be done to improve the quality of both problem-solving procedures and the solutions they generate. A systematic problem-solving procedure is a key factor in improving the overall quality of your group activities because it provides ways for you to maintain a healthy vigilance around your problem-solving choices. Systematic procedures usually produce better decisions than unsystematic discussions.[5] This chapter identifies the nature of problems, reports on factors that improve problem solving, and describes tools for enhancing group problem-solving discussions.

# A Systematic Procedure as the Basis for Problem Solving

There are a number of ways to solve problems. One way is by turning to an expert or someone you consider to be an authority, the way many people turn to doctors for dealing with illnesses. Or, you may solve problems at an unconscious level called *intuition*. For example, you may be wondering what to do about an assignment, and suddenly the answer occurs to you while you're taking a shower.

There's nothing wrong with these methods, particularly for problems that will affect only you. However, intuition can have serious limitations for group problem solving if you use it alone, without also using a systematic procedure for checking out the hunch. Careful, critical analysis of information, like the kind detailed in Chapter 7, is important as well. What would you say if you went to the doctor because of chest pains and, without doing any tests, she said, "My intuition tells me you need a shot of penicillin"? Ideas derived only through intuition must be examined critically before they are implemented because critical thinking can reveal flaws in the ideas that may not be apparent at first. It's possible the hunch is terrific and may only need to be tweaked to solve your problem, but it's also possible that the hunch may cause more problems than it solves. Systematic problem solving is a way for groups to assess ideas and to manage the mountain of information unearthed by the problem-solving process. For example, in our opening case the merger involved keeping track of dozens of details—far more than any one person could have handled. If the steering committee hadn't met regularly and used a systematic process, some of the information would have been lost, and key options might not have been considered. Any less systematic procedure might have produced a successful merger, but chances are some important element would have been overlooked.

Thus, no matter how a group discovers the possible solutions to a problem—through intuition, logic, or authority—the group must use a systematic process and the best creative and critical thinking it can muster to develop solutions and assess how well they will work. There is also an ethical imperative to systematic problem solving. The National Communication Association's Credo of Ethical Communication tells us that one component of ethical communication involves taking responsibility for the short- and long-term consequences of our communication. Being systematic in our problem solving means being responsible. This shows we are willing to carefully consider our choices, realizing that our group decisions have consequences both to the group and to those outside the group who are affected by those group decisions. Those consequences can range from a poor evaluation on a project to the loss of life.

## GLOSSARY

**Problem**

*The difference between what exists presently and what you expect or want*

**Problem Solving**

*Everything you need to do to move from your present undesirable situation to what you want, including creating solutions and choosing among them*

**Decision Making**

*Choosing from available options*

The rest of this chapter is divided into two main sections, each dealing with group problem solving. The first section focuses on the nature of a problem, no matter its specific focus: what defines a problem, how a problem can vary, and how to generate problem questions for discussion. The second section details how you can organize your group problem solving by using a systematic, yet flexible, procedure called the procedural model of problem solving, or P-MOPS.

# Capturing the Problem in Problem Solving

We have been discussing problem solving throughout this book as the central task of groups. Yet we have not yet discussed a key factor: just what is it that groups are solving? This section will clarify what a problem is, regardless of its topical focus, and how varying characteristics of problems can influence the degree of systematic planning necessary to solve them effectively. We will also show you how you can generate sensible problem questions for group work in order to best facilitate creative solutions. This section is important because how a problem gets defined initially can have a profound impact on how the group treats the problem and its assessment in later stages of problem solving.[6]

## HOW DO WE KNOW A PROBLEM WHEN WE SEE ONE?

**Problem** refers to the difference between what exists and what you expect or want. For example, you need your entire group to show up for a class presentation, but on the day of the presentation three members are no-shows. You have a problem!

Problem solving and decision making are related concepts and need to be distinguished before we go further. **Problem solving** involves all the things you have to do to move from the existing situation to the goal. It is a multistep process that includes defining the problem, identifying or creating possible solutions, and choosing among the solutions. **Decision making** refers to the act of selecting one or more available options; it does *not* involve creating possible options. Problem solving is a more comprehensive procedure that includes decision making (choosing). The entire process of solving a problem often involves making many decisions, such as how to define the problem, what solutions to consider, which to suggest or act upon, and how to carry out the chosen solution. The steps you take and the order in which you do them can greatly influence the quality of your final product. Can you imagine cutting out material for a coat without first having a pattern to guide your scissors?

Every problem—whether it is about dealing with absent members, merging two larger groups, improving campus safety, or decreasing gambling debts for college students—has three components that together create what is commonly called a problem. A group needs to understand and talk about these components in detail in order to have a richer understanding of what members will attempt to solve. Neglecting to do this can set your group up for failure.

1. **An undesirable existing situation.**

   If people believe that something is perfectly satisfactory as it is, there is no problem. For example, when Grupo Latino Americano's meeting place was accessible and affordable, it had no problem. But when the landlord suddenly tripled the rent, it needed to find a new place to meet. The undesirable present situation in this case was an exorbitant rent the group couldn't afford.

For more information on the digital divide problem, go to the Online Learning Center at **www.mhhe.com/ adamsgalanes7**

2.  **A desired situation or goal.**

    At the start a goal can vary from a vague image of a better condition (being able to meet) to a very precise, detailed objective (meeting at the Youth Club on F Street). Part of effective problem solving involves establishing a precise goal that is achievable, doesn't suggest a solution, and is understandable to all members. Outstanding groups have clear goals that all members support.[7]

3.  **Obstacles to change.**

    These are conditions and forces that must be overcome by the chosen solution to achieve the goal. Typical obstacles include insufficient information, the competing interests of other people, lack of tools or skills, and insufficient funds. For example, when the Grupo Latino Americano's rent tripled, members had no idea what other facilities were available, what similar facilities rented for, how soon another facility could be located, whether members would be willing to move, what the group could afford, and so forth.

## AREA OF FREEDOM

Once you have a better handle on what the problem is, where you might like to go, and what stands in your way, your group needs to talk about the extent of its power to do anything about the problem it is about ready to tackle. The **area of freedom** is the amount of authority and the limitations given to a group charged with solving a problem. Group members must know, at the beginning, what they are and are not supposed to do. A fact-finding group, for instance, may be asked only to investigate a problem, not solve it. Another small group may have authority only to interpret information, as in the case of a jury that can decide guilt or innocence but not the penalty for guilt. Many advisory

| |
|---|
| **GLOSSARY** |

| |
|---|
| **Area of Freedom** |
| *The amount of authority and the limitations given to a group* |

### Improving Airport Security

**APPLY NOW**

After September 11, 2001, it was clear that the United States had a problem with ensuring security on its airline flights, since terrorists had been able to hijack four different airplanes on the same day. Map this problem according to the problem components described above.

1.  An undesirable existing situation: What was the airplane boarding situation on 9/11? What was undesirable about that situation (e.g., rules permitted box cutter knives to be carried on planes)?

2.  A desired situation or goal: What would the desired situation look like? For instance, passengers would like to board quickly and efficiently, but they would also like to be protected from other passengers carrying weapons.

3.  Obstacles to change: What are obstacles to achieving these goals? For instance, do we lack information about how terrorists bypass safeguards in our system? Do we lack technology at airports to improve baggage screening?

committees and conferences can recommend a solution but not make it binding. For example, in our opening case the facilities subcommittee charged with identifying available space for Ozarks Public Television was not empowered to start modifying that space until the steering committee had evaluated the options and given the go-ahead.

Committee members must understand the exact charge to the group before they proceed to work on any problem. Otherwise, they will waste time and may become frustrated or angry. A committee one of us observed was charged with making recommendations about the types of student activities on campus. Instead, this committee created a sweeping proposal to fire certain individuals and restructure the student activities department. Even though committee members worked long and conscientiously to develop the plan, it was not accepted because the committee went far beyond its area of freedom.

## CHARACTERISTICS OF PROBLEMS

We have shown you the three components that together constitute a problem: discontent over present conditions, a more desirable future goal, and obstacles that prevent movement toward that goal. These need to be talked about by the group, which must also clarify its assignment and any limitations to its problem solving. You can see that by discussing these matters, you are beginning to shape your overall problem-solving procedures to fit the unique details of your problem. To finish this assessment of your problem, you need to ask several questions about the particular nature of your problem so that you can make important adaptations to your problem-solving procedures.

Some problems are complex while others are relatively simple. It makes intuitive sense that you would not use exactly the same process for all problems. Using a systematic process for problem solving doesn't mean force-fitting the procedure onto every kind of problem. Rather, it involves modifying that procedure to fit the particular problem your group faces. The three components we discussed earlier define *any* problem; however, a problem's specific characteristics vary. You could consider many characteristics of problems when you start to modify your problem-solving procedures, but the five we discuss here are among the most important.

**Task Difficulty.**   How complex is the issue or problem? A complicated task is high in difficulty while a simple task is low in difficulty. For a difficult task, members should make sure they fully understand the nature of the problem, do a thorough job of unearthing information, carefully coordinate their efforts, and expect to attend many meetings before they finish. Groups are asked to work on difficult tasks because their solutions are beyond what one person alone can accomplish. Extensive problem mapping will be important.

**Solution Multiplicity.**   Are there many possible ways to solve the group's problem, or is there one correct answer? For instance, there are many fun and appropriate ways to plan your high school class's tenth reunion, but there may be only one solution to a math problem. When a problem has high solution multiplicity—in other words, has many possible solutions—you will want to make sure that your group identifies as many of those solutions as possible. This focus on creatively generating ideas (see Chapter 7) will be the key to success.

**Intrinsic Interests.**   Are group members really interested and excited about working on this problem (that is, is there high intrinsic interest), or would they rather go to the dentist than have to tackle the problem? You learned in Chapter 6 about different member characteristics and motivations that affect group processes. When members are excited and interested, they want to talk about the problem or issue, tell their own stories about it, or vent their feelings. They don't want to be overcontrolled or overstructured in addressing the problem. But when they are bored and uninterested, they will be happy to have someone—probably the group leader—structure the problem and give them specific assignments to complete.

**Member Familiarity.**    Has the group ever confronted a similar problem? Did it solve the problem successfully? If so, the members have high familiarity with the problem. They may want to focus on establishing criteria for evaluating options. But if they have never undertaken anything similar, or if they have just formed a new group, they will need some time to get to know each other and to familiarize themselves with all aspects of the problem (particularly if it is complex). Group members initially do not tend freely to share all their information about a problem but share only information commonly known by the group.[8] Groups need to find out not only what members know in common but what they also know *uniquely* if they hope to find that best solution. Detailed problem mapping helps to pool this information, and using outside experts may also help the group.

**Acceptance Level.**    Is acceptance of the solution by people who will be affected by it critical for success? For instance, if a company is considering changing its overtime policies, lack of employee acceptance can derail the "solution" and cause lasting bad feelings. In such a case, the acceptance level needs to be high, making it crucial for the group to solicit the opinions and ideas of those who will be affected. Before committing fully to the solution, the group may want to suggest partially implementing the solution and reevaluating it with those who are affected. But if the solution won't matter much to most people—such as which party favors to buy for that high school reunion—then members don't need to spend time seeking outside opinions.

Table 8.2 summarizes these five characteristics of problems and also offers suggestions for modifying any problem-solving procedure your group is using. Having a clear picture of the nature of your problem and how it varies in relationship to other problems is necessary prior to moving ahead with your systematic procedure.

Sometimes problems are obvious—your landlord triples the rent, your treasurer empties the bank account, you can't get anyone to come to meetings. But most proactive organizations don't wait for a crisis to identify problems. The Ozark Public Television board didn't wait for the digital equipment conversion deadline to pass before investigating its options. Spotting problems in advance is a good idea.

## IDENTIFYING PROBLEMS WITH A PROBLEM CENSUS

The **problem census** is a posting technique for identifying important problems or issues. It can be used to establish agenda items for future meetings of a committee or to identify problems on the horizon that a group should work on. Sometimes a group leader wants to encourage participation and make group processes more democratic but doesn't know exactly where to begin. The problem census is ideal for all these purposes because it requires all the members of a group to take responsibility for creating the group's work agenda. Members often become more committed to the group's task because they are enthused about working on items they perceive as important to them. For example, its most obvious

| TABLE 8.2 | **Problem Characteristics and the Problem-Solving Process** |
|---|---|

**TASK DIFFICULTY**

*Adaptation for high difficulty:*

1. Plan to meet often.

2. Use detailed problem mapping.

3. Include many subquestions to the problem-solving procedure.

4. Form a detailed implementation plan, in writing.

**SOLUTION MULTIPLICITY**

*Adaptation for high multiplicity:*

1. Use brainstorming or one of its variations to generate many ideas.

2. Use synectics or another creativity-enhancing technique to help members relax and be creative.

3. Leave plenty of time for generating ideas; don't rush the process.

**INTRINSIC INTEREST**

*Adaptation for high interest:*

1. Set aside a "ventilation" period early in the problem-solving process for members to express their feelings.

2. Leave plenty of time for early ventilation.

3. Don't overcontrol the ventilation process or introduce structured procedures too early.

**MEMBER FAMILIARITY**

*Adaptation for high familiarity:*

1. Focus on establishment of clear criteria.

2. Focus on evaluating the options using the criteria developed.

*Adaptation for low familiarity:*

1. Use detailed problem mapping.

2. Use consultants and outside experts for help.

**ACCEPTANCE LEVEL**

*Adaptation for high acceptance requirements:*

1. Include representatives in your group from groups that must accept the decision.

2. Use techniques to spot potential problems before finally deciding on a solution.

3. Pretest a solution by partially implementing it and agreeing to pull back if it doesn't seem to work.

## Characteristics of OPT's Problem

Assume you are members of the Ozarks Public Television (OPT) governing board, and it is early 2000. You know that you have a 2003 deadline for converting to digital equipment, a very expensive proposition. You are currently bringing in enough money for OPT to operate both stations in Springfield and Joplin, Missouri, but you aren't making the kind of extra money you'd need—more than $1 million—to make the digital conversion. You have a problem!

1. Identify the elements of this problem: the undesirable existing situation, the goal, and the obstacles to change.

2. Look at the characteristics of the problem-solving process presented in Table 8.2. Evaluate OPT's problem in terms of these characteristics, explaining your evaluation:

   Task difficulty: High or low? Why?

   Solution multiplicity: High or low? Why?

   Intrinsic interest: High or low? Why?

   Member familiarity: High or low? Why?

   Acceptance level: High or low? Why?

use in educational courses is helping newly formed student groups come up with the problem that will be the focus of their class project. This task often follows quickly after groups are formed, and too often your authors watch groups get frustrated trying to find a problem everyone wants to work on. Using this technique is a way to give structure to the process of finding a problem; it offers a way to get group members committed early to their problem. The following are detailed steps (summarized in Figure 8.1) for conducting a problem census in a face-to-face meeting. Several of these steps are easily handled electronically.

1. **Seat the group in a semicircle facing a chart or board.**

   If you have access to a large computer screen and specialized hardware and software (discussed later), you may also position members at computer terminals facing a large computer screen.

2. **Explain the purpose of the technique.**

   This is to bring out any problems, concerns, questions, or issues any member wants to discuss.

3. **Ask each participant to present one problem or concern in round-robin fashion.**

   After the first person presents one problem, the second presents one, and so forth. Anyone who does not have a problem to list may pass. This continues until all problems are identified. One electronic variation is to ask members to brainstorm problems individually and then send them to the centralized computer screen. That way all

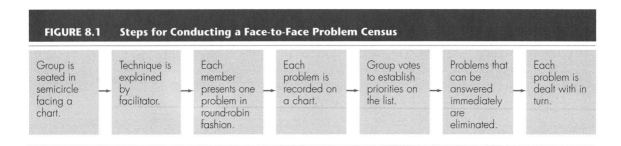

**FIGURE 8.1    Steps for Conducting a Face-to-Face Problem Census**

| Group is seated in semicircle facing a chart. | → | Technique is explained by facilitator. | → | Each member presents one problem in round-robin fashion. | → | Each problem is recorded on a chart. | → | Group votes to establish priorities on the list. | → | Problems that can be answered immediately are eliminated. | → | Each problem is dealt with in turn. |

problems are posted for everyone to see. Another electronic alternative is to ask people to e-mail their lists to the group's leader in advance of the meeting; these are easily compiled into a master list that members can be given ahead of time.

4. **Post each problem on a board or chart as it is presented.**

   As each page of the chart is filled, tape it to the wall so that all problems are visible at all times. The group's recorder must never challenge or disagree but may ask for clarification or elaboration and may rephrase long problems. The recorder should always ask the speaker whether the rephrasing accurately reflects the speaker's intent.

5. **Have a vote to establish priorities on the list.**

   Usually, each member votes individually for three or four top choices. The items are then ranked from most to least votes received. All items remain on the list; voting simply prioritizes the agenda. With certain software this ranking process can be handled electronically as well. Members rank the items individually; the computer automatically tallies and prioritizes the overall list.

6. **Eliminate problems that can be solved immediately.**

   Sometimes group members can answer questions or solve problems to the satisfaction of the person who initially presented the problem. Such questions or issues are removed from the list.

7. **Deal with each problem in turn.**

   Some issues may call for an investigation and report, a lecture, or another informational presentation such as a brochure. Some require the services of outside consultants. However, major problems should be handled by the entire group or a subcommittee, following an appropriate problem-solving procedure.

Once a group has identified the problem it is going to address and discussed the particular nature of the problem, it is ready to begin the task of identifying solutions. Taking time to really talk about the nature of the problem helps a group avoid becoming solution-minded too quickly. This is a common problem in business groups.[9] Jumping into discussions of solutions without a comprehensive, initial understanding of the problem is like a car mechanic telling you that you need new valves without even looking under the hood! Defining the problem and detailing its specifics enables you to make modifications in your problem-solving procedure and provides important initial insight into the problem before you begin the detailed work outlined in the next section of the chapter. The procedure described below is easily modified so you can take advantage of its flexibility and adapt it to the particulars of your group problem that have already been discussed.

# Effective Problem Solving and Decision Making

In the early 1900s, American philosopher John Dewey asked his students to think about a problem they had faced and solved, then to recall the sequence they used to solve the problem. From their reports he created a general sequence of mental steps he called *reflective thinking,* which implied that the students' process was systematic rather than intuitive or haphazard behavior. The individual problem-solving sequence usually goes like this: First, we become aware of a difficulty; then we define and describe it, think of some possible solutions, evaluate these potential solutions, and make a decision about what to do. If possible, when we implement the solution, we monitor it to see how it's working, then keep it, adjust it, or replace it after testing it.[10] Dewey's model has been adapted for groups to use; group problem-solving procedures based on his model go under such names as the standard agenda, ideal solution, and single-question formats.

As Dewey did with individuals, Dennis Gouran, Randy Hirokawa, and their associates have examined problem solving and decision making in *groups.*[11] Their **functional theory** has evolved over the past two decades to describe how communication helps or hinders group problem solving and decision making. It is called "functional" because it focuses attention on the communicative functions that must be performed if a group is to do a good job. Gouran and Hirokawa assume that group members *want* to make a good decision, have all the information and other resources they need to do so, and have the communicative and thinking skills necessary to do a good job. If those conditions are present, whether a group solves problems effectively depends on three factors.

1. **The first factor pertains to the task requirements.**

   According to functional theory, five task requirements must be met for a group to succeed. First, members must understand the problem or issue, a necessity discussed in the previous section of this chapter. Second, they must know the minimum requirements of a successful solution, including what criteria it must meet. For instance, is there a budget members cannot exceed or an outside group whose support is essential? Members of effective groups discuss the criteria openly to ensure that everyone understands them. Third, the group must identify the alternatives from which it will make its choice. Many groups stop identifying or creating alternatives too soon; without sufficient realistic alternatives to choose from, the group may miss the best one. Fourth, the alternatives must be thoroughly evaluated, for both strengths and weaknesses, against the agreed-upon criteria. Finally, the best solution—the one that best meets the criteria—should be chosen.

2. **The second factor pertains to how well members use their communication to overcome obstacles to effective problem solving.**

   For instance, sometimes members fail to discover information pertinent to their problem or fail to share relevant information. We discussed earlier how members tend to share and believe information they have in common (that they all know), but to hold on to unique information that only one or a small number of them know.[12] Sometimes members consider their relationships with each other more important than finding the best solution; in that case members will refrain from disagreeing with each other and may try to pressure others to conform. Finally, some members may be more self-interested than interested in helping the group. How the rest of the group deal with such members directly affects the quality of decisions the group makes.

3. **The third factor pertains to the degree of willingness members have to review their process and reconsider their decisions.**

    If they find flaws, members must be willing to second-guess themselves, even to the point of starting over. They must not remain committed to a solution when it is clear the solution is flawed. Their communication to each other should remind members of the importance of reviewing the process and of being fair in making the ultimate choice.

Many researchers have found that following a planned problem-solving procedure helps groups make better decisions and solve problems more effectively. Such procedures can minimize the bad habits typical of small groups, including getting off track, being pressured by domineering members, prematurely rejecting ideas, and focusing on solutions too early in the process. The procedures help balance participation, improve a group's reflectiveness, coordinate members' thinking, and establish important ground rules for proceeding.[13]

It doesn't seem to matter which problem-solving procedure a group uses; *any* systematic procedure or outline produces better decisions than using no procedure.[14] Step-by-step procedures improve the quality of solutions because they provide logical priorities and steps that must be taken; they remind members of things they might otherwise forget.[15] Evidence suggests that groups arriving at high-quality solutions have made a thorough analysis of the problem, generated a variety of solutions, and conducted a detailed assessment of both the positive and negative aspects of the alternatives being considered.[16] In addition, these groups have focused on a solution's possible problems and have avoided pitfalls.[17] In other words, using a systematic problem-solving procedure encourages a group to consider the functions (according to functional theory) necessary to arrive at an effective solution by helping ensure that an important step doesn't get overlooked.

Group members have said that one of their most urgent needs is for guidance about methods and procedures to use during group work.[18] The lack of strong procedural guidelines is one of their most troublesome barriers to effective problem solving. In particular, participants want methods that help them generate and organize their ideas about complex problems. One such guideline, the procedural model for problem solving, has been used with good success.

### GLOSSARY

**Procedural Model of Problem Solving (P-MOPS)**

*A flexible framework to guide each phase of the problem-solving process*

## THE PROCEDURAL MODEL OF PROBLEM SOLVING (P-MOPS)

Several different guidelines can help groups solve problems effectively; we favor P-MOPS for its adaptability and because it focuses a group's attention on the essential tasks outlined by the functional theory. The **procedural model of problem solving,** based on Dewey's reflective thinking model, is a flexible framework that can guide each phase of problem solving; it applies all the principles we have learned about effective problem solving by groups and individuals.

P-MOPS reminds the group to analyze the problem thoroughly before trying to solve it and to think critically about the positive and negative outcomes likely to occur with each alternative solution. We have shortened its name to P-MOPS to remind you that it will help you "mop up" the details needed for good problem solving. The five steps in this general problem-solving procedure are (1) describing and analyzing the problem, (2) generating and explaining possible solutions, (3) evaluating all solutions, (4) choosing the best solution, and (5) implementing the chosen solution.

**1. Describing and Analyzing the Problem.**    During the first stage of problem solving, the group concentrates on thoroughly understanding the problem. Members should consider all three major elements of the problem: what is unsatisfactory, what is desired, and what obstacles exist. This phase of problem solving may require nothing more than sharing the knowledge members now have, illustrated by the mapping procedure depicted in Figure 8.2. That's easier said than done, though. Group members are apt to share freely that information that they already hold in common.[19] Apparently, shared information is more credible and creates common ground among members, who tend to withhold unique information, but this defeats the purpose. For group problem solving to be most effective, *all* information must be shared.[20] Members have to overcome their natural reluctance to share certain kinds of information and be willing to make whatever they know about a problem the property of the group. The description and analysis of a problem should never be rushed—it is crucial to effective problem solving. If this stage sounds familiar to you, it *should* because it refers to the preliminary work of understanding the problem that we talked about in the first section of this chapter. As we move into a detailed discussion of a systematic procedure for problem solving, we bring this initial work into the first stage of P-MOPS.

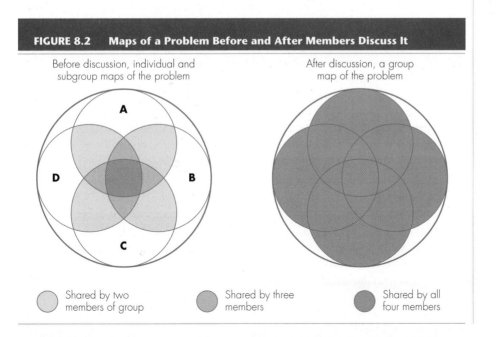

**FIGURE 8.2    Maps of a Problem Before and After Members Discuss It**

Before discussion, individual and subgroup maps of the problem

After discussion, a group map of the problem

Shared by two members of group

Shared by three members

Shared by all four members

**GLOSSARY**

**Charge**

*The group's assignment*

Following are several principles to guide your thinking and discussion in step 1 of problem solving.

1. **Be sure you understand the charge precisely.**

   The **charge** is your assignment of both responsibility and limitations, given by the organization or person who created the group. Getting the charge straight means that you make sure you understand an assignment exactly as intended. Get the charge in writing if possible. A committee should ask for clarification of any unclear terms from the person presenting the charge. For instance, you need to know what form your final product is to take: a recommendation, a research report, a blueprint with perspective drawings, or any other tangible object. You will certainly need to know what limitations are placed on your area of freedom, such as information you can obtain from company records, legal restraints, and spending limits. You will want to know when your work must be done; deadlines are part of most charges to groups. Thus, be sure the charge is clear to all members and that it is understood alike by the small group and the parent organization.

2. **State the problem as a single, clear problem question.**

   A question that suggests the solution biases the group and limits its effectiveness. "How can we convince the administration to put in a new parking lot?" is a *solution question* that assumes the solution to the parking problem is to create a new parking lot. This *problem question* is better: "How can we improve the parking situation on campus?"

3. **Focus on the problem before discussing how to solve it.**

   We mentioned earlier that one common source of poor solutions is getting solution-centered before the problem has been thoroughly investigated, described, and analyzed. If a group member suggests a solution too early, the discussion leader or another member should then remind the group to refrain from any talk about what to do until after the group has completed its analysis of the problem.

4. **Describe the problem thoroughly.**

   Be sure to answer all questions about what is going on and what you hope to accomplish, as well as possible obstacles to that goal—the way a successful investigative reporter or detective does. A good way to describe the problem is to think of it as an uncharted map with only vague boundaries. Your first job as a group is to make a complete, detailed map of the problem. As we mentioned earlier, this process of information sharing is critical—don't be tempted to shortchange it! Table 8.3 outlines questions you will need to answer.

5. **Make an outline and a schedule based on the procedural model of problem solving.**

   This is especially important if it is a major problem requiring extended work over several meetings. This outline and schedule can be modified later if needed, but at least now the group will reap the benefits of a plan before getting too deeply into the problem analysis.

6. **Summarize the problem as a group.**

   This ensures that you act interdependently and that everyone understands it in the same way. In the case of a large problem, this summary may be done in writing by one member and edited by the entire group until all members are satisfied with it.

| TABLE 8.3 | **Questions to Ask as You Analyze the Problem** |
|---|---|

**WHAT ARE ALL THE RELEVANT FACTS?**

**1.** Who is involved? When? Where? How?

**2.** What complaints have been made?

**3.** What is the difference between what is expected and what is actually happening?

**4.** What harm has occurred?

**5.** What exceptions have there been?

**6.** What changes have occurred?

**7.** What other information do we need?

**WHAT MAY HAVE PRODUCED OR CAUSED THE UNSATISFACTORY CONDITION?**

**1.** What events precipitated the problem?

**2.** What other factors may have contributed to the problem?

**WHAT DO WE HOPE TO ACHIEVE?**

**1.** What form will our solution take?

**2.** What would be a minimum acceptable solution for each person concerned?

**WHAT ARE THE CHARACTERISTICS OF OUR PROBLEM?**

**1.** How difficult is our problem?

**2.** How many possible solutions are there to our problem?

**3.** How interested are we personally in this problem?

**4.** How familiar are we with the problem?

**5.** How important is it that those most affected accept the solution?

Sometimes the problem you are addressing will affect a number of people, and you may need information about what is important to them. For instance, merging with Missouri State University was a scary prospect for the Ozark Public Television employees; they had many concerns about whether their jobs would be retained or changed in major ways. Sometimes a particular problem may have several aspects, and you may need to know which ones are the main issues or concerns. For example, work on the license transfer to Missouri State University was a critical step that had to be undertaken first; if the Federal Communication Commission didn't approve the transfer, nothing else mattered. One technique you can use to find out what is important to others is the focus group.

***Spotlighting Key Issues with Focus Groups.***    The **focus group** technique, which encourages unstructured discussion about a given topic, is often used to analyze people's interests and values. It is a great way for a group or an organization to find out what the important issues are regarding a problem facing the group; however, it is such a flexible procedure that it can be used at several steps in the problem-solving process.

In a focus group discussion, the facilitator introduces a topic to the group and instructs group members to discuss the topic any way they choose. The facilitator gives no further direction to the group but may probe or ask questions. Usually, the group discussion is tape-recorded for later analysis. After the group is finished, the facilitator or representatives of the parent organization listen to the tape for usable ideas.

Although focus groups were created within the advertising industry, many other types of organizations use them in a variety of creative ways. For example, a public relations officer at a small campus used a focus group to discover more effective ways of scheduling and promoting evening classes. A group of evening students was instructed simply to talk about what it was like to be an evening student. From the discussion it was clear that evening students were often trying to juggle full-time jobs, families, and other responsibilities in addition to school. The school's schedule was forcing them to come to the campus four nights a week to complete two courses. But the focus group discussion indicated that the students would be happy to stay later in the evening if they could take those two courses by coming to the campus only two nights a week. Campus officials found a way to "stack" the evening classes to allow this. In addition, the student comments spurred many imaginative ideas for advertising and promoting the evening offerings.

## 2. Generating and Explaining Possible Solutions.    The quality of the solution to a problem will not be better than the quality of the pool of ideas the group considers. Studies of problem solving have shown that the ideas discovered later are more likely to be innovative and of higher quality than the ideas first mentioned.[21] Thus, the major issue of step 2 is not "What *should* be done to solve the problem?" but "What *might* be done to solve the problem?" This subtle change in wording is important.

During step 2 the group should focus on creatively finding and listing possible solutions, not on critically determining their relative merits or on trying to decide what to do. Creative thinking is crucial to this step and was discussed in detail in Chapter 7. The leader may need to remind the group not to argue (yet) the relative merits of proposed solutions.

No criticism should be allowed during step 2, but ideas may be explained and clarified. Someone may ask, "What do you mean?" or "Could you please explain how that would work?" Descriptive explanations help everyone understand the idea and may even stimulate further ideas.

Sometimes, while generating ideas, a member will recognize details of the problem that ought to be explored more fully. The group may then cycle back to the P-MOPS step 1 for further exploration of that issue. For example, faculty on a committee charged with revising the communication major realized, in the middle of evaluating options for the revision, that they had forgotten to solicit feedback from an important group—their alumni. The members conducted a quick telephone survey of selected alumni, thus temporarily setting aside their evaluation to return to analysis of the problem. When they finish the additional analysis for step 1, members return to listing alternatives.

Once a group has completed its list of alternatives, it is ready to proceed with evaluating them.

**3. Evaluating All Possible Solutions.**    During the third stage of problem solving, *all* proposed solutions should be evaluated. Critical thinking, as discussed in Chapter 7, is especially crucial during this stage, and you want to avoid groupthink. For instance, arguments in undergraduate groups tend to consist of simple assertions almost half of the time, and members seldom cite rules of logic or criteria as standards.[22] The options must be tested against the criteria the group has established, and members must be sure the solution is consistent with the facts brought out during discussion, the goals of the group, and the restrictions imposed by the group's area of freedom. It is especially important to consider all possible negative consequences of each solution, or new problems it might create for the group or other people.

***Criteria for Evaluating Solutions.***    **Criteria** are statements that set standards and limits for comparing and evaluating ideas. For example, search committee members assessing applicants for a library dean's position streamlined their evaluation process by using criteria sheets the members developed. Committee members made a list of the essential qualifications (e.g., academic degrees required, years of experience required) and the other desirable characteristics (e.g., fund-raising experience, team approach to managing). Then they decided which of the criteria were most important and placed them in a priority listing. This gave each member a set of very specific guidelines to use as he or she read each application.

Serious secondary tension (see Chapter 5) may arise as people argue and disagree while they discuss the pros and cons of proposed solutions. Having agreed-upon criteria helps make arguments as constructive as possible and keeps personal defensiveness to a minimum. Establishing criteria is very important—groups that spend time discussing and establishing criteria are more effective than groups that don't.[23] For example, a public utility where one of us lives recently was criticized by the public for its "excessively" generous employee compensation and benefits packages. To determine fair compensation and benefits, the utility's board of directors examined compensation of other public utilities and private companies of similar size and complexity. The directors used this information to develop objective criteria, based on evidence rather than their own hunches, in redesigning the benefits package. Thus, group members should discuss, agree upon, and possibly rank (from most to least important) the criteria for judging their ideas and solutions.

Some criteria are absolute, which means they *must* be met (e.g., "The library dean must have at least a master's degree in library science from an American Library Association–accredited school"). Other criteria are important but give the group some flexibility (e.g., "A Ph.D. is a preferred qualification for the library dean").

Some criteria are virtually universal in judging among solutions: Will the proposed solution actually solve the problem? Can the proposed solution be done? Will the benefits outweigh the costs? Is this solution within our area of freedom? and How acceptable is this idea to the people most likely to be affected by it? Such criteria encourage the group to consider whether the ideas proposed are legal, moral, workable, within the competence of the group or organization, within the control of the parent organization, and so on.

There is some debate over whether groups need to discuss criteria explicitly. When groups are given their criteria as part of their charge and the criteria are understood by the group, some evidence suggests that groups do not need to discuss criteria.[24] We believe, however, that it is never wrong to discuss criteria because discussion can confirm how much members both understand and agree to the criteria. In addition, discussing criteria exposes

**GLOSSARY**

**Criteria**

*Standards and guidelines used to evaluate ideas and solutions*

the values held by group members, and these value discussions are central to effective consensus building in groups.[25]

***Narrowing a Long List of Proposed Solutions.*** When a list of ideas has been generated by brainstorming or any other technique, the group will need to reduce this list to a manageable size before it discusses the merits of the ideas. This can be done in a number of ways after the group has established its criteria. Here are three useful techniques:

1. Combine any ideas that are similar or overlapping. For example, "Hold a goodwill party" and "Have a get-acquainted cocktail party" could be combined into "Plan a social event."

2. Allow each member (including the leader) to vote for his or her top three choices. Tally the votes. Any proposed solutions that do not have at least two votes may be removed from the list.

3. Give each member a set of 10 or 15 stickers and ask them to "vote" on their preferred solutions. Members can distribute their stickers any way they want. They can put all their stickers on one item, if they strongly prefer that item, or put each sticker on a different item. The items receiving stickers are easy to spot and list in priority order. The group then discusses the pros and cons of the options that received at least one sticker.

***Charting the Pros and Cons.*** During the evaluation discussion, a recorder can help greatly by creating a chart of the ideas being discussed, with the pros and cons mentioned for each idea, as shown in Table 8.4. Instead of *Pros* and *Cons,* the chart headings might be *Advantages* and *Disadvantages, For* and *Against,* or even + and −. Using such a chart that

| **TABLE 8.4** | **Charting the Pros and Cons of Two Proposed Solutions** |
|---|---|

**HOW TO REDUCE PASSENGER INJURIES IN AUTOMOBILE ACCIDENTS**

| **Pass Federal Law to Require Use of Seat Belts** | **Require New Cars to Be Equipped with Airbags** |
|---|---|
| **Pros** | **Pros** |
| • Would reduce or eliminate many injuries. | • Would be extremely effective. |
| • Would be inexpensive. | • Technology currently exists. |
| • Precedent exists in many states. | **Cons** |
| **Cons** | • Would increase the cost of cars. |
| • Infringes on individual rights; expect heated legal fight. | • Infringes on individual rights; expect heated legal battle. |
| • Difficult to enforce. | • Airbags might inflate incorrectly and cause accident. |
| • Some injuries could be worse with seatbelts. | |

everyone can see helps the group remember major arguments and think critically about the proposals under consideration. This, too, can be done electronically, either with specialized software or by ordinary e-mail, with someone compiling the comments.

***Using Technology to Help Group Problem Solving.*** In previous chapters (see especially Chapters 1, 3, and 7) we have touched on the increasing role of computer technology in small groups. Technological hardware and software that years ago were accessible to only a few groups that could afford it are now widely available. These computer tools range from the simple to the highly complex. Electronic mail (e-mail) lets group members communicate via their personal computers asynchronously, whenever it is convenient for them.[26] Group writing systems permit members to simultaneously co-author their writing by allowing them to create, analyze, edit, and revise a single document.[27] Instant messaging (IM) allows for the more rapid-fire exchange of messages than with e-mail and voice mail. People who use IM like how quickly they can access others, but the jury is out on the impact of instant messaging on worker productivity.[28]

Instructors increasingly use asynchronous electronic bulletin board services (BBS) and synchronous chat environments, like the Internet Relay Chat (IRC), to facilitate classroom learning or as part of an online course.[29] These technologies allow teachers and students to talk to each other when it is convenient and can equalize participation, increase student self-responsibility, allow students to see each other's perspectives, give students time to think about their responses, and teach valuable computer-mediated skills for their future professions.

In a comparison of classes using BBS and IRC, BBS was most useful for promoting group critical thinking and reflection, particularly when making decisions and evaluating solutions.[30] The downside is that BBS does not promote collaboration and social interaction, and group members have to be motivated to use it. In contrast, the synchronous character of IRC does promote collaboration and works really well for brainstorming. However, the informal, freewheeling nature of IRC—so important for brainstorming—is dangerous if not monitored because groups can get off track. Whether your group uses chat rooms or electronic bulletin boards because you choose to or an instructor or supervisor requires it, you use them most effectively when you consider their purpose and make use of their strengths. You should not use them just to use them!

**Group support systems (GSS)** are computer technologies designed to improve the quality and speed of group problem solving. Specifically, GSS exists to help groups with such tasks as idea generation, information organization, evaluation of options, and decision making. Many are designed to allow group members to work collaboratively on a problem even though they may be meeting in different locations at different times. Two of the more well-known support systems for problem solving are GroupSystems and Software Assisted Meeting Management (SAMM). Both include modules created to help groups in every area of problem solving.[31] They are particularly helpful during the evaluation stage because they structure the procedure by which members can honestly react to each other's suggestions and ideas.

Such systems have rapidly increased in number, ease of use, and effectiveness, especially as more and more organizations use local area networks that allow several computers to be connected to each other. People can employ GSS for either long-term use or for one problem-solving task. For example, workers in geographically dispersed areas can connect via computer to perform group work even though they may be far apart. Often, however,

## GLOSSARY

**Group Support Systems (GSS)**

*Computer-based systems designed to improve various aspects of group work*

people meet electronically in the same room, each at his or her own computer terminal. This allows several members to "talk" at once by entering their messages into the computer, which compiles them quickly. It also permits anonymity; who submitted a particular comment, idea, criticism, and so forth is not recorded. Some GSS are highly specialized. For example, several are designed to improve the idea-generation step of brainstorming. Others, such as SAMM, are more general and are designed to improve the entire problem-solving and decision-making process, in part by providing structure.

Group decision making using computer support systems seems to be at least as good as traditional group decision making.[32] Members are often more satisfied and like the fact that the computers permit simultaneous talk. Studies conducted in organizations using GSS suggest that bigger groups are even more satisfied than smaller ones, that the systems seem to help group members sustain their task focus better, and that less time seems to be spent in meetings. GSS also helps improve organizational record keeping and memory. In addition, the anonymity such systems provide is important, more so for groups with individuals of widely varied status than for groups of peers. In mixed-status groups, members use the anonymity feature of GSS to their advantage.[33] For example, sex is a status characteristic that, left hidden, can level the influence of members' sex in group interaction. Males generally enjoy more status. Online they tend to reveal that they are male, which circumvents the anonymity feature of GSS, making it more like face-to-face communication. Females, on the other hand, try to preserve their anonymity, hiding their sex so as to be more influential in the group.

Group members should recognize that using GSS is not always beneficial. Problems include some group members' discomfort with using computers, GSS procedures that may structure group interaction too tightly, and managers who may not want group members under their supervision to have full access to information easily obtained via computers.[34]

Be careful with any conclusion drawn about GSS. They are changing daily. They seem to be especially beneficial for certain types of tasks, such as idea generation and decision making.[35] However, face-to-face groups seem to be superior for negotiation and complex, cognitive tasks. Whether GSS improves performance depends on a variety of factors.[36] Groups using support systems generally make better decisions; such groups generate more alternatives; and participation among members is more even. On the other hand, groups take longer to reach decisions, experience less consensus, and are less satisfied than face-to-face groups. An important key to satisfaction appears to be user familiarity—users' reactions are usually negative at first. Several reviews of GSS have found that group members need time to become familiar with the spirit or intention of GSS. As long as a GSS program is used consistently with its intentions, it can be very effective; however, merely using a GSS program without considering its intent may lead to failure. GSS do not do the work *for* the group, nor do they work if group members fail to use good communication skills. The same communication skills crucial to traditional face-to-face problem solving are still needed when groups use GSS as tools. For example, anonymity is usually beneficial; however, members who never see each other may not come to identify with the group or each other like they can in face-to-face groups. Groups should combine both face-to-face and computer-mediated communication.[37] The most we can say definitively is that GSS is generally good for groups although not in every circumstance.[38]

## Using Chat Rooms for GSS

Go to **www.mhhe.com/ adamsgalanes7** for additional weblink activities.

**MEDIA AND TECHNOLOGY**

Group support systems can be as simple as using e-mail to facilitate information exchange between group members or as complex as using specialized group meeting software programs. An important characteristic of effective GSS is anonymity. Group members can feel free to share ideas without fear of reprisal or ridicule if their statements are anonymous. Unfortunately, many e-mail systems make anonymity difficult, and specialized meeting software can be expensive.

One alternative to using GSS is to create a chat room and have group members log on using anonymous nicknames. Chat rooms are special websites that allow any number of users to interact in real time (synchronous communication). Thousands of chat rooms already exist on the Internet. Many online services allow users to create free chat rooms that can be used for private discussions among friends or for anonymous group discussions. Here are directions for creating a free GSS resource for your group:

1. Go to http://groups.yahoo.com/. This page will display general categories of groups available on Yahoo!.

2. Click the "click here to register" button on the left. You should register using anonymous information. Remember to write down your anonymous user identification and passwords so you can access the group in the future.

3. Have one group member (or your teacher) create a new group. As you will discover, groups provide more resources than simply chat rooms, including the ability to create polls, share files, and create databases. You should create a public group so that other group members can easily find it. Let other group members know the name of the group and the category (e.g., School and Education—Classmates—Our Group) you placed the group in.

4. Have each group member log in using anonymous nicknames and then navigate to the newly created club. Members can chat, create discussion boards (discussion boards are saved whereas chats are not), and even take part in polls created by group members.

Resources such as the Yahoo! Groups provide an easy way to create functional GSS for your group. Using Internet chat rooms is easy once you are familiar with their many features. Group members should familiarize themselves with the chat room or group interface before the group uses this technology to facilitate a group discussion.

After all proposals have been thoroughly evaluated, the group has set the stage for the emergence of a final decision on a solution or policy. A favored solution may already have begun to emerge during the discussion.

**4. Choosing the Best Solution.**   Just as groups experience predictable phases in their overall development, they also go through identifiable decision-making phases. Several well-respected researchers have contributed to our understanding of group decision-making phases.[39] For example, Donald Ellis and B. Aubrey Fisher found that many groups first enter an *orientation* phase, proceed to a *conflict* phase when they argue about their various options, and finally enter the phases of *decision emergence* and *reinforcement.*[40] Decision emergence may begin during step 3, as members gradually move toward a consensus and coalesce around one proposal. The members will usually know when this has happened. Often a discussion leader can hasten this by asking something like, "I think we may have decided on a solution. Is that right?" If members agree aloud or nod their heads, having a straw vote or simply asking, "Does everyone agree?" or "Does anyone disagree?" can confirm this consensus.

*Reinforcement* refers to the complimenting and back patting that members give each other after a job well done. They will say things like, "That took a long time, but we really came up with a workable solution," "I really think we did a fine job with that," or "We done good, folks!" Such back patting expresses and reinforces the positive feelings members have toward each other.

Not all groups experience exactly the same phases during decision making. That would be too simplistic. Marshall Poole, for example, found that many factors influence the types of phases groups experience and the order in which they occur.[41] We present the idea of group phases to help you analyze what may be occurring in groups you belong to, but remember that the subject is more complex than we have described here (see Chapter 5).

***Methods of Making Decisions.***   A group can make decisions in many different ways, but some methods are likely to produce worse results than others. In some groups the leader has authority to make decisions and may do so frequently for the group. One person may be perceived as the most expert member on the problem the group is discussing; that person may be asked to make the decision for the group. As a way of avoiding conflict, the group can use a method of chance, such as flipping a coin, drawing straws, or rolling dice. Sometimes numbers can be averaged to produce a decision, such as averaging individual applicant rankings to decide who should be offered a job. Often groups decide by voting, which is mandatory in committees governed by Robert's Rules for Committees.

Common ways of making group decisions are for the leader or another designated member to decide without consulting the group, for the group leader to consult with other members but then make the final decision, for members to vote, or for the group to make the decision by consensus. The first method, decision by leader or designated member, is appropriate for minor decisions, such as where to meet, what refreshments to serve, what color notepads to put in the meeting room, or even whom to ask to type the report. It is also appropriate for those decisions for which the leader (or designated member) has all the information needed to make the decision, and support from group members is expected. The second method, the consultative method, is appropriate when the leader does not have all the needed information, when the group members are likely to accept the decision, when

# The School Board Breaks a Deadlock

The school board in a city near where one of us lives had been stymied for several meetings over an issue related to a tax increase for schools and the arguments members should make in the local media to support the tax increase. Most of the members wanted to stress that the tax increase would mean higher salaries for teachers, more teachers in the system, and smaller class sizes. One very vocal member wanted to emphasize the deterioration of the buildings and the necessity for basic facility maintenance. The board was stuck over this and other issues. Members didn't want to alienate the "buildings" member, so, wanting to be polite, they worked hard to find positive things to say about his arguments. However, this just fueled his enthusiasm. The school board president decided to use the university's "Decision Room," a room that had 20 terminals with capacity for full group support systems (GSS).

Two faculty members assisted the school board; one served as "chauffeur" to run the software while the other served as a neutral facilitator. The school board members typed their ideas into a terminal, where they appeared on a large, overhead screen that all could see. They were able to make anonymous comments about each idea. Finally, they rated each idea on a scale of 1 to 5 and rank-ordered each one as well. The ratings and rankings were instantly tallied, and a bar chart was produced that visually reproduced their numerical assessments. It was clear from the ratings and rankings that the "buildings" member was an outlier in the group. His ideas were not supported at all, which became obvious to everyone in the group, including him. This visual representation on the computer screen got through to him when the members' gentle oral comments had not. He dropped his insistence on the building maintenance platform for the tax levy.

1. What do you think are the advantages and disadvantages of using GSS?

2. Why do you think members were direct and clear using GSS where they had not been in face-to-face discussion?

3. What was persuasive about the visual representation that was not persuasive about the oral discussion?

4. For what other kinds of decisions do you think GSS would be helpful?

5. Are there situations in which you would not want to use GSS?

## GLOSSARY

**Consensus**

*A decision all members agree is the best they can all support but isn't necessarily everyone's first choice*

**RISK Technique**

*A technique to help a group assess potential problems or risks with a potential solution*

members cannot agree but a decision *must* be made, or when time is short. The third method, voting, occurs when the majority decides for the group. This method merely weighs the power of numbers, not the relative merits of ideas. The majority may be wrong and a minority of one member may have the best idea. Further, voting may split a group, with some members resenting the decision and trying to sabotage it. Voting can be used to get a sense of where members stand on an issue or to confirm that a decision has been reached. Scientific research and experience both confirm that you should make a major decision with a majority vote *only* when the group must make a decision without enough time to reach a consensus or when the group has exhausted every possible way of achieving consensus.

A **consensus** decision is one that all members agree is the best one they can make that is acceptable to all; it doesn't necessarily mean that the final choice is anyone's first choice! Do not confuse consensus decision making with a haphazard, coincidental convergence of member opinions. *Consensus* as we mean it here is about both a method of careful, open decision making and a product (or decision) that everyone supports but that may not be the top choice for one or more members.[42] It is a form of decision making preferred by individuals if they have the time and the resources it requires. Consensus decision making is pervasive across all kinds of groups and is even required in some because group members recognize that consensus decision making, done well, builds community and support for the final decision.[43]

We noted earlier that once a solution has been tentatively adopted, it is a good idea to test that decision among the people who will most be affected. It is especially useful to identify any negative consequences that may occur to others but that the committee has overlooked. The RISK technique helps accomplish this.

***Testing a Tentative Solution with the RISK Technique.*** The **RISK technique** is designed to help an organization assess how a proposed change or new policy will negatively affect the individuals and groups most involved. Suppose you are responsible for implementing a new employee benefits program at your company. Before you start putting the plan into effect, you want to make sure all problems that could come up have been identified and, if possible, dealt with in advance. RISK will help you do this. The steps for a face-to-face RISK meeting are summarized in Figure 8.3. Like other group techniques, RISK can also be conducted electronically.

A group may have selected an alternative and discovered, with RISK or some other technique, that the solution is acceptable to all concerned. However, its job still isn't finished! Most groups are then responsible for seeing to it that the solution is implemented.

| **FIGURE 8.3** | **Steps for Conducting the RISK Technique in a Face-to-Face Meeting** |

| Proposed solution presented in detail; members identify risks or problems with it. | Risks posted without evaluation on a chart in round-robin fashion. | Master list of risks compiled and circulated to participants. | Second meeting held to discuss the list; problems perceived as serious retained. | Retained problems processed into an agenda and handled as in the problem census. |

Sometimes, that task is given to another group. Nevertheless, the problem-solving process is not complete until the solution has been put into effect.

**5. Implementing the Chosen Solution.**   The final step in group problem solving is implementing the solution. Sometimes groups break off their discussion as soon as they have decided on a solution without working out a plan to put their decision into effect. They may feel finished, but they truly are not. Good leaders see that the group works out the details of implementation. During this stage of problem solving, the group answers questions such as the following:

- Who will do what, when, and how so that our decision is enacted?

- How will we write and present our report?

- How will we word our motion to the membership meeting, and who will speak in support of it?

- What follow-up should we conduct to monitor how well this solution is working?

Some implementation plans are simple, but others are complicated and detailed, especially if the solution involves many people and numerous assignments. Program evaluation and review technique (PERT) is a procedure designed to help group members track the implementation of a complex solution; however, it is useful for implementing simple solutions as well.

*Using PERT to Implement a Solution.*   **PERT** is a set of concrete suggestions to help a group keep track of who will do what by when. It can be difficult to follow a complicated implementation plan that involves many people, groups, and tasks. PERT helps do this by asking those responsible for implementation to make a chart showing deadline dates for completion of various tasks and the names of individuals or groups responsible.

Following are the main parts of the process:

1.  Determine the final step by describing how the solution should appear when it is fully implemented.

2.  List all the events that must occur before the final goal is realized.

3.  Order these steps chronologically.

4.  For complicated solutions, develop a flow diagram of the procedure and all the steps in it.

5.  Generate a list of all the activities, materials, and people needed to accomplish each step.

6.  Estimate the time needed to accomplish each step; then add all the estimates to find the total time needed for implementation of the plan.

7.  Compare the total time estimate with deadlines or expectations, and correct as necessary by assigning more or less time and people to complete a given step.

8.  Determine which members will be responsible for each step.[44]

Another way to construct a PERT chart is to work backward from a target date. For instance, the students who created the chart in Figure 8.4 worked gradually backward from the due date for their presentation by taking into account how long each major step of the process would take. By doing that, they had a clearer picture of when they'd have to start working on the project to get it completed without undue haste. We recommend PERT to our students whenever they have complex group assignments to complete.

"*You mean no one remembered to bring a rock?*"

**FIGURE 8.4    Sample PERT Chart for a Student Group Project**

| Date | Aretha | Barney | Candy | Denzil | Entire Group |
|---|---|---|---|---|---|
| Tues Apr. 8 | Report on prelim observ. | | Report on prelim observ. | | Decide group to observe; decide variables |
| Thu Apr. 10 | | Prelim report, conflict | Prelim report, ldship | Prelim report, roles | Discuss prelim reports; decide methods of analysis |
| Tues Apr. 15 | | Complete lib research, Conflict | Complete lib research, Leadership | Complete lib research, Roles | |
| Thu Apr. 17 | | Observe group, 8 PM | Observe group, 8 PM | Have observ materials ready: survey, SYMLOG | |
| Tues Apr. 22 | | Complete SYMLOG of group | Complete SYMLOG of group | | Meet after class, discuss preliminary findings |
| Thu Apr. 24 | | | Observe group, 8 PM | Observe group, 8 PM Have tape recorder ready | |
| Tues Apr. 29 | | | | | Discuss overall observations; listen to tape |
| Thu May 1 | | Complete first draft, Conflict | Complete first draft, Leadership | Complete first draft, Roles | |
| Mon May 5 | Begin overall editing and typing | Final draft, Conflict; Intro done | Final draft, Leadership; Conclusion done | Final draft, Roles | Look at each other's sections to improve style |
| Tues May 6 | | | | | |
| Wed May 7 | | | | | |
| Thu May 8 | | | | | |
| Fri May 9 | Editing and typing done | Tables and charts to Aretha (conflict) | Tables/Charts to Aretha (leadership) | Tables/Charts to Aretha (roles) | |
| Sat May 10 | Proof: make copies | | | Proof ; make copies | |
| Sun May 11 | Distribute copies to all by 8 PM | Assemble full report by 5 PM | Assemble full report by 5 PM | Make large charts for class presentation | |
| Mon May 12 | | Read full paper | Read full paper | Read full paper | Rehearsal at Aretha's, 7 PM |
| Tues May 13 | | | | | Final presentation to class |

### Moving to New Facilities

Assume you're a member of the committee responsible for moving Ozarks Public Television to Missouri State University facilities. You're working within a four-month time frame, April through July. OPT will need to decide what is staying, what is coming, and what new digital equipment needs to be ordered. Office equipment will be moved, along with 14 staff people. A room on the MSU campus needs to be emptied and rewired for the new equipment, among other things.

Draw up a PERT chart for the move, covering four months:

1. What activities would have to be done, and in what order? (For instance, you would want the wiring in the new room ready before you installed the new equipment.)

2. How long do you estimate each activity would take? (For instance, assume it takes two months from the time you order new equipment until the time you receive it.)

3. How many "supervisors" would you put in charge of each activity?

4. Where would you put your PERT chart?

Although groups rarely stick *exactly* to the P-MOPS (or to any problem-solving guidelines), if you attempt to follow this sequence in the form of an outline of questions written about the problem, you will help guarantee that no important question, issue, or step is overlooked, and thereby create a good solution. The flexibility of the procedure allows you to tailor it to the characteristics of any problem. So that you can understand better how such adaptations are made, we next present examples of outlines written, adapted, and followed by problem-solving groups.

## Applications of P-MOPS

Use the information about problem characteristics in Table 8.2 to help you determine how to modify the P-MOPS to suit your particular problem.

The first example of a procedural outline, shown in Table 8.5, was created by a self-appointed advisory committee of students concerned about pedestrian safety on a street just east of campus. The group of students first decided on the general problem they wanted to tackle, then created an outline to guide their investigation over a six-week span. They devised possible solutions, decided on what to recommend, and finally presented their report to both the city council and the president of the university. You will notice that it closely follows P-MOPS. The students' work was tragically timely—shortly after their presentation, a student was killed crossing that very street.

The outline in Table 8.6 (p. 247) is much shorter and simpler; it is designed to be used for a brief class discussion.

| TABLE 8.5 | **Sample Outline Using P-MOPS for a Complicated Problem** |
|-----------|-----------------------------------------------------------|

**Problem question: What shall we recommend that city council and university administration do to reduce pedestrian injuries on National Avenue east of campus?**

**I.** What is the nature of our problem involving vehicle-pedestrian accidents on National Avenue east of campus?

  **A.** How do we understand our charge?

    **1.** What freedom do we have in this matter?

    **2.** What limits do we have (such as cost, structure of report, etc.)?

    **3.** To what does the general problem question refer?

  **B.** How do we feel about this problem?

  **C.** What do we find unsatisfactory about the way traffic and pedestrians currently affect each other on National Avenue?

    **1.** Diagram of present street, buildings, crossing, medians, lights, and so on.

    **2.** How serious is the problem of injuries to pedestrians?

      **a.** What kinds of accidents and injuries have occurred?

      **b.** When do these accidents happen?

      **c.** Do they tend to occur at any specific times?

      **d.** What kinds of persons are involved?

      **e.** How does this compare to accidents and injuries elsewhere?

      **f.** Are there any other facts we need to learn?

  **D.** What seems to be causing these accidents?

    **1.** Characteristics of the location?

    **2.** Human behavior?

    **3.** Other factors?

  **E.** What do we hope to see accomplished?

    **1.** In reducing the number of accidents and injuries?

    **2.** In practices of city council and administration?

    **3.** Any other features of our goal?

*(continued)*

| **TABLE 8.5** | *Continued* |
| --- | --- |

    **F.** What obstacles exist to prevent achieving our goal?

        **1.** Financial?

        **2.** Priorities of council or administration?

        **3.** Vested interests, such as businesses?

        **4.** Other?

**II.** What might be done to improve the safety of pedestrians crossing National Avenue east of campus?

    **A.** Brainstorm for ideas.

    **B.** Do we need explanations or descriptions of any of these proposed solutions?

**III.** What are the relative merits of our possible solutions to accidents and injuries on National Avenue?

    **A.** What criteria shall we use to evaluate our list of possible solutions?

        **1.** Costs?

        **2.** Acceptability to involved persons?

        **3.** Probable effectiveness in solving the problem?

        **4.** Appearance?

        **5.** Other?

    **B.** Shall we eliminate or combine any ideas?

    **C.** How well does each remaining potential solution measure up to our criteria and the facts of the problem?

**IV.** What recommendation can we all support?

    **A.** Has a decision emerged?

    **B.** What can we all support?

**V.** How shall we prepare and submit our proposal?

    **A.** In what form shall we communicate with council and administration?

    **B.** How will we prepare the recommendation?

        **1.** Who will prepare the recommendation?

        **2.** How will we edit and approve this report?

    **C.** How will we make the actual presentation?

    **D.** Do we want to arrange for any follow-up on responses to our recommended solution?

| TABLE 8.6 | **Sample Outline Using P-MOPS for a Simple Classroom Discussion** |
|---|---|

**I.** What sort of final exam would we like for Communication 315?

   **A.** What is our area of freedom concerning the exam?

   **B.** What facts and feelings should we consider as we discuss what sort of exam to request?

**II.** What are our criteria in deciding on the type of exam to recommend?

   **A.** Learning objectives?

   **B.** Grades?

   **C.** Preparation and study required?

   **D.** Fairness?

   **E.** Other?

**III.** What types of exams are possible?

**IV.** What are the advantages and disadvantages of each type?

**V.** What will we recommend as the type of final exam?

## RESOURCES FOR REVIEW AND DISCUSSION

**SUMMARY**

- Effective group problem solving uses guidelines to help members think critically rather than relying on their intuition, overrelying on expert authority, or overrelying on personal experience.

- A problem consists of a situation perceived to be unsatisfactory, a desired situation or goal, and obstacles to reaching that goal.

- Five characteristics of problems should be considered by members when they adapt their problem-solving procedures to fit the specific problem: task difficulty, solution multiplicity, intrinsic interest, member familiarity, and acceptance level.

- The functional theory of effective problem solving and decision making identifies important functions that must be fulfilled for a group to solve problems effectively. Members must do a thorough job of meeting the task requirements, use their communication skills to help the group overcome potential problems, be willing to review their process, and even reconsider their solution if necessary.

- The procedural model of problem solving (P-MOPS) provides a flexible sequence of steps, based on extensive research, for effective problem solving. These steps include thoroughly describing and analyzing the problem, listing a variety of solutions, carefully and critically evaluating their positive and negative elements, selecting the one that best meets the criteria, and planning how to implement the chosen solution.

■ Several specific techniques can help at each step. For instance, focus groups can help identify key issues pertaining to the problem; group support systems can help, especially with evaluation; the RISK technique can identify problems with a proposed solution the group is seriously considering; and PERT helps a group implement its solution.

■ Group decisions can be made by the leader, by voting, or by consensus.

1. Think of a current or recent problem you have encountered. Analyze your problem by identifying its component parts (present situation, obstacles, and goal). Pay particular attention to the obstacles you identify. Form into groups of four to six, and discuss each of the problems. Ask your team members to help you brainstorm ways of overcoming the obstacles you have identified.

2. As a class, choose two problems, one that is relatively simple and has few options and one that is relatively complex with high solution multiplicity (such as how the university should spend its contingency reserve money of $500,000). Write a leader's outline for structuring a discussion of each of these two issues by adapting P-MOPS to fit the discussion topic.

    After everyone has created an outline, select two leaders, one to guide each of the discussions using his or her outline. After the discussion, talk about what worked and what did not in the outline. How would you modify each outline to improve it?

3. View Part 3 ("An Ineffective Problem-Solving Discussion") of the videotape *Communicating Effectively in Small Groups* that was designed to accompany this text. This segment depicts a group doing a terrible job of problem solving. After viewing the tape, explain what you would do to correct the deficiencies. The following can guide your critique:

   *a.* Give specific examples of either poor or excellent problem-solving skills demonstrated by the group members.

   *b.* Examine the behavior of the leader, Alyce. What could she have done to improve the discussion process?

   *c.* Ask what specific behaviors helped the problem-solving process and what behaviors hurt it. Why did they have such an effect?

 Go to **www.mhhe.com/adamsgalanes7** and **www.mhhe.com/groups** for self-quizzes and weblinks.

| | | |
|---|---|---|
| Area of Freedom | Focus Group | Problem Census |
| Charge | Functional Theory | Problem Solving |
| Consensus | Group Support Systems (GSS) | Procedural Model of Problem Solving (P-MOPS) |
| Criteria | PERT | RISK Technique |
| Decision Making | Problem | |

 **www.mhhe.com/adamsgalanes7**

Use the flashcards and crossword puzzles on the Online Learning Center to further your knowledge of these key terms.

# Managing Conflicts Productively

**CHAPTER OUTLINE**

What Is Conflict?

Myths about Conflict

Types of Conflict

Computer-Mediated Communication
(CMC) and Conflict Types

Managing Conflict in the Group

**CHAPTER OBJECTIVES**

**After reading this chapter you should be able to:**

*1.* Define conflict.

*2.* Discuss the three prevailing myths about conflict in small groups.

*3.* Differentiate between substantive, procedural, and affective group conflict.

*4.* Compare and contrast the five major conflict styles.

*5.* Explain how group members can disagree ethically.

*6.* Discuss how members can maximize their chances to influence the group.

*7.* List and explain the steps of the nominal group technique.

*8.* Describe the four steps in principled negotiation, and explain how to use them to help resolve a conflict.

## The Cask and Cleaver Work Crew

CASE 9.1

The Cask and Cleaver is a local restaurant in California's Central Valley. Its servers (usually students) meet semiannually to select their shifts. At these meetings eight or nine servers take turns, in round-robin fashion, picking a shift. The server with the most seniority picks first, and so on, until all shifts are covered. The servers want to choose shifts that make the most money in the least time so that they can survive financially and still have enough time to study and play. The stakes are higher for those with greater financial needs because they must live with the schedule for six months.

One recent meeting has become legendary as the most contentious in the restaurant's 20-year history. Mark, the senior server, took charge and chose first. At his fourth turn, he realized an earlier turn had been skipped and servers with less seniority had taken one more turn than he had. Mark suggested that they start over again. Some supported his idea, but Tom and Paul did not. They were pleased with their shifts after having lived with very poor schedules during the previous six months. After discussing it, the group decided to start over. During the second round it became apparent that the members were choosing differently; furthermore, the new schedule heavily favored Mark and Beth (Mark's wife), whereas Tom and Paul were not faring well at all. Opposition to starting over was voiced again with greater emphasis. Mark and Beth became defensive, arguing that it was not their fault Tom and Paul had two night classes. Tom and Paul perceived this reaction as callous and reminded Mark and Beth that they had no alternative class sections to choose from. Mark replied, "That's not my problem." Another server, Nathan, sided with Paul and Tom, forming a clique that characterized Mark and Beth as self-centered and unsympathetic to the financial needs of others. Mark, Beth, and another server, Maria, all believed that the others' school schedules were not their concern and that shift scheduling was a hit-or-miss process anyway: Sometimes you do well and sometimes you don't. To them Tom and Paul were "crybabies" who wanted special treatment because they were university students. Tracey and Jeremy, two other servers, remained neutral, moving between the two cliques, listening to both sides, and conferring between themselves without ever sharing their views of the conflict.

By now you should realize that the payoffs of small group decision making and problem solving can be incredible. Yet these benefits do not just happen—they come after hard work, thoughtful modifications, and the knowledge that conflict will be a part of the process. Members have to work with their collective knowledge and skills, which will sometimes complement each other and sometimes clash. When group members do the work of vigilant problem solving and the critical thinking it requires, disagreement will occur. Conflict, expressed and managed well, can help members sharpen their thinking and decide wisely. In contrast, unexpressed disagreement contributes to groupthink (discussed in Chapters 5 and 7), harms group task and social processes, and can destroy a group. We discuss conflict in this chapter—its myths, the different types and styles you will encounter in your groups, the effects it can have on a group, and ways it can be managed well.

## What Is Conflict?

**Conflict** can range from simple disagreement to war. Joyce Hocker and William Wilmot's definition describes conflict as "an expressed struggle between at least two interdependent parties who perceive incompatible goals, scarce resources, and interference from the other party in achieving their goals."[1] This definition emphasizes the central role of communication. Conflict can be experienced without being expressed; group members can be acutely uncomfortable without saying a word, much like Tracey and Jeremy in our opening case.[2] But how conflict is expressed and how it is handled are communicative acts, which we explore in this chapter.

You have probably observed conflict in a small group, such as when two or more people express different ideas, fight with each other over group procedures, or simply do not like each other. These kinds of primary and secondary tensions (see Chapter 5) in groups are common and have to be managed. For example, suppose Marsha suggests that her group present a skit for its class presentation, but Silvio believes skits are childish. For this group to achieve its goal of a successful presentation, Marsha, Silvio, and the other members must manage this disagreement effectively. Most conflicts you experience in a group will be disagreements similar to this. Like the Cask and Cleaver conflict, they can become heated. But if they are handled well, they can help improve a group's performance.

## Myths about Conflict

You have learned from previous chapters that group members often do not freely express their unique opinions about the task and tend toward early closure in their problem solving. You also have learned that group members do this for all sorts of reasons, which range from general reasons associated with members' personalities and cultures to the specific demands of the situation, such as running out of time. Another reason pertains to the common myths about conflict members bring into the group. We would like to dispel three of the most common ones (summarized in Table 9.1).

### GLOSSARY

**Conflict**

*Occurs when discordant ideas or feelings are expressed or experienced between two interdependent parties*

| TABLE 9.1 | **Myths about Conflict and the Reality** | | |
|---|---|---|

| **Myth 1** | **Myth 2** | **Myth 3** |
|---|---|---|
| • Conflict is harmful and should be avoided. | • Conflict represents a misunderstanding or breakdown in communication. | • Conflicts can be resolved if parties are willing to discuss the issues. |
| **Reality** | **Reality** | **Reality** |
| • Conflict can help members understand an issue more clearly. | • Some conflicts occur over differences in values, goals, methods of achieving goals, and limited resources. | • Conflicts over basic values and goals may not be resolvable. |
| • Conflict can improve group decisions. | | • Conflicts over limited resources and methods of achieving goals may be resolvable through communication if the basic values and goals of the parties are compatible. |
| • Conflict can increase member involvement. | | |
| • Conflict can increase cohesiveness. | | |

1. **Conflict is harmful to a group and should be avoided.**

    We all have seen examples of how conflict can hurt a group. Minor misunderstandings can lead to hurt feelings, and a group may dissolve over a conflict. Clearly, conflict can harm a group. This harm is evident in our Cask and Cleaver crew, with servers throwing all sorts of blame around and showing defensiveness because they feel they are being faulted maliciously. However, many students see only the harm and don't realize that conflict can be beneficial to the group *if it is expressed and managed properly.*

    Conflict can help members understand the issues surrounding a decision or problem more completely. When members disagree, they can discover that there are perspectives other than their own. Karl Smith and colleagues found that when students in learning groups heard other opinions they became uncertain about their own, sought out information about the different positions, and were better able to remember information about both their positions and those of others.[3] Expressed disagreement at the beginning of meetings can help generate learning about issues.[4]

    One of us served on an advisory board for a nonprofit organization. The administrative officer of the organization wanted to fire an employee immediately, without issuing a warning or giving the employee a chance to correct the offending behavior. One member, experienced with personnel laws, disagreed strongly with what appeared to her to be a lack of due process in the proposed dismissal. When the other members understood the legal and ethical problems with discharging employees before giving them a chance to improve their performance, they agreed to give the employee a clear set of guidelines and expectations to be followed. One group member's willingness to disagree enabled the others to understand the issue more completely. This type of disagreement illustrates *idea deviance,* mentioned in Chapters 5 and 7.

Conflict also can improve a group's decision, which is a logical outcome of members understanding an issue more clearly. In the previous example the dismissed employee could have sued the organization and the board for arbitrarily firing him. Clarifying his job duties and the board's expectations gave him the best possible chance to perform effectively. The disagreement helped members understand these possible consequences. Only after they had argued, over the course of several meetings, did they truly appreciate that giving him a chance to improve both was fair to him and protected them in case of legal challenge.

Conflict also tends to increase member involvement and participation. Group discussions can become boring, but when a controversy occurs, members perk up and voice their opinions. In the previous advisory board example, members who had begun to skip meetings started to come regularly again. Usually, members become more interested when they believe their opinions can make a difference in the group's outcomes.

Finally, conflict can increase cohesiveness. Have you ever had an argument with your dating partner, spouse, or friend, then observed how close you both felt after you had made up? If so, you know how conflict can increase your positive feelings toward one another. During the advisory board's discussion about firing the employee, members expressed strong feelings on several sides of the issue. After all members aired their views, the group eventually came to a consensus decision. As consensus emerged, members became closer than ever. Several members expressed their appreciation to the member who initially spoke up against the firing. They believed that her comments forced the group to anticipate possible problems and to create a better solution, although at the time they did not see her disagreement as helpful. Members realized that they could disagree, express themselves in forceful terms, and emerge more united than before the conflict; cohesiveness increased. Consensus decision making, introduced in Chapter 8, is not superficial agreement on issues. It emerges out of members working through often difficult discussions of their values, which eventually converge in collective support of a solution.[5] After the Cask and Cleaver crew managed to deal with their issues constructively, lighthearted banter about this meeting being the "ugliest scheduling meeting of all time" followed, as well as a promise never to let such contention happen again. Both task success and interpersonal tolerance combine to strengthen cohesiveness.

So, although conflict can be harmful to a group, it doesn't have to be. Whether a conflict helps or harms a group depends on a number of other factors, including whether the conflict is resolvable in the first place.

2. **Conflicts stem only from misunderstandings and breakdowns in communication.**
Certainly, *some* conflicts occur due to misunderstandings and communication failures, but others do not. Often conflicts occur when individuals understand each other perfectly well but disagree on basic values or the distribution of rewards. For example, a classroom group trying to agree on whether to recommend the repeal of the *Roe v. Wade* court decision making abortions legal in the United States was unable

to arrive at an answer acceptable to everyone. Several members believed that life begins at conception and that abortion is murder. Other members believed that a woman's life should take precedence over the fetus, at least until the fetus reaches a certain stage of development. Each subgroup understood the position of the other subgroup. Misunderstanding and communication breakdown did not occur. However, the subgroups' differing values and assumptions made agreement impossible.

Managing conflict well entails figuring out *why* the conflict is occurring; assuming that all conflicts occur because communication is the problem is dangerous.[6] When we do this, we trivialize communication by turning it into a cure-all and come to believe that more communication or less will solve the problem. Too often increasing communication may do little to help and may even make a situation worse. We will talk about the different kinds of conflict found in groups in the next section so that you can develop a better sense of how different types of conflict affect small group interaction.

3.  **All conflicts can be resolved if parties are willing to discuss the issues.**

As you can see from the previous example, not all conflicts are resolvable, nor is simply talking more about it always going to help—it may even make it worse. Whether or not a conflict can be resolved depends in part on the underlying reason for the conflict. The conflict over basic values on the abortion question is not resolvable at the present time because it is based on differences in assumptions and values. The two assumptions represented—a fetus is a person from conception and has rights equal to those of the mother versus a fetus becomes a person sometime after conception, until which time the woman's rights take precedence—are not reconcilable. Both cannot be true simultaneously. A group experiencing such a conflict will not be able to come to consensus on a policy regarding abortion.

Conflicts over scarce resources are also difficult, if not impossible, to resolve. One of us served on a library committee with representatives from many areas of the school. Meetings on how to distribute limited funds fairly are usually full of acrimony. Broad agreement is rarely possible. Even members who acknowledge that one area deserves more money for books may vote against that proposal if it means their own areas will receive less money. The problem, recognized by everyone, is that funds to support the legitimate requests of all areas are in short supply.

Conflicts over goals can sometimes be difficult to resolve as well. Assume that you want an A on your group project while someone else is satisfied with a C. If you can't convince the other person of the value of striving for excellence, and the other person can't persuade you to lighten up, you can't resolve this conflict. If your goal of receiving an A is very important to you, you may end up having to do a lot of extra work on the project—yours and the other person's.

Conflicts over how to reach goals are sometimes easier to resolve than other types, especially if the basic values of the individuals are similar. In the project grade example, if you and the other member both want to get As, but you prefer to show a movie and the other member prefers a skit, you may be able to compromise or find a third alternative that satisfies you both. Because your basic values and goals are the same, you are more likely to see each other as allies, not enemies, which makes it easier to resolve the conflict.

**MHHE.com/ groups**
For more information on conflict resolution, go to the Online Learning Center at **www.mhhe.com/ adamsgalanes7**

Conflict itself is not the issue. Any social system, due to the interdependence of the system's components, will experience some kind of conflict. How parties manage the conflict is really the issue. Mishandling of disagreement can produce problematic group outcomes such as faulty decision making. Before we discuss how to manage conflict in groups, let's take a closer look at the different types of conflict you may find in your groups. Identifying the cause of the conflict is important to managing it effectively.

# Types of Conflict

The Cask and Cleaver servers are in conflict over all sorts of things. Mark used his seniority to pressure other members to redo the shift selection procedure they had all agreed to use. An established group norm for fair distribution of shifts was altered and further debated. Some members did not see a problem with the schedules, but others did. Coalitions formed, blame was tossed around, and others just kept quiet. Most obviously, the underlying resources at issue for the servers were money, time, and power. Interestingly, these conflicts over procedure and their relationships are the two most common workplace conflicts encountered by college students in their early workplace experiences.[7] In addition, college students report that it is common for conflict over procedures, such as how to decide shift schedules, to turn into interpersonal conflict between members. Perhaps surprisingly, the third type of conflict, task conflict, is not commonly noted by college students at work, yet it is a regular feature of task groups in business and education.

Conflict in and of itself is neither automatically helpful nor harmful to a group. What *does* matter is what the conflict is about, how it is initiated, and how it is managed. Learning the nuances of the three most common types of conflict—task, affective, and procedural—can help you identify them in your groups and assess how to manage them.

## SUBSTANTIVE CONFLICT

**Substantive conflict** revolves around the task and is found in disagreement over ideas, meanings, issues, and other matters relevant to the task.[8] We introduced you to this kind of conflict in Chapter 5 when we discussed secondary tension in groups. This type of conflict is work-related and is the basis for effective decision making and problem solving. In substantive or task conflict, group members challenge ideas, proposals, evidence, and reasoning and critically evaluate them. Doubts are brought out into the open, and group members work together to find the best solution. The opinion, idea, or innovative deviance referred to in Chapter 5 is usually substantive in nature.

## AFFECTIVE CONFLICT

**Affective conflict** is conflict that originates from interpersonal power clashes, likes and dislikes unrelated to the group's task. It represents the *who* in the conflict and is generally detrimental to the efficient functioning of any group. It is a kind of secondary tension, like the one we referred to as tertiary tension. Much of the Cask and Cleaver server conflict involves power struggles between servers—who gets to decide the rules and change them? These kinds of conflicts also emerge over clashes of personality characteristics, learning styles, and perspectives due to age and culture. Recall Judy in our opening case for Chapter 6 on diversity. Mahmut Bayazit and Elizabeth Mannix found that affective conflict, not task conflict, was the main reason team members gave for expressing a desire to leave the team.[9]

Our observations of numerous groups suggest that much affective conflict is rooted in one member's acting as if she or he is superior, and another member's refusal to accept this difference in status or power. Most of this "I am better, more important, more knowledgeable" signaling is nonverbal, projected by subtle patterns of vocal tones, postures, and head/body angles. Group members are able to tell the difference between more substantive (depersonalized) and affective (personalized) conflict and recognize that affective conflict harms consensus.[10] Deviants who obstruct group processes, as opposed to idea deviants, are perceived less favorably in work groups, and the group tries to reduce the deviant's impact on the group.[11] In addition, these work groups report that the deviant produced more harm to their task cohesion than to the social cohesion.

Inequity may also be at the root of affective, personal conflict. Group members may not carry the same workloads or make equitable contributions to the group. This is why equitable distribution of speaking turns is so important to effective decision making.[12] Inequity reduces satisfaction with the group and is associated with high levels of conflict.[13] In our case study, Mark set off a firestorm by using his seniority to force reconsideration of a procedure already accepted by members as fair. Coalitions of members emerged, quite a common response to the stress of inequity. Coalitions emerge in groups when members with access to few resources, minimal power, or little bargaining leverage seek out other members in an attempt to level the playing field. Coalitions can be functional in groups but are detrimental when members become willing to hurt their own cause in an effort to defeat the member perceived as wielding the heavier bat. Coalitions tend to disappear when group members believe they are on more common ground. In our Cask and Cleaver case, group members altered an established norm of fairness, producing instability, which they then had to manage to prevent servers from quitting or working conditions from deteriorating.

## PROCEDURAL CONFLICT

**Procedural conflict** is a type of substantive conflict over the ways to achieve group goals. This disagreement is about the *how* of group work. For instance, group members may disagree about whether they should make decisions by consensus or whether they should vote. In our Cask and Cleaver case, the conflict began over the procedure members had chosen to use to determine their shifts for six months. However, what on the surface appears to be procedural conflict may actually be a substantive or affective conflict in disguise. This can occur because members genuinely disagree over procedures yet use ineffective behaviors to manage their conflict. In our case the procedural conflict turned into a nasty affective one. In addition, members sometimes withdraw from a substantive conflict by forcing a vote or otherwise regulating the group's work, thus using procedural conflict to steer clear of substantive and affective conflict.[14] In other instances, what may appear as a straightforward conflict over procedures is really a conflict between two different needs for structure. For instance, one group member may like things to occur in a linear fashion while another prefers to weave back and forth between procedures, adapting whatever works at the time.

### GLOSSARY

**Procedural Conflict**

*Conflict resulting from disagreement about how to do something*

# Computer-Mediated Communication (CMC) and Conflict Types

As you will recall, group members can use computers to talk to each other online, and some may use group support systems (GSS) to help them problem solve. In fact, we have discussed how the use of computers has been hailed as a way to reduce a status inequity and to increase member contributions. Early research comparing conflict in CMC with face-to-face (FtF) groups produced inconsistent results.[15] For example, CMC groups engaged in more inflammatory, profane, and negative communication than FtF groups. However, groups that used GSS, like the ones discussed in Chapter 8, exhibited less substantive and affective conflict if members used the methods as they were meant to be used. Thus, we might conclude that if groups using CMC gave members time to get to know each other (a common recommendation when using CMC) and adapted GSS appropriately, then computer use could lessen the potential damaging effects of conflict.

In a rare study comparing type of conflict in CMC and FtF groups, differences were found.[16] CMC groups initially displaying more affective and procedural conflict than FtF groups saw these types of conflicts lessen over time. Both CMC and FtF groups displayed similar amounts of substantive conflict. Due to the anonymity of CMC, CMC groups initially have fewer social norms that can be used to support and maintain positive self-images. The higher levels of procedural conflict in CMC groups are related to members initially not knowing how to use the technology. Other research has found that CMC groups are better able to manage their conflict after they become competent users of the technology.[17]

Although CMC groups do not follow the same pattern of conflict types as FtF groups, they do go on to reach comparable levels. If you use any type of CMC for informal or formal group interaction, make sure you give yourselves time for social development. Groups whose members primarily connect using computers should consider times for meeting face-to-face, especially early on, to give themselves the opportunity to create social and procedural norms acceptable to their group.[18]

Although we describe these types of conflict as though they are distinct, they are not mutually exclusive. One type can lead to another and they often blend. In our Cask and Cleaver case, for instance, the conflict occurred not just because Mark wanted to change a procedure; certainly, groups can revisit established procedures. The conflict emerged due to *how* he moved to change the procedure. Members may not like each other (affective) and may be prone to disagree more often with each other when ideas are challenged (substantive). CMC groups initially show an interrelationship between procedural and affective conflict—struggles with technology get tied into interpersonal struggles—whereas FtF groups show more blending of procedural and substantive conflicts.[19] Learning about these different conflict types and how they are manifested in groups is essential to understanding how conflict can help and hinder a group.[20] Groups have been shown to be rather adept at creating ways to help manage task conflict and steer clear of negative emotions.[21] Substantive conflict is needed in a group, but affective conflict should be managed early to avoid destructive patterns that produce great emotional cost to members.

# Managing Conflict in the Group

We hope we have convinced you of the value of constructive substantive conflict during small group problem solving. Conflict is inevitable when people must reach decisions together. Trying to squelch conflict does not eliminate it—it just sends it underground. If managed inappropriately, conflict can hurt the group and its members and, we would argue, is unethical. All the ethical principles of the National Communication Association's Credo for Ethical Communication (see Chapter 1) remind us that conflict mishandled destroys respect and trust, shuts down honest and open communication, and can be degrading, coercive, and irresponsible. In this section we discuss how to manage conflict productively and ethically.

## CONFLICT MANAGEMENT STYLES

There are many different ways of describing how people manage conflict. Common models describe from two to five styles. We have chosen a typical five-style conflict management model because we believe that it better captures subtle nuances among the styles that can be lost in other, popular three-style models.[22] The five styles we discuss here were described by Kenneth Thomas.[23] Whatever style an individual chooses is based on the answers to two questions: (1) How important is it to satisfy your own needs? and (2) How important is it to satisfy the other person's needs? Figure 9.1 shows how these two dimensions intersect to

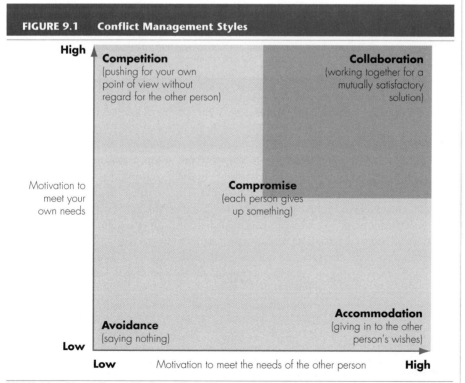

**FIGURE 9.1     Conflict Management Styles**

SOURCE: Adapted from K. Thomas, "Conflict and Conflict Management," *Handbook of Industrial and Organizational Psychology*, ed. by Marvin D. Dunnette (Chicago: Rand McNally, 1976). Used by permission of Marvin D. Dunnette.

| TABLE 9.2 | **Statements That Illustrate the Five Conflict Management Styles** |

Mary, the college financial director, wants the snack shop to close at 5 P.M. Roger, the evening student counselor, wants it to stay open until 8 P.M. Following are examples of how Roger might respond to Mary, using each of the conflict management styles discussed in the chapter:

**Mary:** We'll have to close the snack shop at 5. There isn't any money to keep it open later.

| Avoidance | Accommodation | Competition | Compromise | Collaboration |
|---|---|---|---|---|
| **Roger:** [Says nothing; accepts Mary's statement, even though he disagrees.] | **Roger:** I'd really like to keep it open, but, if there's no money, I guess there's nothing else we can do. | **Roger:** I won't accept that! We can't let the evening students down that way. Cut something else to get the money! | **Roger:** I would accept keeping it open just until 6:30 if you could cut some money from another program. | **Roger:** I understand that it's necessary to contain costs. It's also important to serve evening students. Is there some way we can provide them food service without increasing costs? |

This was an actual problem faced by a student services committee. The solution? Provide vending machine service. This maintained constant labor costs but gave students food service after 5 P.M.

produce the five common conflict management styles of avoidance, accommodation, competition, collaboration, and compromise. Table 9.2 gives examples of statements illustrating each style. *No one conflict style is best to use in all circumstances.* The most appropriate conflict style depends on the situation. Factors to consider include how important the issue is, how serious the consequences will be if the group makes a mistake, whether the group is under any time pressures, whether cultural practices limit what can and cannot be done, and how important it is that the positive relationship between the conflicting parties be maintained. In most groups, preserving and enhancing relationships among the members is important. So conflict management styles incorporating the legitimate needs of all parties are preferable to those producing winners and losers.

The conflict style that group members use depends largely on how they perceive the situation.[24] The situation is more important, in fact, than what members believe "started" the conflict. Factors such as how often the members have been in conflict in the past, how many negative feelings they harbor against each other, how mutual their goals are, and how ambiguous or structured the solution is all affect how a member will approach handling the conflict. Ideally, members recognize that they have a mutual stake in the solution and are motivated to cooperate in resolving the conflict.

**Avoidance.**   **Avoidance** occurs when any group member chooses not to disagree or to bring up a conflicting point, thus downplaying her or his own needs and the needs of others. When group members fight about other people in the group, they tend to avoid

**GLOSSARY**

**Avoidance**

*Conflict style describing a person's unwillingness to confront or engage in conflict*

further conflict with each other. However, if the conflict is about the task, group members tend to be more willing to work together.[25]

   We have talked about the dangers of avoiding conflict, but the avoidance style is sometimes appropriate. If the issue is not very important, and you are certain that the group's decision will not be hurt by your failure to speak up, avoiding a possible conflict is appropriate. One of us served on a committee planning a banquet. The rest of the members favored a different restaurant from the one your author preferred. Both restaurants were comparable in price, service, and atmosphere. Making an issue over this would have been silly because there was no risk of making a serious mistake. This was not an important enough issue to argue about.

**Accommodation.**   **Accommodation** (also called *appeasement* or *giving in*) occurs when one person or faction gives in to the other without arguing strongly for a different point of view. This style is similar to avoidance in that a person downplays her or his own needs, but it differs in that the person works harder to meet the needs of others. You should be honest with yourself if you choose to accommodate. Don't give in if the issue really is important to you. We realize this could be hard for those group members who fear talking in front of others.[26] However, if you give in but privately resent it, in the future you are likely to find yourself arguing with the other person for no apparent reason. On the other hand, if the issue is not crucial to you but you know it is important to the other person, then accommodation is appropriate. For example, a faculty/student committee was charged with redecorating a student lounge. The chemistry professor did not like the color scheme recommended by the art professor and said so. But since the students liked it, the chemistry professor willingly accommodated their preferences. This is an appropriate use of accommodation to resolve conflict.

**Competition.**   **Competition,** sometimes called the *win-lose style,* occurs when you fight hard to win and you don't care whether the other person is satisfied with the solution. Most of the time, highly competitive ways of handling conflict are harmful to a group. If one person tries to impose his or her will on a group, the other members will probably fight back, like Tom and Paul did in our opening case. Competitive tactics often escalate a conflict, especially when people stop listening to understand each other. Each side tries harder and harder to force the other side to go along. For example, at an advisory board meeting, one member, Sherman, argued strongly for one solution to a particular problem. Two members disagreed with Sherman, who then began to use a variety of tactics to win the argument, starting with persuasion but moving quickly to attempted coercion and intimidation. Sherman's behavior indicated that he was more concerned with winning the argument than preserving the group. The visible conflict ended when the rest of the group reacted negatively to the intimidation tactics by voting against Sherman's suggestion.

   When a group is doing something you believe is harmful or wrong or goes against your values and beliefs, then competition is appropriate. Don't accommodate or avoid conflict if you think your basic values are being compromised or if you think the group is about to make a major mistake. The member opposed to firing the employee, described earlier in this chapter, behaved competitively. She was willing to face the group's disapproval because she genuinely believed they were about to make a big mistake, and she was not willing to compromise. Remember, though, that a conflict where one person wins but others feel like

## GLOSSARY

**Accommodation**

*Conflict style describing a person's willingness to engage in conflict; however, she or he backs away from the conflict by giving in to appease the other party*

**Competition**

*Conflict style showing a preference for coming out ahead in the conflict at the expense of the other party*

*"The motion has been made and seconded that we stick our heads in the sand."*

Avoiding conflict, even if desired, may not be the best choice. © The New Yorker Collection; 1986 Mischa Richter from cartoonbank.com. All Rights Reserved.

a decision has been forced down their throats will almost certainly erode teamwork. Until the other members came to agree with her position, the member who disagreed about the firing was left out of the group's informal camaraderie and felt very uncomfortable.

**Collaboration.** **Collaboration,** the win-win style of conflict management, occurs when the people in the conflict want to meet opposing parties' needs along with their own. Like competition, collaboration assumes individuals may argue strongly for their points of view. Unlike competitors, collaborators take care not to attack each other as people or to say or do anything that will harm the relationship. They behave ethically by treating each other as equals. They invest a great deal of energy in searching for a solution that will satisfy everyone. Group members whose communication is collaborative are more satisfied with their group outcomes than members who avoid conflict.[27]

Collaboration can reveal options that other styles miss. For example, the student services committee that served as the model for Table 9.2 initially struggled with two apparently competing goals—making sure that evening students had food available and making sure overhead costs stayed the same. During the discussion, characterized by genuine attempts to help both Mary and Roger achieve their goals, another member suggested the creative option of expanding vending services. This would meet student needs while costing the college nothing, since the vending company would pay for machine costs. But if the committee had voted without discussing the issues, or if either Mary or Roger had kept quiet, this option would never have surfaced.

You may think that collaborative solutions are ideal for groups because they attempt to preserve positive relationships among conflicting parties while members hammer out mutually acceptable solutions. However, collaborative solutions often require much time and energy, which groups don't always have. Not all decisions are important enough for the group to commit the time or energy to create a collaborative solution. If basic values differ or trust is lacking, collaboration may be impossible.

**Compromise.**     **Compromise** represents a middle-ground conflict management style that can be called a *partial-win/partial-lose solution* for each party. Unlike collaboration, parties using compromise give up something to get something in return. This type of horse-trading is typical of labor-management and government bargaining: "I'll settle for a $1-per-hour raise if you give up the demand for mandatory overtime," or "I'll vote for your bill if you support my amendment." If you know you are going to have to compromise, you will be tempted to inflate your original demands. For instance, if you know you will have to settle for less money than you want, you'll ask at first for a higher figure than you really need.

Although there may be problems with compromising, it is appropriate for many conflicts. When collaboration is impossible due to time pressures or differences in values, compromise may represent the best option available. With compromise each party does not completely receive what it wanted to begin with. However, if what each party had to give up seems balanced and the solution appears *fair* to all sides, then compromise can work quite well. *We cannot emphasize too strongly the importance of fairness.* A compromise can work only if all parties feel the solution is fair, and that no one has *won.* But parties cannot assume they know what "fair" means. Instead, both parties should explain honestly what they believe is fair, and these individual conceptions of fairness should be included as absolute criteria by which to evaluate the final decision.

There are appropriate times and situations to use each of the conflict management styles described here. However, approaches that are *integrative*—in other words, that focus on helping participants integrate their goals and needs—generally lead to better group decisions for complex tasks. Tim Kuhn and Marshall Scott Poole looked at naturally occurring groups in two major U.S. organizations.[28] Integrative conflict styles—collaboration and sometimes compromise—were more effective than avoidance and confrontational styles. In addition, groups that managed their conflicts productively also did other things that made the groups more satisfying to their members, such as establishing stable roles, relationships, and norms for accomplishing tasks.

The groups Kuhn and Poole studied tended to formulate norms for handling conflict early in their development and generally didn't change their patterns much. This means it is especially important to pay attention to a group's emerging norms for handling conflict and to discuss such norms if you believe they are counterproductive to good decision making.

In an insightful study of the process of consensus in a naturally occurring group, Mary Ann Renz showed how groups who value consensus develop norms that allow them to deal with the push and pull between their efforts to be open with each other and the demands to finish the task.[29] This kind of tension can produce frustration and conflict in consensus decision-making groups. Building consensus over time involves making lots of little decisions and requires that groups maintain a willingness to review their process and make adaptations. So what happens when a previous proposal has been accepted but someone now wants to challenge it? Renz discovered that one particular group used C. T. Butler and Amy Rothstein's 1991 book *On Conflict and Consensus,* which they called their "little white book," as a procedural guide to help them decide what they should do if

> ## GLOSSARY
>
> **Compromise**
>
> *Conflict style showing a preference for giving a little and gaining a little to manage the issue*

someone was blocking consensus on a proposal. This worked for them because they had all decided on the validity of the little white book and agreed to follow its recommendations; the guidelines had already been determined to be fair. This is one example of how a group effectively developed its own norms for managing conflict—in this case procedural conflict—fairly.

No single conflict style is always best. Each one can be evaluated not only in terms of its effectiveness but also in terms of its appropriateness.[30] Effectiveness is judged by the person engaging in the action, and appropriateness is judged by the other members in accordance with social norms. For instance, more collaborative styles are seen as both effective and appropriate, whereas competition can be effective in reaching your goals but probably will not be seen as appropriate by others. In our Cask and Cleaver server group, Mark probably thought he was being effective in pursuing his interests, but others certainly did not see his behavior as appropriate. Often we fail to see that what is happening in our group conflicts is a clash between effectiveness and appropriateness.[31] Conflict management styles are based on cultural norms and expectations like the ones we talked about in Chapter 6. The advice we give you here, particularly about openly expressing your disagreement, is consistent with norms for the individualistic cultures of the United States and Western Europe. An analysis of conflict management studies has questioned the view that it is always better to express conflict directly.[32] In Asian cultures, which tend to be collectivist, preserving harmony and helping others save face are paramount in group work. A more direct, competitive behavior may be effective in getting something done in a group but would not be seen as appropriate by those who are more collectivist or interdependent with others. Open disagreement is considered rude, in part because it can damage relationships. Avoidance, accommodation, and indirect expression of disagreement are considered appropriate responses.

Although more collectivist cultures such as Japan may prefer collaborative styles that value harmony and preserving the self-esteem of others, they may change the style depending on whom the conflict involves and what it concerns. In conflicts over values and opinions, Japanese tend to avoid conflict with acquaintances more than with close friends; they are more collaborative with close friends.[33] They can act collectivist and interdependent with members of their in-groups but can turn very competitive toward members of out-groups; thus, their intergroup communication is not the same as their intragroup communication.[34]

Each style is appropriate under certain circumstances, but having a more collaborative style is preferred in most problem-solving discussions. You may have found yourself in temporary task groups like the ones found in many small group courses. You usually have not met your group members before, do not plan on seeing them after the class is finished, and have only a short amount of time—at least it certainly feels like it—to finish your task. In temporary, highly task-focused groups, members generally perceive collaborative styles as more competent and avoidance styles as incompetent.[35] However, time may leave little room for collaborative styles. Confrontational, competitive styles may be effective for finishing the task under the gun, but they are not perceived as appropriate by other members. So what do you do if you want to be both effective and appropriate? Stay solution-oriented in your conflict strategies, and stay away from avoidance styles. If you believe the circumstance calls for more controlling behaviors, which can be effective but which may jeopardize appropriateness, then alert members to what you are doing—explain your

| TABLE 9.3 | **How to Disagree Productively** |
|---|---|

**EXPRESS YOUR DISAGREEMENT**

**1.** Remember that failure to express doubts and disagreements deprives the group of potentially valuable information and reasoning.

**EXPRESS DISAGREEMENT IN A TIMELY WAY**

**1.** Don't wait until the deadline is near to speak.

**EXPRESS DISAGREEMENTS WITH SENSITIVITY TOWARD OTHERS**

**1.** Disagree with the idea, but do not criticize the person.

**2.** Use neutral, not emotionally charged, language.

**3.** Be respectful of different face needs of members.

**REACT TO DISAGREEMENT WITH A SPIRIT OF INQUIRY, NOT DEFENSIVENESS**

**1.** Ask for criticism of your ideas and opinions.

**2.** Show you are interested in the other's opinion by listening actively and sincerely.

**3.** Clarify misunderstandings that may have occurred.

behavior so you don't seem arbitrarily confrontational. A comment such as "We are running out of time, and I know this will sound pushy, but could we consider voting on this to see where we all stand?" could act to soften the attempt at control.

## EXPRESSING DISAGREEMENT ETHICALLY

When you express disagreement, the *how* is just as important as the *what*. This distinction is significant; no matter how valid your disagreement is, if you express it in a tactless or arrogant way, you hurt your chance of benefiting the group. A legitimate concern (the *what*) can be expressed so insensitively (the *how*) that even a rational group member becomes defensive rather than receptive to what you have to say. The following suggestions, summarized in Table 9.3, will help you disagree without damaging relationships with other group members.

1. **Express your disagreement.**

   A disagreement has no chance of helping a group if it is not expressed. An unexpressed disagreement does not disappear—it goes underground, to resurface in inappropriate ways. Avoiding a conflict is only a temporary "solution." Issues can pile up so that eventually a large blowup occurs when each issue could have been handled individually. Remember that disagreements can help a group arrive at the best possible decision or solution, and that failure to express disagreements can lead to poor decision making.

2. **Express your disagreement in a timely way.**

   Research demonstrates that *when* you disagree may be just as important as what you say.[36] When group members approach a deadline or have already decided on a proposal, they are less tolerant of a member who introduces a dissenting opinion or wants to reconsider a previous decision because this threatens closure.[37] Members can respond rather emotionally to a late disagreement. Group members should check regularly with each other on their positions and watch nonverbal behavior for signs of dissent. Another idea is to hold smaller informal meetings specifically to talk about proposals, which encourages more reticent members to voice their concerns. Some groups also use "second-chance" meetings to try to avoid late disagreement.

3. **Express your disagreements with rhetorical sensitivity toward the rest of the group.**

   Disagree with the idea, or parts of the idea, without criticizing the person. Suppose you have just suggested that your campus shut down its snack bar at 5 P.M. to cut costs. Which response would you rather hear: "That's stupid! What are the evening students supposed to do, starve?" or "One problem I see is that your suggestion does not consider evening students' needs for food service"? The first response implies that the speaker is stupid, arouses defensiveness, and cuts off further examination of the issue. The second response describes a major problem with the suggestion but leaves room for discussion regarding how to cut food service costs. The second response is helpful; the first is not.

   Another way to show your sensitivity is to use neutral instead of emotionally charged language. Name-calling or otherwise pushing people's emotional buttons is never helpful. One of us recently attended a meeting where one member, John, who disagreed with another member, Janos, made a snide play on words using Janos's last name. Naturally, Janos was offended, and the atmosphere remained tense until John apologized. Disagreeing by making fun of others does not improve the group's decision-making process. Steer clear of words that you think might be offensive; be rhetorically sensitive.

   The material on managing tensions in your group in Chapter 5 and on working with diversity in Chapter 6 offers additional suggestions for being rhetorically sensitive to others. Recall that the central feature of working with diversity is human respect and the belief that fairness applies to everyone.[38] We all, no matter what our cultural backgrounds, have face needs, but we achieve them differently. Stella Ting-Toomey suggests that more of us need to "give face" more often to others.[39] For someone who is more individualistic, this means avoiding behaviors that would humiliate another member in front of others. For someone who is more collectivist, this means attending more to substantive issues rather than being relationally focused all the time.

4. **React to disagreement with a spirit of inquiry, not defensiveness.**

   Whether you are the group's leader or just a member, you have a lot of power to determine the atmosphere in your group. When someone disagrees with you, if you show that you are interested in what the other member is saying and in his or her reasons for disagreeing, you send the right message to the rest of the group. Even if the disagreement was expressed poorly, you do not have to let someone else's insensitivity control your reaction. Group members' reactions to argument are more important than the arguments themselves in creating group divisiveness over issues.[40] Listen actively to the person who disagrees, make sure that person has understood your position accurately, clarify any misunderstandings that may have occurred, and show that you are willing to work together to find the best possible solution.

For example, Kareema's committee had worked for several months on a proposal to change the criteria for promotion in her department. A new member, appointed to the committee to replace someone who had left the department, questioned the committee's preliminary investigation, saying, "I don't see how that's going to work. Seems to me you'll have more problems than you had before." Although Kareema *felt* defensive, she reacted calmly and asked, "Derek, what problems do you see with the proposal?" Derek explained his concerns, several of which uncovered problems Kareema's committee had overlooked. The committee's revised proposal accommodated Derek's concerns. The final proposal was much stronger and was overwhelmingly approved by the rest of the department. Examples like this show how you can make disagreement and conflict work *for* your group rather than against it.

## MAXIMIZING YOUR CHANCES TO INFLUENCE THE GROUP

Expressing your disagreement is the only way to make your ideas and reasoning available to the group. Even so, it is often difficult for people who are perceived as group deviants, even beneficial idea deviants, to influence the other members of the group. Whether you stand alone as an idea deviant or belong to a minority subgroup, the following suggestions will help you maximize your influence when you express your disagreement.

1. **Make sure your arguments are of high quality.**

   This is the single most important thing that you can do. Rick Garlick and Paul Mongeau found that, although several factors—including the idea deviant's expertise, attractiveness, and job status—affect that person's status within the group, only the quality of the deviant's argument directly influences the other members' attitude change.[41] That means you must think the problem through carefully and be willing to listen to the objections others may have.

2. **Make sure your arguments are consistent.**

   Lisa Gebhart and Renee Meyers found that subgroups expressing minority opinions are more successful if they generally stick to a consistent message.[42] This is especially important during the latter part of a discussion. These authors recommend, however, that a minority subgroup not be so consistent that it appears rigid and unable to understand others' views.

3. **If you are a member of a subgroup, make sure all the subgroup members publicly agree with each other.**

   Subgroups, or coalitions, are a powerful way group members have of influencing each other in conflict.[43] They occur for a variety of reasons. Some form around popular members, some because members are not sure who has the power and who does not. Often, group members form coalitions because they lack resources or power and hope to increase their influence—"power in numbers." However,

**GLOSSARY**

**Nominal Group Technique**

*A technique that alternates between individual work and group work to help a group hear from every member when discussing a controversial issue*

coalitions containing members who disagree with each other are less influential than coalitions presenting a united front.[44] The subgroup members should meet privately and hash out any disagreements among themselves before they meet with the rest of the group so that they can agree on a consistent message.

## THE NOMINAL GROUP TECHNIQUE

A major advantage of group over individual problem solving is that several heads can be better than one. But capitalizing on that advantage can be difficult. While the number of ideas increases with additional members, the opportunity for conflict also increases. One technique, the **nominal group technique,** can be used by a group to help members reach a decision on a controversial issue without bitterness from a win-lose conflict.

Nominal means "in name only." The nominal group technique capitalizes on the finding that sometimes people working individually while in the presence of others generate more ideas than while interacting as a group. In addition, sometimes dominant members inhibit the participation of quieter members. The nominal group technique gets around this potential problem by alternating between solitary work and group interaction. One organization used the nominal group technique as part of a detailed decision analysis procedure to decide what type of computer system to buy. This complex organization consisted of many different units and subunits that coordinated work with each other, but it also had unique computing needs that had to be satisfied. The nominal group technique helped all these individual units achieve consensus about the best computer system to buy. Participants were satisfied with both the process and the outcome.[45]

In the nominal group technique, members (usually six to nine) work individually in each other's presence by writing their ideas. Then members record the ideas on a chart, discuss them as a group, and finally evaluate them by a ranking procedure until members reach a decision. The following steps, summarized in Figure 9.2, make up the process.

---

**FIGURE 9.2    Steps for Conducting the Nominal Group Technique**

1. **The problem, situation, or question is stated clearly and concisely.**

   Elements of the problem or question are described, and discrepancies between what is desired and what currently exists are explained, often by a member of top management. Care must be taken not to mention possible solutions. Group members can ask questions to clarify or add information about the problem. If the group is large, it may be subdivided into smaller groups, each with its own facilitator.

2. **The coordinator asks participants to generate a list of the features or characteristics of the problem or question.**

   Steps 1 and 2 may be combined; the facilitator presents the problem and moves the group directly to step 3.

3. **The coordinator gives the group 5–15 minutes to work silently.**

   Each person brainwrites as many solutions or answers to the original question as possible.

4. **Each suggestion is listed and recorded in round-robin fashion on a chart visible to all members.**

   The first person gives one item from his or her list, and the recorder lists it. Then the next person gives one item, and so forth, until the master list is complete. If any additional ideas or items occur to people while the list is being compiled, they should add them to the master list. During this step no discussion of the merits of the suggestions is permitted.

5. **Members clarify the items but do not yet evaluate them.**

   The group discusses each item on the list, but only to clarify or elaborate on it. Any member may ask what a particular item means, but arguing, criticizing, and disagreeing are not permitted during step 5.

6. **Each person chooses his or her top-ranked items.**

   The easiest way to do this is to give each person a set of stickers to place next to his or her most important items. Sometimes participants are instructed to place one sticker by the five most important items. Other times participants are told they can distribute their stickers however they want, including placing all five on one item. Then the items with the most stickers become the agenda items for the group's discussion.

7. **The group engages in full discussion of the top-rated items.**

   This discussion should be a freewheeling and thorough evaluative discussion. Critical thinking, disagreement, and exhaustive analysis of the items are encouraged.

8. **A decision is reached.**

   Often the discussion in step 7 will produce a consensus decision. If so, the group's work is completed. If not, group members can revote on the items and continue their discussion. Steps 6 and 7 may be repeated as often as necessary until support for one idea, or for a combination of ideas, emerges. The decision is then acted on by the group or the parent organization that established the group.

This technique minimizes the disadvantages of group discussion and maximizes the benefits. The solitary work neutralizes the stifling effect of domineering members and the tendency for lazy or shy members to let others carry the ball. The open discussion frequently produces well-thought-out group decisions. However, be careful not to overuse this technique when you wish to create a sense of teamwork. It doesn't always create cohesiveness and sometimes produces lower satisfaction ratings than normal discussion.

Both of us have used this technique, or modifications of it, with great success. One of us employed it to help a major manufacturer identify problems with package instructions for a product and to suggest possible solutions for these problems. Recently, we used a modification of the nominal group technique with students to help plan changes to the communication curriculum. In each case it was not important for the group members providing the information to develop a sense of cohesiveness; thus, the nominal group technique was ideally suited for the situations.

In addition to knowing how to express disagreements, group members need tools to help them arrive at fair solutions. One such technique for managing serious intragroup conflict is named *principled negotiation.*

## STEPS IN PRINCIPLED NEGOTIATION

Each member of a group, along with the group's leader, is responsible for helping manage the conflicts that arise within the group. However, even though you may want to resolve a conflict effectively, you may not know how to proceed. The following helpful steps are suggested by Roger Fisher and William Ury in their book *Getting to Yes: Negotiating Agreement Without Giving In.*[46] Following these suggestions will help a group engage in **principled negotiation,** a conflict management procedure that encourages people to search for ways of meeting their own needs without damaging their relationships with others. Members can use this procedure collectively, or the designated leader or other facilitator can guide members through the process to a solution.

1. **Separate the people from the problem.**

   Sometimes conflict produces such strong emotions that people cannot be objective. What may start as a disagreement about how to get something done becomes a personal declaration of war in which combatants try to hurt each other. Our Cask and Cleaver crew started out selecting shifts and ended up calling each other names. Earlier, when we discussed conflict types, we explained how important it is to separate the people from the issues. People believe and act in ways that make sense to them. Try not to take disagreement personally—usually, it is the result of strong beliefs that someone else holds. The administrative headquarters of a church recently experienced serious conflict among administrators. Members on both sides of the fence began to talk about the other side as *the enemy.* After several long sessions with a trained mediator, people on each side began to listen carefully to those on the other side. Each side learned that the other side cared deeply about the issues; they also realized that they shared many concerns. Eventually, the conflict was resolved and the bad feelings healed. This occurred in part because both sides demonstrated that they cared about each other and because they focused on the issues that divided them rather than on personalities.

2. **Focus on interests, not positions.**

   Group members are tempted to stake out positions from which they cannot be budged. If Roger says, "I insist that we keep the snack bar open in the evening,"

## Helping the Cask and Cleaver Crew

The Cask and Cleaver work crew still must come up with the next six-month shift schedule. They almost had their schedule until Mark discovered he had been skipped. Now they are taking sides, acting defensive, and calling each other names. Your job is to take the role of each crew member and use the nominal group technique to create a shift schedule that is satisfactory to all the crew. Mark and Beth are married, and Beth has major health problems. Mark is a full-time student, and Beth works full time. Maria is married and recently started her own business. Tom and Nathan are students at a local university working toward a teaching credential. Paul is a graduate student and single. Tracey is an undergraduate and recently divorced. Jeremy, an undergraduate, is single and lives at home with his parents.

Select a facilitator to help the "crew" go through the eight steps of the nominal group technique. After a solution is derived, the class can discuss the following:

1. What was difficult about the procedure?

2. Did the "crew" think that the technique helped in any way? If so, how? If not, why?

3. Read ahead and see if this crew's solution is anything like the one the real crew devised.

and Mary says, "We have to close the snack bar in the evening to save money," there is no way to reconcile those positions—they are incompatible. The harder individuals cling to them, the more difficult it will be to resolve the conflict. However, people stake out positions for reasons that seem good to them. It is the *reasons* for the positions (personal interests) that should be the focus of the negotiation. In our earlier example, Mary wanted to save the campus money while Roger wanted to make sure the evening students were provided with food service. Not only are these legitimate interests, but they also are probably interests common to *both* Roger and Mary. Roger cared about financial solvency, and Mary cared about serving evening students, but each of them emphasized a different priority. One way to resolve this issue was to close the snack shop at 5 P.M. (thereby saving on labor and utility costs) but provide vending machines with a variety of sandwiches and snacks. In this way, the legitimate interests of each individual were served. The work crew of the Cask and Cleaver all had reasons for their positions. Mark and Beth faced huge doctor bills because Beth has a congenital heart defect. Maria recently started a new business. Paul, Mark's former roommate, felt hurt by Mark's indifference to his schedule. All were legitimate feelings and interests and had to be dealt with in the discussion if members were to manage their conflict productively.

3. **Invent new options for mutual gain.**

Group members should become creative at inventing alternatives. A number of techniques, such as brainstorming, are designed to help groups become more inventive. If Roger and Mary's committee had assumed there were only two available options—keeping the snack shop open past 5 P.M. or closing it—members could never have resolved the issue. The same committee later resolved a similar issue with the bookstore by inventing a solution that was not apparent when the committee first began to discuss the issue. You can probably remember other examples in which a group was able to invent a new option that met everyone's interests.

In our Cask and Cleaver case, the only options initially presented were to start all over again or keep going and ignore Mark's skipped turn. Another option, one that the crew did not consider, was to go back to the point where Mark was skipped, keep everything the same up until then, and start anew from Mark's skipped turn. In fact, Tracey's option effectively solved the problem. She pointed out that while it was not Mark and Beth's fault that Paul and Tom had night classes, it also was not Paul and Tom's fault that Beth needed surgery. She suggested that Mark give his night shift to Tom so he and Beth, who didn't work that night, could spend some time together. Mark saw the logic in Tracey's solution and gave his valued shift to Tom. All members apologized to those whom they had offended. The crew was able to come up with an option that gave them mutual gain given their reasons for their positions.

4. **Insist on using objective criteria.**

Much wasted time can be saved if members use criteria they agree are fair and appropriate for evaluating solutions, much like the "little white book" in an earlier example. For example, the *Kelley Blue Book* establishes a price range that helps both used-car buyers and sellers determine the fair price for a car. You may want $10,000 for your 15-year-old Toyota Corolla, but both you and potential buyers know that you won't get it! Using prices supplied by the *Blue Book* as criteria allows the negotiation to take place within narrower, more realistic limits.

The same use of objective criteria occurs in other situations, too. One of us served on a church finance committee charged with reviewing salaries and recommending adjustments. The salaries for the organist and choir director had not been reviewed in several years. Not knowing whether these salaries were reasonable, the committee called the local Council of Churches director, who had data about how much organists and choir directors with comparable responsibilities received at other churches of similar size. When the finance committee presented the recommendations to the full board of directors, the recommendations were easy to defend because of the objective criteria used.

One of our students, a residence hall adviser, recently used the principled negotiation technique with four roommates having problems devising an equitable schedule for leaving their suite clean at the end of the school year. Instead of doing what she normally would do (that is, assigning specific responsibilities to each roommate), Amanda met with all four women together and asked them what was

## Should He Go Back to School?

Sam and Tashie have been married for 12 years. Sam wants to quit his job because he is bored and believes they had an agreement that he would be able to complete his education after they had been married a few years. Tashie owns her own company, which is finally getting off the ground, and she doesn't believe they have the money for Sam to leave his job. Select two students to role-play the discussion between Sam and Tashie in front of the class. After the role-play, use the principled negotiation procedure with the entire class to help Sam and Tashie manage the conflict.

1. **People:** Ask the role-players how they feel about the argument, themselves, and the other person. Emphasize the importance of recognizing feelings.

2. **Interests:** Distinguish between the irreconcilable positions and the interests behind each position. Have the class and the role-players participate in discovering what each person's interests may be.

3. **Options:** Ask the class and the role-players to brainstorm creative options for this couple. Emphasize the point that interests may be met in a variety of ways, one of which is bound to be acceptable to both.

4. **Criteria:** Explore whether any objective criteria might apply to this couple's dilemma.

most important to each regarding this end-of-year task. It turned out that each woman wanted the tasks to be divided fairly and to be assured that the last woman to leave the suite would not be stuck with tasks the others had not completed. Amanda asked them how they would divide the tasks and establish consequences to ensure that each woman completed her assigned duties. The roommates themselves divvied up the work and suggested several options for holding one another accountable. Amanda was delighted because the women owned the solution and were more likely to carry it out than one she had imposed on them.

Even with the best of intentions, sometimes a group becomes deadlocked when it tries to resolve a conflict. We recommend that groups try to resolve their own conflicts first, but if that isn't possible, a group can try mediation or arbitration. The principled negotiation procedure can be used by an outside facilitator. This may be necessary if the leader has been actively involved in the conflict. Finally, a group may bring in an outside arbitrator with power to settle the dispute. However, these are last resorts. It is far better if a group can resolve its own conflicts.

## RESOURCES FOR REVIEW AND DISCUSSION

**SUMMARY**

- Three common myths about conflict are that conflict is always harmful, it is due to misunderstandings, and it can be resolved by good communication.

- Three conflict types in groups involve the task, procedures, and relationships between group members.

- The five common conflict management styles of avoidance, accommodation, competition, collaboration, and compromise are each appropriate in certain circumstances, but styles that encourage members to look for ways to satisfy all participants are usually preferable.

- Group members can use the nominal group technique, which balances solitary and group work, to help work through potentially contentious discussions.

- Group members can also use procedures such as principled negotiation, which focuses on people's interests rather than positions, finding creative options, and using objective criteria to resolve conflicts.

**EXERCISES**

1. Rent either *Twelve Angry Men* or *Lord of the Flies*. Watch the movie and observe types of conflicts: how these conflicts were handled, what the effects of the conflicts were on the group, how decision making was affected by the various conflicts, and what the group could have done to improve its ability to manage conflict. You can do this yourself, or you can discuss your observations with others in class who have also watched the video.

2. Think of a group you currently belong to. Recollect two recent conflicts in the group. Write an essay describing the conflict, labeling the type of conflict, and reporting how it was managed. Draw some conclusions about conflict in group interaction from these observations.

3. Divide yourselves into groups and come to a consensus regarding what you would do about each of the following group problems.

*a.* Ann has missed the first three meetings of the group. For the first two she said she had to work, but she offered no reason for missing the last one. She also has completed none of the work she agreed to do for the group.

*b.* Bob is a domineering individual who attempts to control the direction of the group. He evaluates each idea as soon as it is presented. As a result, the rest of the members have stopped volunteering suggestions and ideas.

*c.* The members of the group have fallen into two subgroups, and competition has arisen between the subgroups. If you didn't have to work together, you would have split apart long ago.

 Go to **www.mhhe.com/adamsgalanes7** and **www.mhhe.com/groups** for self-quizzes and weblinks.

KEY TERMS • CONCEPTS

Accommodation

Affective Conflict

Avoidance

Collaboration

Competition

Compromise

Conflict

Nominal Group Technique

Principled Negotiation

Procedural Conflict

Substantive Conflict

**www.mhhe.com/adamsgalanes7**

Use the flashcards and crossword puzzles on the Online Learning Center to further your knowledge of these key terms.

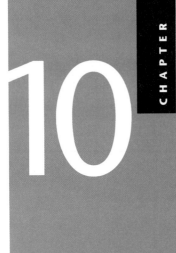

# 10

# Applying Leadership Principles

## CHAPTER OUTLINE

Leadership and Leaders

Myths about Leadership

Current Ideas about Leadership

What Good Leaders Do

Encouraging Distributed Leadership

Ethical Guidelines for Group Leaders

## CHAPTER OBJECTIVES

**After reading this chapter you should be able to:**

1. Distinguish between leadership and a leader; differentiate a designated from an emergent leader.

2. Describe the seven sources of a leader's power, and give an example of each.

3. List and discuss the myths of leadership.

4. Discuss current thinking about leadership.

5. Describe the administrative duties leaders are expected to perform, and explain how leaders can perform these effectively.

6. List and explain six tips for leading group discussions.

7. Explain how establishing a climate of trust, developing teamwork, and promoting cooperation can help develop the group.

8. Define *distributed leadership* and discuss what it means to encourage it.

9. List and explain the ethical guidelines for group leaders.

## The College Service Club

CASE 10.1

TerryAnn was so envious of the close, cohesive executive committee of her service club that she decided to run for office so she could be part of the team. When she was elected president as a junior, she was thrilled. She wanted the club and the executive committee to continue experiencing the same success she had witnessed as a member. Unfortunately, things wouldn't turn out that way. TerryAnn and the rest of the executive committee met soon after the spring election to make plans for the upcoming fall. Although many good ideas surfaced at this meeting, no one wrote them down. TerryAnn was somewhat intimidated by all the seniors on the executive committee, and she was reluctant to assign tasks or even ask the other members to do things. No one else picked up the ball either. Consequently, no one remembered what they had decided or knew who was supposed to do what. Committee members lost valuable summer planning time because they weren't organized. When fall came, they had to scramble to catch up.

TerryAnn's reluctance to guide the process affected both the executive committee and the regular organizational meetings. She made no effort to start the meetings on time, so members got into the habit of coming late. Because there was no agenda, members did not know what they would be discussing or what materials they should bring to the meetings. Discussion was haphazard, jumping from one topic to the next without ever finishing a single subject. No meeting minutes were ever compiled or distributed, so members weren't sure what actions had been decided or who was assigned to what tasks. As a result of the disorganization in the executive committee, service club members became disenchanted with the organization. Membership decreased. As the frustrating year drew to a close, TerryAnn was increasingly depressed because her high hopes for the club had not come close to being realized.

This story could have had a different ending if TerryAnn had known what the other members expected of her. Because she was afraid to be seen as a dictator, she did the exact opposite. But the group members were practically begging for TerryAnn to give them structure and organization so that the club's jobs would get done. TerryAnn's "leadership" did not match what the group needed and expected from her.

In this chapter we will differentiate leadership from leaders, describe the sources of a leader's power, discuss myths about leadership and current thinking about effective leadership, and explain the typical duties of designated small group leaders. In addition, we suggest guidelines to encourage distributed leadership and describe ethical leader behavior.

# Leadership and Leaders

Effective leadership is an essential element in successful groups. Most scholars believe that *every* member of a group, not just the leader, can help provide leadership. We now look more closely at how leaders and members actually provide leadership to the group.

## WHAT IS LEADERSHIP?

Michael Hackman and Craig Johnson define **leadership** as "human (symbolic) communication which modifies the attitudes and behaviors of others in order to meet shared group goals and needs."[1] This definition acknowledges that communication is the central, essential activity of leading and implies three things. First, leadership is accomplished through communication—what a group member actually says and does in person-to-person interaction. Leadership involves persuasion and discussion, not psychological coercion or physical force. Second, leadership consists of those behaviors that *help* the group achieve shared goals. A rebel—even a popular one others admire—would not be considered a group leader if the rebellious actions interfered with the group's accomplishment of its goals. Finally, the term *modifies* in the definition suggests that group leaders must be adaptable to the changing conditions of the group. Thus, leadership is a dynamic process of exchange, not a fixed quality. To modify others' behaviors in support of group goals, leaders must be aware of the others' needs, beliefs, and attitudes. Leadership does not exist in a vacuum; it is a shared property of the group that is created through communicative interaction.

## SOURCES OF POWER AND INFLUENCE

Leadership implies **influence,** which is the use of interpersonal power to modify others' actions—a communicative activity. The capability to influence is the central defining characteristic of leadership.[2] Where does this ability to influence others come from? Why do some people have an easy time getting others to work for them, but others do not? Bertram Raven and John French identified five sources of interpersonal power that capture the different kinds of influence between leaders and followers: legitimate, reward, punishment, expert, and referent.[3] Although these five sources of power are the most widely cited, we will also include two other sources of power recognized in theories of leadership: informational and ecological.[4] Table 10.1 summarizes the seven.

A member's title or position confers **legitimate power.** For instance, other members expect their president or chair to call meetings, establish an agenda, and coordinate tasks. Just having the title of "chair," whether the individual was appointed or elected to the position, gives that individual the ability and right to influence the others. TerryAnn did not recognize that she had the legitimate power, as president, to do such things as asking another member to take meeting notes or assigning tasks.

| TABLE 10.1 | **Sources of Power and Influence** |
| --- | --- |

**LEGITIMATE POWER**
Leader is elected or appointed; has a title (chair, coordinator).

**REWARD OR PUNISHMENT**
Leader can give or take away items of value; may be tangible (money, promotion, titles) or intangible (praise, acceptance).

**EXPERT POWER**
Leader has information, knowledge, or skills needed and valued by the group.

**REFERENT POWER**
Leader is admired and respected; other group members try to copy his or her behavior.

**INFORMATION POWER**
Leader has access to information and controls distribution of information.

**ECOLOGICAL POWER**
Leader directs how a task is organized and can alter a group's working physical environment.

**Reward power** comes from someone's ability to give others what they want and value, and **punishment power** comes from the ability to take those things away. Both rewards and punishments can be tangible or intangible. For instance, Sandra rewards her fellow members with praise and encouragement. These intangible items, along with others such as attention and smiling, have great power to influence others. Similarly, frowning, ignoring someone, asking a member to redo an assignment, and so forth are intangible ways of punishing group members. Tangible rewards can include such things as special privileges, monetary bonuses, and promotions. Tangible punishments may include taking away special privileges, giving someone undesirable assignments or work shifts, or even firing a member. **Coercion** is one extreme form of punishment involving threats or force to make a member comply. Such tactics can breed resentment, sabotage, and rebellion. We think coercion is inappropriate to use in small groups.

Another form of power is expertise. An individual with **expert power** is perceived by other members to have knowledge or skill valuable to the group. For instance, Becky's group called her the "PowerPoint Queen" because she could do anything with PowerPoint and had a good eye for design. Members took her advice whenever they had to design a public presentation of any kind. Interestingly, expert power does not guarantee that a member will be the leader of a group. Sometimes, for example, the most analytical member of a group can demonstrate the most influence yet not be recognized by members as the group's leader.[5]

A person with **referent power** is someone others admire and want to be like. Most of us want the people we like to like us back. That desire gives them tremendous power over us.

Since we want them to like us, we will often do what we think they want us to do—even, sometimes, when we know that what they're asking us to do is wrong! In high school one of us belonged to a social group led by a "cool" informal leader with considerable referent power. Members of her group accepted Sue's opinions about a variety of issues: how to dress, whom to date, what school activities to join. One day Sue suggested that the group ditch school for the afternoon. Group members did—much to their dismay when they all got caught!

Two other sources of power extend our understanding of the kind of influence leaders enact in groups.[6] **Information power** involves the degree of control a leader can have over information. This control can involve the actual amount of information a leader has as well as the leader's access to information useful to the group, which can impact the leader's perceived expertise. A leader's control of information can leave her or him as the group's only source of important information, thus increasing members' dependence on the leader. We pointed out in Chapter 5 that sometimes managers resist the adoption of new technology because they do not want others having access to that information. In addition, a leader's distribution of information can greatly influence how others interpret the information. For example, if a leader wants increased support for his or her position, he or she can edit out information that might weaken evidence supporting that position.

Finally, **ecological power** involves a form of indirect influence stemming from the ability to control the organization of work and the physical environment of the group. We often do not recognize that something as simple as being able to arrange a group's working environment can influence member behavior. Recall from Chapter 4 that who sits next to whom, for example, guides who has access to whom in a group. In addition, directing the procedures a group will use to complete its task or influencing the kind of technology the group will use influences members' satisfaction and their relationships to each other. Because TerryAnn did not want to jeopardize her acceptance by others, she was reluctant to take charge by organizing the group's processes. This lack of ecological power then reduced her power in other ways—such as her legitimate power as designated leader.

A group leader's influence usually stems from more than just one of these power sources. Sue, for example, had referent power because she was cool. But she also had power to reward and punish—she could invite you to her next party, or she could punish you by leaving you out. President George W. Bush, too, possesses referent power among his closest circle of advisers, as well as legitimate power, and the ability to reward and punish. Much debate also surrounds his ability to control the information coming out of the White House. This ability to control information would not be so controversial if it were not associated with power—who has it and who does not. As you can guess, the more sources of power within a group, the greater the leader's ability to influence others.

Thus far, we have equated group leadership with the ability to influence others, and we have examined the sources from which that influence may stem. Now we turn our attention to the specific people who exercise influence—the leaders of a group.

## WHAT IS A LEADER?

A **leader** is *any* person who exercises interpersonal influence to help a group attain its goals. That's what makes distributed leadership, discussed in Chapter 1, possible. There are several important implications to this statement. First, this definition of *leader* implies that all individuals in a group can (and should) supply some of the needed leadership services to the group. Second, it does not require that a leader hold a particular title or office. Any member of a group, with or without a title, can at times function as a group's leader. Third, the definition assumes that *communication* is the process through which a person actually leads others. In other words, rather than assuming that leaders are born or must have particular titles, this definition suggests that leaders *perform behaviors* that help a group achieve its goals. We next discuss the two types of leaders found in groups.

**Designated Leader.**  The **designated leader** is the group's legitimate leader who holds a title (e.g., chair, coordinator, moderator, facilitator, president) that identifies him or her as having a specific position in the group. Usually, group members expect the designated leader to perform a variety of coordination functions for the group. For example, Michael Kramer found in his study of a community theater group that members expected their designated leader to provide the directions for completing the task, coordinate other secondary leaders in the group, and provide them with a vision.[7] The designated leader may be elected to the position by group members, or may be appointed by the group's parent organization or supervisor.

**Emergent Leader.**  An **emergent leader** is a person with the same status as other members in a group of peers, but who gradually emerges as an informal leader. Sue, in our earlier example, was an emergent leader—her group didn't elect her to the post, but by virtue of her personality and influence, she emerged as the group's leader. Many of the groups you will belong to will have designated leaders; however, you will also belong to several that do not. Typically, for instance, the groups you are in as part of course assignments do not have designated leaders, so understanding how informal leaders emerge will give you insight into what constitutes effective group leadership.

Studies conducted at the University of Minnesota reveal how informal leaders emerge from an initially leaderless group.[8] Researchers observed college students placed in leaderless task groups and found that, at first, all members initially have the potential to be recognized as leader by the others. However, members who don't speak up or are uninformed are quickly eliminated from consideration. Next to be eliminated are members who, compared to the rest, are overly bossy or dogmatic. Those who remain as potential leaders speak frequently, are well informed on the issues facing the group, and are open-minded, democratic, sensitive, and skilled in expressing ideas for the group. The individual who ultimately emerges as a group's leader is the member who seems able to provide the best blend of task and people skills for that particular group. Especially important is the ability to coordinate the work of other members by communicating effectively with them. Subsequent studies have found that communication relevant to the group's task is the one factor that significantly predicts leadership emergence.[9]

Other behaviors or characteristics related to leadership emergence have been found. They include effective listening,[10] self-monitoring (the ability to pay attention to how others are responding to you and to adjust your own behavior in response),[11] being extraverted and sociable,[12] and intelligence.[13] Although early small group research suggested that men usually emerge as leaders, biological sex now seems irrelevant, although psychological gender is not. Task-oriented women emerge as group leaders as often as task-oriented men. In one study of groups of women, those who emerged as leaders combined intelligence with the personality characteristics of masculinity or androgyny (exhibiting both masculine and feminine characteristics).[14] In mixed-gender groups, regardless of sex, masculine and androgynous members emerged as leaders more often than feminine and undifferentiated members.[15] Groups appear to choose leaders based on performance. Research into gender and leadership shows that men and women lead equally well, and group members are equally satisfied with both male and female leaders.[16]

Although most groups have a designated leader, the process of leadership emergence teaches you two things about being a designated leader. First, emergent leaders influence primarily through referent, expert, reward, informational, and ecological power. Without a title they must rely on communication skills to lead the group. By definition, they have the support of other group members. So, even though you may hold the title of leader (or chair, president, coordinator, and so forth) in your group, it will benefit you to act like the kind of person who would also emerge as the group's leader. Second, the person who emerges as a leader in one group may not emerge as leader in another. Each group's situation is different, requiring a different blend of leader skills. The type of task as well as the personalities and preferences of the members influence what type of leadership is comfortable to a given group. For example, in graduate school one of us participated in a group where all other members were engineers. They were highly task-oriented and impatient with chitchat, which they saw as irrelevant to the task. In contrast, many groups of communication students are sociable and would perceive an exclusively task-focused leader as hostile or uncaring. As leader pay attention to the group's needs so you can adjust your behavior appropriately.

Now that we have talked about leadership and leaders, including how they emerge in a group, we will turn our attention to several misconceptions people have about leadership.

## Informal Leadership in the Group

**APPLY NOW**

Think of a group you belong to that does not have an official leader. Most such groups will have an informal leader. Picture that person as you answer the questions below. When you are finished, divide into groups of five or six, and share your observations with one another. Are there any common characteristics or behaviors that the emergent leaders demonstrate?

1. What are the sources of power that give your informal leader the ability to influence? List as many as apply, and provide specific examples of how your leader used his or her power.

2. If you found yourself in a high-stakes project group with this person (e.g., in a group that had to complete a project for a major portion of a course grade), would this person emerge as leader in that group? Would this person's leadership skills be a good fit for the project group? Why or why not?

3. Are there other individuals in the group who demonstrate leadership skills? If so, who are they? What sources of power do they possess? Provide examples.

# Myths about Leadership

Students usually say that leaders "control the actions of the other members," "give orders," and generally "tell people what to do." In this section we examine several other pervasive myths about leadership.

1. **Leadership is a personality trait that individuals possess in varying degrees.**

   From the time of Plato to the 1950s, the study of leadership consisted of a search for the traits that make people leaders. These traits included intelligence, attractiveness, psychological dominance, group size, and, most recently, communication traits such as communication apprehension, verbal aggressiveness, and ability to argue a position well, or argumentativeness.[17] However, strict trait approaches to studying leadership have several flaws. First, there is no trait or set of traits that leaders have but followers do not. No trait differentiates leaders from members.

   A second flaw in the trait approach is the underlying assumption that all leadership situations call for the same trait or set of traits. Think about this for a moment. Does the leader of a classroom discussion group need the same traits as the leader of a military platoon? Do both situations require the same approach? No single set of traits will identify the best leader for any given group or situation.

   A third flaw in the trait approach relates directly to the concept of *trait* as something innate, the belief that leaders are born, not made. If you aren't born with the characteristics of a leader (whatever those may be), you will not become a leader. Instead, leadership consists of *behaving in ways that can be learned* (at least up to a point). Consider, for a moment, Candy Lightner, the woman who developed MADD (Mothers Against Drunk Driving). Lightner was an ordinary single parent, not a recognized leader, before a drunken driver killed her daughter. Nothing in her previous background or experience could have predicted that she would become the leader of a national organization. But she cared enough to do the hard work of learning to lead. So can you.

2. **There is an ideal leadership style, no matter what the situation.**

   Since the 1950s a number of researchers have examined the behaviors associated with leadership, including the styles displayed by various leaders. Several studies indicated that leaders perform both *task-oriented* and *relationship-oriented* behaviors.[18] Leaders could rate high on either, neither, or both of these dimensions. Many people believed that the ideal style of leadership was one rated high on both task and relationship dimensions, so many organizations instituted training programs to teach their employees how to be simultaneously task- and relationship-oriented.

   Other researchers have examined different kinds of leadership styles, summarized in Table 10.2. First, we will talk about the three most common styles: autocratic (authoritarian), democratic (participatory), and laissez-faire (noninvolved). *Autocratic* leaders are primarily task-oriented people who personally make the decisions for the group and control the group's process. They say things like, "Here's what I've decided we'll do." They alone decide the group's agenda, select procedures the group will follow, and decide who will speak when. Highly authoritarian leaders can stifle group members who are expert, creative, and enthusiastic, but their groups can be very productive.

For more information on analyzing famous leaders, go to the Online Learning Center at **www.mhhe.com/ adamsgalanes7**

| TABLE 10.2 | **Styles of Leadership** |
|---|---|

**AUTOCRATIC LEADERSHIP**
Characterized by decisions made solely by the leader, with little to no consultation with group members and a primary focus on the task but not relationships.

**DEMOCRATIC LEADERSHIP**
Characterized by decisions made by leaders in consultation with group members and a primary focus on both task and social dimensions of the group equally.

**LAISSEZ-FAIRE LEADERSHIP**
Characterized by a passive, hands-off attitude that translates into behavior providing little leadership; requires that others step in and take over if the group is to succeed.

**TRANSACTIONAL LEADERSHIP**
Characterized by the exchange of resources between the leader and followers as a way to influence member behavior.

**TRANSFORMATIONAL LEADERSHIP**
Characterized by a leader's ability to inspire followers to act toward a greater good beyond their own self-interests.

**CHARISMATIC LEADERSHIP**
Characterized by a leader whose power is connected to his or her perceived extraordinary qualities.

*Democratic* leaders want all the group members to participate in decision making, and so are more relationship-oriented than autocratic leaders. They say things like, "What ideas do you have for solving our problem?" Democratic leaders suggest but do not coerce. They try to discover the wishes of the group members and help them achieve their common goals. They encourage members to develop the group's agenda and to determine what procedures the group will use. Discussants can speak freely within the group. When members propose ideas, they are considered to be the property of the group as a whole. Democratic leaders see their function as helping the group accomplish what the members want, as long as it is part of the group's purpose or charge. Members of groups with democratic leaders tend to be more satisfied, to participate more actively in meetings, to demonstrate more commitment to group decisions, and to be more innovative than members of groups with either autocratic or laissez-faire leaders.[19]

*Laissez-faire* "leaders," who consider themselves to be no different from the other members, display a hands-off style that really does not provide much leadership.

They say things like, "Do what you want; it doesn't matter to me." They create a void that forces the other members to step in or flounder without coordination. This is the mistake TerryAnn made, but the others weren't able or willing to step into the void she created. Occasionally, the other members of groups led by laissez-faire leaders blend their efforts to lead the group successfully, but more often such groups end up wasting a lot of time or following the structure provided by an autocratic leader who emerges and takes charge. Only groups of highly motivated experts tend to be more productive and satisfied with laissez-faire leaders than democratic leaders.[20] Kramer's study of the community theater group supported this conclusion.[21] When this group's designated leader failed to lead, both its secondary leaders and other members stepped up to fill the void. Kramer noted, however, that these members were highly motivated and speculated that had they not been motivated from the beginning their production probably would have failed.

Research looking for an ideal leadership style came up with inconsistent findings. While most group members prefer the democratic to the autocratic style, some groups composed of authoritarian members actually prefer the more authoritarian style. Plus, autocratic groups sometimes complete more work than democratic groups. About the only consistent finding was that groups prefer either the democratic or the autocratic style to the laissez-faire style.

A recent review of studies of democratic and autocratic leadership suggests that several factors in combination with leadership style influence a group's productivity.[22] Democratic leadership seems to be more productive when it occurs in natural, real-life settings and when the group's task is a complex one. In addition, member satisfaction with democratic leadership is not guaranteed.

Other leadership styles have also captured the attention of organizational and management researchers.[23] You may have heard, for instance, about transactional, transformational, and charismatic leadership styles. All three of these styles provide a way for people to capture the more emotional and symbolic attributes of leadership in addition to the more common focus on leadership's rational processes. Leaders, after all, are not only a part of group experience; they also influence the meaning given that experience (see, for example, the process of symbolic convergence in Chapter 7). *Transactional leadership* involves a leader's willingness to trade or exchange one resource for another. Political leaders, for example, trade votes for funding of hometown pet projects. *Transformative leadership,* in contrast, involves a higher degree of symbolic behavior in that the leader is able to rally others to buy into and support a common good beyond that of any one person. These leaders are often called visionary leaders who inspire and motivate their followers. Gandhi and Martin Luther King Jr. were associated with this kind of leadership. Closely related and often used interchangeably with transformational leadership is charismatic leadership. While both involve leaders who communicate a vision to followers, *charismatic leadership* is more focused on the leader and his or her extraordinary qualities that move followers to act. Thus, followers are more dependent on charismatic leaders whereas transformative leaders behave in ways to empower their followers and can be found in any group at any level.[24] While discussions of these styles are usually found in management studies, the styles are similar to those studied in small group research in that they involve sets of behaviors relevant to leadership: trading resources, encouraging members to work for something greater than themselves, and reflecting the power of one person's character to move people.

The styles approach oversimplifies the complexities of groups as open systems. For example, consider the following two groups: (1) an advertising agency's creative team, in which the members have worked together successfully for two years, and (2) an outdoor survival group of adolescent boys, strangers to each other, none of whom has ever been camping. Would you recommend the same style of leadership to the coordinator of the creative team and to the adult adviser of the survival group? Everything suggests a democratic approach with the creative team and a more controlling approach with the young boys. Most of us would agree that no one style is right for all situations.

The styles approach also assumes that a particular group will have the same needs over its lifetime. But just as different groups vary in their needs for different leadership services, a single group's needs will change greatly over time as well. Early in a group's history, the more inexperienced members may appreciate a take-charge leader, but as group members become more experienced, they may prefer less control.

Most people today discredit the idea that there is an ideal leadership style no matter what the occasion. Rather, a number of factors, such as how experienced the members are, how long they have been together, how successful they have been in the past, how interesting the job is, and whether there is an impending deadline, all contribute to determining the most appropriate style.

3. **Leaders get other people to do the work for them.**

When some students are elected or appointed to leadership positions, they assume that their job is to tell other people what to do and often seem surprised that it doesn't work. Recently, the president of a campus organization was disgusted that a colleague failed to complete an assignment for the organization. "I told her what to do, and I told her we needed the information for today's meeting," she said. She didn't understand that just telling someone to do something doesn't ensure that it will happen. If you think your position as leader makes your job easier, think again.

# Current Ideas about Leadership

**GLOSSARY**

**Functional Concept**

*The idea that groups need to have certain functions performed, and all group members can and should perform needed functions*

Now that you know that small group leadership isn't a trait, a style, or the act of bossing people around, let's discuss what it *does* involve. Several contemporary ideas about leadership will help you be more effective as a group leader. The ideas we discuss next complement each other.

## THE FUNCTIONAL CONCEPT OF GROUP LEADERSHIP

The **functional concept** of leadership contains two premises. First, this concept assumes that certain important functions must be performed for the group to reach its goals: task-related and people-related functions. Task-related functions, such as initiating discussion or action, offering opinions, making suggestions, and elaborating on other members' ideas, are behaviors directly related to getting the group's job done. People-related functions, such as harmonizing, gatekeeping, and relieving tension, help members work as a team.

Second, the functional concept suggests that performing those functions is the responsibility of *all* the group members, not just the individual designated as the group's leader. One individual cannot give a group everything it needs. We haven't seen anyone with all that knowledge and skills. Also, having only the leader supply everything a group needs deprives the other members of the chance to develop their skills and talents. People want to contribute. Every member of a group needs to know that he or she is valued. When that occurs, members tend to be committed and loyal, and group cohesiveness is high.

For example, one project manager at a Fortune 500 corporation was terrific at motivating and developing her staff. Staff member Tina was a fabulous presenter. Carol could interpret data and incorporate it effectively into the group's reports. Roger was a gifted writer, and Ty was super-organized, with the ability to keep track of where everyone was on a project. Tamika had a quirky sense of humor and could always lighten things up if meetings got tense. These staff members worked as a *team,* with no one member dominating and the leader encouraging them to use all their talents on behalf of the team.

If all members are responsible for providing needed leadership functions, what is your job as a group's leader? In Chapter 1 we suggested that the leader's job is *completing* the group by supplying any needed functions (services) that other members are not providing or at least seeing that someone supplies them.[25] This gives the designated leader a lot to do. The leader must constantly monitor the group's progress, identify what the group needs at any time, decide whether those functions are currently being performed adequately by other members, and, if not, provide them or encourage someone else to do so. For example, when John notices that Rada has not offered an opinion about an important issue, he deliberately asks Rada her opinion. If the group seems confused, John summarizes and clarifies or calls on Kim, the group's recorder, to reorient the group. When he sees the group becoming tense, he may offer a joke or suggest a 10-minute break.

The functional approach requires leaders to diagnose what functions are needed and to supply them. That means you have to be smart, to figure out what is needed, and flexible, to adapt accordingly. But you can call on your fellow members to help you, because this approach assumes that all members can learn a variety of behaviors and can function as leaders in certain circumstances. Kramer's study of the community theater group provides support for this key assumption of the functional approach.[26] Even when the designated leader failed to lead, the other group members were capable of stepping in at various times to supply the needed guidance and attention the group needed to mount a successful production. Group members attended to both task and relational functions; they did so directly by stating what needed to be done and how it could be done and indirectly by starting the task or suggesting what needed to be done and how.

## THE CONTINGENCY CONCEPT OF GROUP LEADERSHIP

Related to the functions approach, the **contingency concept** holds that appropriate leadership behavior depends on the situation. As we noted earlier, it doesn't seem reasonable that the same leadership style should be used for a classroom discussion group as for a platoon during a firefight. TerryAnn's laid-back manner of leading did not work in her particular service club, but with a group of experienced pros, it could have been quite effective. There are several contingency approaches; we will focus on those developed by Paul Hersey and Kenneth Blanchard.

**GLOSSARY**

**Contingency Concept**

*The idea that features of the situation determine appropriate leadership behavior*

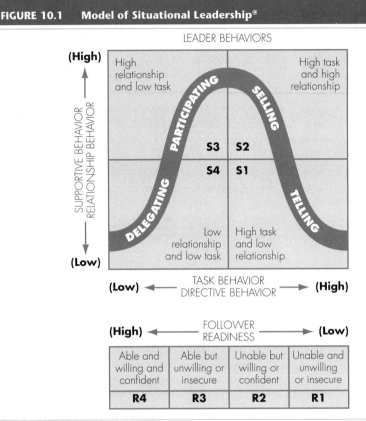

**FIGURE 10.1     Model of Situational Leadership®**

Contingency approaches suggest that leaders should consider several factors before deciding on the specific leadership services appropriate for the group. Among these factors are the type of task, how well the members work together, and how well members work with the leader.[27] A major factor that affects the way a leader should act is the maturity level, or readiness, of the followers.[28] Hersey and Blanchard have provided a model, shown in Figure 10.1, to help match leadership style to the readiness level of the followers. In general, the more experienced, interested, and motivated the members are, the less direction is needed from the leader.

Hersey and Blanchard's model, tempered with your common sense and knowledge of group leadership, helps you know how to adapt. If group members are unable or unwilling or don't have enough information to complete the task on their own, they are low in readiness. *Telling* can be an effective leadership style. The leader needs to give them specific instructions and provide close supervision of their work: "Our goal is to increase sales by 15 percent, and here's what I want you to do . . ." The leader tells the members what, how, and when to do something, and the members have little say in the matter. Telling demonstrates high-task and low-relationship behavior.

With low to moderate readiness, group members are usually willing but do not have the skills or experience necessary to perform well. In this case the leader takes a *selling* approach by providing much of the direction but seeking members' support for this direction: "One of our goals is to increase sales by 15 percent, and I'd really like your input about how we can do that." Two-way communication occurs as the leader encourages members to ask for explanations and additional information. The leader's goal is to promote member enthusiasm while providing the guidance needed to complete the task well. Selling is both high-task and high-relationship oriented.

With members of moderate to high readiness, the leader can pay less attention to the demands of the task and concentrate instead on the relationships among members: "How is the sales campaign going? What can I do to help you?" Here, followers have the skills to perform the job but may feel insecure about taking action or need coordination to work out a set of roles and division of labor. The leader's supportive, democratic style is called *participating* because decision making is shared and the leader's role is mostly one of facilitation and coordination. All members share in leading the group. When members reach this level of readiness, anyone in the group could probably serve as its designated leader.

In a fully ready, mature group, members are both able and willing to perform. They need little task-related supervision or encouragement. In this situation the *delegating* style is appropriate; the leader turns the responsibility for the group over to the group: "Let me know if you need anything." All members (including the leader) are equal in responsibility. This relatively low-task, low-relationship style is appropriate where a more active leadership style might be perceived as interference. However, even when the group is fully ready, the leader must still monitor the changing conditions of the group and be ready to step in to perform additional services the group may need. This was TerryAnn's style, but her followers were not at this level of readiness.

The contingency approach to leadership is highly popular and used widely to train leaders in the military, management, and education.[29] Interestingly, it has received mixed results when tested in research. For instance, there is not conclusive evidence that if leaders follow the guidelines in Hersey and Blanchard's model they will be more effective. However, studies of this model have shown the importance of paying attention to members who are low in readiness and mentoring them into higher levels of maturity. Leaders are warned not to make oversimplified generalizations from the model and force-fit members into categories but to remain flexible and alert to the nuances of interpersonal relationships between themselves and their followers.[30] At minimum, this model reminds us to take the group members' level of readiness and the group's situation into account.

One theme unites the contingency and functional approaches to leadership: Leadership is a property of the *group,* not of the individual who happens to have the title of "leader." This is called **distributed leadership,** which explicitly acknowledges that each group member should perform the communication behaviors needed to move the group toward its goal. Our society's democratic values suggest that participation by everyone is a healthy and desirable goal. John Gastil, making a case for democratic leadership, argues that "democratic group leadership amounts to giving group members responsibility, improving the general abilities and leadership skills of the other members, and assisting the group in its decision-making process."[31] This is precisely what the functional approach to leadership

## GLOSSARY

**Distributed Leadership**

*The idea that each group member can and should provide leadership services to a group*

suggests: All group members are capable of performing the variety of functions a group needs, even though no *one* person is capable of supplying everything. In one study, over-all leadership activity by all members was found to be more related to productivity than activity of the designated leader alone.[32] Distributing the leadership functions is good not only for the members themselves but for the group as well. We talk more about how to encourage distributed leadership later in this chapter.

We have discussed major myths surrounding group leadership, presented current thinking about leadership, and promoted the idea of distributed leadership. It is now time to investigate what members expect from their leaders.

# What Good Leaders Do

A group leader has a lot of work to do, sometimes more than any other member. Recent studies have described what good group leaders do to help their teams succeed.[33]

1. **Good leaders establish the group's goal and make sure the group starts in the right direction.**

   Usually, the goals are put into writing, perhaps as part of a team charter that spells out the charge, area of freedom, and scope of the project. They take the time to ensure that everyone understands and supports the goal, even to the extent of asking a completely unsupportive member to leave the team.

2. **Good leaders mold the group members into a team with a collaborative climate for working together.**

   They take team building seriously and recognize that to accomplish good group work members must trust one another and feel free to contribute. Good leaders constantly monitor the group's interactions to ensure that members are working collaboratively and intervene when they perceive a problem.

3. **Good leaders never lose sight of the group's task and its progress toward completion of that task.**

   That means they keep track at all times of where the group is in relation to its goals. Along with keeping the group moving forward, they are able to paint the "big picture" so that members know what has been accomplished and what still needs to be done. In that regard they manage group members' uncertainty about complex tasks. They manage the group's priorities, in part so the group does not get bogged down in unessential matters. They also manage the individual members' performance by making sure members are contributing appropriately and by working with them as needed if they are not.

4. **Consistent with the leadership approaches discussed earlier, good leaders develop their members' talents by encouraging them to assume leadership responsibilities for the group.**

   That builds members' confidence in themselves and the team. Good leaders also demonstrate appreciation for the work members do on behalf of the team.

5. **Good group leaders do not take their leadership for granted.**

   They work at it, think about it, and consciously try to improve their own leadership skills.

## Which Contingency Style Is Most Appropriate?

You have been asked to conduct a workshop on group leadership for a major corporation in your city. You have selected the contingency approach to leadership as the focus of your workshop. The corporation has asked that your workshop contain several activities to give the participants "hands-on" experience with current thinking about group leadership. You have decided that one of those activities will involve application of the contingency model to several different kinds of groups. Your task now is to construct the activity. To do so, you need the materials to set up the activity and the answers to the activity.

You first will ask the participants to create a matrix that lists the four Hersey and Blanchard leadership styles (participating, selling, delegating, and telling) across the top. Under each style, list the contingencies that make that style appropriate, along with how each contingency is likely to affect the style. Next, you will give participants a list of situations and ask them to determine what style is most appropriate using their matrix. The list of situations includes the following:

- A group of college students studying together for a final exam
- A heart transplant team
- A task force of neighbors trying to rid the neighborhood of crack dealers
- A group of student senators planning the senate agenda for the following month
- A self-managed work group of employees assembling an automobile
- A group of four grown children planning their parents' fiftieth wedding anniversary party

You will ask participants to use their matrix to determine the appropriate style for each of these. To be prepared to direct discussion after the participants have finished this part of the activity, you must first participate in the activity yourself.

**1.** Construct the matrix, as you will ask the participants to do.

**2.** Apply the matrix to the six situations listed.

## WHAT GROUP MEMBERS EXPECT LEADERS TO DO

Group members expect that their leaders will be competent and committed and will work for the good of the group. In particular, most group members in the United States assume that their designated leaders will provide services in three major categories, described briefly in Table 10.3: performing administrative duties, leading group discussions, and developing the group.[34] The behaviors of good leaders presented earlier fall into these

| | |
|---|---|
| **TABLE 10.3** | **Major Duties Leaders Are Expected to Perform** |
| **PERFORMING ADMINISTRATIVE DUTIES** | Planning and preparing for meetings; keeping members informed; following up between meetings; making sure the group keeps complete written records |
| **LEADING GROUP DISCUSSION** | Starting discussions and keeping them on track; encouraging participation; stimulating members' creative and critical thinking |
| **DEVELOPING THE GROUP** | Fostering a productive and supporting climate; developing teamwork, cooperation, and trust |

three categories. The following information can serve as your concise leader's manual whenever you find yourself elected or appointed designated leader of a group.

## PERFORMING ADMINISTRATIVE DUTIES

Leaders should plan for meetings, follow up on members' assignments, and make sure the group's written records are complete. TerryAnn's performance was particularly weak in these areas.

**Planning for Meetings.** As leader you must plan meetings so you don't waste other members' time. Here is a set of guidelines you can follow.

1. **Define the purpose of the meeting and communicate it clearly to the members.**

   Don't have a meeting if there is no reason for it. If a meeting is needed, state the purpose clearly. "To talk about what we're going to do this year" is too vague; "to establish a list of priorities we want to accomplish within the next six months" is clear and specific. Tell the members exactly what outcomes should be produced at the meeting, such as a written report, an oral recommendation, plans for a party, or a decision.

2. **Make sure members know the place, starting time, and closing time for the meeting.**

   Let members know this ahead of time, and stick to those starting and ending times. In addition, state the meeting place exactly. "At the library" is vague and confusing. Some members may go to the lobby while others go to the student lounge. "In room 302 of the library" eliminates confusion.

   Although the leader is responsible for communicating this information to members, this task can be delegated to someone else (e.g., a secretary).

3. **If special resource people are needed at the meeting, advise and prepare them.**

   Groups often need information and advice from specialists. A personnel committee may need the advice of a psychologist or lawyer; a student group may need to consult with the parking services manager before recommending changes in parking policies. Make sure invited guests know what to prepare and what to expect at the meeting.

*"How about some little pads and pencils?"*

It's the leader's responsibility to make sure members have all the supplies they need. © The New Yorker Collection; 1985 Arnie Levin from cartoonbank.com. All Rights Reserved.

4. **Make all necessary physical arrangements.**

   Reserve the room, arrange the seats properly, and bring needed materials (e.g., notepads, pencils, microphones, tape recorders).

**Following Up on Meetings.**   Generally, two kinds of follow-up are needed: reminding group members of assignments, and serving as liaison with other groups.

1. **Keep track of member assignments.**

   The leader must make sure that members know what their assignments are and when they are due. Keep written records of assignments, perhaps as part of the group's regular minutes. Keep in touch with members between meetings by telephone or e-mail to monitor their progress. Had TerryAnn done these things throughout the summer following her initial planning meeting as president, her term might have been memorable for positive rather than negative reasons.

2. **Serve as liaison with other groups.**

   The leader is the group's spokesperson. This means the leader represents the group to other groups and the media, answers questions about the group and its work, and keeps the parent organization informed. For example, the chair of each subcommittee working on the Ozarks Public Television merger with the university, described in Chapter 8, was simultaneously a member of the steering committee overseeing the merger. This made liaison and coordination easy.

**Managing the Group's Written Communication.**    Any group needs written messages to provide continuity from meeting to meeting and to serve as the group's collective memory. We learned in Chapters 7 and 8 that a group without memory loses track of arguments, can get off topic, and may tend toward premature closure on a decision. The management of written communication in a group is a key tool groups can use to archive their work. As leader you may delegate these activities to a secretary or ask for a volunteer, but you are still responsible for making sure they get done.

1. **Send a meeting notice and agenda to each member before each meeting.**

   Meeting notices are reminders of a meeting's date, starting and ending times, location, and purpose. Often, a meeting notice is mailed or e-mailed along with the meeting's **agenda,** the list of items to be discussed at the meeting in chronological order. The agenda helps members prepare for the meeting—nothing wastes time like having a meeting where members have no clue what will be discussed and no ability to prepare. If a meeting involves consideration of something like a special report, that report should be provided along with the agenda. In this age of computers and faxes, it is easy to help members do a good job by giving them all the relevant information they need ahead of time.

2. **Keep personal notes to keep track of what is going on.**

   Taking notes helps you focus your listening so you won't forget what the group is discussing. These should be very brief—just enough to help you keep track of such things as key facts, proposed ideas, major interpretations, assignments you and others have accepted, and anything else important to the discussion.

3. **Keep minutes of each meeting so you will have a record of what you did.**

   **Minutes** are notes of what occurred at each meeting. They are distributed to members after the meeting and are legally required for some groups, such as governmental committees. Even if not required, keeping minutes is a good idea—otherwise, like TerryAnn's group, members forget important information and neglect to complete assignments. Minutes contain summary information, not details. Records of important actions should be noted in a group's minutes, including all conclusions, decisions, and assignments. However, because members need to express themselves freely, some things should *not* be recorded in group minutes. These include such things as confidential and sensitive information, as well as who proposed a course of action, how anyone voted (unless that is required by law), or who provided what information. Minutes can be presented in a variety of formats, two of which are shown in Figure 10.2.

4. **Keep in a permanent file copies of any reports, resolutions, or recommendations made by a group.**

   As with minutes, these should become part of the group's permanent record. Often a group's end product is a major written report submitted to the parent organization, with a brief oral presentation by the designated leader. The leader is responsible for submitting the report by a particular deadline, but normally one or two members actually write the report. Usually, a draft is given to all members ahead of time for suggestions and revisions, followed by discussion and agreement on the final version. All committee members sign the final report.

**FIGURE 10.2    Examples of Group Minutes Using Two Different Formats**

**Minutes of November 16, 2008, Meeting of Committee A (Version 1)**

Committee A held a special meeting at 1:30 p.m. on Wednesday, November 16, 2008, in room 14 of the Jones Library.

Attendance: Walter Bradley, Marlynn Jones, George Smith, Barbara Trekheld, Michael Williams

Absent: Jantha Calamus, Peter Shiuoka

1. The minutes of the November 6 meeting were approved as distributed.

2. Two nominations for membership in the graduate faculty were considered. A subcommittee of Bradley and Trekheld reported that their investigation indicates that Dr. Robert Jordan met all criteria for membership. It was moved that Professor Jordan be recommended to Dean Bryant for membership in the graduate faculty. The vote was unanimously in favor.

   The nomination of Professor Andrea Long was discussed; it was concluded that she met all criteria, and that the nomination had been processed properly. It was moved that Professor Long be recommended for appointment to the graduate faculty. The motion passed unanimously.

3. Encouragement of grant activity. Discussion next centered on the question of how to encourage more faculty members to submit proposals for funding grants. Several ideas were discussed. It was moved that we recommend to President Yardley that

   *a.* A policy be established to grant reduced teaching loads to all professional faculty who submit two or more grant proposals in a semester.

   *b.* Ten percent of all grant overhead be returned to the department that obtained the grant for use in any appropriate way.

This motion was approved unanimously.

*(continued)*

**FIGURE 10.2** *Continued*

### Minutes of November 16, 2008, Meeting of Committee A (Version 2)

Attendance: Walter Bradley, Marlynn Jones, George Smith, Barbara Trekheld, Michael Williams (chair)

Members absent: Jantha Calamus, Peter Shiuoka

| Topic | Discussion | Actions/recommendations |
|-------|-----------|------------------------|
| Minutes of 11/16/08 | None | Approved as distributed |
| Nominations for graduate faculty membership | Subcommittee of Bradley and Trekheld reported that both Dr. Robert Jordan and Dr. Andrea Long meet all criteria and should be recommended to Dean Bryant for membership. | Recommendation passed unanimously, for Drs. Jordan and Long |
| Grant activity | Discussion centered on how to encourage faculty members to submit proposals for funding grants. After discussion of several proposals, motion was made to recommend to President Yardley that | Motion to submit the two recommendations to Pres. Yardley passed unanimously |
| | 1. Professional faculty who submit two or more grant proposals in a semester be given reduced teaching loads. | |
| | 2. Ten percent of all grant overhead be returned to the department that obtained the grant, to use in any appropriate way. | |

Respectfully submitted,

George Smith, Secretary

Sometimes a group's final product is a resolution of a motion the leader will make during a meeting of the parent organization. In that case members of the group often accompany the leader and are available to answer questions, make supporting speeches, and counter objections. A common format for motions and resolutions can be found in any comprehensive parliamentary manual, such as *Robert's Rules of Order Revised,* if the organization does not have its own manual that must be followed.

## LEADING GROUP DISCUSSIONS

One of your most important duties as designated leader is coordinating discussions so that they are productive. Plan how you will start the meeting, keep the discussion organized, encourage all members to participate, and stimulate both creative and critical thinking. You also should monitor the group so that what is not accomplished at one meeting can be addressed at the next. This was TerryAnn's most crucial failing.

**Initiating Discussions.**    Opening remarks set the stage for the meeting and help members begin to focus on the group's task. Here are guidelines for you to follow.

1. **Help reduce primary tensions, especially with new groups.**

   Members may need to be introduced to each other. Name tags may be needed. An icebreaker or other social activity may be used to help members get to know one another.

2. **Briefly review the purpose of the meeting, the specific outcomes desired, and the area of freedom of the group.**

   Members should have been informed of these before the meeting, but some members may want clarification. Discussing them early helps prevent misunderstandings later. Food helps! It's amazing what coffee and snacks can do to relax people.

3. **Give members informational and organizational handouts.**

   These may include informational sheets, an agenda, outlines to guide the discussion, and copies of things to be discussed.

4. **See that special roles are established as needed.**

   Decide what roles are needed and how they will be handled. Most groups appoint a recorder to keep written records of meetings. Decide whether these positions will be rotated or handled by only one individual.

5. **Suggest procedures to follow.**

   Members should know whether decisions will be made by consensus or majority vote and whether the group will follow the small group procedures recommended by *Robert's Rules of Order Revised* or another group technique. We recommend that you suggest procedures to the group, then ask the members to accept, modify, or suggest alternative procedures. (If bylaws or other laws impose specific procedures on the group, such as on a jury, you won't have this flexibility.)

6. **Ask a clear question to help members focus on the first substantive issue on the agenda.**

   This helps launch the group into the substantive portion of the meeting. You may want to review the examples of discussion questions in Table 4.2. A group leader might open the group's meeting this way: "At this meeting we must decide which

Go to
**www.mhhe.com/
adamsgalanes7**
for additional
weblink activities.

## Group Leaders and the Use of Technology

**MEDIA AND TECHNOLOGY**

This chapter has introduced a number of leadership functions. The leader must facilitate communication before, during, and after meetings; ensure that appropriate materials are provided to group members; and guarantee that a historical record of the meeting, usually in the form of minutes, is kept.

Technology can help group leaders manage information. For example, e-mail can be used to disseminate agendas and other written material before meetings; Web pages can display minutes of previous meetings; and computer networks can store documents and other materials used by the group.

For groups with virtually unlimited access to technology, someone must help coordinate how technology will be used. If you were designing a "wish list" for technology resources for a group you belong to (e.g., a study group, a student group, a work team), what would you want? Your group may already have access to e-mail, for example. How should group members use e-mail? What other technology resources would be useful to your group, and how would you suggest using them?

two of our five job applicants we should interview in person. You all received copies of the résumés prior to the meeting. Unless you'd rather proceed in a different way, I suggest we go in alphabetical order and assess each person's strengths and weaknesses against the criteria we adopted at our last meeting. After we've talked about each one, we can compare them to determine our top two. Does that seem OK? [Wait for feedback.] Fine, then let's look at James Adams's résumé first." Such a statement makes the meeting's goals, procedures, and desired outcomes clear from the beginning.

**Structuring Discussions.**   Once the group members know each other and are oriented to the task, the leader should organize the discussion. Effective leaders help maintain productive relationships among the members, but their primary focus should be on the group's task. This is what most group members expect.[35] That includes constantly monitoring the group's process and making needed adjustments. Following are some suggestions.

1. **Keep the group goal-oriented; watch for digressions and topic changes.**

   Be sure the members understand and accept the goal. A certain amount of digression is normal and desirable because it can foster team spirit. You don't want to stifle every digression, but if a lengthy digression occurs, help bring the group back on track: "We seem to be losing sight of our objective" or "We're getting off track. What we were talking about was . . ." Topic switches are common, so be on constant watch for them. When you notice one, point it out and suggest that the group finish one topic before going on to another: "We're jumping ahead. Let's finish our parking recommendation before we start talking about scholarships." When a change of issue, irrelevant topic, or premature solution crops up, ask if that person would mind waiting until the group has finished its analysis of the current issue or post it on a flip chart—the "parking lot"—for later consideration.

2. **Put the discussion or problem-solving procedure on the board or in a handout.**

   If the group is using a procedure such as brainstorming, help the group remember the steps by summarizing them briefly in writing. This helps keep comments to the point.

3. **Summarize each major step or decision.**

   It is easy for members to lose track of what the group is doing. Before the group proceeds to the next issue or agenda item, help all members keep track by summarizing and asking members for feedback. In many cases a secretary can help summarize. This also helps make a clear transition to the next step in the discussion.

4. **Structure the group's time.**

   Nothing is more frustrating than running out of time before you have a chance to discuss an issue important to you. Since members often get caught up in a discussion, it is up to the leader to keep track of time and remind the group of what still needs to be done and how much time is available.

5. **Bring the discussion to a definite close.**

   Do this no later than the scheduled ending time for the meeting, unless all members agree to extend the time. In your conclusion, include a brief summary of progress the group has made, a review of assignments given, a statement of how reports of the meeting will be distributed to members and others, comments about preparation for the next meeting, commendations for a job well done, and, periodically, your evaluation of the meeting to improve the group's future interactions.

**Equalizing Opportunity to Participate.**    Along with keeping the group's discussion organized, the leader is responsible for seeing to it that everyone has an equal opportunity to speak. This is central to democratic participation discussed earlier in the chapter and to working with diversity (Chapter 6) and problem solving (Chapter 8). You can do several things to produce such equality.

1. **Address your comments to the group rather than to individuals.**

   Unless you are asking someone for specific information or responding directly to what a member has said, speak to the group as a whole. Make eye contact with everyone, especially the less-talkative members. It is natural to pay the most attention to those who talk a lot, but this may further discourage quiet members.

2. **Control dominating or long-winded speakers.**

   Occasionally, a member monopolizes the discussion so much that others give up. This imbalance can destroy a group. The other members expect you to control domineering members and will thank you for it. Here are several techniques to try. First, avoid direct eye contact. Second, sit where you can overlook them naturally when you ask questions of the group. Third, cut in tactfully and say something like, "How do the *rest* of you feel about that point?" Fourth, help the group establish rules about how long someone may speak; then appoint a timekeeper to keep track of members' remarks. Fifth, describe the problem openly to the group, and ask the members to deal with it as a group. Sometimes even more drastic measures are needed, such as talking with the offending individual privately or even asking the person to leave the group. This is a last resort; use it only when other measures have failed.

3. **Encourage less-talkative members to participate.**

   Quiet members may feel overwhelmed by talkative ones. Encourage less-talkative members: "Roger, finances are your area of expertise. Where do you think the budget could be cut?" or "Maria, you haven't said anything about the proposal. Would you like to share your opinion?" Make a visual survey of members continuously to look for nonverbal signs that a member wants to speak, seems upset, or disagrees with what someone else is saying. Give such members a chance to speak by asking a direct question such as, "Did you want to comment on Navida's suggestion?"

   Other techniques for increasing the participation of quiet members include assigning them to investigate needed information and reporting back to the group or inviting them to contribute with their special areas of knowledge or skill. You might say, "Kim, you're a statistical whiz. Will you take charge of the data analysis for the project?" Listen with real interest to what an infrequent participant says and encourage others to do so as well. Nothing kills participation faster than the other members' apparent lack of interest.

4. **Avoid commenting after each member's remark.**

   Some discussion leaders comment after each person has spoken. Eventually, members start waiting for the leader to comment, which inhibits the free flow of conversation. Listen, speak when you are really needed, but as a rule don't repeat or interpret what others say.

5. **Bounce questions of interpretation back to the group.**

   Some groups blindly follow the designated leader's opinions. (See Chapters 5 and 9 for more on groupthink.) Especially in a new group, hold back until others have had a chance to express their views. Then offer yours only as another point of view to be considered. If a member asks, "What do you think we should do?" you can reply, "Let's see what everyone else thinks first. What do the rest of you think about . . . ?"

6. **Remain neutral during arguments.**

   If you are heavily involved in an argument, you will have a harder time being objective, encouraging others to participate, and seeing that each point of view is represented. If you stay neutral, you can legitimately serve as a mediator for resolving disputes. Of course, feel free to support decisions as they emerge and encourage critical thinking by all members.

**Stimulating Creative Thinking.**    Many problem-solving groups create mediocre solutions. Sometimes inventive solutions are needed. Chapter 7 discussed the importance of creative thinking. Here we elaborate further on how to encourage group creativity.

1. **Suggest discussion techniques that are designed to tap a group's creativity.**

   Several techniques, such as brainstorming, synectics, and mind mapping, are designed especially to help a group create inventive solutions. Many techniques employ deferred judgment—the group postpones evaluation until all possible solutions are presented. When people know their ideas will not be judged, they feel freer to suggest wild and crazy ideas, many of which may turn out to be useful.

2. **When the flow of ideas has dried up, encourage the group to search for a few more alternatives.**

   Often the best ideas appear late in a period of creative brainstorming. You might use these idea-spurring questions: "What else can we think of to . . . ?" or "I wonder if we can think of any more possible ways to . . . ?" In addition, you can take a break and return to the activity later (see Chapter 7).

3. **Discuss the components of a problem one at a time.**

   For instance, ask, "Is there any way to improve the appearance of . . . ?" or ". . . the durability of . . . ?"

4. **Watch for suggestions that open up new areas of thinking and then pose a general question about them.**

   For example, if someone suggests putting up signs in the library that show the cost of losses to the users, you might capitalize on that idea by asking, "How else could we publicize the cost of losses to the library?"

5. **Force an alternative perspective or switch senses.**

   For example, if you're trying to find a new way to remove plaque from blood vessels, pretend you are a microbe traveling along the bloodstream, getting a microscopic view of clogged arteries. Or if your problem is visual ("How can we create an eye-catching graphic for the new store?"), think in sound ("What would an attention-getting ad for the new store *sound* like?")

**Stimulating Critical Thinking.**    Chapter 7 also covered critical thinking in detail. We remind you here of your responsibility as leader for ensuring that group members carefully evaluate the decisions they make. Here are specific suggestions.

1. **Encourage group members to evaluate information and reasoning.**

   Ask questions to make sure the group evaluates the source of evidence ("Where did that information come from?" "How well respected is Dr. Gray in the field?"), the relevance of the evidence ("How does that apply to our problem?"), the accuracy of the information ("Is that information consistent with other information about the issue?" "Why does this information contradict what others have said?"), and the reasoning ("Are the conclusions logical and based on the information presented?"). Bring in outside experts to challenge the views of the group or to help evaluate information.

2. **See that all group members understand and accept the standards, criteria, or assumptions used in making judgments.**

   Fair, unbiased judgments are based on criteria that are clear to all members. You might ask, "Is that criterion clear to us all?" "Is this something we want to insist on?" or "Do we all accept this as an assumption?" Criteria were discussed in Chapter 8.

3. **See that all proposed solutions are tested thoroughly before they are accepted as final group decisions.**

   Make sure that group members discuss tentative solutions with relevant outsiders, that pros and cons of each solution have been evaluated, and that members have

## Red Ribbon Committee and Sober Graduation

The Red Ribbon Committee is a community group in California's Central Valley. The committee develops, plans, and presents several community events each year that promote a sober and drug-free lifestyle. Each year the committee debates whether the sober graduation party should last all night or end at 2 or 3 A.M. Students, noting that their parents would not approve of an all-night event, have said they'd be willing to go even if it was not all night. Lupe (a 50-year-old Hispanic woman with strong community ties) and Tracy (a divorced Caucasian woman in her late 40s who is quite vocal about how things should be done) argue that it should end early because the students and chaperones get too tired. In addition, they note that the majority of problems usually happen after 2 A.M. They suggest that the main goal of sober graduation is to get as many students as possible to attend, and that means guaranteeing their safety. The other four members of the group (a Caucasian female and former school board member, a wealthy female Portuguese dairy owner who is feared in the community, a Portuguese man who is very active in the community, and a young Caucasian man employed by the school district) argue that the goal is to ensure the kids are safe *all* night. Traditionally, they add, these events have been all-night affairs. Lupe and Tracy have become increasingly adamant; they want the others to try their idea at least once to see how it would work.

You are the leader of this group. At this point, how would you stimulate creative and critical thinking in this group?

1.  Offer suggestions, relevant to this committee, about how members can stimulate creative thinking?

2.  Offer ways the group can critically examine the suggestions generated by creative thinking?

had a chance to play devil's advocate in challenging proposals. For a major problem, propose holding a second-chance meeting, where all doubts, concerns, or untested assumptions can be explored.

4. **Establish a devil's advocate individual or competing subgroups to poke holes in potential solutions.**

Assigning one or more group members the role of devil's advocate, described in Chapter 7, encourages group members to spot flaws in an argument or problems with a solution. Establishing two subgroups in friendly competition with one another can be a fun way to think critically. Ask each group to find as many problems as possible with the options the group is considering. Whichever group "wins" gets treated to dinner or drinks. This forces the group to consider deficiencies in possible solutions, but does so in an entertaining way.

**Fostering Meeting-to-Meeting Improvement.** Effective group leaders spend time evaluating each meeting to discover how it could have been improved. Ask the group itself to participate in evaluation. Usually, you will privately review your notes to determine whether the major meeting goals were met and how smoothly the meeting went. Then, establish your goals for improving future meetings and adjust your own behavior accordingly to meet the group's goals.

Several studies of effective leaders have shown that good leaders adjust their behavior from one meeting to the next, depending on the specific goals of the meeting. Good leaders monitor their own and the other members' behaviors so they can modify their actions to help the group.

1. **Review personal notes of the meeting.**

   Keep personal notes of important happenings during the meeting. After the meeting, ask yourself, Did we accomplish our purpose? Did everyone have a chance to participate? Did anyone hog the floor? Was the group both creative and critical in its thinking? and, most importantly of all, What could I personally have done to ensure a better meeting?

2. **Decide how the meeting could have been improved.**

   The answers to the previous questions will guide you. For example, if Sonya believes that the group jumped on an early solution without carefully assessing the problem just to get the meeting over with, she might decide that the group needs to look at the problem again. If TerryAnn had evaluated her meetings, she would have discovered that the group needed more direction and guidance than she was providing.

3. **Establish specific improvements as goals for the next meeting.**

   After determining where the meeting could have been improved, incorporate this information into planning for the next meeting. Sonya, for example, could place the problem back on the agenda, explain to the group that she perceived a lack of critical thinking, and invite the group to assess the problem again.

4. **Adjust behavior accordingly.**

   Once you, as leader, have diagnosed areas of group communication where improvement could occur and have decided what needs to be done, you should adjust your behavior to help ensure improvement. For example, TerryAnn needed to be more clear, direct, and concise in her communication. She also needed to keep the group on track instead of letting them digress. Notice that these are *communication* behaviors (not personality characteristics) that TerryAnn should change.

We now consider specific areas in which the designated small group leader can help group members develop, a topic we explored in detail in Chapter 5.

## DEVELOPING THE GROUP

One of the most important functions of the leader is to assist in the group's development from a collection of individuals to a productive unit. This involves such things as establishing a climate of trust, promoting teamwork and cooperation, and evaluating the group's progress.

**Establishing a Climate of Trust.**   Groups perform more effectively when members trust one another. The following suggestions help establish a climate of trust.

1. **Establish norms that build trust.**

   Norms building trust encourage respectful active listening, cooperation, confidentiality, timely completion of assignments, and the freedom to disagree without being considered deviant. Many leaders are far too slow to speak to members who are manipulative, do poor work, or act out of self-interest harmful to the group.[36]

2. **Function as a coordinator rather than a dictator.**

Foster a climate of trust by serving the needs of the group, not by ordering people around to serve your personal interests. That way, members feel free to express themselves and to develop skills needed by the group. Ask for volunteers to do jobs for the group rather than ordering: "Cal, could you please get the . . ."

3. **Encourage members to get to know each other.**

Usually, members trust each other and feel safe in the group if they know one another as individuals. Sometimes an unstructured social period helps create a sense of teamwork. Graduate teaching assistants in one department have a tradition of planning a float trip at the beginning of each fall semester. Social gatherings like this help people get to know each other.

### Developing Teamwork and Promoting Cooperation.

Although the leader's principal responsibility is to see that the group accomplishes its task, the development of teamwork can help group members work productively. Here are suggestions you can use.

1. **Speak of *us* and *we,* rather than *I* and *you.***

Calling the group members *we* implies commitment to the group and its values. Ask what it means if another member speaks of the group as "you."

2. **Develop a name or another symbol of group identification.**

Such items as T-shirts, logos, "inside" jokes, and slogans can display shared identification. For example, a successful advertising agency creative group called itself the "Can-Do Team."

3. **Watch for evidence of hidden agenda items that conflict with group goals.**

If you suspect a hidden agenda item is interfering with the group's agenda, promptly bring it to the attention of the group. Ignoring such problems makes them worse, not better.

4. **Use appropriate conflict management approaches and procedures.**

Conflict that is allowed to proceed too long or to become personal can cause lasting damage. Help prevent this by keeping arguments focused on facts and issues and by immediately stopping members who attack another's personality or character. Look for a broader goal that can bring together two or more competing subgroups, one that is more important to members than their individual subgroup goals and behind which they can rally.

Sometimes, despite the best intentions of the leader, a group becomes deadlocked. If this happens, look for a basis on which to compromise. Maybe you can synthesize parts of one person's ideas with parts of another's to create a compromise or consensus solution. Perhaps you can serve as mediator. If you have been performing your job well as the group's leader, you have remained detached from the fray. This gives you a broader perspective from which to see a solution all parties can accept. It also helps your credibility—you'll be seen as fairer and more objective. We discussed conflict in detail in Chapter 9.

## Marcos and His Fraternity

Marcos was appointed chair of the service committee of his college fraternity. He and Luis were the only experienced members on the committee; the other three members were new to the fraternity. His committee was responsible for organizing the fraternity's service projects and recruiting frat members to participate. The inexperienced members were excited about working on the committee, but they were not aware of all the fraternity's activities, procedures, and past efforts. Marcos faced a challenge. He did not want to stifle the enthusiasm, dominate the group, or do most of the work for the group. On the other hand, he did not want to lose valuable time while the new members felt their way along. He preferred working on a committee where all members could contribute equally, but he believed that, at least at first, these members weren't ready to contribute fully—they needed strong direction.

He and Luis worked together between the committee meetings to establish an agenda and select some of the early goals and service activities for the committee. During these meetings Marcos kept close control over the agenda and the discussion. He assigned specific tasks, always making sure the tasks were acceptable to members. He also encouraged newer members to contribute to the group until they could speak on their own. As he recognized that the newer members were becoming capable of acting on their own, he began to encourage them to take over more planning and decision-making responsibilities. He eventually became less involved in the details of committee work, focusing more on the process of discussion and decision making during meetings. He moved from functioning as a director to functioning as a coordinator.

Marcos recently heard about TerryAnn's problems with her service club from a disgruntled committee member. Concerned that he may not be as effective as he thinks he is, he comes to you, a buddy, for advice. He knows you are taking a small group communication course.

1. What are his strengths, and what may be his weaknesses?
2. Given the information Marcos has provided and the material you have read about performing administrative duties, leading group discussions, developing the group, and managing the group's written communication, devise a list of specific questions you think are important to ask if you want to get a good handle on Marcos's situation.

5. **Share rewards with the group.**

Leaders often receive praise from the group's parent organization, but wise leaders give credit to the group. Your comments about what *the group* has done, your pride in membership, and your acknowledgment of the service provided by members foster cohesiveness and team spirit.

6. **Have fun; share a laugh or joke with the group.**

Don't let the discussion get so serious that people can't enjoy themselves. Humor and fantasy help reduce tensions and make people feel good about each other. Most groups take mental "work breaks" in which they digress from the task. Wise leaders let the group develop fantasy chains that enrich the group's life and that help establish shared beliefs and values. The result can be more concerted work effort in the long run. Bring the group back to the task once the joke is over or the fantasy has chained out.

As you can see, any group's designated leader is expected to perform a variety of duties associated with the title *leader*. Far from being the person who orders others around, the leader serves the group by making sure it has what it needs.

# Encouraging Distributed Leadership

We have encouraged you to think about group leadership in a way that may be different from how you've thought about it in the past. We suggested that you as leader encourage other group members to assume responsibility for leading the group. Distributing the leadership in this way helps you, in the long run, by using all members' abilities and talents to the fullest. It helps the other members develop leadership skills and also makes a wider scope of abilities available to serve the group.

## The Great Leader

**APPLY NOW**

The following quote is attributed to Chinese philosopher Lao Tse:
*The wicked leader is he whom the people despise.*

*The good leader is he whom the people revere.*

*The great leader is he about whom the people say, "We did it ourselves."*

What do you understand this quote to mean? How can a leader lead and still have people say, "We did it ourselves"?

SOURCE: Quote from Peter M. Serge, "The Leader's New Work: Building Learning Organizations," *Sloan Management Review* Reprint Series 32 (Fall 1990), p. 22.

At first, our support of distributed leadership with a democratic focus may seem to contradict our earlier support of the contingency concept of leadership. We see distributed leadership as being an ideal to strive for, but it requires a certain maturity and self-confidence on the part of members. That takes time to develop, as Marcos recognized. You can't assume, as TerryAnn did, that members are fully ready to take over and run the group! In the community theater group Kramer studied, the members were ready to take over.[37] But until members achieve this level of skill and maturity, you'll need to be astute in supplying just the right amount of direction, particularly as members try to grapple with the initial ambiguity that typically faces a newly formed group. Another lesson from

Kramer's study is that this ideal of shared leadership does not resemble equal distribution at all times. Instead, who is doing what for the group shifts, and over time a sense of "sharedness" and "equity" emerges—the key is balance and distribution.

As you can see, to be an effective leader in a variety of situations, you must perceive what is happening with the individual members and the group as a whole, and adapt your behavior accordingly. Being perceptive requires listening ability, knowledge of group processes and procedures, and analytical ability. Adapting your behavior requires mastering a variety of leader skills.

We think distributed leadership is the ideal. Most groups you belong to will have a designated leader, and we are not suggesting doing away with designated leaders. We *are* saying that, even if a group has a designated leader, the other members have capabilities that should be developed and used in service to the group. You may not be able to reach the ideal right away; you may never even see a group that has achieved that ideal. However, distributed leadership is the best way of ensuring that everybody's talents are used.

This section contains several suggestions for effectively leading a group where leadership is distributed. These suggestions do not ask you to change your personality. Instead, they ask you to focus on your *communication behavior* and adapt it appropriately.

1.  **Be perceptive; analyze the needs of the group.**

    Effective leaders understand people. They know how to help others motivate themselves to contribute their best.[38] In part they do this by listening carefully— actively—to what is going on in the group. For example, if group members appear confused, you know that the group should spend some time clarifying the discussion. Consider the following dialogue:

    | | |
    |---|---|
    | **Jerry:** | Yeah, we've got to finish everything Monday night, the charts and all, with the easel, and get the stuff to Maryann. Our presentation on Tuesday should be pretty good. |
    | **Maryann:** | [Becoming agitated and visibly upset] That's not going to give me nearly enough time to type them! I have to have them by Friday at the latest! How can you expect me to type the charts, fix the table of contents, copy the paper, and have it ready to turn in by Tuesday if I don't get the stuff before Monday night? |
    | **Sheri:** | [Trying to calm Maryann but also somewhat annoyed at her tone of voice] Lighten up, Maryann. It won't take that long—we've only got two charts to do, and I can help you. |
    | **Terrell:** | [The group's coordinator, sensing this argument stems from a misunderstanding] Hold on, guys. I think we're talking about two different sets of charts. If I remember right, we promised we'd get the data tables that are supposed to go into our written report to Maryann by Friday so she can type them over the weekend. But I thought Sheri and I were supposed to make the two chart posters for our class presentation on Monday night. Isn't that what we decided? |

    Here, Terrell senses that the argument is over a misunderstanding and attempts to clarify it for the group. Notice that he states his clarification ("If I remember right" and "Isn't that what we decided?") provisionally, so others can disagree or improve on his understanding if he has been mistaken. Terrell can perform this function for the group only because he has been paying attention and listening actively.

2. **Adapt your behavior to fit the needs of the group; be a completer.**

   Groups need different things at different times. In addition to being able to analyze your group's needs, you must be able to adapt your behavior to perform a variety of functions, but it doesn't make sense to perform functions that others are already performing well. In the previous example, if Sheri had clarified Maryann's and Jerry's misunderstanding, there would have been no reason for Terrell to do so. Terrell jumped in because clarification was needed and no one else was providing it. He served as a completer by "plugging in the holes" for the others.

3. **Focus primarily on task needs rather than social relationships.**

   The person most likely to emerge as a leader is a task-oriented individual who clearly helps the group achieve its goal. This doesn't mean you should never tend to relationship issues, but it does mean that you should always keep one eye on the task. This helps you make the best use of the members' time and provide the appropriate amount of coordination and structure for your group.

4. **Balance your active participation with good listening.**

   Emergent leaders are active group participants; your fellow members expect you to take an interest and contribute. However, balance your talking with good listening so you don't dominate the group. Don't feel you have to comment on everything. Let the discussion flow freely without overcontrolling it.

5. **Express yourself clearly and concisely.**

   When you do talk, get to the heart of the matter being discussed, clarify, and summarize what is being said. Don't ramble; be well organized, coherent, and relevant. The ability to verbalize the group's goals, procedures, ideas, values, and ideals is an important leadership skill.

6. **Be knowledgeable about group processes and group techniques.**

   This point may seem obvious, but many designated group leaders are clueless about how to lead a group. Too often, a committee head is appointed without anyone checking that the individual has had adequate training to perform well. Like TerryAnn you may be willing to do the job, but if you don't know what you are doing, you can make a shambles of what could have been a productive group. To be effective, know what to expect, what your skills are, and what your group needs.

You also should be familiar with a variety of small group techniques, including computer-based group support systems, and suggest them when appropriate. Using GSS successfully depends on several factors, such as whether the group has good facilitative leadership with a leader sensitive to group dynamics.[39] Sometimes members can become caught up with the "bells and whistles" of GSS and lose sight of its purpose. Effective group leaders use these computer programs wisely and help members overcome their anxiety or lack of interest in computer technology.

# Ethical Guidelines for Group Leaders

We pointed out earlier that the essence of leadership is interpersonal influence and power. The issue most germane to leadership is not power itself but how that power is used and the ethics of leadership. Michael Hackman and Craig Johnson suggest that leaders be held to the highest possible ethical standards.[40] We refer once again to the National Communication Association's Credo for Ethical Communication, introduced in Chapter 1, for the following guidelines to help you maintain the highest ethical standards as a group leader.

1. **Do not lie or intentionally send deceptive or harmful messages.**

   Not only should leaders tell the members the truth, but they also should hold truth to be the standard for the group's decision making. That means, for instance, that you should welcome all relevant information in the group, whether it supports your preference or not. It also means that you must be willing to subject your ideas to the same standards of evaluation as the others' ideas.

2. **Place your concern for the group and for others ahead of your own personal gain.**

   In addition to willingly committing your time and energy to serving the group, never take advantage of your power as leader for personal gain or advantage. Leaders' hidden agendas are as counterproductive to the group as members' hidden agendas are.

3. **Be respectful of and sensitive to the other members.**

   Groups are effective problem solvers because several heads are better than one, but only if the members feel free to share their thoughts and ideas within the group. Never do anything intentionally to ridicule members or their ideas or to discourage their participation.

4. **Stand behind the other members when they carry out policies and actions approved by the leader and the group.**

   Don't try to enhance your own position by betraying your fellow members. If something goes wrong with a decision the group has made, assume personal responsibility for the decision.

5. **Treat members with equal respect, regardless of sex, ethnicity, or social background.**

   Respond to members without regard to their sex, ethnicity, social background, age, or other personal or social attributes. Members should be valued for their contributions to the group, not their sex or race. As an ethical leader, minimize status differences to encourage everyone's participation.

6. **Establish clear policies that all group members are expected to follow.**

   Group rules and procedures should be clearly understood. Group members should be encouraged to participate in establishing the group's procedures and policies.

7. **Follow the group rules, just as you expect the others to do.**

   Because of your status as the group leader, you may be given some leeway to violate rules others are expected to follow. Do not abuse this privilege. If others are expected to arrive on time, so should you. If you reprimand members for failing to complete assignments, make sure your own assignments are completed well and on time. As much as possible, be a model member for the group.

As Lao Tse said: "The great leader is he about whom the people say, 'We did it ourselves.'" Will you be that kind of leader?

## Your Needs or the Team's Needs?

**ETHICAL DILEMMA**

In 1971, after the *Swann* v. *Charlotte-Mecklenburg Board of Education* decision that permitted busing to achieve racial integration, schools were required to become integrated immediately.* In Alexandria, Virginia, the previously all-white high school was closed, and students were absorbed into the previously all-black school. Bob Yardley, who had been the winning, successful head football coach of the all-white school, expected to be named head football coach of the integrated school. However, Horace Bond, a young African American coach new to the community, was offered the position. At first reluctant to accept the offer, Bond was encouraged by town leaders; he eventually accepted. Bond considered for a long time what he might do to bring his black and white players together—particularly when neither set of students wanted to be brought together! He offered an assistant coaching position to Bob Yardley.

If you were Bob Yardley, what would you do? You think you should have had the head coaching spot, and it's not fair that you didn't get the offer. But you also think that achieving racial integration is a positive step, and you want to help the school achieve it. You have several choices.

1. You could accept, refuse, accept and try to sabotage Coach Bond's efforts, and so forth. List at least five options in this situation.

2. Assume you decided to accept Coach Bond's offer. What would be your communication behavior toward him? Respectful? Disdainful? How would you show your feelings through your communication behavior?

3. You truly believe the top spot should have been yours, but assume that you've decided you want to make a positive contribution here. What would you do? How would you behave toward Bond and the players?

4. How would you describe the ethical dilemma you face and on what basis would you make your ethical decision?

*This story is used with permission of Robin Swanson. Names of the schools and individuals have been changed. The actual outcome was positive—the coaches found a way to work together, the players were forced to operate as a team (although they initially resisted), and the team won the regional championship in an undefeated season.

**RESOURCES FOR REVIEW AND DISCUSSION**

**SUMMARY**

- Leadership consists of using communication to modify others' behaviors to meet group goals; a leader is anyone who exerts influence to help a group. Designated leaders are appointed or elected, whereas emergent leaders surface naturally from within a group of peers.

- Leaders derive their ability to influence others from seven sources of power: reward, punishment, legitimate, expert, referent, informational, and ecological. The more sources of power a leader has, the greater is that leader's ability to influence the other group members.

- Three common myths about leadership are that leaders have special traits that followers don't, that there is an ideal leadership style, and that leaders get other people to do all the work for them.

- The functional approach to leadership encourages all group members to perform whatever functions a group needs. The contingency approach assumes that the type of leadership a group needs depends on the group's situation.

- Both approaches suggest that the leader serve as a completer, supplying whatever necessary functions the other members are not providing.

- Group members expect leaders to perform four broad types of tasks: providing administrative services for a group, structuring a group's discussions, helping a group develop as a team, and managing a group's written messages.

- Distributed leadership, in which each member takes responsibility for providing leadership services to a group, is an ideal worth striving for.

- Ethical leaders tell the truth, are sensitive to and respectful of others, support the other members, establish clear rules that they expect to follow themselves, and put group concerns ahead of their own personal gain.

**EXERCISES**

1. View Part 1 ("Leadership") of the video *Communicating Effectively in Small Groups,* and discuss the following questions:

   *a.* What functions did the leader perform?

   *b.* How effective was each function? How appropriate?

   *c.* Were there any points during the discussion where the leader failed to supply needed leadership service? Did anyone else step in to provide it? Was the group hurt?

   *d.* On a scale of 1 to 10, how effective was the leader? Why do you say this?

2. Select five members from your class to act as a problem-solving group. Assign one of the members to be the leader of the group. Ask the group to tackle the following problem:

   **The Teacher's Dilemma**
   *An English teacher in a consolidated, rural school has had extensive dramatic experience. She was chosen by the principal to direct the first play in the new school. The play will be the first major production for the school. Its success may determine whether there will be any future plays produced at the school, and if well done, it could bring prestige to both the teacher and the school. As a result, the teacher is exhausting every means available to her to make the play an artistic success. She has chosen all the cast except for the leading female part. The principal's daughter wants the part, and the principal told the teacher he*

*really wants his daughter to have it. But she is a poor actress and would jeopardize the success of the show. Tentatively, the teacher has chosen someone who should do an excellent job in the role, but the principal has implied that if his daughter is not selected, he will appoint another director in the future. What should she do?*

Place the group of five in the middle of the class and surround it with the rest of the class members. They are to watch this group's discussion and to evaluate the leader on his or her ability to lead the group discussion. How well did he or she do? On what do you base your evaluation?

3. Form small groups of four to six members. Discuss the "ideal" group leader. Each group is

to address not only the specific duties leaders should perform but also the communicative skills leaders should exhibit and the ethical principles they should both exhibit and uphold. Each group should create a "Guidelines for Group Leaders" manual that could be distributed to student leaders at your school. Discuss each group's guidelines to determine which ones tend to be common to all groups. Why do you think these tend to be the most common?

 Go to **www.mhhe.com/adamsgalanes7** and **www.mhhe.com/groups** for self-quizzes and weblinks.

**KEY TERMS * CONCEPTS**

| | | |
|---|---|---|
| Agenda | Emergent Leader | Leadership |
| Coercion | Expert Power | Legitimate Power |
| Contingency Concept | Functional Concept | Minutes |
| Designated Leader | Influence | Punishment Power |
| Distributed Leadership | Information Power | Referent Power |
| Ecological Power | Leader | Reward Power |

 **www.mhhe.com/adamsgalanes7**

Use the flashcards and crossword puzzles on the Online Learning Center to further your knowledge of these key terms.

## PART FIVE

# Small Group Public Presentations

Just as it is important to figure out the leadership roles and who will perform them, a group must also assess its strengths and difficulties when it comes to oral presentations. Up to now, we have discussed the complex nature of small group interactions as they occur within group meetings. The successful development of small group interaction helps ensure a more professional and successful oral presentation by individuals and group members. In Part Five, we discuss a three-step process to prepare your group's oral presentation, by focusing on the planning, organizing, and presenting stages of these presentations.

# 11

# Planning, Organizing, and Presenting Small Group Oral Presentations

## CHAPTER OUTLINE

The Planning Stage

The Organizing Stage

The Presenting Stage

What Makes a Good Oral Presentation?

## CHAPTER OBJECTIVES

**After reading this chapter you should be able to:**

1. Explain the different choices group members can make in the planning, organizing, and presenting stages.

2. Compare and contrast the three types of public discussions.

3. Discuss the role of the moderator in any type of public discussion.

4. Explain the essential parts of the introduction, the body, and the conclusion of an oral presentation.

5. Compare and contrast the four methods of presenting a speech.

6. Describe and apply relevant criteria to evaluate an oral presentation.

## Food for the Homeless

Six students in a small group communication class spent more than half the semester discussing the problems faced by a local homeless shelter. One especially significant problem they noted was the great reduction in contributions, especially of food, during the summer. The shelter seemed to get more than enough donations during the fall and winter holiday seasons, when everyone seemed to be in a giving mood, but contributions dropped significantly during the summer months. As part of the solution section of their report, the students recommended a way of getting more edible leftovers from local restaurants to the shelter, a program they had discovered already in operation in a few other communities across the nation.

The students' report earned them an A. Their instructor was so impressed that he showed the report to a close friend, the president of the local restaurant association. She, too, thought the students were on to something and invited them to make a 15-minute presentation about their project at the association's monthly meeting. The students were excited that their work might become something more than a classroom exercise and that they might be able to help the homeless shelter, but they did not know how they should respond to this invitation. Should they let their chair represent them? Should they all go and each say a few words? Should they let their most talkative member make the presentation or the one who seemed to be the best critical thinker? The meeting was coming quickly, and they did not know what to do.

We spend so much time focusing on the work that group members engage in while problem solving that we can forget many problem-solving groups are not finished when they select a solution to their problem. Many groups, even those who can implement their solutions, are asked and even required to orally present their group work to others. Now the group must turn its attention to figuring out how to best create and deliver an oral presentation under specified conditions.

# The Planning Stage

The moment your group is informed that a presentation will be needed, you should schedule a planning meeting to work through key details. Planning to speak to an audience requires advance assessment of the upcoming speaking situation. Practicing engineers, for instance, report that while oral presentations are a key part of their jobs, often the time and effort they spend preparing for these presentations is more important to and demanding on them than the actual presentation.[1] The most important areas of assessment include your group's audience, occasion, purpose, topic, member strengths/difficulties, and supplemental logistics. This initial assessment, as well as plenty of preparation, is essential for a smooth production. In this section we look at each area of assessment and describe different types of oral presentations that groups often deliver.

## YOUR AUDIENCE

Assessing your audience is important for creating a comfortable speaking environment, not only for your audience but also for your group. Although we often *think* about our audience when giving presentations, too often we do not carefully figure out who this group of listeners is to us.[2] **Audience analysis** is a systematic approach to gathering as much information as possible about the audience for the purpose of tailoring your presentation to the information you uncover in that analysis.[3] Audience members listen to material presented to them through their *own* perspectives, not those of the person presenting the material. This is why it is so important to gather information systematically about the people hearing what you have to say. In professional contexts such as engineering, for instance, the ability to communicate main ideas in a multitude of ways is critical.[4] Engineers speak to audiences that can include clients, engineers like themselves, staff members, and federal and local agencies—all with varying technological competence. Engineers thus need at least "a dozen ways to state and clarify any individual idea or piece of technical information."[5]

How might these perspectives affect how audience members listen to your group presentation? Let's explore audience attitudes toward topics.[6] If you know that your audience is not familiar with your topic, then you should stay with basic facts and provide background information. If your group's topic is new to the audience, such as material on pollution rates during peak traffic hours, then you should show why listeners should care about the topic and demonstrate how this issue relates to air quality issues they *do* know about. If your audience holds attitudes against your topic, then create a common ground with the audience and relate your group's main points to audience perspectives. For example, suppose your group believes it is necessary to use marijuana for medical purposes; however, you know your audience is against drug use. Show how your group and the audience care about health care for loved ones, and then relate your main points to the audience's beliefs about health care for those they love. If your audience is strongly against your group's main points, then consider altering your positions or make sure you build a sound case for your points. All these recommendations are grounded in *knowing* your audience.

You can find out information about your audience in a variety of ways.[7] If you want targeted information about a particular audience, interview them or conduct a survey. This is easy if your audience will be members of your class. Interviews can be composed of open-ended questions and closed-ended questions. We offer examples of these kinds of questions in Chapter 7. You can also answer your questions by giving your audience a written survey. If you want only general information about your audience, you can access published polls, which can give you information about attitudes on current topics. For example, the Roper Center for Public Opinion holds the largest collection of polls and surveys in the United States (www.ropercenter.uconn.edu). A variety of demographic statistics about the United States can be found on the U.S. Census Bureau's website (www.census.gov).

Once you are aware of *who* your audience is, you can determine the knowledge they may or may not have about the topic you are considering for discussion. As a group you should answer specific questions about your audience. Will you be speaking only to your class, or will your instructor be part of the audience? Will it be the entire membership of your fraternity or just the executive committee? Will it be people you know, or will most of them be strangers? Will the audience members be there voluntarily, or is someone forcing them to attend? The mood of your audience can depend on whether your audience feels required to be there.

A captive or required audience member is going to need a presentation with lots of enthusiasm and reasons why they should listen. What can you add to their knowledge of or attitude toward your topic? You do not want to bore an audience by repeating what they already know, nor do you want to talk over their heads about complex issues. Don't hesitate to ask if you can observe, interview, or survey your audience before the speaking engagement. Remember, for more opportunities of audience inclusion, find out as much as possible about the audience before you start writing your presentation.

## YOUR OCCASION

Depending on who has invited your group to speak, you may be able to get much of your information about the audience and the occasion from this lead contact person. Ask if you can visit the facility and room you will be speaking in before the event occurs; also check and recheck the time of the event, as well as the major purpose and context. How many people are expected? Where will you be placed in the speaking lineup, and how much control do you have over your setting? Before your group begins serious purpose and topic planning, make sure you clarify why you have been asked to speak to this audience and whether there is a specific goal that needs to be met. If you are preparing for a classroom presentation of your small group project, you already know the time and place for your presentation. Clarify with your instructor the purpose and requirements of the presentation and how you can use the room for the presentation.

## YOUR PURPOSE

Typically, a speaker wants to have a general purpose of informing, persuading, or entertaining an audience. Knowing what you are trying to accomplish is an essential step in any effective presentation. If your group is unaware of the purpose of your presentation, how can the audience members make sense of what they are supposed to do with the information you present? The **informative speech** is used when your group wants to educate, enlighten, or inform. For example, if your group is reporting on a new community service group that has just moved into the area, and you are offering information that describes who they are, where they come from, and what they offer, your purpose is to

## GLOSSARY

**Informative Speech**

*A speech given with the primary purpose of teaching something to an audience*

inform. If your group wanted the audience to donate time or money to this community service organization, your purpose would be to persuade.

A **persuasive speech** is defined by the call to action. Your purpose, as a group, is to get your audience to do something with the information you have given them. Another example of a persuasive purpose would be trying to influence your fraternity or sorority to try a new fund-raising technique. You want your audience members to agree with you and adopt your suggestion(s).

On occasion you may be asked to give an **entertainment speech,** such as to wrap up the year's events or "roast" a colleague at the annual company picnic. You want the audience members to enjoy themselves, to laugh and have a good time. Sometimes it is hard to get an audience to warm up to jokes and different types of humor, so be prepared if you do not get the response you want. Also, be aware that most jokes are directed at or said at the expense of others, so be very careful that your humor is appropriate and tasteful, and does not turn off audience members. What is funny on Comedy Central may not be appropriate for your audience. You're speaking to make a connection with your audience, not to alienate them.

Although your purpose may be to entertain, this speech could easily inform or persuade as well. We have heard speeches on many serious issues that were delivered in a thoughtful and entertaining manner.

## YOUR SUBJECT OR TOPIC

As soon as you determine the general purpose, establish a specific subject or topic of your presentation. Your instructor or employer often will tell you what to talk about, but sometimes, the choice of a specific topic will be left up to you. This step is often one of the most difficult. Where do you start? The best topics come from your own experiences, beliefs, or skills. As a group, sit down and brainstorm different topic ideas from your own individual experiences. What are your interests and hobbies? What subjects do you enjoy, read about, and find interesting? Often you are selected to speak because of some expertise you possess. You can also ask whoever asked you to speak which of several topics the audience would find most appealing.

Undoubtedly, there will be a time limit for your presentation. You may have 5 minutes or 20, or you may be told simply to "be brief" or to "fill us in." Keep your time limit in mind when selecting what to say about your subject. Inexperienced speakers often make the mistake of coming to the podium with enough material for two or three speeches. As a result the audience gets restless or your instructor tells you to stop so that others in the class have time to speak. Don't try to cover everything you know about a subject; select those matters that are most important to you and of special interest to your audience.

## MEMBER STRENGTHS AND FEARS

Knowing the strengths and fears that your members may have with oral presentations will help in the organizing and presenting stages. What information does each individual group member have about the topic that has been chosen for discussion? What contacts or research leads do you have as a group? What is the attitude of the group toward the topic? After assessing the strengths of group members, deciding who will present different points will be easier. Also, if a question-and-answer period will follow your presentation, knowing members' strengths will help in determining who is best qualified to answer the specific questions that are asked.

In addition to looking at the strengths of 45 members, the group should focus on member difficulties in making oral presentations. Anxiety can prevent members from having a confident and effective delivery. If your group does an early assessment of this communication apprehension, it will be easier to combat the problem. A group must not rely on the stereotype that "any leader can lead an effective oral presentation." Anxiety is normal and may be experienced in different ways. Just because your group leader or president has no problem speaking to *your* group as a whole doesn't mean she or he will be comfortable speaking to a group that may be larger or unknown to the speaker. Knowing a member's difficulty with public speaking will allow your group to organize different presenting strategies that take the focus off of one person. This knowledge will also be a helpful reminder that your group should practice the delivery to ease tensions.

## SUPPLEMENTAL LOGISTICS

Near the end of your planning stage, your group should be more knowledgeable about what you need. Will you need supplies to set up your speaking environment? Are you using a visual aid? What will you need to run this visual aid properly (e.g., TV, DVD player, laptop computer, projector, audio player, slide machine)? Speakers often forget a simple item, such as tape, and end up worrying about the poster that will not stand up straight instead of focusing on the words that are just as important as the visual aid. Do not expect a member of your audience, your teacher, or a contact person to provide you with these items. It is your responsibility to remember these essential supplemental tools for your presentation. It never hurts to be overprepared. A good rule of thumb is to be prepared enough to give your group presentation without any audio and visual aids should something go wrong. Remember, these tools only supplement your presentation; they do not take the place of your presentation.

Take, for example, the community service story discussed earlier. If your group hasn't gone the extra mile to find pamphlets, booklets, handouts, buttons, balloons, fact sheets, or other items that this homeless shelter has for distribution, then you may be missing out on updated information. Many organizations would be happy to have a volunteer group inform others about their needs and services, and your presentation would look that much more professional because you obtained original, from-the-source information about your topic.

## TYPES OF GROUP ORAL PRESENTATIONS

Once you have completed your presentation assessment, you must decide which presentation format best fits the purpose and occasion of your presentation. These formats allow for differing viewpoints to be expressed and are often followed by comments and questions from the audience. The three most common group presentation formats are the panel discussion, symposium, and forum (see Table 11.1).

**Panel Discussion.** A **panel discussion** is a public interaction between a small number of people, often selected because of their knowledge of a topic and usually holding conflicting viewpoints. The purpose of a panel is to make the audience more aware of a significant topic or to persuade them to act in a certain way (e.g., vote for a specific issue or candidate). For example, your group may be asked by your instructor to serve as a panel and explain your semester project and conclusions to the rest of your class.

> **GLOSSARY**
>
> **Panel Discussion**
>
> *One of three kinds of group public discussions, in which panel members often bring different points of view to the discussion*

| TABLE 11.1 | **Types of Group Presentations** | |
|---|---|---|
| **Panel: Conversation among Experts** | **Symposium: Individual Uninterrupted Presentations** | **Forum: Questions and Comments from Audience** |
| Topics outlined in advance | Different aspects of topic discussed by panelists | Different viewpoints encouraged |
| Controversy encouraged | No interaction among panelists | Questions directed at individuals or at entire group |
| Moderator acts as traffic cop | Moderator introduces topic and panelists | Moderator selects audience participants |

The procedure to follow for a panel discussion includes the following:

1. Select a **moderator** to maintain order, see that all the major issues are covered, and ensure that everyone gets to speak. The moderator introduces the members of the panel and keeps the discussion moving by calling on speakers as necessary. The moderator acts as a conversational traffic cop, directing questions to the appropriate panelists and clarifying issues and statements as necessary. The moderator also makes appropriate opening and closing remarks and directs any subsequent audience participation.

2. Before the discussion, make an outline of all the important points the group wants to cover, and decide in what order to cover them. Follow this outline closely during the panel discussion. What might this outline look like? Often your presentation outline mirrors whatever problem-solving agenda your group used to arrive at a solution for your problem—if that was your task. For instance, if you used the procedural model of problem solving (P-MOPS), detailed in Chapter 8, then your presentation agenda would look like the outlines found in Tables 8.5 and 8.6.

3. Make appropriate physical arrangements:

    a. Seat panelists so they can see each other and make eye contact with the audience; a semicircle is appropriate.

    b. Seat panelists at a table or desk so it is easy for them to write notes.

    c. Identify panelists with a name card on the table in front of them or their names on a blackboard behind them. The audience can then address questions to specific panelists easily.

    d. If the discussion is to be held in a large auditorium, place microphones on the table for the panelists to share. If audience participation will follow, strategically locate at least one standup microphone in the auditorium.

    e. Make provisions for panelists to present visual aids. Provide an easel or chalkboard that is easy to reach and will not block the view of the audience or panel.

## GLOSSARY

**Moderator**

*A participant in a public group presentation whose main responsibility is to regulate the discussion and guide any audience participation*

4.  Recognize that the panelists should not hesitate to disagree with each other, but should do so politely. Even when they are not talking, the audience can see them, so they should refrain from inappropriate nonverbal communication. Remember that just because you might not be speaking at the moment, you are still an active part of the presentation and should look as if you are attentive to the event.

**Symposium.**  A **symposium** is much more structured than a panel discussion. Instead of a relatively free interchange of ideas, the topic is divided into segments, and each discussant presents an uninterrupted speech on a portion of the topic. The purpose of a symposium is similar to that of a panel: to enlighten an audience on a subject of importance. For example, on September 11, 2001, after the horrific attacks on the World Trade Center in New York City, Governor George Pataki and Mayor Rudy Giuliani and other New York dignitaries presented a news conference to disseminate information to the public. After these attacks New York and the rest of the world wanted and needed information in a quick, controlled manner. This symposium allowed each presenter to deliver information in an uninterrupted format. Most symposiums are usually followed by a forum, which allows the audience to question the panelists and permits the discussants to answer these questions and comment on each other's presentations. In the New York City press conference, reporters asked questions after the concluding remarks, leaving time for each member to comment from his or her own expertise. For example, Mayor Giuliani provided information from a city perspective, working hard to unite his community and dispense information, while Governor Pataki expressed what the state could be providing and how he was working with the president and other authorities to keep things running smoothly. Procedures for a symposium are as follows:

1.  Select a moderator to introduce the speakers, introduce the topic, and make concluding remarks.
2.  Select a small group of experts to present different aspects of the issue. Because each individual presentation is uninterrupted, make sure there will not be much repetition among the speakers. Pay particular attention to how you will transition between speakers so that the overall presentation is coherent.
3.  As with the panel presentation, make appropriate physical arrangements. In a class group presentation, this means knowing what in the classroom can be moved, how the room can best be arranged, and where the group will be placed relevant to the audience. Do not wait for others, including your instructor, to make these physical arrangements for you. Take the initiative, and be ready to set up the classroom when it is your turn to speak.

**Forum Discussion.**  A **forum discussion** allows members of an audience for a speech, symposium, panel discussion, debate, or other public presentation an opportunity to comment on what they have heard and to ask questions of the speakers. All sides of the question should be given an equal amount of presentation time, and no speaker should be allowed to monopolize the floor. The moderator's role is crucial. Some suggestions for the moderator are:

1.  Let audience members know that a forum will follow the panel or symposium so they can prepare their questions or comments.

---

**GLOSSARY**

**Symposium**

*One of three kinds of group public discussions, in which participants deliver uninterrupted speeches on a selected topic*

**Forum Discussion**

*Structured audience participation after a speech, symposium, panel, or debate*

2. Make sure everyone understands any special rules of the forum segment. How will audience members be recognized? They might raise their hands or step forward to an audience microphone. Will speakers from the audience be allowed to ask a follow-up question? Will someone who has not spoken have preference over someone who has already spoken? If there is a time limit for questions, make sure it is announced and followed.

3. Make sure everyone knows when the forum will end, and do not accept questions once that time has been reached. Offer a warning before the last question or two.

4. Try to ensure that a diversity of views is offered. Ask for comments opposed to those that have just been expressed. On a very controversial issue, the moderator might deliberately alternate between a spokesperson from one side and the other.

5. Make sure everyone can hear questions or comments. If necessary, repeat them for the audience.

6. Following the last question or comment, offer a brief summary and thank everyone for their participation.

### What Type of Group Presentation Should the Group Make to the Restaurant Association?

**APPLY NOW**

Form groups of about six people, and discuss how you feel about making oral presentations. Next, pretend that you are the members of the discussion group described in Case 11.1, and decide how you would respond to the invitation from the restaurant association.

1. Would you prefer to work together and put on a panel or a symposium? If so, whom would you select to be the moderator? Why?

2. Would you prefer to send a single representative? If so, which of you would you send? Why?

3. Compare your group's answers to these questions with those of the other groups in your class. How do you account for differences and similarities?

# The Organizing Stage

The success of the organizing stage depends on how well group members interact and listen to one another. If the group allows one person to take the lead, expecting that this person will plan and organize the presentation, many problems will arise. Not only will only one person know what is going to be discussed, but also resentment on both sides may arise. As with every other stage, it is important to have every member present during the organizing stage. In this section on organization, we focus on the importance of delegating member duties, we explain different types of verbal and visual materials that the group can use, and we provide a speaker's blueprint for organizing these materials and the presentation.

## DELEGATING DUTIES

Although the delegation of duties may sound like a function of the leader, this is not always the case. After assessing the strengths and fears of each member, it is important to determine what each member feels most comfortable with and where his or her presentation strengths lie. If you don't speak up at this crucial time of organizing, you might be stuck with a job that you don't know how to perform or have no desire to do. When presenting on specific areas, examine the different backgrounds and experiences of your members, and analyze where their strengths lie. Think about the different majors in a college classroom. If these students had to build a presentation about the parking problem on their campus, which areas of the presentation would be best delegated to whom? For example, math majors could demonstrate, with the use of numbers, car/space ratios, or funding issues. History majors could give background to this ongoing problem. An art major would be our first choice when deciding on visual aids, and communication majors might have the duty of surveying students and administration on solutions to this problem.

Knowing each group member's responsibilities will help when you plan speaking duties and each member's order in the presentation. After you are aware of who is speaking when and about what, you will want to discuss who will obtain verbal and visual aid materials. Who will be required to set up the TV/VCR, turn the lights off during the slide show, or set up a meeting with an outside agency? Each duty is extremely important to the success of the group and its presentation and should be planned *before* the day of the event.

## GATHERING VERBAL AND VISUAL MATERIALS

**Verbal Materials.**   Once your group is aware of each member's duties, you can now conduct much more focused research on each person's item for discussion. Often speakers will try to approach the audience with only the information they know, without obtaining supporting material. Listed are three of the most important types of verbal supporting materials: examples, statistics, and statements by authorities, or testimony.

- **Examples:** Aristotle said that examples become "witnesses and a witness is everywhere persuasive."[8] Examples are used in inductive reasoning, where a generalization is drawn from a number of specific instances. Examples can range from detailed factual ones (the story of a rape victim, complete with dialogue, names, and dates), to undeveloped factual examples (a listing of the countries in the world where war is presently occurring), to hypothetical ones (how much a dollar will be worth in 10 years given a certain rate of inflation). You should choose typical examples and offer enough to make your point believable.

- **Statistics:** Statistics are numbers or quantification used to explain or support your position. Audience members can be easily confused by statistics, so make your statistics clear and meaningful. For instance, it is hard to imagine how large a country is if the speaker tells us only that it is 200,000 square miles in area. More helpful is a comparison: about the size of California and Oregon combined. To emphasize how large the state budget in California was in 2000 ($61.53 billion), point out that to spend that much, the state had to spend $168.5 million a day, $7 million per hour, or $19,511 per second.

- **Testimony:** Some people are recognized as authorities on certain issues. To support your position, you may want to quote directly or paraphrase what these authorities have said or written about your topic. Obtain this from library research or interviews or over the Internet. The group mentioned in Case 11.1 got useful materials from interviewing the director of the homeless shelter and from newspaper articles about similar shelters across the country.

Three common types of testimony are lay, expert, and celebrity. *Lay testimony* is a statement taken from an ordinary individual. Information that is reported by a person who has special training or knowledge about the topic is *expert testimony.* A person who is famous would offer *celebrity testimony.* Let's imagine that your group has decided to give an informative presentation on tips for a long-lasting, happy marriage. Who might you interview for lay, expert, and celebrity testimony? Think about the problems that might arise if you chose testimony from someone who is known too well by the audience. For example, picking Britney Spears as your celebrity testimony might cause problems. Although Britney Spears might offer interesting tips for your presentation, the public knowledge of her divorce might taint her message.

The bottom line when assessing verbal supporting material is to be aware of the attitudes that your audience might have toward your research—who or what is seen as more credible?

**Visual Materials.**    Look also for visual materials to keep the audience's interest. Keep in mind what successful attorneys know: A visual aid helps your audience remember your main points. Most lawyers know that juries pay closer attention, understand technical points better, and remember more when oral testimony is coupled with a visual prop. Many will never forget the images of Johnnie Cochran slipping on the leather glove while repeating, "If it doesn't fit, you must acquit" in the courtroom while he was defending O.J. Simpson, on trial for murder. If visual images were not important, we would not have an obsession with television. Imagine listening to your news, sports, and favorite television programming only on the radio.

Now that you have a better understanding of the importance of these images, here are a number of possibilities that can enhance your presentation.

- **Object:** If what you are speaking about is small enough, bring it with you. A small animal is a very effective prop if your talk is about birth control for pets or overcrowding at animal shelters. If your subject is too large or noisy to bring with you, use a model or picture instead.

- **Model:** A plastic model of the object can allow the audience to see what you are talking about when the real object is too large. The space shuttle will be unable to land on your campus, but a model can easily be displayed on a small table in the front of the classroom.

- **Picture or video:** A photograph, slide, or videotape can focus the audience's attention on your topic. To show the problem of traffic congestion in your city, for instance, take a video of rush hour on a busy street. Slide shows need to be planned and rehearsed well in advance of the performance. Your group does not want to be known as the group with the upside-down slides.

- **Map:** Most Americans' knowledge of geography is weak. Don't assume that just because you know where a city is, everyone in your audience will, too. Give them a map of the place itself, and show it in relation to other familiar points of interest.

- **Transparency:** Putting an outline of your presentation on an overhead projector allows the audience to see your main points and relieves you of having to use the chalkboard. Make sure the projector is centered with your screen, and reveal only part of the outline at a time to keep the listeners focused on what you are saying and not looking ahead to what comes next. If too much information is given, in the form of an outline, audience members will wonder why you are reading to them and quickly get bored. Never put every detail of your speech on the outline; include only the main points so the audience has a map to follow.

- **Chart:** Charts are especially useful for showing statistics. Numbers are sometimes hard to grasp in a speech, especially when there are a lot of them. Make it easy for your listeners by putting the figures on a chart. If you are going to compare statistics, consider making a pie chart to demonstrate percentages, a bar graph to exhibit comparisons, and/or a line graph to illustrate increases and decreases.

- **Handout:** Many items mentioned earlier can be put on a handout and given to the audience before the presentation begins. If you distribute an outline, leave some blanks so listeners can take notes and stay involved with your presentation. Don't forget to look into free handouts that might be provided by local organizations or businesses.

- **Chalkboard:** Use the board only to illustrate something you are saying at the same time. For example, if you use an unfamiliar technical term, write it on the board. But audiences should not have to watch you make a chart on the board of the increase in automobile accidents over the past 30 years. Make a chart of this the night before, and have it ready to go when you get to that part of your speech.

- **Multimedia:** Presentation software, such as Microsoft PowerPoint or Adobe Persuasion, can make your presentation polished and professional. You can program everything from charts and slides to video clips with sound for presentation in your speech. You can even create a link to the Internet that the audience can view on your screen. You will need access to a television monitor, a computer-projection table, or an LCD panel that can be placed on a regular overhead projector.

There are a number of do's and don'ts to keep in mind when using visual aids. First, personally make sure that any equipment you are using is in operating order before the presentation. Be prepared to give the speech even if your equipment fails. Second, make sure the visual is large enough for those in the back of the room to see easily. A Polaroid snapshot may picture exactly what you want to show, but unless it is blown up, even the front row may have difficulty seeing it. In addition, hold your visual up or tape it up long enough for everyone to see. Otherwise, someone looking away momentarily may miss it. Third, practice with the visual. Know exactly when you are going to use it in your speech. Students have been known to prepare visual aids and then, in their nervousness and excitement, forget to show their hard work. Fourth, don't pass anything around during your presentation. Your audience's attention will be on the object itself or on the person handing the material to them rather than on you. Pass something out before you begin, or tell your listeners that they will receive it after you have concluded. Fifth, use a visual aid only if it pertains to your speech. Although visual aids can make a great contribution to your presentation, this same visual aid will seem "thrown in" or "in the way" if it has no relationship to the topic.

Go to
**www.mhhe.com/
adamsgalanes7**
for additional
weblink activities.

**MEDIA AND TECHNOLOGY**

## Using Presentation Technology

The availability and simplicity of presentational software such as Power-Point have increased audience expectations for the use of professionally created visuals to aid in understanding presentation content. Despite the pervasiveness of this type of technology, many public speaking professionals question whether multimedia visual aids help or hinder speakers. Thus, practitioners recommend using the following guidelines when using PowerPoint:

1. **Don't let technology dictate content.** Determine the most appropriate content, and then begin to think about how you can use the presentation software to enhance how the material is conveyed to your audience.

2. **Ensure that special effects have a purpose.** Although they may be fun to include (and show off your knowledge of the software), they distract from your content.

3. **Keep wording clear and simple.** Abbreviate your message by outlining thoughts that provide a memory trigger for you and the audience. Use a consistent font size and style with a combination of upper- and lowercase lettering.

4. **Keep a consistent design.** Use color sparingly, with backgrounds that allow your text to stand out. A slide is of little use if the audience can't read the material.

Consult the following sources for more information on what to do and what to avoid with PowerPoint presentations:

**www.anandnartrajan.com/FAQs/powerpoint.html** and
**www.crocker.k12.mo.us/tech/pptrules.html**

## ORGANIZING MATERIALS AND THE PRESENTATION

The verbal and visual information you have gathered will be a valuable asset as you plan the organization and writing of your presentation. Look at this step of organizing your materials as drawing a road map of how the audience should follow your speech. As with any road map, directions must be clear, so the audience can understand how and why you are taking them through your chosen topic. Every speech should have an introduction, a body, and a conclusion, with major transitions between major ideas. Earlier we pointed out that presentation outlines often follow the problem-solving agenda used by the group to arrive at a solution to their problem question. Again you can refer to Tables 8.5 and 8.6 to get an idea of how to organize your oral presentation. Plan to get the audience's attention, explain what you are going to be talking about, talk about it, and then summarize what you have said.

**Introduction.**    An **introduction** has three essential elements: an attention step, a need step, and a thesis statement. First, your goal is to motivate your audience to listen. This is called the *attention step,* and you can choose from a number of ways to capture an audience's attention.

1. **Use humor.**

   One way of getting audience members to listen to you is to make them laugh. However, be careful if you use this approach. First, what you say must be funny to others, not just to you. Preview the joke or story to other people before you use it in your presentation. If your friends enjoy it, chances are your audience will, too. The humor also must be in good taste. You do not want to offend anyone. You want favorable attention, with people wanting to listen to you. Don't risk alienating anyone by telling a story that is going to offend. Finally, your humor should be relevant to your topic or to the audience and occasion. Something that David Letterman said the night before may be humorous, but if it is not related to what you want to talk about, find something more appropriate and relevant.

2. **Ask a question.**

   A second way of getting attention is by asking the members of the audience a question. If you are going to talk about parking problems on your campus, ask, "How many of you have been late to a class because you could not find a close place to park?" or "How many of you have gotten a parking ticket from the campus gestapo this semester?" If you want an answer, tell them how to respond: "Please raise your hand." However, don't make your question so personal that you won't get an accurate response. "How many of you use cocaine on a regular basis?" will probably get a laugh, but no hands will go up. Finally, use the information as a transition into the topic of your speech: "That's what I thought. Too many of us are spending too much money on parking tickets when the university should be building more parking structures." You must be able to use any answer as a transition. If no one raised a hand, say something like, "Well, you guys are lucky. In my research I've found too many of us spending . . ."

   A rhetorical question is a question that the speaker asks but does not want the audience to answer aloud. The speaker will answer the question as part of the speech: "Is there any way to stop college students from binge drinking? I think there is, and today I am going to offer you three practical solutions to what seems to be a growing problem at our school and at other colleges across the country." The audience will think about the question, but the speaker will provide the answer.

3. **Make a striking statement.**

   Say something at the start of your speech to grab the audience's attention and make them want to listen. Saying, "I can guarantee you an A in this course and in every other course you take this semester" will probably gain the attention of every student in your class. Likewise, "Our division has been wasting at least $50,000 a year for the past three years" will gain the attention of your employer. You have to be able to carry out your promise in the rest of your speech, but you can be sure that for the first few minutes, at least, people will be listening to you. Another good example of a striking statement is the tagline used by news programs or talk shows

**GLOSSARY**

**Introduction**

*The first of three components of a speech, designed to catch the attention of the audience, show a need to listen, and clarify the main point of the speech*

to get you to stay tuned to an upcoming segment. This statement should make your audience feel like they want and need to listen to what your group has to say during the presentation.

4. **Offer a striking quotation.**

Giving a vivid quotation can attract attention. For example, if your group has been doing research on date rape, quoting a victim's own words about how she felt during the attack will attract attention to your topic. Reading a quotation from a song or a poem is another way of attracting favorable attention. Quoting someone familiar and well liked or someone saying something unexpected or out of character can gain attention. For example, a student giving a presentation on myths in student academic performance began this way: "I've heard it said that 'a theory is a thing of beauty, until it gets run over by a fact.' Nowhere is this more true than in the field of education." Although the quote does not directly relate to education, the speaker makes the connection for the audience while grabbing their attention with vivid imagery.

5. **Tell a short story.**

People are interested in other people. Telling a story related to your topic is a great way to gain attention. The story can be true or fictional, but it must help you make your point. If a character in the story is someone audience members can relate to, so much the better.

The second essential part of an introduction is the *need step.* Follow your attention step with a short statement that shows audience members why they need or can benefit from the information you are about to give them. A direct purpose statement shows audience members how the presentation is relevant to their lives and how they can directly benefit by listening. If you are talking about a new medical discovery, tell the audience that your information could help save a life. If your topic is the outrageous prices at the college bookstore, tell them you can save them money. An indirect need step implies that, because the topic is so significant, everyone should know something about it: "What happens to Social Security will affect all of us no matter how young or old we are today."

The third element of a good introduction is the *thesis statement* and *preview.* Here you tell the audience what specifically you will be talking about. Like a road map, it shows your listeners where you are going, making it easier for them to follow along. Use enumeration (i.e., words like *first, second,* and *third*) so listeners know how many main points you will cover. A completed introduction will gain the audience's attention, establish the need to listen, and demonstrate the purpose and main points of your speech.

**Body.**    The **body** of the speech is the main portion of the presentation, in which you actually talk about the ideas you want to cover. Present your ideas in an easily recognized pattern so your audience can see the relationship among them. If your group's task was to solve a problem, then the body of your oral presentation contains the most important information from your problem-solving agenda (see Chapter 8), used during your group discussions and perhaps in your final written report. Remember to use transition statements that help move your speech smoothly from one point to the next. The following are some of the most common patterns of organization.

- **Problem-solution:** The problem-solution pattern is especially important if you are trying to persuade your audience to accept your recommendation. You state the

*"The main body of this Inaugural Address is great, but he wants a happier ending."*

problem, discuss its causes and significance, and then present your proposal as a solution for the problem. This pattern is also easy to use if you want to inform, such as by showing how a problem has already been solved. "How New York City dealt with the devastating loss of the World Trade Center" could be discussed using this pattern.

- **Chronological:** A chronological order is a discussion of things as they happen in time. Talking about how something is made, explaining a historical event, or listing the steps one needs to follow when searching for a job naturally calls for a chronological order. The history of your sorority or the development of the motion picture industry likewise calls for chronological order.

- **Spatial:** A spatial order is used to describe things as they exist in space. A presentation describing the best areas to ski in California could go from north to south within the state or from east to west.

- **Cause and effect or effect to cause:** Explaining how a particular virus affects millions of people is an example of cause and effect organization. You describe how the virus was discovered and how it works and then discuss the suffering of the people who have contracted it. You can also reverse the process by first talking about the people who are suffering and then describing why this situation exists.

- **Topical:** A topical organization examines the inherent parts of a topic, its essential components. For instance, our American system of government is made up of the executive, legislative, and judicial branches. To cover the entire topic, you have to mention all three parts.

You may discover that pairing some of the organizational styles works more efficiently. No organization style is the best, but using some type of systematic approach is essential to the development of your main purpose and ideas. A stream of consciousness is not considered a typical pattern. Members of the audience may not think along the same lines you do. Instead of presenting a topic in exactly the same way the ideas came to you, you are better off choosing a pattern with which audience members are likely to be familiar.

**Conclusion.**   If your purpose was to inform, your **conclusion** should be a summary of the main points you want the audience to remember. What do you hope listeners retain after they leave the room, even if they forget everything else? That should be in your conclusion. Your conclusion is similar to your introduction, but your final summary should be more concrete. Remind the audience of the specific items you covered and, while summarizing your position, explain what you want them to remember.

If your purpose is to persuade, this is your last chance to get the audience emotionally involved in your topic. Use this opportunity to reconnect with your audience, offer a challenge, or help them to see how things could change for better or worse if action is or is not taken.

# The Presenting Stage

Surveys show that many Americans fear public speaking more than they fear spiders, snakes, or even death.[9] You may be in a group communication class because you were trying to avoid "the dreaded speech." However, as a group member, you may be faced with this feared endeavor. Many times in your career you may need to speak to a committee or larger audience, so it is wise to work through this fear of making an oral presentation now. We offer advice for checking your language, practicing your speech out loud, and, finally, evaluating your speech or the speeches of others.

## CHECKING YOUR LANGUAGE

In the English language we have approximately half a million words to express our ideas. The average college student can recognize 60,000 words and actually uses about 20,000.[10] The more word choices speakers have, the better able they are to make language do their bidding and fulfill their purposes.[11] Speakers often forget that writing the speech is only half the battle; the delivery is just as important. Trying to make your audience feel compelled to listen, participate, and take action requires effective use of language. Speak to your audience in a conversational style, just as if you are giving the speech to friends, and not in a dry monotone or reading manner. Generally, speakers should strive for a style that is clear, vivid, and appropriate.

*Clarity* requires language that is concrete rather than abstract. Note the difference between explaining that last night you saw Tom "coming down the street" and saying you saw him "staggering" or "crawling" or "stumbling" or "skipping down the street." Clarity also requires that you avoid jargon and use words that your audience will understand.

*Vividness* attracts our attention. Using figurative language, repetition, and amplification (supporting details that develop or reinforce an idea) will add vividness to your presentation and make it easier for your audience to pay attention. Try to imagine Martin Luther King's famous "I Have a Dream" speech without repetition or figurative language—part of what made his speech so memorable.

Finally, make sure your language choices are *appropriate* for the audience and the occasion. A formal classroom presentation probably should not be filled with expletives or street language unless they are being used to illustrate something in the speech.

## PRACTICE ALOUD

There are four ways of delivering an oral presentation: manuscript, memorization, impromptu, and extemporaneous. Each method has advantages and disadvantages.

If you write out everything you want to say, word for word in a **manuscript,** you won't leave anything out when you present the speech. Everything you want to say is right there in front of you. Unfortunately, many speakers become so dependent on their manuscripts that they pay little attention to the audience. They have little eye contact with listeners and may not notice whether listeners understand the material presented. Listeners may feel that the speaker has little interest in them and may find the speech boring. News broadcasters and many political figures avoid this problem by using a TelePrompTer that makes it seem as if they are looking directly at their listener, but such equipment is probably not available to you. If you must use a manuscript, work diligently to make a connection with your audience through eye contact and body language while occasionally looking down to find your next point.

You could also **memorize** your speech. Thus, you make sure you don't leave anything out and at the same time maintain eye contact with your audience. However, this requires that you have a good memory and do not forget even minor points. No situation is more uncomfortable for a speaker than drawing a blank about what comes next. If you are going to attempt a memorized presentation, make sure it really is committed to memory and that it does not sound memorized. The delivery of a memorized speech often sounds robotic. Because the speaker spends many hours working on the memorization of the material, she or he doesn't have time to work on a natural, conversational delivery. Even good eye contact will not fool an audience if you do not sound interested in the subject or in them.

An **impromptu speech** is one delivered off-the-cuff. There are no notes and no specific preparation; you speak from the knowledge that you have gained over a lifetime. Not having to prepare in advance is an advantage, but a disadvantage is that such speeches can sound disorganized or incoherent. The perfect example that might have easily explained your second point may not come to mind until you are well into your third point. The audience is left to put all the little pieces of information together. In a panel presentation individual panelists may present impromptu when they answer a moderator's question if they do not have the questions beforehand. Anytime forums are involved, where audience members can ask spontaneous questions, a respondent's answer will be impromptu.

An **extemporaneous speech** is a prepared speech, but instead of writing out a manuscript or memorizing it, you write an outline of what you want to cover, using as few or as many notes as you need to present your ideas. This type of speech is one typically required of students in small group discussion courses and the most preferred because it can offer the most immediacy with the audience. Don't prepare too many notes or you might as well read a manuscript. However, make sure that everything is in your note cards: ideas, statistics, quotations, a final statement. The exact wording of the speech will be different every time you present it, but the main points will always be there. This method permits you to have much eye contact with the audience. It also allows you to react to your audience's feedback without fear of losing your place or forgetting something you want to say. If you realize that some of your listeners do not understand you, you can offer another example or repeat your point in a different way to make the point clear, then return to where you left off in your notes.

Once you have selected the method of delivery, practice your speech out loud. Thinking the speech silently to yourself does not take as much time as saying it aloud does, so you may misjudge the length. You also need to hear what the speech sounds like, because you may find that something said easily in your head is a real tongue twister when said aloud. A colleague of ours remembers his embarrassment when he wanted to say "needy student" but "nudey student" came out. After a second and then a third unsuccessful attempt at "needy," he was forced to switch to "impecunious." If possible, get someone to listen to your speech before you present it to an audience. That person will be able to tell you what you can do to improve the speech.

Group presentations call for not only individual practice of speeches but also *group* practice. Find the time to go through your presentation together, concentrating on how you will shift between speakers, how you will act while others are speaking, what members can do to help if someone forgets to say something, and so on. Showing a sense of continuity and togetherness during a presentation that involves more than one person is challenging and needs to be rehearsed. You would also do well to talk about how the group will handle any spur-of-the-moment failure of equipment and how the group can complete a presentation should a member be unable to attend and you cannot reschedule it.

# What Makes a Good Oral Presentation?

Since the time of the ancient Greeks and Romans, a number of criteria have been generally agreed upon as artistic standards to evaluate oral performances. These standards are called the *canons of rhetoric.* Karyn and Donald Rybacki write: "Because rhetorical theory was an outgrowth of observations of the practice of public speaking in classical cultures, the canons are particularly appropriate to the analysis of speeches."[12] The five classical canons were invention, arrangement, style, delivery, and memory. You can use these elements to render an overall evaluation of any presentation, to compare it to other presentations you have heard, or to offer suggestions for improvement. We will concentrate on the first four canons because memory—the use of codes and mnemonic devices the speaker relied on to recall lengthy speeches—has generally been replaced by written notes and the use of TelePrompTers (see Table 11.2).

| **TABLE 11.2**     **Criteria for Evaluation (Canons)** |
| --- |
| 1. **Invention:** raw materials and adaptation to audience |
| 2. **Arrangement:** organization |
| 3. **Style:** choice of language |
| 4. **Delivery:** oral presentation |

## Preparing an Individual Presentation

**APPLY NOW**

Congratulations! The group mentioned in Case 11.1 has selected you to make the oral presentation to the restaurant association. Although the other members will be present to help answer questions, the primary responsibility for the presentation rests with you.

1. Based on the information you already have, go through the planning stages of preparing an oral presentation. For example, decide whether you are going to try to persuade your listeners to act or to inform them of what your group has discovered. What do you think the audience will be like? How will audience members respond to you? What makes you think so?

2. List the verbal and visual materials you plan to use. Be specific. What types of visual aids would be effective? What kinds of statistics?

3. Assuming that all these materials are available, what pattern of organization would be most effective in presenting them? What type of introduction would best attract the audience's attention?

4. Compare your answers with those of the other members of your class.

The canon of **invention** deals with the raw materials of the speech and how they are adapted to a particular audience. Did the speaker choose an appropriate topic? Did the speaker select interesting examples and illustrations to explain an informative thesis? Did the speaker use significant and sufficient examples and statistics to support a thesis when attempting to persuade? Did the speaker relate the topic and show its significance to the audience? Did the speaker adhere to the ethics of communication (see National Communication Association Credo for Ethical Communication in Chapter 1), using accurate information, respecting the views of others, and adapting to the needs of the audience? Did the speaker complete the presentation within any assigned time limits?

In a panel or symposium, did the speakers work together to present varied aspects of the issue? Did the moderator keep the discussion focused? Did the panel cover all the material that would be of interest to the audience?

The canon of **arrangement** is concerned with how the speech is put together or organized. Were the main points clear and easy to follow? Was there an interesting introduction that captured the audience's attention and previewed the body of the speech? Were there effective transitions? Did the conclusion summarize the main points and reinforce the central idea?

In a symposium did the moderator provide the audience with transitions between the individual presentations? Was there a clear introduction and a conclusion to the discussion? In a panel did the participants stick to the topic and make clear when they were moving from one aspect to another? Did the individual presentations work together to present a coherent whole?

The canon of **style** is concerned with the distinctive manner and appropriateness of the speech's language. Was the language clear and accurate? Was it appropriate to the audience

### GLOSSARY

**Invention**

*A canon of rhetoric identifying the raw materials of the speech and how they are adapted to a particular audience*

**Arrangement**

*One of the canons of rhetoric, specifying how a speech is ordered or put together*

**Style**

*One of the canons of rhetoric, referring to the individual manner in which a speech is delivered*

## Using the Canons to Evaluate

**APPLY NOW**

Demosthenes, the great Greek orator of antiquity, is supposed to have claimed that the most important canon was delivery, the second most important was delivery, and the third most important was delivery.

1. Which canon do you think is the most important? How would you divide 100 points among the four canons to show their relative importance?

2. In a small group, discuss which of the canons you feel to be most important, rank them from 1 (most important) to 4 (least important), and figure out the average score for each based on the 100-point scale.

3. Can your group offer any examples of contemporary or historical public speakers who rate high on all the canons? Who rates poorly on all?

4. Compare your responses to those of the other groups in your class.

and occasion? Was it free of grammatical errors that make it hard to understand? Was the language vivid and likely to hold the audience's attention? Did the speaker use language ethically, without demeaning or intimidating the audience?

The canon of **delivery** deals with how the presentation is offered to the audience. Did the speaker maintain eye contact with the audience? Did the speaker avoid any distracting movements and gestures? Did the speaker vary his or her pitch and rate? Was the speaker confident? Were appropriate movements and gestures used?

In group presentations do the speakers work with each other and not against each other? Does the presentation flow and convey a sense of cooperativeness, cohesion, and continuity between individual speeches? Did the gestures and movements of nonspeakers distract from the speaker?

### RESOURCES FOR REVIEW AND DISCUSSION

**SUMMARY**

- Small groups are often called upon to make oral presentations of their work, so members need to understand how to be effective presenters.

- Public presentation sessions include panels and symposiums, where speakers publicly discuss an issue before an audience; a forum often follows, where the audience can address or question the speakers.

- In preparing a speech, the speaker must first determine whether the purpose is to inform, persuade, or entertain.

- Speakers must analyze the audience to understand how to get their attention; find the most appropriate and interesting ideas, supporting materials, and visuals aids to present; and organize the material so that it is easy for the audience to follow the presentation.

■ An effective presentation includes an introduction, body, and conclusion.

■ Oral presentations can be evaluated using four criteria, based on the canons of rhetoric, which include invention, arrangement, style, and delivery.

1. C-SPAN is a nonprofit cooperative of the cable industry. C-SPAN programming covers a variety of political events, including congressional hearings, press conferences, public policy conferences, and so forth. Watch C-SPAN for examples of panels, forums, or symposiums.

   a. Could you distinguish which kind of public presentation was taking place?

   b. Was there a moderator? How effective was the moderator? Why?

   c. What did you find interesting about how the public presentation was conducted? What did you see that was problematic?

   d. Did the public presentation meet with your expectations? Were you surprised? Why?

   e. Did you get any ideas about how you might or might not conduct your own public presentation?

2. Take some time to listen to the persuasive speech of a car salesperson and a minister. Compare and contrast the "sales pitch" of both. Both presentations are persuasive in nature, but they are delivered to different audiences. How are their oral presentations the same? How are their oral presentations different?

3. Various videos and CD-ROMs contain the text of famous speeches. You can rent these at your local or school library. Find one with excerpts or the entire speech of someone famous who interests you. Watch the speech and evaluate according to the four canons: invention, style, delivery, and arrangement.

 Go to **www.mhhe.com/adamsgalanes7** and **www.mhhe.com/groups** for self-quizzes and weblinks.

| | | |
|---|---|---|
| Arrangement | Forum Discussion | Memorization |
| Audience Analysis | Impromptu Speech | Moderator |
| Body | Informative Speech | Panel Discussion |
| Conclusion | Introduction | Persuasive Speech |
| Delivery | Invention | Style |
| Entertainment Speech | Manuscript | Symposium |
| Extemporaneous Speech | | |

 **www.mhhe.com/adamsgalanes7**

Use the flashcards and crossword puzzles on the Online Learning Center to further your knowledge of these key terms.

# Techniques for Observing Problem-Solving Groups

## Consulting to the Technical College Executive Committee

The technical college's executive committee meetings were boring. Members agreed that communication among the various departments was essential for the college to function effectively, but the weekly staff meetings somehow were not satisfying this need. Real communication about problems, solutions, and goals of the various departments was done outside the meetings. Members didn't complain much, but they showed little enthusiasm for the meetings. The chair of the committee, Basil, was concerned. He asked Gloria to observe the meetings, figure out what was wrong, make recommendations for improvement, and conduct training sessions to help members interact more effectively during the meetings.

For two months Gloria systematically observed, analyzed, and evaluated the staff meetings. First, she attended meetings, took notes, and completed a content analysis that showed Basil doing most of the talking. He was almost the only member to initiate new ideas during the meetings. Other members contributed only when addressed directly by Basil. Thus, a *wheel* interaction pattern (with Basil at the hub and everyone else as an individual spoke) had become the group's norm. On a questionnaire asking about effectiveness, Basil indicated that he believed the meetings were very effective, most other members thought they were moderately effective, and two members rated them completely ineffective. Gloria followed up the questionnaire by interviewing each staff member to determine how the meetings could be improved. She paid particular attention to the comments of the two dissatisfied members.

Gloria concluded that Basil dominated the meetings but that he was unaware he was doing so. Members felt stifled during the meetings but didn't know how to express those feelings to Basil or to change the pattern of their meetings. Members wanted to discuss freely the problems that had come up in their respective departments, and they hoped the staff meetings would provide an open forum for exchanging information and ideas. The two members who were most dissatisfied were quite knowledgeable about college operations and felt particularly ignored. Members were suppressing disagreements for fear of retribution by Basil; although Basil was not a tyrant, he made it clear from his behavior (rolling his eyes, interrupting people, speaking sarcastically) that he did not like it when others disagreed with his ideas. In short, this committee displayed some obvious and some hidden problems, all of which could be overcome with training and desire.

This story highlights the value of having someone observe a group, describe its behavior, evaluate that behavior, and make recommendations to improve the functioning of the group. In this appendix we will present a variety of techniques to help you do that.

## The Role of the Observer

The role of group observer can be valuable and helpful if the observer knows how to function. Most group members have not been trained to be effective group participants, so it's especially important for those who do know something about small group communication to monitor the group's discussions and help the group perform as well as possible. Knowledgeable observers function like athletic coaches, helping players improve their performance as a team.

In Chapter 1 we described the participant-observer, a group member who makes available his or her knowledge and skills to help a group perform more effectively. A second type of observer is the **consultant-observer,** an outsider brought in to observe, evaluate, and make recommendations to the group. The consultant-observer may be a member of the organization the group belongs to or an outside consultant trained in small group communication. When executives learn that someone within the organization has small group communication expertise, they often ask that person to apply his or her skills to help the group. That was Gloria's situation when she observed the technical college executive staff, and that may also be your position someday.

Participant- and consultant-observers have unique advantages and disadvantages. The consultant-observer may be able to maintain more objectivity regarding group members and group processes, but the participant-observer may have inside information that gives insight regarding what is happening in the group. A group that has been experiencing serious conflict may view the consultant-observer as a hatchet person for an executive. On the other hand, a participant-observer may be seen as biased rather than objective, thereby undermining his or her effectiveness as an adviser to the group.

**GLOSSARY**

**Consultant-Observer**

*An outsider who observes and evaluates a group*

In general, observers seek to answer two questions: How well is this group performing? and How can it improve? However, *many* elements contribute to a group's performance. Observers cannot look at everything at once, or they will become overwhelmed. They plan their observation strategy in advance. Table A.1 lists questions you can use as a general guide for observing. Don't try to answer all the questions; instead, use the list to screen out elements that seem to be working well so you can concentrate your observation on those that can be improved.

Both participant- and consultant-observers should follow several guidelines when they are giving feedback to a group:

1. **Stress the positive** and point out what the group or the leader is doing well.

2. **Do not overwhelm the group** by telling the members each and every thing you think should be improved. Instead, emphasize one or two things that most need improvement.

3. **Avoid arguing** when you present your observations and advice. Leave the group members free to decide whether and how your advice will be used.

4. **Do not interrupt the whole meeting** to give advice to the group's leader during a meeting. Instead, whisper or write your suggestions.

5. **Speak clearly and concisely** when you are giving feedback. Do not ramble or belabor your points. Consider the following remarks by Larry, who observed that group members were switching to new topics without completing the original one:

   *One of the problems I see is that you are having trouble staying on track with your discussion! In the past five minutes, you have talked about a pedestrian overpass at Grand and National, why money was spent on artificial turf instead of library books, how you can handle a landlord who won't repair plumbing, and several other topics. Your discussion would be more efficient if you helped each other focus on the original question: How can pedestrian/car accidents be eliminated on National Avenue?*

   In this example of giving feedback, Larry states the problem he has observed, gives a few (rather than 10 or 20) examples to clarify what he means, and provides a suggestion that makes the whole group responsible for solving the problem. He doesn't ramble endlessly about the problem or blame individual members.

6. **Prepare members to use special procedures** by explaining the procedure or giving them a handout that outlines the key steps. (Feel free to use the figures in this book, as long as you give credit to the source.)

7. **Make individual critical comments in private** to the appropriate person so that he or she will not feel attacked or publicly humiliated.

Now that you have an idea of what observers look for and how they present their findings, here are a variety of instruments to help you gather information about your group.

# Observation Instruments and Techniques

The following techniques and instruments may be used by group members as part of a self-evaluation of the group or by observers. They can be used as is or adapted to suit particular situations and groups.

| TABLE A.1 | **Questions to Guide Your Observations** |
|-----------|------------------------------------------|

**GROUP GOALS**

- Are there clear and accepted group goals?
- How well does the group understand its charge?
- Does the group know and accept limits on its area of freedom?
- Do members know what output they are supposed to produce?

**SETTING**

- Does the physical environment (seating arrangements, privacy, attractiveness) facilitate group discussions?

**COMMUNICATION SKILLS AND INTERACTION PATTERNS**

- How clearly do members express their ideas and opinions?
- Do members complete one topic before they switch to another?
- Is verbal participation balanced equally among all members?
- Is the pattern of interaction evenly distributed or unduly restricted?

**COMMUNICATION CLIMATE AND NORMS**

- Does the group climate seem supportive and cooperative or defensive and competitive?
- What attitudes do the members exhibit toward themselves and each other?
- Do any hidden agenda items seem to interfere with group progress?
- Do any norms seem to interfere with group progress or cohesiveness?

**LEADERSHIP AND MEMBER ROLES**

- What style of leadership is the designated leader providing?
- Is the leadership appropriate for the group's needs?
- Are the roles performed by members appropriate both for their skills and for the needs of the group?
- Are there any needed functions not being provided by anyone?

**DECISION-MAKING AND PROBLEM-SOLVING PROCEDURES**

- Are members adequately prepared for meetings?
- Does the group use an agenda? How well is it followed? Does it serve the group?
- Is anyone providing periodic internal summaries so members can keep track of major points of discussion?
- Are decisions, assignments, and proposals being recorded?
- How are decisions being made?
- Has the group defined and analyzed the problem before developing solutions?
- Do members understand and agree on criteria in making decisions?
- How creative is the group in generating potential solutions?
- Do members defer judgment until all solutions have been listed and understood?
- Are information and ideas being evaluated critically or accepted at face value?
- Do you see any tendency toward groupthink?
- Has the group made adequate plans to implement decisions?
- Are special procedures (brainstorming, focus groups, etc.) being used as needed?
- Could procedural changes benefit the group?

**FIGURE A.1    Verbal Interaction Diagram**

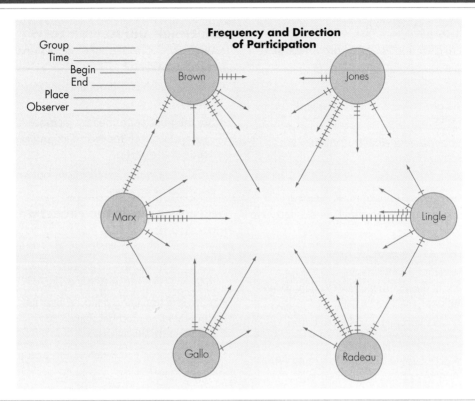

VERBAL INTERACTION ANALYSIS

A **verbal interaction analysis** shows who talks to whom, how often each member speaks, and whether the group participation is balanced or dominated by one or more individuals. A model interaction diagram is shown in Figure A.1. The names of all participants are located around the circle in the same order in which they sit during the discussion. Whenever a person speaks, an arrow is drawn from that person's position toward the individual to whom the remark was addressed. Subsequent remarks in the same direction are indicated by the short cross marks on the base of the arrow. (For example, Gallo addressed three remarks to Brown in the model diagram.) The longer arrow pointing toward the center indicates remarks made to the group as a whole.

An interaction diagram can look messy or confusing. For easier interpretation, display the numbers and percentages in a chart (see Figure A.2). From the frequency of participation to the group as a whole and to specific members, who might you guess is the leader of this group? Do you consider the participation balanced? Does anyone appear to dominate the discussion?

GLOSSARY

**Verbal Interaction Analysis**

*A technique to discover who talks to whom*

**FIGURE A.2    How to Display Data from a Verbal Interaction Diagram**

Group    CURRICULUM COMMITTEE                    Place    CRAIG HALL

Observer    SMITH                    Date    9-5-2007

Beginning time    9:00 a.m.                    Ending time    10:30 a.m.

TO:

| FROM: | Brown | Jones | Lingle | Radeau | Gallo | Marx | Group | Total |
|---|---|---|---|---|---|---|---|---|
| Brown | – | 5 | 2 | 4 | 2 | 5 | 5 | 23 / 16.1 |
| Jones | 3 | – | 3 | 4 | 4 | 3 | 13 | 30 / 21 |
| Lingle | 2 | 2 | – | 3 | 2 | 4 | 12 | 25 / 17.5 |
| Radeau | 3 | 3 | 4 | – | 0 | 2 | 12 | 24 / 16.8 |
| Gallo | 3 | 3 | 2 | 0 | – | 0 | 6 | 14 / 9.8 |
| Marx | 8 | 2 | 2 | 3 | 2 | – | 10 | 27 / 18.9 |
| Total number | 19 | 15 | 13 | 14 | 10 | 14 | 58 | 143 |
| Total percent | 13.3 | 10.5 | 9.1 | 9.8 | 7 | 9.8 | 40.6 | 100 |

## CONTENT ANALYSIS PROCEDURES

**Content analysis procedures** examine the *type* of remarks being made by specific members. In Figure A.3 specific task, maintenance, and self-centered behaviors are listed along the left margin and the participants' names across the top. Each time a member speaks, the observer places a mark in the appropriate box according to the type of remark made. The tally marks are converted to percentages, as shown in Figure A.4. Who is probably the task leader of this group? Who is the maintenance leader? Are any individuals acting in self-centered ways?

Any category system can be used as the basis for a content analysis diagram. For example, you may want to focus on the defensive and supportive behaviors described in Chapter 5. In that case you would record all the individual defensive and supportive communication categories (control, superiority, provisionalism, empathy, etc.) along the left side.

**GLOSSARY**

**Content Analysis Procedures**

*Techniques to help analyze the types of remarks being made*

**FIGURE A.3** **Content Analysis of Task, Maintenance, and Self-Centered Behaviors**

Group _____ Place _____ Observer _____

Date _____ Beginning time _____ Ending time _____

Participants' Names

| Behavioral Functions | | | | | | |
|---|---|---|---|---|---|---|
| 1. Initiating and orienting | | | | | | |
| 2. Information giving | | | | | | |
| 3. Information seeking | | | | | | |
| 4. Opinion giving | | | | | | |
| 5. Opinion seeking | | | | | | |
| 6. Clarifying | | | | | | |
| 7. Elaborating | | | | | | |
| 8. Summarizing | | | | | | |
| 9. Consensus testing | | | | | | |
| 10. Recording | | | | | | |
| 11. Suggesting procedure | | | | | | |
| 12. Gatekeeping | | | | | | |
| 13. Supporting | | | | | | |
| 14. Harmonizing | | | | | | |
| 15. Tension relieving | | | | | | |
| 16. Dramatizing | | | | | | |
| 17. Showing solidarity | | | | | | |
| 18. Withdrawing | | | | | | |
| 19. Blocking | | | | | | |
| 20. Status and recognition seeking | | | | | | |
| 21. Playing | | | | | | |
| 22. Acting helpless | | | | | | |

Task-Oriented (items 1–11)
Maintenance (items 12–17)
Self-Centered (items 18–22)

Group __EXECUTIVE COMMITTEE__          Place __CU LOBBY__

Observer __ANDY__          Date __8-28-07__

Beginning time __4:30 p.m.__          Ending time __6:30 p.m.__

| | Behavioral Functions | Mary | John | Edna | Dave | Jodi | Total number percent |
|---|---|---|---|---|---|---|---|
| Task-Oriented | 1. Initiating and orienting | 5 | 3 | | | | 8 / 5.7 |
| | 2. Information giving | 6 | 5 | | 2 | 3 | 16 / 11.4 |
| | 3. Information seeking | | | 3 | | | 3 / 2.1 |
| | 4. Opinion giving | 8 | 8 | 4 | 2 | 1 | 23 / 16.4 |
| | 5. Opinion seeking | | | 2 | | | 2 / 1.4 |
| | 6. Clarifying | | | 3 | | | 3 / 2.1 |
| | 7. Elaborating | 2 | 4 | | | 1 | 7 / 5 |
| | 8. Summarizing | 2 | | | | | 2 / 1.4 |
| | 9. Consensus testing | 8 | | | | | 8 / 5.6 |
| | 10. Recording | | | | 3 | | 3 / 2.1 |
| | 11. Suggesting procedure | | | 5 | | | 5 / 3.5 |
| Maintenance | 12. Gatekeeping | 3 | | 6 | | | 9 / 6.3 |
| | 13. Supporting | | | 1 | 5 | | 6 / 4.2 |
| | 14. Harmonizing | 2 | | 2 | 6 | | 10 / 7 |
| | 15. Tension relieving | | | | 3 | 2 | 5 / 3.5 |
| | 16. Dramatizing | | | | | 6 | 6 / 4.2 |
| | 17. Showing solidarity | | 5 | | | 3 | 8 / 5.6 |
| Self-Centered | 18. Withdrawing | | | | 4 | | 4 / 2.8 |
| | 19. Blocking | | 1 | | | | 1 / .7 |
| | 20. Status and recognition seeking | 2 | 5 | | | | 7 / 4.9 |
| | 21. Playing | | | 4 | | | 4 / 2.8 |
| | 22. Acting helpless | | | | | 2 | 2 / 1.4 |
| | Total number percent | 38 / 26.8 | 31 / 21.9 | 30 / 21.1 | 25 / 17.6 | 18 / 12.6 | 142 / 100 |

Participants' Names

| FIGURE A.5 | All-Purpose Discussion Rating Scale |
| --- | --- |

Date _____                Group _____

Time _____                Observer _____

| Group Characteristic | 5 Excellent | 4 Good | 3 Average | 2 Fair | 1 Poor |
| --- | --- | --- | --- | --- | --- |
| Organization of discussion | | | | | |
| Equality of opportunity to speak | | | | | |
| Cooperative group orientation | | | | | |
| Listening to understand | | | | | |
| Evaluation of ideas | | | | | |
| Comments: | | | | | |

Other types of content analyses can be performed. For example, you might want to trace the development of any fantasy chains in the group, the progression of an idea from its original introduction by one member through all its modifications by the rest of the group, the types of conflicts, or the types of arguments members use to support their ideas. It is easier if you tape-record (with permission, of course) the group's interaction first.

## RATING SCALES

**Rating scales** are questionnaires that ask members or observers to assess any aspect of a group, such as group climate, cohesiveness, efficiency, satisfaction, freedom to express disagreement, and organization of discussion. For example, the question "How well did the committee chair keep the discussion organized?" asks you to rate the leader's ability to conduct a systematic discussion. Scale questions may be closed-ended, in which the responses are already provided for you (such as *very well, adequately,* and *very poorly*), or open-ended, in which you are free to respond any way you choose. The following figures provide a number of examples of rating scales. Figure A.5 is a general scale to evaluate any group discussion, and Figure A.6 is a scale adapted from one developed by Patton and

## · FIGURE A.6    *Problem-Solving Process Rating Scale*

*Instructions:* Indicate the degree to which the group accomplished each identified behavior. Use the following scale for your evaluations:

| Poor | Fair | Average | Good | Excellent |
|------|------|---------|------|-----------|
| 1 | 2 | 3 | 4 | 5 |

Circle the appropriate number in front of each item.

1   2   3   4   5     1. The concern of each member was identified regarding the problem the group attempted to solve.

1   2   3   4   5     2. This concern was identified *before* the problem was analyzed.

1   2   3   4   5     3. In problem analysis, the present condition was carefully compared with the specific condition desired.

1   2   3   4   5     4. The goal was carefully defined and agreed to by all members.

1   2   3   4   5     5. Valid (and relevant) information was secured when needed.

1   2   3   4   5     6. Possible solutions were listed and clarified before they were evaluated.

1   2   3   4   5     7. Criteria for evaluating proposed solutions were clearly identified and accepted by the group.

1   2   3   4   5     8. Predictions were made regarding the probable effectiveness of each proposed solution, using the available information and criteria.

1   2   3   4   5     9. Consensus was achieved on the most desirable solution.

1   2   3   4   5     10. A detailed plan to implement the solution was developed.

1   2   3   4   5     11. The problem-solving process was systematic and orderly.

Giffin to identify deficiencies in problem-solving procedures. Figure A.7 is the Seashore Index of Group Cohesiveness, which measures cohesiveness of a work group.[1] We encourage you to modify these scales or create your own.

---

**FIGURE A.7        Seashore Index of Group Cohesiveness**

---

Check one response for each question.

1. Do you feel that you are really a part of your work group?

_____ Really a part of my work group

_____ Included in most ways

_____ Included in some ways, but not in others

_____ Don't feel I really belong

_____ Don't work with any one group of people

_____ Not ascertained

2. If you had a chance to do the same kind of work for the same pay in another work group, how would you feel about moving?

_____ Would want very much to move

_____ Would rather move than stay where I am

_____ Would make no difference to me

_____ Would want very much to stay where I am

_____ Not ascertained

3. How does your group compare with other similar groups on each of the following points?

| | Better than Most | About the Same as Most | Not as Good as Most | Not Ascertained |
|---|---|---|---|---|
| a. The way the members get along together | _____ | _____ | _____ | _____ |
| b. The way the members stick together | _____ | _____ | _____ | _____ |
| c. The way the members help each other on the job | _____ | _____ | _____ | _____ |

SOURCE: From Stanley Seashore, *Group Cohesiveness in the Industrial Work Group* (Ann Arbor: Institute for Social Research, University of Michigan, 1954).

| **FIGURE A.8** | **Postmeeting Reaction Form** |
|---|---|

1. How do you feel about today's discussion?

   Excellent ___ Good ___ All right ___ So-so ___ Bad ___

2. What were the strong points of the discussion?

3. What were the weaknesses?

4. What changes would you suggest for future meetings?

(You need not sign your name.)

## POSTMEETING REACTION FORMS

**Postmeeting reaction (PMR) forms** are questionnaires designed to get feedback from members about a particular meeting. PMR forms may focus on a particular aspect (such as leadership) or deal with several broad aspects (such as how effective members believe the meetings are). The leader, a member, or an observer distributes the PMR forms; members complete them anonymously, the results are tallied, and the findings are reported to the group as soon as possible. The findings provide a basis for the group to discuss how to improve its communication and effectiveness. Basil, the group leader in our introductory example, could have used PMR forms himself to get feedback from the other members about how the group's discussions could be improved.

PMR forms are tailored to fit the purposes and needs of the group. Questions may concern substantive items, interpersonal relationships, matters of procedure, or a mixture of all three. Two different examples of PMR forms are shown in Figures A.8 and A.9.

# Evaluating Individual Participants

In addition to evaluating general group processes, it is often useful to evaluate behaviors of individual participants. An observer or the members themselves may complete the following forms. Figure A.10 is a simple rating form that focuses on some of the most important aspects of participation. A more detailed form is shown in Figure A.11. Figure A.12 is a scale to evaluate leadership, and Figure A.13 is a leader's self-rating scale.

**GLOSSARY**

**Postmeeting Reaction (PMR) Forms**

*Questionnaires members complete after a meeting to evaluate that particular meeting*

**FIGURE A.9    Postmeeting Reaction Form**

*Instructions:* Circle the number that best indicates your reactions to the following questions about the discussion in which you participated:

1. *Adequacy of Communication.* To what extent do you feel members were understanding each others' statements and positions?

| 0 | 1 | 2 | 3 | 4 | 5 | 6 | 7 | 8 | 9 | 10 |
|---|---|---|---|---|---|---|---|---|---|----|

Talked past each other; misunderstanding

Communicated directly with each other; understanding well

2. *Opportunity to Speak.* To what extent did you feel free to speak?

| 0 | 1 | 2 | 3 | 4 | 5 | 6 | 7 | 8 | 9 | 10 |
|---|---|---|---|---|---|---|---|---|---|----|

Never had a chance to speak

Had all the opportunity to talk I wanted

3. *Climate of Acceptance.* How well did members support each other, show acceptance of individuals?

| 0 | 1 | 2 | 3 | 4 | 5 | 6 | 7 | 8 | 9 | 10 |
|---|---|---|---|---|---|---|---|---|---|----|

Highly critical and punishing

Supportive and receptive

4. *Interpersonal Relations.* How pleasant and concerned were members with interpersonal relations?

| 0 | 1 | 2 | 3 | 4 | 5 | 6 | 7 | 8 | 9 | 10 |
|---|---|---|---|---|---|---|---|---|---|----|

Quarrelsome, status differences emphasized

Pleasant, empathic, concerned with persons

5. *Leadership.* How adequate was the leader (or leadership) of the group?

| 0 | 1 | 2 | 3 | 4 | 5 | 6 | 7 | 8 | 9 | 10 |
|---|---|---|---|---|---|---|---|---|---|----|

Too weak ( ) or dominating ( )

Shared, group-centered, and sufficient

6. *Satisfaction with Role.* How satisfied are you with your personal participation in the discussion?

| 0 | 1 | 2 | 3 | 4 | 5 | 6 | 7 | 8 | 9 | 10 |
|---|---|---|---|---|---|---|---|---|---|----|

Very dissatisfied

Very satisfied

7. *Quality of Product.* How satisfied are you with the discussions, solutions, or learnings that came out of this discussion?

| 0 | 1 | 2 | 3 | 4 | 5 | 6 | 7 | 8 | 9 | 10 |
|---|---|---|---|---|---|---|---|---|---|----|

Very displeased

Very satisfied

8. *Overall.* How do you rate the discussion as a whole apart from any specific aspect of it?

| 0 | 1 | 2 | 3 | 4 | 5 | 6 | 7 | 8 | 9 | 10 |
|---|---|---|---|---|---|---|---|---|---|----|

Awful; waste of time

Superb; time well spent

**FIGURE A.10     Participating Rating Scale**

Date _____

Observer _____

_____
(Name of participant)

1. Contributions to the *content of the discussion?* (well prepared, supplied information, adequate reasoning, etc.)

| 5 | 4 | 3 | 2 | 1 |
|---|---|---|---|---|

Outstanding in quality and quantity       Fair share       Few or none

2. Contributions to *efficient group procedures?* (agenda planning, relevant comments, summaries, keeping on track)

| 5 | 4 | 3 | 2 | 1 |
|---|---|---|---|---|

Always relevant, aided organization       Relevant, no aid in order       Sidetracked, confused group

3. Degree of *cooperating?* (listening to understand, responsible, agreeable, group-centered, open-minded)

| 5 | 4 | 3 | 2 | 1 |
|---|---|---|---|---|

Very responsible and constructive       Self-centered

4. *Speaking?* (clear, to group, one point at a time, concise)

| 5 | 4 | 3 | 2 | 1 |
|---|---|---|---|---|

Brief, clear, to group       Vague, indirect, wordy

5. *Value* to the group? (overall rating)

| 5 | 4 | 3 | 2 | 1 |
|---|---|---|---|---|

Most valuable       Least valuable

Suggestions:

**FIGURE A.11     Participating Rating Scale**

Participant's name _____

*Instructions:* Circle the number that best reflects your evaluation of the discussant's participation on each scale.

| Superior | | | | Poor | |
|---|---|---|---|---|---|
| 1 | 2 | 3 | 4 | 5 | 1. Was prepared and informed. |
| 1 | 2 | 3 | 4 | 5 | 2. Contributions were brief and clear. |
| 1 | 2 | 3 | 4 | 5 | 3. Comments relevant and well timed. |
| 1 | 2 | 3 | 4 | 5 | 4. Spoke distinctly and audibly to all. |
| 1 | 2 | 3 | 4 | 5 | 5. Contributions made readily and voluntarily. |
| 1 | 2 | 3 | 4 | 5 | 6. Frequency of participation (if poor, too low [ ] or high [ ]). |
| 1 | 2 | 3 | 4 | 5 | 7. Nonverbal responses were clear and constant. |
| 1 | 2 | 3 | 4 | 5 | 8. Listened to understand and follow discussion. |
| 1 | 2 | 3 | 4 | 5 | 9. Open-minded. |
| 1 | 2 | 3 | 4 | 5 | 10. Cooperative and constructive. |
| 1 | 2 | 3 | 4 | 5 | 11. Helped keep discussion organized, following outline. |
| 1 | 2 | 3 | 4 | 5 | 12. Contributed to evaluation of information and ideas. |
| 1 | 2 | 3 | 4 | 5 | 13. Respectful and tactful with others. |
| 1 | 2 | 3 | 4 | 5 | 14. Encouraged others to participate. |
| 1 | 2 | 3 | 4 | 5 | 15. Overall rating in relation to other discussants. |

Comments                        Evaluator _____

**FIGURE A.12    Barnlund-Haiman Leadership Rating Scale**

*Instructions:* This rating scale may be used to evaluate leadership in groups with or without official leaders. In the latter case (the leaderless group), use part A of each item only. When evaluating the actions of an official leader, use parts A and B of each item on the scale.

## Influence in Procedure

*Initiating Discussion*

A. 3                    2                    1                    0                    1                    2                    3

| Group needed more help in getting started | | Group got right amount of help | | | Group needed less help in getting started | |

B. The quality of the introductory remarks was:

| Excellent | Good | Adequate | Fair | Poor |

*Organizing Group Thinking*

A. 3                    2                    1                    0                    1                    2                    3

| Group needed more direction in thinking | | Group got right amount of help | | | Group needed less direction in thinking | |

B. If and when attempts were made to organize group thinking, they were:

| Excellent | Good | Adequate | Fair | Poor |

*Clarifying Communication*

A. 3                    2                    1                    0                    1                    2                    3

| Group needed more help in clarifying communication | | Group got right amount of help | | | Group needed less help in clarifying communication | |

B. If and when attempts were made to clarify communication, they were:

| Excellent | Good | Adequate | Fair | Poor |

*Summarizing and Verbalizing Agreements*

A. 3                    2                    1                    0                    1                    2                    3

| Group needed more help in summarizing and verbalizing agreements | | Group got right amount of help | | | Group needed less help in summarizing and verbalizing agreements | |

B. If and when attempts were made to summarize and verbalize, they were:

| Excellent | Good | Adequate | Fair | Poor |

*Resolving Conflict*

A. 3                    2                    1                    0                    1                    2                    3

| Group needed more help in resolving conflict | | Group got right amount of help | | | Group needed less help in resolving conflict | |

B. If and when attempts were made to resolve conflict, they were:

| Excellent | Good | Adequate | Fair | Poor |

*(continued)*

SOURCE: From D. C. Barnlund and F. S. Haiman, *The Dynamics of Discussion* (Boston: Houghton-Mifflin, 1960), pp. 401–4. Used by permission of Robert Goldsmith, M.D., executor of Barnlund estate.[2]

**FIGURE A.12     *Continued***

## Influence in Creative and Critical Thinking

*Stimulating Critical Thinking*

A.  3 | 2 | 1 | 0 | 1 | 2 | 3
--- | --- | --- | --- | --- | --- | ---

Group needed more stimulation in creative thinking

Group got right amount of help

Group needed less stimulation in creative thinking

B.  If and when attempts were made to stimulate ideas, they were:

| Excellent | Good | Adequate | Fair | Poor |
| --- | --- | --- | --- | --- |

*Encouraging Criticism*

A.  3 | 2 | 1 | 0 | 1 | 2 | 3
--- | --- | --- | --- | --- | --- | ---

Group needed more encouragement to be critical

Group got right amount of help

Group needed less encouragement to be critical

B.  If and when attempts were made to encourage criticism, they were:

| Excellent | Good | Adequate | Fair | Poor |
| --- | --- | --- | --- | --- |

*Balancing Abstract and Concrete Thought*

A.  3 | 2 | 1 | 0 | 1 | 2 | 3
--- | --- | --- | --- | --- | --- | ---

Group needed to be more concrete

Group achieved proper balance

Group needed to be more abstract

B.  If and when attempts were made to balance abstract and concrete thought, they were:

| Excellent | Good | Adequate | Fair | Poor |
| --- | --- | --- | --- | --- |

## Influence in Interpersonal Relations

*Climate-Making*

A.  3 | 2 | 1 | 0 | 1 | 2 | 3
--- | --- | --- | --- | --- | --- | ---

Group needed more help in securing a permissive atmosphere

Group got right amount of help

Group needed less help in securing a permissive atmosphere

B.  If and when attempts were made to establish a permissive atmosphere, they were:

| Excellent | Good | Adequate | Fair | Poor |
| --- | --- | --- | --- | --- |

*Regulating Participation*

A.  3 | 2 | 1 | 0 | 1 | 2 | 3
--- | --- | --- | --- | --- | --- | ---

Group needed more regulation of participation

Group got right amount of help

Group needed less regulation of participation

B.  If and when attempts were made to regulate participation, they were:

| Excellent | Good | Adequate | Fair | Poor |
| --- | --- | --- | --- | --- |

*Overall Leadership*

A.  3 | 2 | 1 | 0 | 1 | 2 | 3
--- | --- | --- | --- | --- | --- | ---

Group needed more control

Group got right amount of control

Group needed less control

B.  If and when attempts were made to control the group, they were:

| Excellent | Good | Adequate | Fair | Poor |
| --- | --- | --- | --- | --- |

**FIGURE A.13    Leader Self-Rating Scale**

*Instructions:* Rate yourself on each item by putting a check mark in the "Yes" or "No" column. Your score is five times the number of items marked "Yes." Rating: *excellent,* 90 or higher; *good,* 80–85; *fair,* 70–75; *inadequate,* 65 or lower.

|  | Yes | No |
|---|---|---|
| 1. I prepared all needed facilities. | ___ | ___ |
| 2. I started the meeting promptly and ended on time. | ___ | ___ |
| 3. I established an atmosphere of permissiveness and informality. I was open and responsive to all ideas. | ___ | ___ |
| 4. I clearly oriented the group to its purpose and area of freedom. | ___ | ___ |
| 5. I encouraged all members to participate and maintained equal opportunity for all to speak. | ___ | ___ |
| 6. I used a plan for leading the group in an organized consideration of all major phases of the problem. | ___ | ___ |
| 7. I listened actively and (if needed) encouraged all members to do so. | ___ | ___ |
| 8. I saw to it that the problem was discussed thoroughly before solutions were considered. | ___ | ___ |
| 9. I integrated related ideas or suggestions and urged the group to arrive at consensus on a solution. | ___ | ___ |
| 10. My questions were clear and brief. | ___ | ___ |
| 11. I saw to it that unclear statements were paraphrased or otherwise clarified. | ___ | ___ |
| 12. I prompted open discussion of substantive conflicts. | ___ | ___ |
| 13. I maintained order and organization, promptly pointing out tangents, making transitions, and keeping track of the passage of time. | ___ | ___ |
| 14. I saw to it that the meeting produced definite assignments or plans for action, and that any subsequent meeting was arranged. | ___ | ___ |
| 15. All important information, ideas, and decisions were promptly and accurately recorded. | ___ | ___ |
| 16. I actively encouraged creative thinking. | ___ | ___ |
| 17. I encouraged thorough evaluation of information and all ideas for solutions. | ___ | ___ |
| 18. I was able to remain neutral during constructive arguments and otherwise encourage teamwork. | ___ | ___ |
| 19. I suggested or urged establishment of needed norms and standards. | ___ | ___ |
| 20. I encouraged members to discuss how they felt about the group process and resolve any blocks to progress. | ___ | ___ |

## RESOURCES FOR REVIEW AND DISCUSSION

**SUMMARY**

- A consultant-observer is an outsider brought in to observe a group; such observers may be more objective than participant-observers.

- Participant- and consultant-observers cannot look at everything at once, so they concentrate on those elements a group needs to improve most.

- When they give feedback, they focus on a few elements rather than risk overwhelming the group.

- Observers and group members themselves can use a variety of methods to gather information, including verbal interaction analyses, content analyses, and rating scales.

**KEY TERMS • CONCEPTS**

Consultant-Observer

Content Analysis Procedures

Postmeeting Reaction (PMR) Forms

Rating Scales

Verbal Interaction Analysis

## Chapter 1

1. Synthesized from information in Samantha Glen, *Best Friends: The True Story of the World's Most Beloved Animal Sanctuary* (New York: Kensington Books, 2001), and from the Best Friends Animal Society website, accessed January 7, 2007: www.bestfriends.org and www.bestfriends.org/aboutus/oldhistory/intro.htm.

2. Best Friends Animal Society website, accessed January 7, 2007: www.bestfriends.org/aboutus/oldhistory/story5.htm.

3. About Women's History website, accessed January 11, 2007: http://womenshistory.about.com/cs/quotes/a/qu_margaretmead.htm. The origin of this quote is unknown, but Margaret Mead is believed to have said this spontaneously and then been quoted in a newspaper report.

4. Michelle Tullier, "The Skills You Have . . . and the Skills They Want," accessed January 12, 2007: http://campus.monster.com.hk/articles/7346/.

5. Ellen Neuborne, "Companies Save, but Workers Pay," *USA Today,* February 25, 1997, pp. 1B–2B.

6. Neuborne, "Companies Save," p. 1B.

7. Daniel McGinn, "Mired in Meetings," *Newsweek,* October 16, 2000, pp. 52–54.

8. Lawrence R. Frey, "The Call of the Field: Studying Communication in Natural Groups," in *Group Communication in Context,* ed. Lawrence R. Frey (Hillsdale, NJ: Lawrence Erlbaum, 1994), pp. ix–xiv.

9. Charles C. DuBois, "Portrait of the Ideal MBA," *The Penn Stater,* September/October 1992, p. 131.

10. Joann Keyton, "Relational Communication in Groups," in *Handbook of Group Communication Theory & Research,* ed. Lawrence R. Frey (Thousand Oaks, CA: Sage, 1999), p. 192.

11. Glen, *Best Friends.*

12. Ibid., p. 116.

13. This line of research began in 1928 and continues to the present. For a concise summary of the research up to 1980, see Marvin E. Shaw, *Group Dynamics,* 3rd ed. (New York: McGraw-Hill, 1981), pp. 57–64.

14. Herm W. Smith, "Group versus Individual Problem Solving and Type of Problem Solved," *Small Group Behavior* 20 (1989), pp. 357–74.

15. Janis Andersen, Jon Nussbaum, Loretta Pecchioni, and Jo Anna Grant, "Interaction Skills in Instructional Settings," in *Teaching Communication,* 2nd ed., eds. Anita Vangelisti, John A. Daly, and Gustav W. Friedrich (Mahwah, NJ: Lawrence Erlbaum, 1999), pp. 359–74.

16. Robert G. Powell and Dana Caseau, *Classroom Communication and Diversity: Enhancing Instructional Practice* (Mahwah, NJ: Lawrence Erlbaum, 2004), pp. 193–94.

17. Dennis S. Gouran and Randy Y. Hirokawa, "Counteractive Functions of Communication in Effective Group Decision Making," in *Communication and Group Decision Making,* eds. Randy Y. Hirokawa and Marshall Scott Poole (Beverly Hills, CA: Sage, 1986), pp. 81–90.

18. Associated Press, "Second Opinion Can Spark Big Changes," accessed January 11, 2007: http://www.msnbc.msn.com/id/16430071/.

19. Shaw, *Group Dynamics,* p. 8.

20. Paul V. Crosby, ed., *Interaction in Small Groups* (New York: Macmillan, 1975), p. 7.

21. Steven A. Beebe and John T. Masterson, *Communicating in Small Groups,* 7th ed. (Boston: Allyn & Bacon, 2003), pp. 6–9.

22. Frank LaFasto and Carl Larson, *When Teams Work Best: 6,000 Team Members and Leaders Tell What It Takes to Succeed* (Thousand Oaks, CA: Sage, 2001), pp. xii–xiii.

23. Randy Y. Hirokawa, Robert S. Cathcart, Larry A. Samovar, and Linda D. Henman, "Part IV: Group Processes," in *Small Group Communication: Theory and Practice,* 8th ed., eds. Randy Y. Hirokawa, Robert S. Cathcart, Larry A. Samovar, and Linda D. Henman (Los Angeles, CA: Roxbury, 2003), p. 83.

24. Sandra Ketrow, "Nonverbal Aspects of Group Communication," in *Handbook of Group Communication Theory & Research,* ed. Lawrence R. Frey (Thousand Oaks, CA: Sage, 1999), pp. 251–87.

25. John F. Cragan and David W. Wright, *Communication in Small Groups: Theory, Process, Skills,* 5th ed. (Belmont, CA: Wadsworth, 1999), pp. 20–21.

26. William C. Schutz, *FIRO: A Three-Dimensional Theory of Interpersonal Behavior* (New York: Rinehart, 1958).

27. Thomas J. Socha, "Communication in Family Units," in *Handbook of Group Communication Theory & Research,* ed. Lawrence R. Frey (Thousand Oaks, CA: Sage, 1999), pp. 475–92.

28. Carolyn M. Anderson and Matthew M. Martin, "The Effects of Communication Motives, Interaction Involvement, and Loneliness on

Satisfaction: A Model of Small Groups," *Small Group Research* 26 (February 1995), pp. 118–37.

29. Kevin Wright, "Perceptions of On-Line Support Providers: An Examination of Perceived Homophily, Course Credibility, Communication and Social Support Within On-Line Support Groups," *Communication Quarterly* 48 (Winter 2000), pp. 44–59.

30. Susan A. Wheelan and Alan R. List, "Cohort Group Effectiveness and the Educational Achievement of Adult Undergraduate Students," *Small Group Research* 31 (December 2000), pp. 724–38.

31. Joseph M. Putti and Wong K. Choeng, "Singapore's Positive Experience with Quality Circles," *National Productivity Review* 9 (Spring 1990), pp. 193–200.

32. Henry P. Sims, Jr., and James W. Dean, Jr., "Beyond Quality Circles: Self-Managing Teams," *Personnel Journal* (1985), pp. 25–32.

33. Suggestions synthesized from Neil Clark, *Teambuilding: A Practical Guide for Trainers* (New York: McGraw-Hill, 1994); Glenn M. Parker, *Team Players and Teamwork* (San Francisco: Jossey-Bass, 1991); and Glenn H. Varney, *Building Productive Teams: An Action Guide and Resource Book* (San Francisco: Jossey-Bass, 1989).

34. Sharon L. Murrell, "The Impact of Communicating Through Computers," unpublished doctoral dissertation, State University of New York at Stony Brook, 1983.

35. *The Random House Dictionary of the English Language,* 2nd ed. unabridged (New York: Random House, 1987), p. 665.

**Chapter 2**

1. Dawn Steel (Producer) and Jon Turtetaub (Director), *Cool Runnings* [Film]. Distributed by Walt Disney Pictures (1993) and available on video.

2. Em Griffin, *A First Look at Communication Theory,* 2nd ed. (New York: McGraw-Hill, 2003), p. 4.

3. Daniel Katz and Robert Kahn, *The Social Psychology of Organizations,* 2nd ed. (New York: Wiley, 1978).

4. Benjamin J. Broome and Luann Fulbright, "A Multistage Influence Model of Barriers to Small Group Problem Solving: A Participant-Generated Agenda for Small Group Research," *Small Group Research* 26 (February 1995), pp. 25–55.

5. Linda Putnam and Cynthia Stohl, "Bona Fide Groups: An Alternative Perspective for Communication and Small Group Decision Making," in *Communication and Group Decision Making,* 2nd ed., eds. Randy Hirokawa and Marshall Poole (Thousand Oaks, CA: Sage, 1996), pp. 147–78.

6. Broome and Fulbright, "A Multistage Influence Model."

7. Randy Y. Hirokawa and Joann Keyton, "Perceived Facilitators and Inhibitors of Effectiveness in Organizational Work Teams," *Management Communication Quarterly* 8 (May 1995), pp. 424–46.

8. Deborah G. Ancona and David F. Caldwell, "Bridging the Boundary: External Activity and Performance in Organizational Teams," *Administrative Science Quarterly* 37 (December 1992), pp. 634–65.

9. Cynthia Stohl and Kasey Walker, "A Bona Fide Perspective for the Future of Groups," in *New Directions in Group Communication,* ed. Lawrence R. Frey (Thousand Oaks, CA: Sage, 2002), pp. 237–52.

10. Ibid.

11. Ronald Brownstein, "Tapping Talent, Not Just Names," *Los Angeles Times,* July 4, 2004, pp. A1, A21.

12. Amy Tessler, Norm Wada, and Bob Klein, "Quality Function Deployment (QFD) at PG&E: Applying Quality Function Deployment to the Residential Services of Pacific Gas & Electric," accessed January 6, 2007: www.ams-inc.com/publications/reprints.asp?id=6.

13. Beth Bonniwell Haslett and John R. Ogilive, "Feedback Processes in Task Groups," in *Small Group Communication: Theory and Practice,* 8th ed., eds. Randy Hirokawa, Robert Cathcart, Larry Samovar, and Linda Henman (Los Angeles: Roxbury, 2003), pp. 97–108.

14. Ibid.

15. Ibid.

16. Ibid.

17. Abran J. Salazar, "Understanding the Synergistic Effects of Communication in the Small Group: Making the Most of Group Member Abilities," *Small Group Research* 26 (May 1995), pp. 169–99.

18. Stephen W. Littlejohn, *Theories of Human Communication,* 7th ed. (Belmont, CA: Wadsworth/Thomson Learning, 2002).

19. Jeremy Rose, "Communication Challenges and Role Functions of Performing Groups," *Small Group Research* 25 (August 1994), pp. 411–32.

## Chapter 3

1. Richard West and Lynn H. Turner, *Introducing Communication Theory: Analysis and Application,* 2nd ed. (New York: McGraw-Hill, 2004).

2. Julia T. Wood, *Communication Theories in Action: An Introduction,* 3rd ed. (Belmont, CA: Thomson Wadsworth, 2004).

3. Ibid.

4. Martin Fackler, "Homeward Bound: Carefully Worded Letter to China Earns Release of Crew Members," *San Francisco Chronicle,* April 12, 2001, pp. A1, A17.

5. Frank E. X. Dance, "A Helical Model of Communication," in *Foundations of Communication Theory,* eds. Kenneth K. Sereno and C. David Mortensen (New York: Harper & Row, 1970), pp. 103–07.

6. Paul Watzlawick, Janet H. Beavin, and Don D. Jackson, *The Pragmatics of Human Communication* (New York: Norton, 1967).

7. Kittie W. Watson, "Listener Preferences: The Paradox of Small-Group Interactions," in *Small Group Communication: Theory and Practice,* 7th ed., eds. Robert S. Cathcart, Larry A. Samovar, and Linda Henman (Madison, WI: Brown & Benchmark, 1996), pp. 268–82.

8. Dan B. Curtis, Jerry L. Windsor, and R. D. Stephens, "National Preferences in Business and Communication Education," *Communication Education* 38 (1989), pp. 6–14.

9. John Gastil, "Identifying Obstacles to Small Group Democracy," *Small Group Research* 24 (February 1993), pp. 5–27.

10. Curt Bechler and Scott D. Johnson, "Leadership and Listening: A Study of Members' Perceptions," *Small Group Research* 26 (February 1995), pp. 77–85.

11. Lyman K. Steil, Larry L. Barker, and Kittie W. Watson, *Effective Listening: Key to Your Success* (Reading, MA: Addison-Wesley, 1983), pp. 21–22.

12. Kenneth N. Leone Cissna and Evelyn Sieburg, "Patterns of Intentional Confirmation and Disconfirmation," in *Bridges, Not Walls,* 4th ed., ed. John Stewart (New York: Random House, 1986), pp. 231–39.

13. Watson, "Listener Preferences," pp. 271–75.

14. Ibid., p. 270.

15. George R. Bach and Peter Wyden, *The Intimate Enemy* (New York: Avon, 1968).

16. David M. Berg, "A Descriptive Analysis of the Distribution and Duration of Themes Discussed by Task-Oriented Small Groups," *Speech Monographs* 34 (1967), pp. 172–75.

## Chapter 4

1. Joseph A. DeVito, *The Communication Handbook: A Dictionary* (New York: Harper & Row, 1986).

2. Wendy Leeds-Hurwitz, *Communication in Everyday Life: A Social Interpretation,* 3rd ed. (Norwood, NJ: Ablex, 1992).

3. Marshall S. Poole, David R. Siebold, and Robert D. McPhee, "Group Decision Making as a Structurational Process," *Quarterly Journal of Speech* 71 (1985), pp. 74–102; and Marshall S. Poole, "Group Communication and the Structuring Process," in *Small Group Communication: A Reader,* 6th ed., ed. Robert S. Cathcart and Larry A. Samovar (Dubuque, IA: Wm. C. Brown, 1992), pp. 147–57.

4. Meredith May, "Talkin' off the Hizzle with Homeys," *San Francisco Chronicle,* April 29, 2001, pp. A1, A17.

5. Ibid., p. A17. (You can still purchase the *Berkeley High Slang Dictionary* for $5 by contacting Rick Ayers at rickilene@igc.org.)

6. Dale G. Leathers, "Process Disruption and Measurement: Small Group Communication," *Quarterly Journal of Speech* 55 (1969), pp. 288–98.

7. This example is a modification of a case where a Fresno, California, high school student was suspended from school for using "nigga" to greet a friend on school grounds.

8. John Stewart and Carol Logan, *Together: Communicating Interpersonally,* 5th ed. (New York: McGraw-Hill, 1998).

9. Ibid.

10. Ray L. Birdwhistell, lecture at Nebraska Psychiatric Institute, Omaha, Nebraska, May 11, 1972.

11. Dana R. Carney, Judith A. Hall, and Lavonia Smith LeBeau, "Beliefs About the Nonverbal Expression of Social Power," *Journal of Nonverbal Behavior,* 29 (2) (Summer 2005), pp. 105–21.

12. Timothy P. Mottet, Steven A. Beebe, Paul C. Raffeld, and Michelle L. Paulsel, "The Effects of Student Verbal and Nonverbal Responsiveness on Teachers' Liking of Students and Willingness to Comply with Student Requests," *Communication Quarterly,* 52 (1) (Winter 2004), pp. 27–38.

13. Kory Floyd and George Ray, "Adaptation to Expressed Liking and Disliking in Initial

Interactions: Response Patterns for Nonverbal Involvement and Pleasantness," paper presented at the International Communication Association Conference, New York, May 26–30, 2005.

14. Sandra Ketrow, "Nonverbal Aspects of Group Communication," in *The Handbook of Group Communication Theory & Research,* ed. Lawrence R. Frey (Thousand Oaks, CA: Sage, 1999), pp. 251–87.

15. Ibid.

16. Robert Freeman, *The Beatles: A Private View* (New York: Barnes & Noble, 1990).

17. Ibid., p. 46.

18. Edward T. Hall, *The Silent Language* (Garden City, NY: Doubleday, 1959).

19. Ketrow, "Nonverbal Aspects of Group Communication."

20. Ibid.

21. Judee K. Burgoon, Don W. Stacks, and Steven A. Burch, "The Role of Interpersonal Rewards and Violations of Distancing Expectations in Achieving Influence in Small Groups," *Communication: Journal of the Association of the Pacific* 11 (1982), pp. 114–28.

22. Ketrow, "Nonverbal Aspects of Group Communication."

23. P. Eckman, P. Ellsworth, and W. V. Friesen, *Emotion in the Human Face: Guidelines for Research and an Integration of Findings* (New York: Pergamon, 1971).

24. Mark Frank, Anastacia Kurylo, Kang Sinuk, AmyMarie Keller, Malgorzata Habasz, and Courtney Nolan, "I See How You Feel: Training Laypeople and Professionals to Recognize Fleeting Emotions," paper presented at the International Communication Association conference, New York, May 26–30, 2005.

25. A. E. Scheffler, "Quasi-Courtship Behavior in Psychotherapy," *Psychiatry* 28 (1965), pp. 245–56.

26. Edward A. Mabry, "Developmental Aspects of Nonverbal Behavior in Small Group Settings," *Small Group Behavior* 20 (1989), pp. 190–202.

27. Martin Remland, "Developing Leadership Skills in Nonverbal Communication: A Situational Perspective," *Journal of Business Communication* 3 (1981), pp. 17–29.

28. Judee K. Burgoon and Thomas Saine, *The Unknown Dialogue: An Introduction to Nonverbal Communication* (Boston: Houghton Mifflin, 1978).

29. Joel D. Davitz and Lois Davitz, "Nonverbal Vocal Communication of Feelings," *Journal of Communication* 11 (1961), pp. 81–86.

30. Ketrow, "Nonverbal Aspects of Group Communication."

31. Pino Cutrone, "A Case Study Examining Backchannels in Conversations Between Japanese-British Dyads," *Multilingua,* 24 (3) (2005), pp. 237–74.

32. Han Z. Li, "Backchannel Responses as Misleading Feedback in Intercultural Discourse," *Journal of Intercultural Communication Research* 35 (2) (July 2006), pp. 99–116.

33. Donald Klopf, *Intercultural Encounters: The Fundamentals of Intercultural Communication* (Englewood, CO: Morion, 1987), p. 177.

34. R. G. Harper, A. N. Weins, and J. D. Matarazzo, *Nonverbal Communication: The State of the Art* (New York: Wiley, 1978).

35. Hall, *The Silent Language,* pp. 175–76.

36. Ketrow, "Nonverbal Aspects of Group Communication."

37. Ibid.

38. Craig R. Scott, "New Communication Technologies and Teams," in *Small Group Communication: Theory and Practice,* 8th ed., eds. Randy Hirokawa, Robert Cathcart, Larry Samovar, and Linda Henman (Los Angeles: Roxbury, 2003), pp. 134–47.

39. Jennifer Zaino, "Employee Collaboration on the Upswing," *InformationWeek.com* (February 11, 2002). Retrieved June 28, 2004, from www. Informationweek.com/story/IW20020202750008.

40. Tyrone Adams and Norman Clark, *The Internet: Effective Online Communication* (Fort Worth, TX: Harcourt, 2001), pp. 112–19.

41. S. R. Hiltz and M. Turoff, "Virtual Meetings: Computer Conferencing and Distributed Group Support," in *Computer Augmented Teamwork: A Guided Tour,* eds. R. P. Bostrom, R. T. Watson, and S. T. Kinney (New York: Van Nostrand Reinhold, 1992), pp. 67–85.

42. Everett M. Rogers, *Communication Technology: The New Media in Society* (New York: Free Press, 1986).

43. Compiled from Larry L. Barker, Kathy J. Wahlers, Kittie W. Watson, and Robert J. Kibler, *Groups in Process: An Introduction to Small Group Communication,* 3rd ed. (Englewood Cliffs, NJ: Prentice-Hall, 1987), p. 208, and Robert J. Johansen, J. Vallee, and K. Spangler, *Electronic*

*Meetings: Technical Alternatives and Social Choices* (Reading, MA: Addison-Wesley, 1979), pp. 113–15.

44. Jennifer M. Heisler and Scott L. Crabill, "Who Are 'stinkybug' and 'Packerfan4'? Email Pseudonyms and Participants' Perceptions of Demography, Productivity, and Personality," *Journal of Computer-Mediated Communication,* 12 (1) (November 2006), pp. 114–35.

**Chapter 5**

1. Robert F. Bales, "The Equilibrium Problem in Small Groups," in *Working Papers in the Theory of Action,* eds. Talcott Parsons, Robert F. Bales, and Edward A. Shils (New York: Free Press, 1953), pp. 111–61.

2. The terms *primary* and *secondary tension* were first used by Ernest G. Bormann; elaboration of the concepts may be found in Bormann, *Discussion and Group Methods: Theory and Practice,* 2nd ed. (New York: Harper & Row, 1975), pp. 181–90.

3. Donald G. Ellis and B. Aubrey Fisher, *Small Group Decision Making: Communication and the Group Process,* 4th ed. (New York: McGraw-Hill, 1994), p. 38.

4. Bormann, *Discussion and Group Methods.*

5. Ellis and Fisher, *Small Group Decision Making,* p. 38.

6. Katherine E. Finkelstein, "Tempers Seem to Be Shorter in Many Jury Rooms," *New York Times* (August 3, 2001). Retrieved July 8, 2004, from www.nytimes.com/2001/08/03/nyregion/ 03JURY.htm?ex=1089604800&en= 9dlfl46719a4ab93&ei=5070&ex=997841696&.

7. David M. Ryfe, "Narrative and Deliberation in Small Group Forums," *Journal of Applied Communication Research* 34 (1) (2006), pp. 72–93.

8. Joseph B. Walther and Judee K. Burgoon, "Relational Communication in Computer-Mediated Interaction," *Human Communication Research* 19 (1992), pp. 50–88.

9. Bruce Tuckman, "Developmental Sequence in Small Groups," *Psychological Bulletin* 63 (1965), pp. 384–99; Bruce Tuckman and Mary Ann Jensen, "Stages of Small-Group Development Revisited," *Group & Organization Studies* 2 (4) (1977), pp. 419–27.

10. Connie Gersick, "Time and Transition in Work Teams," in *Small Group Communication: Theory & Practice,* 8th ed., eds. Randy Hirokawa, Robert Cathcart, Larry Samovar, and Linda Henman (Los Angeles: Roxbury, 2003), pp. 59–75.

11. Carolyn M. Anderson, Bruce L. Riddle, and Matthew M. Martin, "Socialization Processes in Groups," in *Handbook of Group Communication Theory & Research,* ed. Lawrence R. Frey (Thousand Oaks, CA: Sage, 1999), pp. 139–63.

12. Ibid., p. 142.

13. Ibid.

14. Ibid.

15. Joann Keyton, *Group Communication* (Mountain View, CA: Mayfield, 1999), p. 115.

16. Anderson et al., p. 147.

17. Ibid., p. 148.

18. Ibid., p. 149.

19. Stewart Sigman, "The Applicability of the Concept of Recruitment to the Communication Study of a Nursing Home: An Ethnographic Case Study," *International Journal of Aging and Human Development* 22 (1985–86), pp. 215–33. See also Melanie Booth-Butterfield, Stephen Booth-Butterfield, and Jolene Koester, "The Function of Uncertainty Reduction in Alleviating Primary Tension in Small Groups," *Communication Research Reports* 5 (1988), pp. 146–53.

20. Anderson et al., "Socialization Processes in Groups," p. 151.

21. K.E.W. Morrison, "Information Usefulness and Acquisition During Organizational Encounter," *Management Communication Quarterly* 9 (1995), pp. 131–55.

22. Anderson et al., p. 152.

23. Ibid., p. 164.

24. Joann Keyton, "Group Termination: Completing the Study of Group Development," *Small Group Research* 24 (1993), pp. 84–100.

25. Stephanie Zimmerman, "Social Cognition and Evaluations of Health Care Team Communication Effectiveness," *Western Journal of Communication* 58 (Spring 1994), pp. 116–41.

26. Peter E. Mudrack and Genevieve M. Farrell, "An Examination of Functional Role Behavior and Its Consequences for Individuals in Group Settings," *Small Group Research* 26 (November 1995), pp. 542–71.

27. Aitor Aritzeta, Barbara Senior, and Stephen Swailes, "Team Role Preferences and Cognitive Styles: A Convergent Validity Study," *Small Group Research* 36 (4) (August 2005), pp. 404–36.

28. Craig R. Scott, "New Communication Technologies and Teams," in *Small Group Communication: Theory & Practice,* 8th ed., eds. Randy Hirokawa, Robert Cathcart, Larry Samovar, and Linda Henman (Los Angeles: Roxbury, 2003), pp. 134–47.

29. Michael K. Kramer, Communication in a Community Theatre Group: Managing Multiple Group Roles," *Communication Studies* 53 (2002), pp. 151–70.

30. Ibid.

31. Susan B. Shimanoff, "Coordinating Group Interaction via Communication Rules," in *Small Group Communication: A Reader,* 6th ed., eds. Robert Cathcart and Larry Samovar (Dubuque, IA: Wm. C. Brown, 1992), p. 255.

32. Daniel Feldman, "Development and Enforcement of Group Norms," *Academy of Management Review* 9 (1984), pp. 47–53.

33. Stanley Schacter, "Deviation, Rejection, and Communication," *Journal of Abnormal and Social Psychology* 46 (1951), pp. 190–207, and Harold Leavitt, *Managerial Psychology,* 2nd ed. (Chicago: University of Chicago Press, 1964), pp. 270–74.

34. Ronald R. Sims, "Linking Groupthink to Unethical Behavior in Organizations," *Journal of Business Ethics* 11 (September 1992), pp. 651–62.

35. Katherine W. Hawkins and Bryant P. Fillion, "Perceived Communication Skill Needs for Work Groups," *Communication Research Reports* 16 (Spring 1999), pp. 167–74.

36. Joseph P. Folger and Marshall S. Poole, *Working Through Conflict: A Communication Perspective* (Glenview, IL: Scott, Foresman, 1984), p. 84.

37. Hawkins and Fillion, "Perceived Communication Skill Needs for Work Groups," pp. 167–74.

38. Carl E. Larson and Frank M. J. LaFasto, *TeamWork: What Must Go Right, What Can Go Wrong* (Newbury Park, CA: Sage, 1989).

39. M. E. Johnson and J. G. Fortman, "Internal Structure of the Gross Cohesiveness Scale," *Small Group Behavior* 19 (February 1988), pp. 187–96.

40. C. N. Greene, "Cohesion and Productivity in Work Groups," *Small Group Behavior* 21 (February 1989), pp. 221–25.

41. Brian Mullen, Tara Anthony, Eduardo Salas, and James E. Driskell, "Group Cohesiveness and Quality of Decision Making: An Integration of Tests of the Groupthink Hypothesis," *Small Group Research* 25 (May 1995), pp. 189–204.

42. Claus W. Langfred, "Is Group Cohesiveness a Double-Edged Sword? An Investigation on the Effects of Cohesiveness on Performance," *Small Group Research* 29 (1996), pp. 124–43.

43. Irving L. Janis, *Groupthink: Psychological Studies of Policy Decisions and Fiascoes,* 2nd ed. (Boston: Houghton Mifflin, 1983), pp. 14–47.

44. Jack R. Gibb, "Defensive Communication," *Journal of Communication* 11 (1961), pp. 141–48.

**Chapter 6**

1. Marvin E. Shaw, *Group Dynamics; The Psychology of Small Group Behavior,* 2nd ed. (New York: McGraw-Hill, 1971), pp. 219–36.

2. See, for example, Warren E. Watson, Kamalesch Kumar, and Larry K. Michaelson, "Cultural Diversity's Impact on Interaction Process and Performance: Comparing Homogeneous and Diverse Task Groups," *Academy of Management Journal* 36 (1993), pp. 590–602.

3. William B. Johnston and Arnold E. Packer, *Workforce 2000: Work and Workers for the 21st Century* (Indianapolis, IN: Hudson Institute, 1987).

4. G. M. Parker, *Team Players and Teamwork: The New Competitive Business Strategy* (San Francisco: Jossey-Bass, 1990), and R. A. Eisenstat, "Fairfield Systems Group," in *Groups That Work and Those That Don't,* ed. J. R. Hackman (San Francisco: Jossey-Bass, 1990), pp. 171–81.

5. Kim M. Shapcott, Albert V. Carron, and Paul A. Estabrooks, "Member Diversity and Cohesion and Performance in Walking Groups," *Small Group Research* 37 (6) (December 2006), pp. 701–20.

6. Robert Freed Bales, *Personality and Interpersonal Behavior* (New York: Holt, Rinehart & Winston, 1970).

7. Carolyn M. Anderson and Matthew M. Martin, "Communication Motives (State vs. Trait?) and Task Group Outcomes," *Communication Research Reports* 19 (Summer 2002), pp. 269–82.

8. Ibid., p. 193.

9. Dirk Scheerhorn and Patricia Geist, "Social Dynamics in Groups," in *Managing Group Life,* eds. Lawrence R. Frey and J. Kevin Barge (Boston: Houghton Mifflin, 1997), pp. 80–103.

10. Carolyn M. Anderson and Matthew M. Martin, "The Effects of Communication Motives, Interaction Involvement, and Loneliness on Satisfaction: A Model of Small Groups," *Small Group Research* 26 (February 1995), pp. 118–37.

11. John G. Oetzel and Keri Bolton-Oetzel, "Exploring the Relationship Between Self-Construal and Dimensions of Group Effectiveness," *Management Communication Quarterly* 10 (3) (February 1997), pp. 289–315.

12. Torsten Reimer, Sascha Kuendig, Ulrich Hoffrage, Ernest Park, and Verlin Hinz, "Effects of the Information Environment on Group Discussions and Decisions in the Hidden-Profile Paradigm," *Communication Monographs* 74 (1) (March 2007), pp. 1–28.

13. William F. Owen, "Metaphor Analysis of Cohesiveness in Small Discussion Groups," *Small Group Behavior* 16 (1985), pp. 415–26.

14. David A. Kolb, *Experiential Learning: Experience as the Source of Learning and Development* (Englewood Cliffs, NJ: Prentice-Hall, 1984).

15. Synthesized from Isabel Briggs Myers, *Introduction to Type: A Description of the Theory and Application of the Myers-Briggs Type Indicator* (Palo Alto, CA: Consulting Psychologists Press, 1987); Otto Kroeger and Janet A. Thuesen, *Type Talk: The 16 Personality Types That Determine How We Live, Love, and Work* (New York: Dell, 1988); Otto Kroeger with Janet A. Thuesen, *Type Talk at Work: How the 16 Personality Types Determine Your Success on the Job* (New York: Dell, 1992); and Paul D. Tieger and Barbara Barron-Tieger, *Nurture by Nature: Understand Your Child's Personality Type—And Become a Better Parent* (Boston: Little, Brown, 1997), pp. 5–62.

16. See, for example, John G. Oetzel, "Culturally Homogeneous and Heterogeneous Groups: Explaining Communication Processes Through Individualism-Collectivism and Self-Construal," *International Journal of Intercultural Relations* 22 (2) (May 1998), pp. 135–61; John G. Oetzel, "Explaining Individual Communication Processes in Homogenous and Heterogeneous Groups Through Individualism-Collectivism and Self-Construal," *Human Communication Research* 25 (2) (December 1998), pp. 202–24; and Kim M. Shapcott, Albert V. Carron, and Paul A. Estabrooks, "Member Diversity and Cohesion and Performance in Walking Groups," *Small Group Research* 37 (6) (December 2006), pp. 701–20.

17. The following information about culture is synthesized from a number of sources, including Edward T. Hall, *Beyond Culture* (New York: Anchor Press, 1977); Geert Hofstede, *Culture's Consequences: International Differences in Work-Related Values,* 2nd ed. (Beverly Hills, CA: Sage, 2001); William B. Gudykunst and Stella Ting-Toomey, *Culture and Interpersonal Communication* (Newbury Park, CA: Sage, 1988); Myron Lustig and Jolene Koester, *Interpersonal Competence: Interpersonal Communication Across Cultures* (New York: HarperCollins, 1993); and Myron W. Lustig and Laura L. Casotta, "Comparing Group Communication Across Culture: Leadership, Conformity, and Discussion Procedures," in *Small Group Communication: A Reader,* 6th ed., eds. Robert S. Cathcart and Larry A. Samovar (Dubuque, IA: Wm. C. Brown, 1992), pp. 393–404.

18. Larry A. Samovar and Richard E. Porter, *Communication Between Cultures,* 4th ed. (Belmont, CA: Wadsworth, 2001), pp. 52–88.

19. Min-Sun Kim and William F. Sharkey, "Independent and Interdependent Construals of Self: Explaining Cultural Patterns of Interpersonal Communication in Multicultural Organizational Settings," *Communication Quarterly* 43 (Winter 1995), pp. 20–38.

20. Oetzel, "Culturally Homogeneous."

21. Judith N. Martin and Thomas K. Nakayama, *Experiencing Intercultural Communication: An Introduction* (Mountain View, CA: Mayfield, 2001), pp. 166–67.

22. This section is a summary of Oetzel, "Culturally Homogeneous," and Oetzel, "Explaining Individual."

23. This information is synthesized from Michael L. Hecht, Mary Jane Collier, and Sidney A. Ribeau, *African American Communication: Ethnic Identity and Cultural Interpretation,* vol. 2, Language and Language Behaviors series (Newbury Park, CA: Sage, 1993), especially Chap. 3, pp. 82–113, and Anita K. Foeman and Gary Pressley, "Ethnic Culture and Corporate Culture: Using Black Styles in Organizations," *Communication Quarterly* 35 (Fall 1987), pp. 293–307.

24. Rebecca Leonard and Don C. Locke, "Communication Stereotypes: Is Interracial Communication Possible?" *Journal of Black Studies* 23 (March 1993), pp. 332–43.

25. Mark P. Orbe, "Remember, It's Always Whites' Ball: Descriptions of African American Male Communication," *Communication Quarterly* 35 (Fall 1987), pp. 293–307.

26. C. Kirchmeyer and A. Cohen, "Multicultural Groups: Their Performance and Reactions with Constructive Conflict," *Group & Organization Management* 17 (1992), pp. 153–70, and C. Kirchmeyer, "Multicultural Task Groups: An

Account of the Low Contribution Level of Minorities," *Small Group Research* 24 (February 1993), pp. 127–48.

27. Hofstede, "Culture's Consequences."

28. Nina M. Reich and Julia T. Wood, "Sex, Gender and Communication in Small Groups," in *Small Group Communication: Theory and Practice,* 8th ed., eds. Randy Y. Hirokawa, Robert S. Cathcart, Larry A. Samovar, and Linda D. Henman (Los Angeles: Roxbury, 2003), pp. 218–29.

29. Andrew J. Flanagin, Vanessa Tiyaamornwong, Joan O'Connor, and David R. Seibold, "Computer-Mediated Group Work: The Interaction of Member Sex and Anonymity," *Communication Research* 29 (February 2002), pp. 66–93.

30. Lindsey M. Grob, Renee A. Meyers, and Renee Schuh, "Powerful/Powerless Language Use in Group Interactions: Sex Differences or Similarities?" *Communication Quarterly* 45 (3) (Summer 1997), pp. 282–303.

31. Ibid.

32. Scott A. Krebs, Elizabeth V. Hobman, and Prashant Bordia, "Virtual Teams and Group Member Diversity," *Small Group Research* 37 (6) (December 2006), pp. 721–41.

33. This information is taken primarily from Rick Hicks and Kathy Hicks, *Boomers, Xers, and Other Strangers: Understanding the Generational Differences That Divide Us* (Wheaton, IL: Tyndale House, 1999), especially pp. 229–353. Other sources of information include Morris E. Massey, *The People Puzzle: Understanding Yourself and Others* (Reston, VA: Reston, 1979); Don Tapscott, *Growing Up Digital: The Rise of the Net Generation* (New York: McGraw-Hill, 1998); and Lynne C. Lancaster and David Sillman, *When Generations Collide* (New York: HarperCollins, 2002).

34. Franklin B. Krohn, "A Generational Approach to Using Emoticons as Nonverbal Communication," *Journal of Technical Writing and Communication* 34 (4) (2004), pp. 321–28.

35. Watson, Kamalesh, and Michaelson, "Cultural Diversity," and Leisa D. Sargent and Christina Sue-Chan, "Does Diversity Affect Group Efficacy? The Intervening Role of Cohesion and Task Interdependence," *Small Group Research* 32 (August 2001), pp. 426–50.

36. Stella Ting-Toomey, *Communicating Across Cultures* (New York: Guilford Press, 1999), pp. 45–54, 261–76.

37. Ernest G. Bormann, "Symbolic Convergence Theory and Communication in Group Decision Making," in *Communication and Group Decision Making,* 2nd ed., eds. Randy Y. Hirokawa and M. Scott Poole (Thousand Oaks, CA: Sage, 1996), pp. 81–113.

38. Catherine Cobb Morocco, "Development and Function of Group Metaphor," *Journal for the Theory of Social Behavior* 9 (1979), pp. 15–27.

39. Bormann, "Symbolic Convergence," pp. 229–30.

40. Complete information on constructing a SYMLOG diagram, along with an abbreviated explanation of SYMLOG theory, may be found in a workbook, R. F. Bales, *SYMLOG Case Study Kit* (New York: Free Press, 1980). An even more simplified explanation of SYMLOG theory and method for constructing a diagram may be found in Joann Keyton, "Coding Communication in Decision-Making Groups," in *Managing Group Life: Communicating in Decision-Making Groups* (Boston: Houghton Mifflin, 1997), pp. 236–69. For readers who are interested in details of both the theory and methodology, we refer them to R. F. Bales and Stephen P. Cohen, *SYMLOG: A System for the Multiple-Level Observation of Groups* (New York: Free Press, 1979).

41. Richard V. Polley, SYMLOG computer software, Lewis and Clark University, Portland, OR.

42. Ting-Toomey, *Communicating Across Cultures.*

**Chapter 7**

1. Sunwolf, "Getting to 'GroupAha!' Provoking Creative Processes in Task Groups," in *The Handbook of Group Communication Theory & Research,* ed. Lawrence R. Frey (Thousand Oaks, CA: Sage, 1999), p. 205.

2. Susan Jarboe, "Group Communication and Creativity Processes," in *The Handbook of Group Communication Theory & Research,* ed. Lawrence R. Frey (Thousand Oaks, CA: Sage, 1999), p. 336.

3. David F. Caldwell and Charles A. O'Reilly, III, "The Determinants of Team-Based Innovations in Organizations: The Role of Social Influence," *Small Group Research* 34 (August 2003), pp. 497–517.

4. Paul G. Bain, Leon Mann, and Andrew Pirola-Merlo, "The Innovation Imperative: The Relationship Between Team Climate, Innovation, and Performance in Research and Development Teams," *Small Group Research* 32 (February 2001), pp. 55–73.

5. Bernard A. Nijstad and Paul B. Paulus, "Group Creativity: Common Themes and Future

Directions," in *Group Creativity: Innovation Through Collaboration,* eds. Paul B. Paulus and Bernard A. Nijstad (New York: Oxford University Press, 2003), pp. 326–39.

6. John J. Sosik, Bruce J. Avolio, and Surinder S. Kahai, "Inspiring Group Creativity: Comparing Anonymous and Identified Electronic Brainstorming," *Small Group Research* 29 (1998), pp. 3–31.

7. Nijstad and Paulus, "Group Creativity," p. 330.

8. Jarboe, "Group Communication and Creativity Processes," pp. 336–41.

9. Nijstad and Paulus, "Group Creativity," pp. 326–32.

10. Antonio Chirumbolo, Lucia Mannetti, Antonio Pierro, Alessandra Areni, and Arie W. Kruglanski, "Motivated Closed-Mindedness and Creativity in Small Groups," *Small Group Research* 36 (February 2005), pp. 59–82.

11. Alex Osborn, *Applied Imagination,* rev. ed. (New York: Scribner, 1957).

12. M. Basadur and R. Thompson, "Usefulness of the Ideation Principle of Extended Effort in Real World Professional and Managerial Problem Solving," *Journal of Creative Behavior* 20 (1982), pp. 23–34.

13. Chirumbolo et al., "Motivated Closed-Mindedness."

14. Hamit Coskun, "Cognitive Stimulation with Convergent and Divergent Thinking Exercises in Brainwriting: Incubation, Sequence Priming, and Group Context," *Small Group Research* 36 (August 2005), pp. 466–98.

15. Chirumbolo et al., "Motivated Closed-Mindedness."

16. R. Brent Gallupe, Alan R. Dennis, William H. Cooper, Joseph S. Valacich, Lame M. Bastianum, and Jay F. Nunamaker, Jr., "Electronic Brainstorming and Group Size," *Academy of Management Journal* 35 (June 1992), pp. 350–70. See also Joseph S. Valacich, Alan R. Dennis, and T. Connolly, "Idea Generation in Computer-Based Groups: A New Ending to an Old Story," *Organizational Behavior and Human Decision Processes* 57 (1994), pp. 448–68.

17. Russell L. Ackoff and Elsa Vergara, "Creativity in Problem Solving and Planning," in *Handbook for Creative and Innovative Managers,* ed. Robert L. Kuhn (New York: McGraw-Hill, 1988), pp. 77–90.

18. Accessed June 14, 2004, www.ideafinder.com/history/inventions//story015.htm.

19. Del Jones, "GE Leader Recalls 'Eureka' Moment: Being No. 1 Was Limiting Opportunity," *The Cincinnati Enquirer,* April 8, 2001, pp. D1–2.

20. See Tony Buzan with Barry Buzan, *The Mind Map® Book* (New York: Plume, 1996), for a detailed description of the process with examples and information about the theoretical underpinnings of mind mapping.

21. Sunwolf, "Getting to 'GroupAha!,'" p. 209.

22. R. L. Firestein, "Effects of Creative Problem-Solving Training on Communication Behaviors in Small Groups," *Small Group Research* 21 (1990), pp. 507–21.

23. For a clear review of these issues, see Dale E. Brashers, Mark Adkins, and Renee A. Meyers, "Argumentation and Computer-Mediated Group Decision-Making," in *Group Communication in Context,* ed. Lawrence R. Frey (Hillsdale, NJ: Lawrence Erlbaum, 1994), pp. 263–82.

24. D. Christopher Kayes, "From Climbing Stairs to Riding Waves," *Small Group Research* 37 (December 2006), pp. 612–30, and D. Christopher Kayes, "Dilemma at 29,000 feet: An Exercise in Ethical Decision Making Based on the 1996 Mt. Everest Disaster," *Journal of Management Education* 26 (2002), pp. 307–21.

25. Columbia Accident Investigation website, "Columbia Accident Investigation Board Press Briefing," August 26, 2003, accessed June 5, 2004, www.caib.us/events/press_briefings/20030826/transcript.html.

26. Marcia Dunn, "NASA Chiefs: Managers Must Embrace Change," Yahoo! News, accessed April 14, 2004, http://story.news.yahoo.com/news.

27. Dennis S. Gouran, Randy Y. Hirokawa, and Amy E. Martz, "A Critical Analysis of Factors Related to Decisional Processes Involved in the *Challenger* Disaster," *Central States Speech Journal* 37 (1986), pp. 119–35.

28. Chirumbolo et al., "Motivated Closed-Mindedness."

29. Brashers et al., "Argumentation and Computer-Mediated Group Decision-Making."

30. Sarah J. Tracy, "When Questioning Turns to Face Threat: An Interactional Sensitivity in 911 Call-Taking," *Western Journal of Communication* 66, pp. 129–57.

31. Richard Huseman, Glenn Ware, and Charles Gruner, "Critical Thinking, Reflective Thinking, and the Ability to Organize Ideas: A Multivariate Approach," *Journal of the American Forensic Association* 9 (1972), pp. 261–65.

32. Torsten Reimer, Sascha Kuendig, Ulrich Hoffrage, Ernest Park, and Verlin Hinz, "Effects of the

Information Environment on Group Discussions and Decisions in the Hidden-Profile Paradigm," *Communication Monographs* 74 (1) (March 2007), pp. 1–28.

33. M. Neil Browne and Stuart M. Keeley, *Asking the Right Questions: A Guide to Critical Thinking,* 3rd ed. (Englewood Cliffs, NJ: Prentice-Hall, 1992), pp. 3–5.

34. Tyrone Adams and Norman Clark, *The Internet: Effective Online Communication* (Fort Worth, TX: Harcourt, 2001), pp. 166–75.

35. Ibid., pp. 3–7.

36. Brashers et al., "Argumentation and Computer-Mediated Group Decision-Making," pp. 263–82.

37. Gouran et al., "A Critical Analysis of Factors Related to Decisional Processes Involved in the *Challenger* Disaster," p. 130.

38. Mark F. Stasson and Scott D. Bradshaw, "Explanations of Individual-Group Performance Differences: What Sort of 'Bonus' Can Be Gained Through Group Interaction?" *Small Group Research* 26 (May 1995), pp. 296–308.

39. Richard Paul and Linda Elder, *The Thinker's Guide to Fallacies: The Art of Mental Trickery and Manipulation* (Dillon Beach, CA: Foundation for Critical Thinking, 2004).

40. Daniel C. Vock and Pauline Vu, "Va. Tech Tragedy Revives Gun Controversy," accessed June 13, 2007: http://www.stateline.org/live/details/ story? contentId=199281; and Whitney Hodgin, "Concealed-Carry Controversy Ongoing After Va. Tech Shootings," accessed June 13, 2007: http://media.www.kstatecollegian.com/media/ storage/paper1022/news/2007/04/23/News/ ConcealedCarry.Controversy.Ongoing.After.Va. Tech.Shootings-2871377.shtml.

41. For a more detailed description of and source for these GSS tools and their potential impact on group critical thinking, see Brashers et al., "Argumentation and Computer-Mediated Group Decision-Making."

42. D. Cole, "Meetings That Make Sense," *Psychology Today* (May 1989), pp. 14–15.

43. David Henningsen, Mary Lynn Miller Henningsen, Jenifer Eden, and Michael Cruz, "Examining the Symptoms of Groupthink and Retrospective Sensemaking," *Small Group Research* 37 (2006), pp. 36–64.

44. Brian Mullen, Tara Anthony, Eduardo Salas, and James E. Driskell, "Group Cohesiveness and Quality of Decision Making: An Integration of the Groupthink Hypothesis," *Small Group Research* 25 (May 1994), pp. 189–204.

45. Irving L. Janis and Leon Mann, *Decision Making: A Psychological Analysis of Conflict, Choice, and Commitment* (New York: Free Press, 1977).

46. Lucia Savadori, Lyn M. Van Swol, and Janet A. Sniezek, "Information Sampling and Confidence Within Groups and Judge Advisor Systems," *Communication Research* 28 (December 2001), pp. 737–71; Michael G. Cruz and David D. Henningsen, "The Presence of Norms in the Absence of Groups?" *Human Communication Research* 26 (January 2000), pp. 104–24; Mark Schiettekatte and Alain Van Niel, "Effects of Partially Shared Information and Awareness of Unshared Information on Information Sampling," *Small Group Research* 25 (May 1994), pp. 189–204.

47. Janis and Mann, *Decision Making.*

48. Charles R. Franz and K. Gregory Jin, "The Structure of Group Conflict in a Collaborative Work Group During Information Systems Development," *Journal of Applied Communication Research* 23 (1995), pp. 108–27.

49. Markus Brauer, Charles M. Judd, and Vincent Jacquelin, "The Communication of Social Stereotypes: The Effects of Group Discussion and Information Distribution on Stereotypic Appraisals," *Journal of Personality and Social Psychology* 81 (3) (2001), pp. 463–75.

50. R. Spears and M. Leah, "Panacea or Panopticon? The Hidden Power in Computer-Mediated Communication," *Communication Research* 21 (1994), pp. 427–59.

**Chapter 8**

1. Jay Hall, "Decisions, Decisions, Decisions," *Psychology Today* (November 1971), pp. 51–54, 86–87; Jay Hall and W. H. Watson, "The Effects of a Normative Intervention on Decision-Making Performance," *Human Relations* 23 (1970), pp. 299–317; Irving L. Janis, *Groupthink: Psychological Studies of Policy Decisions and Fiascoes,* 2nd ed. (Boston: Houghton Mifflin, 1982); Randy Y. Hirokawa, "Consensus Group Decision-Making, Quality of Decision and Group Satisfaction: An Attempt to Sort Fact from Fiction," *Central States Speech Journal* 33 (1982), pp. 407–15; Lester Coch and J. R. P. French, Jr., "Overcoming Resistance to Change," *Human Relations* 1 (1948), pp. 512–32; and Myron W. Block and L. R. Hoffman, "The Effects of Valence

of Solutions and Group Cohesiveness on Members' Commitment to Group Decisions," in *The Group Problem-Solving Process,* ed. L. Richard Hoffman (New York: Praeger, 1979), p. 121.

2. Kathleen M. Propp, "In Search of the Assembly Bonus Effect: Continued Exploration of Communication's Role in Group Memory," *Human Communication Research* 29 (4) (2003), pp. 600–606.

3. Patrica Fandt, "The Relationship of Accountability and Interdependent Behavior to Enhancing Team Consequences," *Group and Organization Studies* 16 (1991), pp. 200–212.

4. Charles Pavitt and Kelly Kline Johnson, "An Examination of the Coherence of Group Discussions," *Communication Research* 26 (June 1999), pp. 303–21.

5. Hirokawa, "Consensus Group Decision-Making," pp. 407–15; Hirokawa, "Why Informed Groups Make Faulty Decisions: An Investigation of Possible Interaction-Based Explanations," *Small Group Behavior* 18 (1987), pp. 3–29; and Hirokawa, "Discussion Procedures and Decision-Making Performance: A Test of the Functional Perspective," *Human Communication Research* 12 (1985), pp. 203–24.

6. Karen Tracy and Heidi Mueller, "Diagnosing a School Board's Interactional Trouble: Theorizing Problem Orientation," *Communication Theory* 11 (2001), pp. 84–104.

7. Carl E. Larson and Frank M. J. LaFasto, *TeamWork: What Must Go Right, What Can Go Wrong* (Newbury Park, CA: Sage, 1989), pp. 27–38.

8. David Dryden Henningsen and Mary Lynn Miller Henningsen, "Examining Social Influence in Information-Sharing Contexts," *Small Group Research* 34 (August 2003), pp. 391–412.

9. For example, see Randy Hirokawa, "Group Communication and Problem Solving Effectiveness: An Investigation of Group Phases," *Human Communication Research* 9 (1983), pp. 291–305.

10. John E. Dewey, *How We Think* (Boston: D.C. Heath, 1910).

11. This research is synthesized in Dennis S. Gouran and Randy Y. Hirokawa, "Effective Decision Making and Problem Solving in Groups," in *Small Group Communication: Theory and Practice,* 8th ed., eds. Randy Y. Hirokawa, Robert S. Cathcart, Larry A. Samovar, and Linda D. Henman (Los Angeles: Roxbury, 2003), pp. 27–38.

12. Lucia Savadori, Lun M. Van Swol, and Janet A. Sniezek, "Information Sampling and Confidence Within Groups and Judge Advisor Systems," *Communication Research* 28 (2001), pp. 737–71; Michael G. Cruz and David Dryden Henningsen, "The Presence of Norms in the Absence of Groups?" *Human Communication Research* 26 (2000), pp. 104–24.

13. Susan Jarboe, "Procedures for Enhancing Group Decision Making," in *Communication and Group Decision Making,* 2nd ed., eds. Randy Y. Hirokawa and Marshall Scott Poole (Thousand Oaks, CA: Sage, 1996), pp. 345–83.

14. Marshall S. Poole, "Decision Development in Small Groups II: A Study of Multiple Sequences in Decision Making," *Communication Monographs* 50 (1983), pp. 224–25, and "Decision Development in Small Groups III: A Multiple Sequence Model of Group Decision Development," *Communication Monographs* 50 (1983), pp. 321–41.

15. Randy Y. Hirokawa, "Group Communication and Decision-Making Performance: A Continued Test of the Functional Perspective," paper presented at the annual convention of the Speech Communication Association, Boston, 1987; Randy Y. Hirokawa and Kathryn M. Rost, "Effective Group Decision Making in Organizations: Field Test of the Vigilant Interaction Theory," paper presented at the annual convention of the Speech Communication Association, Atlanta, 1991.

16. Elizabeth E. Graham, Michael J. Papa, and Mary B. McPherson, "An Applied Test of the Functional Communication Perspective of Small Group Decision Making," *Southern Communication Journal* 62 (Summer 1997), pp. 269–79.

17. Among these studies were John K. Brilhart and Lurene M. Jochem, "Effects of Different Patterns on Outcomes of Problem-Solving Discussion," *Journal of Applied Psychology* 48 (1964), pp. 175–79; Ovid L. Bayless, "An Alternative Model for Problem Solving Discussion," *Journal of Communication* 17 (1967), pp. 188–97; Carl E. Larson, "Forms of Analysis and Small Group Problem Solving," *Speech Monographs* 36 (1969), pp. 452–55; and Hirokawa, "Discussion Procedures and Decision-Making Performance."

18. Benjamin J. Broome and Luann Fulbright, "A Multistage Influence Model of Barriers to Group Problem Solving: A Participant-Generated Agenda for Small Group Research," *Small Group Research* 26 (February 1995), pp. 25–55.

19. Joseph A. Bonito, "An Information-Processing Approach to Participation in Small Groups,"

*Communication Research* 28 (June 2001), pp. 275–303; Michael G. Cruz, Franklin J. Boster, and Jose I. Rodriquez, "The Impact of Group Size and Proportion of Shared Information on the Exchange and Integration of Information in Groups," *Communication Research* 27 (June 1997), pp. 291–313.

20. Michael E. Mayer, Kevin T. Sonoda, and William B. Gudykunst, "The Effect of Time Pressures and Type of Information on Decision Quality," *Southern Communication Journal* 62 (Summer 1997), pp. 280–92.

21. For example, see Sidney J. Parnes, "Effects of Extended Effort in Creative Problem Solving," *Journal of Educational Psychology* 52 (1961), pp. 117–22.

22. Renee Meyers, David Seibold, and Dale Brashers, "Argument in Initial Group Decision-Making Discussions: Refinement of a Coding Scheme and a Descriptive Quantitative Analysis," *Western Journal of Speech Communication* 55 (Winter 1991), pp. 47–68.

23. Graham, Papa, and McPherson, "An Applied Test of the Functional Communication Perspective of Small Group Decision Making."

24. Randy Y. Hirokawa, John G. Oetzel, Carlos G. Aleman, and Scott E. Elston, "The Effects of Evaluation Clarity and Bias on the Relationship Between Vigilant Interaction and Group Decision-Making Efficacy," paper presented at the Speech Communication Association convention, November, 1991.

25. Mary Ann Renz, "Paving Consensus: Enacting, Challenging, and Revising the Consensus Process in a Cohousing Community," *Journal of Applied Communication Research* 34 (May 2006), pp. 163–90.

26. Sue Barnes and Leonore M. Grueller, "Computer-Mediated Communication in the Organization," *Communication Education* 43 (April 1994), pp. 129–42.

27. Annette C. Easton, Nancy S. Eickelmann, and Marie E. Flately, "Effects of an Electronic Meeting System Group Writing Tool on the Quality of Written Documents," *Journal of Business Communication* 31 (1994), pp. 27–40.

28. Mathew Schwartz, "The Instant Messaging Debate," *Computerworld* 36 (January 2002), p. 40.

29. Judith Pena-Shaff, Wendy Martin, and Geraldine Gay, "An Epistemological Framework for Analyzing Student Interactions in Computer-Mediated Communication Environments," *Journal of Interactive Learning Research* 12 (Spring 2001), pp. 41–62.

30. Ibid.

31. For a more detailed description of these support systems, see Joseph E. McGrath and Andrea B. Hollingshead, *Groups Interacting with Technology* (Thousand Oaks, CA: Sage, 1994).

32. Leonard M. Jessup and Joseph S. Valacich, eds., *Group Support Systems: New Perspectives* (New York: Macmillan, 1993).

33. Andrew Flanagin, Vanessa Tiyaamornwong, Joan O'Connor, and David Seibold, "Computer-Mediated Group Work: The Interaction of Member Sex and Anonymity," *Communication Research* 29 (February 2002), pp. 66–93.

34. S. Opper and H. Fresko-Weiss, *Technology for Teams: Enhancing Productivity in Networked Organizations* (New York: Van Nostrand Reinhold, 1992).

35. Andrea B. Hollingshead, Joseph E. McGrath, and Kathleen M. O'Connor, "Group Task Performance and Communication Technology: A Longitudinal Study of Computer-Mediated versus Face-to-Face Work Groups," *Small Group Research* 24 (August 1993), pp. 307–33.

36. Izak Benbasat and Lai-Huat Lim, "The Effects of Group, Task, Context, and Technology Variables on the Usefulness of Group Support Systems: A Meta-Analysis of Experimental Studies," *Small Group Research* 24 (November 1993), pp. 430–62.

37. Craig R. Scott, "The Impact of Physical and Discursive Anonymity on Group Members' Multiple Identifications During Computer-Supported Decision Making," *Western Journal of Communication* 63 (Fall 1999), pp. 456–87.

38. Poppy McLeod, "New Communication Technologies for Group Decision Making: Toward an Integrative Framework," in *Communication and Group Decision Making,* 2nd ed., eds. Randy Y. Hirokawa and Marshall Scott Poole (Thousand Oaks, CA: Sage, 1996), pp. 426–61.

39. Robert F. Bales, *Interaction Process Analysis* (Reading, MA: Addison-Wesley, 1950); Donald G. Ellis and B. Aubrey Fisher, *Small Group Decision Making: Communication and the Group Process,* 4th ed. (New York: McGraw-Hill, 1994); and Poole, "Decision Development in Small Groups II."

40. Ellis and Fisher, *Small Group Decision Making,* pp. 144–57.

41. Poole, "Decision Development in Small Groups II."

42. Renz, "Paving Consensus: Enacting, Challenging, and Revising the Consensus Process in a Cohousing Community."

43. Ibid.

44. David R. Seibold, "Making Meetings More Successful: Plans, Formats, and Procedures for Group Problem Solving," in *Small Group Communication: A Reader,* 5th ed., eds. Robert S. Cathcart and Larry A. Samovar (Dubuque, IA: Wm. C. Brown, 1988), pp. 219–20.

**Chapter 9**

1. Joyce L. Hocker and William W. Wilmot, *Interpersonal Conflict,* 3rd ed. (Dubuque, IA: Wm. C. Brown, 1991), p. 12.

2. Ana Zornoza, Pilar Ripoll, and José M. Peiró, "Conflict Management in Groups That Work in Two Different Communication Contexts: Face-to-Face and Computer-Mediated Communication," *Small Group Research* 33 (October 2002), pp. 481–508.

3. Karl Smith, David W. Johnson, and Roger T. Johnson, "Can Conflict Be Constructive? Controversy versus Concurrence Seeking in Learning Groups," *Journal of Educational Psychology* 73 (1981), pp. 654–63.

4. Charles R. Franz and K. Gregory Jin, "The Structure of Group Conflict in a Collaborate Work Group During Informational Systems Development," *Journal of Applied Communication* 23 (May 1995), pp. 108–27.

5. Mary Ann Renz, "Paving Consensus: Enacting, Challenging, and Revising the Consensus Process in a Cohousing Community," *Journal of Applied Communication Research* 34 (May 2006), pp. 163–90.

6. Rob Anderson and Veronica Ross, *Questions of Communication: A Practical Introduction to Theory,* 3rd ed. (Boston: Bedford/St. Martin's, 2002), p. 53.

7. Laura L. Myers and R. Sam Larson, "Preparing Students for Early Work Conflict," *Business Communication Quarterly* 68 (September 2005), pp. 306–17.

8. Harold Guetzkow and John Gyr, "An Analysis of Conflict in Decision-Making Groups," *Human Relations* 7 (1954), pp. 367–82.

9. Mahmut Bayazit and Elizabeth A. Mannix, "Should I Stay or Should I Go?: Predicting Team Members' Intent to Remain in the Team," *Small Group Research* 34 (2003), pp. 290–321.

10. Roger C. Pace, "Personalized and Depersonalized Conflict in Small Group Discussions," *Small Group Research* 21 (1990), pp. 79–96.

11. Jackie M. Wellen and Matthew Neale, "Deviance, Self-Typicality, and Group Cohesion: The Corrosive Effects of the Bad Apples on the Barrel," *Small Group Research* 37 (April 2006), pp. 165–86.

12. John G. Oetzel, "Explaining Individual Communication Processes in Homogenous and Heterogeneous Groups Through Individualism-Collectivism and Self-Construal," *Human Communication Research* 25 (2) (December 1998), pp. 202–24.

13. Victor D. Wall, Jr., and Linda Nolan, "Small Group Conflict: A Look at Equity, Satisfaction, and Styles of Conflict Management," *Small Group Behavior* 18 (1987), pp. 188–211.

14. Linda L. Putnam, "Conflict in Group Decision Making," in *Communication and Group Decision Making,* eds. Randy Y. Hirokawa and Marshall Scott Poole (Beverly Hills, CA: Sage, 1986), pp. 16–23.

15. Elizabeth Hobman, Prashant Bordia, Bernd Irmer, and Artemis Chang, "The Expression of Conflict in Computer-Mediated and Face-to-Face Groups," *Small Group Research* 33 (2002), pp. 439–65.

16. Ibid.

17. Laku Chidambaram, Robert P. Bostrom, and Bayard E. Wynne, "A Longitudinal Study of the Impact of Group Discussion Support Systems on Group Development," *Journal of Management Information Systems* 7 (Winter 1990/91), pp. 7–25.

18. Hobman et al., "The Expression of Conflict in Computer-Mediated and Face-to-Face Groups."

19. Ibid.

20. Myers and Larson, "Preparing Students for Early Work Conflict."

21. Karen Jehn, "A Qualitative Analysis of Conflict Types and Dimensions in Organizational Groups," *Administrative Science Quarterly* 42 (1997), pp. 530–57.

22. Michael Song, Barbara Dyer, and R. Jeffrey Thieme, "Conflict Management and Innovation Performance: An Integrated Contingency Perspective," *Journal of the Academy of Marketing Science* 34 (2006), pp. 341–56.

23. Kenneth Thomas, "Conflict and Conflict Management," in *Handbook of Industrial and Organizational Psychology,* ed. Marvin Dunnette (Chicago: Rand McNally, 1976), pp. 890–934.

24. Hal Witteman, "Analyzing Interpersonal Conflict: Nature of Awareness, Type of Initiating Event, Situational Perceptions, and Management Styles," *Western Journal of Communication* 56 (Summer 1992), pp. 248–80.

25. Victor D. Wall and Linda L. Nolan, "Small Group Conflict: A Look at Equity, Satisfaction, and Styles of Conflict Management," *Small Group Behavior* 18 (1987), pp. 188–211.

26. Renee Meyers and Dale Brashers, "Influence Processes in Group Interaction," *The Handbook of Group Communication Theory and Research,* ed. Lawrence Frey (Thousand Oaks, CA: Sage, 1999), pp. 288–312.

27. Victor D. Wall, Gloria J. Galanes, and Susan B. Love, "Small Task-Oriented Groups: Conflict, Conflict Management, Satisfaction, and Decision Quality," *Small Group Behavior* 18 (1987), pp. 31–55.

28. Tim Kuhn and Marshall Scott Poole, "Do Conflict Management Styles Affect Group Decision Making?" *Human Communication Research* 26 (October 2000), pp. 558–90.

29. Renz, "Paving Consensus: Enacting, Challenging, and Revising the Consensus Process in a Cohousing Community."

30. Michael A. Gross, Laura K. Guerrero, and Jess K. Alberts, "Perceptions of Conflict Strategies and Communication Competence in Task-Oriented Dyads," *Journal of Applied Communication Research* 32 (August 2004), pp. 249–70.

31. Ibid.

32. Min-Sun Kim and Truman Leung, "A Multicultural View of Conflict Management Styles: Review and Critical Synthesis," *Communication Yearbook* 23, ed. Michael E. Roloff (Thousand Oaks, CA: Sage, 2000), pp. 227–69.

33. Judith Martin and Thomas K. Nakayama, *Experiencing Intercultural Communication: An Introduction* (Boston: McGraw-Hill, 2001), pp. 173–74.

34. John G. Oetzel, "Explaining Individual Communication Processes in Homogenous and Heterogeneous Groups Through Individualism-Collectivism and Self-Construal."

35. Gross et al., "Perceptions of Conflict Strategies and Communication Competence in Task-Oriented Dyads."

36. Arie W. Kruglanski and Donna M. Webster, "Group Members' Reactions to Opinion Deviates and Conformists at Varying Degrees of Proximity to Decision Deadline and of Environmental Noise," *Journal of Personality and Social Psychology* 61 (1991), pp. 212–26.

37. Renz, "Paving Consensus: Enacting, Challenging, and Revising the Consensus Process in a Cohousing Community."

38. Stella Ting-Toomey, *Communication Across Cultures* (New York: Guilford Press, 1999).

39. Ibid.

40. Steven M. Alderton and Lawrence Frey, "Argumentation in Small Group Decision Making," in *Communication and Group Decision Making,* eds. Randy Hirokawa and Marshall Scott Poole (Beverly Hills, CA: Sage, 1986), pp. 157–73.

41. Rick Garlick and Paul A. Mongeau, "Argument Quality and Group Member Status as Determinants of Attitudinal Minority Influence," *Western Journal of Communication* 57 (Summer 1993), pp. 289–308.

42. Lisa J. Gebhart and Renee A. Meyers, "Subgroup Influence in Decision-Making Groups: Examining Consistency from a Communication Perspective," *Small Group Research* 26 (May 1995), pp. 147–68.

43. Dale Brashers and Renee Meyers, "Tag-Team Argument and Group Decision Making: A Preliminary Investigation," *Spheres of Argument: Proceedings of the Sixth Speech Communication Association/American Forensics Association Conference on Argumentation,* ed. Bruce Gronbeck (Annandale, VA: Speech Communication Association, 1989), pp. 542–50.

44. Gebhart and Meyers, "Subgroup Influence."

45. James B. Thomas, Reuben R. McDaniel, Jr., and Michael J. Dooris, "Strategic Issue Analysis: NGT and Decision Analysis for Resolving Strategic Issues," *Journal of Applied Behavioral Science* 25 (May 1989), pp. 189–201.

46. Roger Fisher and William Ury, *Getting to Yes: Negotiating Agreement Without Giving In* (New York: Penguin Books, 1983).

**Chapter 10**

1. Michael Z. Hackman and Craig E. Johnson, *Leadership: A Communication Perspective,* 2nd ed. (Prospect Heights, IL: Waveland Press, 1996), p. 14.

2. Gary Yukl, *Leadership in Organizations,* 5th ed. (Upper Saddle River, NJ: Prentice-Hall, 2002).

3. John R. P. French and Bertram Raven, "The Bases of Social Power," in *Group Dynamics: Research and*

*Theory,* 3rd ed., eds. Dorwin Cartwright and Alvin Zander (New York: Harper & Row, 1968), pp. 259–69.

4. Yukl, *Leadership in Organizations.*

5. S. M. Ketrow, "Nonverbal Aspects of Group Communication," in *The Handbook of Group Communication and Research,* eds. Lawrence R. Frey, Dennis S. Gouran, and Marshall Scott Poole (Thousand Oaks, CA: Sage, 1999), pp. 251–87.

6. Yukl, *Leadership in Organizations.*

7. Michael W. Kramer, "Shared leadership in a Community Theater Group: Filling the Leadership Role," *Journal of Applied Communication Research* 34 (May 2006), pp. 141–62.

8. Ernest G. Bormann, *Discussion and Group Methods: Theory and Practice,* 2nd ed. (New York: Harper & Row, 1975), pp. 253–69, and John C. Geier, "A Trait Approach to the Study of Leadership in Small Groups," *Journal of Communication* 17 (1967), pp. 316–23.

9. Katherine W. Hawkins, "Effects of Gender and Communication Content on Leadership Emergence in Small Task-Oriented Groups," *Small Group Research* 26 (May 1995), pp. 234–49.

10. Scott D. Johnson and Curt Bechler, "Examining the Relationship Between Listening Effectiveness and Leadership Emergence," *Small Group Research* 29 (August 1998), pp. 452–71.

11. David A. Kenny and Steven J. Zaccaro, "An Estimate of Variance Due to Traits in Leadership," *Journal of Applied Psychology* 68 (1983), pp. 678–85; Robert J. Ellis and Steven F. Cronshaw, "Self-Monitoring and Leader Emergence: A Test of Moderator Effects," *Small Group Research* 23 (February 1992), pp. 113–29; and Steven F. Cronshaw and Robert J. Ellis, "A Process Investigation of Self-Monitoring and Leadership Emergence," *Small Group Research* 22 (September 1991), pp. 403–20.

12. Simon Taggar and Rick Hackett, "Leadership Emergence in Autonomous Work Teams: Antecedents and Outcomes," *Personnel Psychology* 52 (Winter 1999), pp. 899–926.

13. Robert S. Rubin, Lynn K. Bartels, and William H. Bommer, "Are Leaders Smarter or Do They Just Seem That Way? Exploring Perceived Intellectual Competence and Leadership Emergence," *Social Behavior & Personality* 30 (2) (2002), pp. 105–18; Simon Taggar and Rick Hackett, "Leadership Emergence in Autonomous Work Teams: Antecedents and Outcomes,"

*Personnel Psychology* 52 (Winter 1999), pp. 899–926; Robert G. Lord, Christy L. deVader, and George M. Alliger, "A Meta-Analysis of the Relation Between Personality Traits and Leadership Perceptions: An Application of Validity Generalization Procedures," *Journal of Applied Psychology* 71 (August 1986), pp. 402–10.

14. Amy B. Gershenoff and Roseanne J. Foti, "Leader Emergence and Gender Roles in All-Female Groups: A Critical Examination," *Small Group Research* 34 (April 2003), pp. 170–96.

15. Judith A. Kolb, "Are We Still Stereotyping Leadership? A Look at Gender and Other Predictors of Leader Emergence," *Small Group Research* 28 (August 1997), pp. 370–93.

16. Susan B. Shimanoff and Mercilee M. Jenkins, "Leadership and Gender: Challenging Assumptions and Recognizing Resources," in *Small Group Communication: Theory and Practice,* 8th ed., eds. Randy Y. Hirokawa, Robert S. Cathcart, Larry A. Samovar, and Linda Henman (Los Angeles: Roxbury, 2003), pp. 184–98.

17. M. Sean Limon and Betty H. La France, "Communication Traits and Leadership Emergence: Examining the Impact of Argumentativeness, Communication Apprehension, and Verbal Aggressiveness in Work Groups," *Southern Communication Journal* 70 (Winter 2005), pp. 123–33.

18. Ralph M. Stogdill, Carrol L. Shartle, Willis L. Scott, Alvin E. Coons, and William E. Jaynes, *A Predictive Study of Administrative Work Patterns* (Columbus: The Ohio State University, Bureau of Business Research, 1956); Ralph M. Stogdill and Alvin E. Coons, eds., *Leader Behavior: Its Description and Measurement* (Columbus: The Ohio State University, Bureau of Business Research, 1957); and Robert Blake and Jane Mouton, *The Managerial Grid* (Houston: Gulf, 1964).

19. Hackman and Johnson, *Leadership: A Communication Perspective.*

20. Ibid., p. 27.

21. Kramer, "Shared Leadership."

22. John Gastil, "A Meta-Analytic Review of the Productivity and Satisfaction of Democratic and Autocratic Leadership," *Small Group Research* 25 (August 1994), pp. 384–410, and John Gastil, *Democracy in Small Groups* (Philadelphia: New Society Publishers, 1993).

23. Yukl, *Leadership in Organizations.*

24. Ibid.

25. William C. Schutz, "The Leader as Completer," in *Small Group Communication: A Reader,* 3rd ed., eds. Robert S. Cathcart and Larry A. Samovar (Dubuque, IA: Wm C. Brown, 1979), pp. 454–60.

26. Kramer, "Shared Leadership."

27. Fred Fiedler, *A Theory of Leadership Effectiveness* (New York: McGraw-Hill, 1967).

28. Paul Hersey and Kenneth H. Blanchard, *Management of Organizational Behavior,* 4th ed. (Englewood Cliffs, NJ: Prentice-Hall, 1982).

29. Robert P. Vecchio, R. Craig Bullis, and Donna M. Brazil, "The Utility of Situational Leadership Theory: A Replication in a Military Setting," *Small Group Research* 37 (October 2006), pp. 407–24.

30. Ibid.

31. Gastil, "A Meta-Analytic Review," p. 403.

32. J. Kevin Barge, "Leadership as Medium: A Leaderless Group Discussion Model," *Communication Quarterly* 37 (Fall 1989), pp. 237–47.

33. This information is synthesized from Frank LaFasto and Carl Larson, *When Teams Work Best: 6000 Team Members and Leaders Tell What It Takes to Succeed* (Thousand Oaks, CA: Sage, 2001), and Gloria J. Galanes, "In Their Own Words: An Exploratory Study of Bona Fide Group Leaders," *Small Group Research* 34 (December 2003), pp. 741–70.

34. Much of the following information is discussed in detail in John K. Brilhart and Gloria J. Galanes, *Effective Group Discussion,* 8th ed. (Madison, WI: Brown & Benchmark, 1995), pp. 177–202.

35. Katherine W. Hawkins, "Effects of Gender and Communication Content on Leadership Emergence in Small Task-Oriented Groups," *Small Group Research* 26 (May 1995), pp. 234–49.

36. Carl Larson and Frank M. J. LaFasto, *Team Work: What Must Go Right/What Can Go Wrong* (Newbury Park, CA: Sage, 1989), pp. 27–33.

37. Kramer, "Shared Leadership."

38. Dong L. Jung and John J. Sosik, "Transformational Leadership in Work Groups: The Role of Empowerment, Cohesiveness, and Collective-Efficacy on Perceived Group Performance," *Small Group Research* 33 (June 2002), pp. 313–36.

39. P. H. Andrews and R. T. Herschel, *Organizational Communication: Empowerment in a Technological Society* (Boston: Houghton Mifflin, 1996).

40. Hackman and Johnson, *Leadership: A Communication Perspective.*

**Chapter 11**

1. Ann L. Darling and Deanna P. Daniels, "Practicing Engineers Talk About the Importance of Talk: A Report on the Role of Oral Communication in the Workplace," *Communication Education* 52 (January 2003), pp. 1–16.

2. Cindy Griffin, *Invitation to Public Speaking* (Belmont, CA: Thomson Wadsworth, 2004), chap. 5.

3. Dan O'Hair, Rob Stewart, and Hannah Rubenstein, *A Speaker's Guidebook: Text and Reference* (Boston: Bedford/St. Martin's, 2004), chap. 6.

4. Darling and Daniels, "Practicing Engineers Talk," p. 13.

5. Ibid, p. 13.

6. Ibid., p. 88.

7. Ibid., pp. 96–99.

8. George Kennedy (trans.), *Aristotle, On Rhetoric* (New York: Oxford, 1991), p. 181.

9. *Spectra* IX (December 1973), n.p.

10. Jane Blankenship, *A Sense of Style* (Belmont, CA: Dickenson, 1968), p. 12.

11. Ibid., p. 41.

12. Karyn Rybacki and Donald Rybacki, *Communication Criticism: Approaches and Genres* (Belmont, CA: Wadsworth, 1991), p. 40.

**Appendix**

1. Stanley Seashore, *Group Cohesiveness in the Industrial Work Group* (Ann Arbor: University of Michigan Institute for Social Research, 1954).

2. Dean C. Barnlund and Franklyn S. Haiman, *The Dynamics of Discussion* (Boston: Houghton Mifflin, 1960), pp. 401–4.

**BIBLIOGRAPHY**

## Chapter 1

Galanes, Gloria J., and Katherine Adams. *Effective Group Discussion,* 12th ed. New York: McGraw-Hill, 2007.

LaFasto, Frank, and Carl Larson. *When Teams Work Best: 6,000 Team Members and Leaders Tell What It Takes to Succeed.* Thousand Oaks, CA: Sage, 2001.

## Chapter 2

Fisher, Aubrey, and Donald Ellis. *Small Group Decision Making: Communication and the Group Process,* 4th ed. New York: McGraw-Hill, 1994.

Von Bertalanffy, Ludwig. *General Systems Theory: Foundations, Development, Applications.* New York: Braziller, 1968.

## Chapter 3

Cathcart, Robert S.; Larry A. Samovar; and Linda Henman, eds. *Small Group Communication: Theory & Practice,* 7th ed. Madison, WI: Brown & Benchmark, 1996, sections 5 and 6.

Ellis, Donald G., and Aubrey B. Fisher. *Small Group Decision Making,* 4th ed. New York: McGraw-Hill, 1994, chap. 4.

Galanes, Gloria J., and Katherine Adams. *Effective Group Discussion,* 12th ed. New York: McGraw-Hill, 2007, chap. 2.

Steil, Lyman K., and Larry Barker. *Effective Listening: Key to Your Success.* Reading, MA: Addison-Wesley, 1983.

Watzlawick, Paul; Janet A. Beavin; and Don D. Jackson. *The Pragmatics of Human Communication.* New York: Norton, 1967.

## Chapter 4

Anderson, Peter A. "Nonverbal Communication in the Small Group." In *Small Group Communication: A Reader,* 6th ed., eds. Robert S. Cathcart and Larry A. Samovar. Dubuque, IA: Wm. C. Brown, 1992, pp. 272–86.

Burgoon, Judee K. "Spatial Relationships in Small Groups." In *Small Group Communication: Theory & Practice,* 7th ed., eds. Robert S. Cathcart, Larry A. Samovar, and Linda Henman. Madison, WI: Brown & Benchmark, 1996, pp. 241–53.

Galanes, Gloria J., and Katherine Adams. *Effective Group Discussion,* 12th ed. New York: McGraw-Hill, 2007, chaps. 2 and 3.

Ketrow, Sandra. "Nonverbal Aspects of Group Communication." In *The Handbook of Group Communication Theory & Research,* ed. Lawrence R. Frey. Thousand Oaks, CA: Sage, 1999, pp. 251–87.

## Chapter 5

Anderson, Carolyn N.; Bruce L. Riddle; and Matthew M. Martin. "Socialization Processes in Groups." In *The Handbook of Group Communication Theory & Research,* ed. Lawrence R. Frey. Thousand Oaks, CA: Sage, 1999, pp. 139–66.

Bormann, Ernest G. *Discussion and Group Methods: Theory and Practice,* 2nd ed. New York: Harper & Row, 1975, chaps. 8 and 9.

Ellis, Donald G., and B. Aubrey Fisher. *Small Group Decision Making,* 4th ed. New York: McGraw-Hill, 1994, chaps. 5 and 8.

Galanes, Gloria J., and Katherine Adams. *Effective Group Discussion,* 12th ed. New York: McGraw-Hill, 2007, chap. 8.

## Chapter 6

Bales, Robert Freed, and Stephen P. Cohen. *SYMLOG: A System for the Multiple-Level Observation of Groups.* New York: Free Press, 1979.

Hecht, Michael L.; Mary Jane Collier; and Sidney A. Ribeau. *African American Communication: Ethnic Identity and Cultural Interpretation,* vol. 2. Language and Language Behaviors series. Newbury Park, CA: Sage, 1993, especially chap. 3.

Hicks, Rick, and Kathy Hicks. *Boomers, Xers, and Other Strangers: Understanding the Generational Differences That Divide Us.* Wheaton, IL: Tyndale House, 1999.

Kolb, David. *Experiential Learning: Experience as the Source of Learning and Development.* Englewood Cliffs, NJ: Prentice-Hall, 1984.

Kroeger, Otto, with Janet A. Thuesen. *Type Talk at Work: How the 16 Personality Types Determine Your Success on the Job.* New York: Dell, 1992.

Samovar, Larry A., and Richard E. Porter. *Communication Between Cultures,* 4th ed. Belmont, CA: Wadsworth, 2001, in particular chap. 3, "Cultural Diversity in Perception: Alternative Views of Reality," pp. 52–88.

Tannen, Deborah. *You Just Don't Understand: Women and Men in Conversation.* New York: Ballantine Books, 1990.

Ting-Toomey, Stella. *Communication Across Cultures.* New York: Guilford, 1999.

## Chapter 7

Browne, M. Neil, and Stuart M. Keeley. *Asking the Right Questions: A Guide to Critical Thinking,* 8th ed. Englewood Cliffs, NJ: Prentice-Hall, 2007.

Buzan, Tony, with Barry Buzan. *The Mind Map® Book.* New York: Plume, 1996.

Jarboe, Susan. "Group Communication and Creativity Processes." And Keyton, Joann. "Relational Communication in Groups." In *The Handbook of Group Communication Theory & Research,* ed. Lawrence R. Frey. Thousand Oaks, CA: Sage, 1999.

Nijstad, Bernard A., and Paul B. Paulus. "Group Creativity: Common Themes and Future Directions." In *Group Creativity: Innovation Through Collaboration,* eds. Paul B. Paulus and Bernard A. Nijstad. New York: Oxford University Press, 2003, pp. 326–39.

Sunwolf. "Getting to 'GroupAha!' Provoking Creative Processes in Task Groups." In *The Handbook of Group Communication Theory and Research,* ed. Lawrence R. Frey. Thousand Oaks, CA: Sage, 1999.

**Chapter 8**

Broome, Benjamin J., and Luann Fulbright. "A Multistage Influence Model of Barriers to Group Problem Solving: A Participant-Generated Agenda for Small Group Research." *Small Group Research* 26 (February 1995), pp. 25–55.

Dewey, John. *How We Think.* Boston: D.C. Heath, 1910.

Gouran, Dennis S., and Randy Y. Hirokawa. "Effective Decision Making and Problem Solving in Groups: A Functional Perspective." In *Small Group Communication: Theory and Practice,* 8th ed., eds. Randy Y. Hirokawa, Robert S. Cathcart, Larry A. Samovar, and Linda D. Henman. Los Angeles: Roxbury, 2003, pp. 27–38.

Larson, Carl E., and Frank M. J. LaFasto. *TeamWork: What Must Go Right, What Can Go Wrong.* Newbury Park, CA: Sage, 1989.

McGrath, Joseph E., and Andrea B. Hollingshead. *Groups Interacting with Technology.* Thousand Oaks, CA: Sage, 1994.

**Chapter 9**

Fisher, Roger, and Scott Brown. *Getting Together: Building a Relationship That Gets to Yes.* Boston: Houghton Mifflin, 1988.

Fisher, Roger, and William Ury. *Getting to Yes: Negotiating Agreement Without Giving In.* New York: Penguin Books, 1983.

Janis, Irving L. *Groupthink: Psychological Studies of Policy Decisions and Fiascoes,* 2nd ed. Boston: Houghton Mifflin, 1983.

Meyers, Renee, and Dale Brashers. "Influence Processes in Group Interaction." In *The Handbook of Group Communication Theory and Research,* ed. Lawrence Frey. Thousand Oaks, CA: Sage, 1999, pp. 288–312.

Thomas, Kenneth W. "Conflict and Conflict Management." In *Handbook of Industrial and Organizational Psychology,* ed. Marvin Dunnette. Chicago: Rand McNally, 1976.

**Chapter 10**

Galanes, Gloria J. "In Their Own Words: An Exploratory Study of Bona Fide Group Leaders," *Small Group Research* 34 (December 2003), pp. 741–70.

Galanes, Gloria J., and Katherine Adams. *Effective Group Discussion,* 12th ed. New York: McGraw-Hill, 2007, chaps. 9 and 10.

Hirokawa, Randy Y.; Robert S. Cathcart; Larry A. Samovar; and Linda D. Henman. *Small Group Communication: Theory and Practice, An Anthology,* 8th ed. Los Angeles: Roxbury, 2003, section 7, pp. 169–213.

LaFasto, Frank, and Carl Larson. *When Teams Work Best: 6000 Team Members and Leaders Tell What It Takes to Succeed.* Thousand Oaks, CA: Sage, 2001, particularly section 4, pp. 97–154.

Robert, Henry M. *Robert's Rules of Order Revised.* Glenview, IL: Scott, Foresman, 1981.

Tropman, John E. *Making Meetings Work: Achieving High Quality Group Decisions.* Thousand Oaks, CA: Sage, 1996.

**Chapter 11**

Griffin, Cindy. *Invitation to Public Speaking.* Belmont, CA: Thomson Wadsworth, 2004.

Lucas, Stephen. *The Art of Public Speaking.* New York: McGraw-Hill, 1998.

O'Hair, Dan; Rob Stewart; and Hannah Rubenstein. *A Speaker's Guidebook: Text and Reference.* Boston: Bedford/St. Martin's, 2004.

Rybacki, Karyn, and Donald Rybacki. *Communication Criticism: Approaches and Genres.* Belmont, CA: Wadsworth, 1991.

**A**

Abstract, 108

Abstract conceptualization learning style, 146

Abstract words, 79, 80–81

Acceptance level, 223, 224

Accommodation, 260, 261

Acting helpless, 121

Action-oriented listener, 65–66

Action questions, 87

Active experimentation learning style, 146

Active listening, 69–71

Ad hoc committees, 19

*Ad hominem* attacks, 205

Adams, C., 205

Adobe Persuasion, 325

Affection, 16

Affective Conflict, 256

African Americans, 156–159

Agenda, 294

All-purpose discussion rating scale, A–8

Ambiguous, 200

Analogies, 206

Anderson, Carolyn, 113, 143

Androgynous members, 281–282

Annotated bibliographies, 195

Anonymity, 160, 258

Antecedent stage, 115, 116

Anticipatory stage, 115, 116–117

Appearance, 94–95

Appeasement, 260, 261

Arbitration, 273

Area of freedom, 221–222

Arguments, 189

Aristotle, 323

Arrangement, 332–333

Asian Americans, 156–159

*Asking the Right Questions: A Guide to Critical Thinking* (Browne/Keeley), 198

Assembly effect, 44, 218

Assessing information needs, 193–194

Assimilation stage, 115, 117

Assuming meaning, 65, 67

Asynchronous communication, 59, 101

Attacking person instead of argument, 205

Attention step, 327

Attitude, 191–193

Audience analysis, 316

Audio conference, 100

Audition practices, 117

Authoritarian leaders, 283

Autocratic leadership, 283, 284

Avatar, 92

Avoidance, 260–261

Ayers, Rick, 79

**B**

Baby boomers, 162, 163, 165

Back-channel sounds, 97, 158

Bales, Robert F., 107, 142

Barnlund-Haiman leadership rating scale, A–15 to A–16

Bay of Pigs, 132

Bayazit, Mahmud, 257

Beatles, The, 94

Beebe, Staven, 13

Beechnut, 128

Behavioral roles, 119

Berg, David, 68

Best Friends Animal Society, 3, 6

Bibliography, B–1 to B–2

Blanchard, Kenneth H., 288, 289

Blitzer, Irving, 29

Blocking, 121

Blushing, 91

Body, 328–330

Body movements, 97

Boeing 767 airplane, 39

Bona Fide Group, 38

Bona Fide Group Perspective, 37, 38

Boomers, 162, 163, 165

Brainstorming, 184–185

Brainwriting, 185

Briggs, Katherine, 147

Broome, Benjamin J., 38

Brown, M. Neil, 198

Bryant, Kobe, 200

Builders, 162, 163

Bush, George W., 280

*Business Periodicals Index,* 195

Butler, C.T., 263

Bypassing, 79, 80

**C**

Canons of rhetoric, 332–334

Captive audience, 318

Caseau, Dana, 8

Cases

Cask and Cleaver work crew, 251

college service club, 277

deadlock-school board, 239

dean search committee, 75

food for the homeless, 315

Jamaican bobsled team (Cool Runnings), 29

*Man of La Mancha* cast and crew, 105

misfit, 139

NASA failures, 190

observing technical college executive committee, A–00 to A–1

Ozarks Greenways, Inc., 179

Cases—*Cont.*

   Ozarks Public Television-MSU Merger, 217

   Students for Alternative Medicine, 53

Cask and Cleaver work crew, 251

Causal relationships, 205–206

Cause and effect organization, 329

Celebrity testimony, 324

Certainty, 134

Chalkboard, 325

*Challenger* space shuttle disaster, 45, 190, 192

Charge, 230

Charismatic leadership, 285

Chart, 329

Chat rooms, 237

Chronological order, 329

Clarifying, 119

Climate, 129–135. *See also* Group climate

Climate of trust, 303–304

Closed-ended questions, 198

Closed system, 40

CMC. *See* Computer-mediated communication (CMC)

CNN, 45, 48

CNN's reporting disaster, 45

Co-culture, 156, 162

Coalitions, 267

Cochran, Johnnie, 324

Coercion, 279

Cohesiveness, 132–133, 254

Cohort groups, 19

Collaboration, 260, 262–263

Collectivist, 151

College service club, 277

*Columbia* space shuttle disaster, 23, 190

ComAbstracts, 196

Commitment to the group, 21

Committee, 19

Communication

   characteristics, 55–60

   defined, 14, 55

   listening, 63, 71

   nonverbal. *See* Nonverbal behaviors

   sender and receiver phenomenon, 58

   relational, 6

   small group, 61–62

   structuration, 77

   synchronous/asynchronous, 59

   verbal message. *See* Language

Communication apprehension, 116

Communication richness, 59

Competition, 260, 261–262

Complexity, 44

Compromise, 260, 263–264

Computer conference, 100

Computer-mediated communication (CMC), 37, 59, 60, 100, 258. *See also* Internet; Technology

   anonymity, 160

   conflict types, 258

   communication richness, 59

   defined, 42, 60

   disadvantages, 42

   face-to-face meetings, compared, 100, 258

   net conference, 100–101

   Postmes study, 7

Conclusion, 330

Concrete experience learning style, 145–146

Concrete language, 79, 80–81

Conference committees, 20

Conflict, 252

   arbitration, 273

   expressing disagreement, 265–267

   maximizing chance to influence group, 267–268

   mediation, 273

   myths about conflict, 252–256

   nominal group technique, 268–270

   principled negotiation, 270–273

   styles of, 259–265

Conflict management styles, 259–265

Conflict Types, 256–259

   affective, 256

   procedural, 257

   substantive, 256

Confusing causal relationships, 205

Consensus, 240

Consensus testing, 170

Constructive debate, 180–182

Consultant-observer, A–1

Consultative method, 240

Content analysis procedures, A–5 to A–8

Content dimension, 60

Content-oriented listener, 65, 66

Context, 152, 153

Contingency concept, 287–290

Continuing small groups, 13

Control, 16, 134

Convergence, 212

Convergent thinking, 180

*Cool Runnings,* 29

Cragan, John, 5

Creative thinking, 180–189

   brainstorming, 184–185

   defined, 180

   environmental factors, 182

   group factors, 181

   individual factors, 180

   leaders, 300–302

   mind mapping, 187–189

   syntectics, 185–187

Creativity, 180. *See also* Creative thinking

Criteria, 233–234

Critical feedback, 43

Critical thinking, 189–213

    attitudes, 191–193

    counterproductive attitudes, 193

    defined, 189

    errors in reasoning (fallacies), 203–207

    evaluating information, 197–203

    gathering information, 193–197

    leaders, 300–302

    probing questions, 192

Cultural differences, 150–167

Culture, 150

Cyborg decision-making groups, 15

**D**

Daft, R., 59

Dance, Frank, 56

de Mestral, George, 185

Deadlock—school board, 239

Dean search committee, 75

Decision by leader or designated member, 238–239

Decision emergence, 238

Decision making, 220, 238–239. *See also* Group problem-solving problems

Defensive behaviors, 134

Defensive responding, 67, 68–69

Delegating style of leadership, 289

Delivery, 331–332, 334

Democratic leaders, 284

Demographic statistics, 317

Description, 134

Designated leader, 281

Developing Norms, 125

Deviants, 127

Devil's advocate, 211

Dewey, John, 227

Dialect, 98

Direct observation, 194

Direct purpose statement, 328

Disagreement, expressing, 265–267

Discussion questions, 85–89

Distributed leadership, 289, 306–309

Divergent thinking, 180

Diversity, 150–174

    cultural differences, 150–167

    defined, 141

    fantasy, 168–169

    gender differences, 159–161

    generational differences, 161–167

    group identity, 169–169, 173–174

    learning styles, 143–146

    motives for joining a group, 142–143

    overcoming the problems, 167–173

    personality differences, 146–149

    race/ethnic differences, 155–159

    SYMLOG, 169–173

Double-barreled question, 88–89

Dow Chemical, 20

Downed U.S. EP-3E surveillance plane, 56

Dramatizing, 121

Dyad, 13

**E**

E-mail, 112

Eastman Kodak, 4

EBSCOhost, 196

Ecological power, 280

Effect to cause organization, 329

Effective Decision Making Theory (EDMT), 155

Egalitarian attitudes, 22

Either-or questions, 88

Either-or thinking, 206

Elaborating, 119

Elder, Linda, 204

Electronic brainstorming, 185

Electronic bulletin boards, 16

Electronic databases, 195–196

Ellis, Donald, 238

Emergent leader, 281–282

Emoticons, 101

Emotional expression, 96–97

Emotive words, 69, 79, 82–83

Empathy, 134

Encounter stage, 115, 117

Entertainment speech, 318

Environment, 36–37

Equality, 134

Equalizing opportunity to participate, 299–300

Equilibrium Problem, 107

ERIC, 196

Errors in reasoning, 205–207

Ethical Formation Behavior, 135

Ethical group member, 21–24

Ethics, 21, 309–310

Ethnic groups, 155–159

Euro-Disney, 154

European Americans, 156

Evaluation, 134

Evaluating Web-Based Sources, 196

Evidence, 189

Examples, 323

Exit stage, 115, 117–118

Expert power, 279

Expert testimony, 324

Expressing disagreement, 265–267

Expressive behaviors, 159

Extemporaneous speech, 331–332

Extraversion/introversion dimension, 147

Extravert, 147, 148

Eye contact, 96–97

**F**

Face-to-face meetings, 100

Face-to-face problem census, 225–226

Facial expressions, 96–97

Facts, 199

Fallacies, 203–207

False dilemma, 206

Fantasy, 168–169

Faulty analogy, 206

Feedback, 43

Feeler, 148, 149

Female-male differences, 159–161, 281–282

Figurative language, 330–331

Fisher, B. Aubrey, 238

Fisher, Roger, 270

Flaming, 126

Floyd, Kory, 91

Focus group, 232

Focusing on irrelevancies, 67, 68

Food for the homeless, 315

Folger, Joseph, 129

Forcefulness, 159

Ford Motor Company, 20

Formal roles, 118

Formal rules, 124

Forum discussion, 321–322

French, John R., 278

Frey, Lawrence, 4

FtF communication, 100

Fulbright, Luann, 38

Fun, 306

Functional concept, 286–287

Functional theory, 227

**G**

Garlick, Rick, 267

Gastil, John, 289

Gatekeeping, 120

Gebhart, Lisa, 267

Gen Xers, 163, 165

Gender, 159

Gender differences, 159–161, 281–282

General Electric (GE), 187

General Motors (GM), 20

Generalization, 205

Generalized system theory, 30. *See also* Systems theory

Generational differences, 161–167

Gersick, Connie, 112

"Get to know you" time, 173

*Getting to Yes: Negotiating Agreement Without Giving In* (Fisher/Ury), 270

Giuliani, Rudolph, 321

Giving in, 260, 261

Glen, Samantha, 6

GM, 20

Gouran, Dennis S., 192, 227

Griffin, Em, 30

Grob, Lindsey, 161

Group, 4–9

climate, 129–135

defined, 11

leaders, 278–310. *See also* Leadership

life cycle, 106–107

participating in, 6–7

stages of socialization, 115–118

primary/secondary, 16–21

problem solver, as, 6, 8–11

roles, 118–123

rules and norms, 123–129

socialization of members, 113–118

small. *See* Small group

virtual, 39

Group climate, 129–135

cohesiveness, 132–133

defined, 132

supportiveness, 133–135

trust, 130–131

Group creativity, 180–189. *See also* Creative thinking

Group discussions, 297–303

Group diversity. *See* Diversity

Group drive, 132

Group ecology, 95

Group functions, 107–108

Group identity, 168–169, 173–174

Group leaders. *See* Leadership

Group norms, 123–129

changing, 128–129

development of, 125

enforcement, 126–127

Group orientation, 159

Group presentations, 319–322. *See also* Oral presentations

Group problem-solving, 221–247

adapting procedures to fit the problem, 222–223

area of freedom, 221–222

components of problem situation, 220–221

face-to-face problem census, 225–226

functional theory, 227

identifying the problem, 223, 225–226

individual problem solving, compared, 8–11, 218

P-MOPS, 228–247. *See also* Procedural model of problem-solving (P-MOPS)

problem characteristics, 222–223, 224

Group roles, 118, 123
  emergence of roles, 121–123
  individual roles, 121
  maintenance roles, 120–121
  task roles, 119–120
  types of roles, 118–119
Group socialization, 113–118
  phases, 115–118
Group support system (GSS), 207, 235–238
Group turnover, 118
Grouphate, 11, 116
GroupSystems, 235
Groupthink, 132, 208–213
GSS, 207, 235–238

**H**

Hackman, Michael Z., 278
Hall, Edward T., 95
Handout, 325
Harmonizing, 121
Helix, 56–57
Hersey, Paul, 288, 289
Heterogeneity, 141
Hiaasen, Carl, 154
Hicks, Rick and Kathy, 162
Hidden agenda, 131
High-context culture, 152–153
High-power-distance cultures, 152–153
Hirokawa, Randy Y., 227
Hispanic Americans, 156
Hocker, Joyce, 252
Homeostasis, 46
Homogeneity, 141
Human language. *See* Language
Humor, 110, 306, 327
Hunch, 219

**I**

"I Have a Dream" speech, 331
Idea deviance, 254
Ideal leadership style, 283–286
Impromptu speech, 331
Incomplete comparisons, 206
Independent, 155
Indirect need step, 328
Individual creativity, 180
Individual roles, 121
Individualism/collectivism, 151–153
Individualistic culture, 151
Individuals *vs.* groups creativity, 180–181
  male-female differences, 159
  problem solving, 8–11, 218
Inference, 199, 200
Influence, 278, 279
Informal roles, 119
Information gathering, 193–197
Information giving, 119
Information lists, 194
Information power, 280
Information questions, 87
Information seeking, 119
Information sources, 194–197
Informative speech, 317
InfoTrac, 196
Initiating and orienting, 119
Inputs, 33–34, 41–42
Instrumental behaviors, 201
Interaction diagram, A–4
Interdependence, 32, 33
Interdependent, 155
Internet, 42. *See also* Computer-mediated communication (CMC); Technology evaluate accuracy of information, 196
  information source, as, 195
  norm enforcement, 126–127

Internet mailing lists, 126
Interpersonal Communication, 15
Interpersonal trust, 130–131
Interpretation questions, 87
Interviews, 197, 198
Intrapersonal Communication, 15
Intrinsic interests, 222–223, 224
Introduction, 327–328
Introvert, 147, 148
Intuition, 222–223, 224
Intuitor, 147, 148
Invention, 332, 333

**J**

Jamaican Winter Olympic bobsled team, 29
Janis, Irving, 132, 208
Johnson, Craig E., 278
Johnson, Tom, 45
Johnston, William, 142
Joking, 110–111, 277
Judger, 148, 149
Jung, Carl, 147
Jury deliberations, 161

**K**

Kahn, Robert, 33
Katz, Daniel, 33
Keeley, Stuart, 198
*Kelley Blue Book,* 272
Kennedy, John F. 132
Keyton, Joann, 118
Kolb, David, 145
Kolb learning cycle, 145
Kraft, 46
Kramer, Michael, 281, 285, 287
Kuhn, Tim, 263

**L**

LaFasto, Frank, 14, 132
Laissez-faire leaders, 284–286

Language, 78
   clarity, coherence, 86
   concrete vs. abstract, 79, 80–81
   discussion questions, 85–89
   emotive words, 79, 82–83
   follow the rules, 79–80
   organize remarks, 79, 83–85
   symbolic nature of, 79, 80
Lao Tse, 310
Larson, Carl, 14, 132
Laughing, 110–111, 277
Lay testimony, 324
Lea, M., 7
Leader, 280
Leader self-rating scale, A–17
Leadership, 278–312
   administrative duties, 292–297
   characteristics of good
      leaders, 290
   contingency concept, 287–290
   defined, 278
   developing the group, 303–306
   distributed, 306–308
   equalizing opportunity to
      participate, 299–300
   ethical guidelines, 309–310
   expectations of group members,
      292–306
   functional concept, 286–287
   gender, 281–282
   group discussions, 298–303
   influence and power, 278–280
   meetings, 2292–293
   myths about, 283–286
   stimulating creative thinking,
      300–301
   stimulating critical thinking,
      301–302
Leadership emergence, 281–282
Learning groups, 19
Learning styles, 143–146

Leaving a group, 117–118
Legitimate power, 278, 279
Lengel, R., 59
Lennon, John, 94
Less-talkative members, 300
Letterman, David, 327
LexisNexis, 196
Life cycle, 106
Lightner, Candy, 283
Listening, 63–71
   active, 69–71
   defined, 63
   group socialization, 115–118
   poor listener, 65–69
   preferences, 64–66
Listening preferences, 64–66
Listservs, 126
Little League baseball team (Tucson
   Diamondbacks), 45
Logan, Carol, 90
Logos, 174
Long-winded speakers, 299–300
Low-context culture, 152–153
Low-power-distance cultures,
   152–153

**M**

Mabry, Edward A., 97
Maintenance roles, 120–121
Majority vote, 240
Male-female differences, 159–161,
   281–282
Mallia, Karen L., 42
*Man of La Mancha* cast and
   crew, 105
Mannix, Elizabeth, 257
Manuscript, 331
Map, 325
Martin, Matthew, 113, 143
Materson, John, 13
MBTI, 147

McPhee, Robert, 77
Mead, Margaret, 4
Media richness, 59
Mediation, 273
Meeting environments, 16
Meeting notice, 292
Meetings, 292–293
Member diversity. *See* Diversity
Member familiarity, 223, 224
Member roles, 119
Memorized presentation, 331
Message, 75
Metaphors, 185–187
Meyers, Renee, 267
Mind assault, 65, 67
Mind mapping, 187–189
Mindful communication, 167
Minutes, 294–296
Misfit, 39
Model, 324
Model of situational leadership, 288
Moderator, 321
Mongeau, Paul A., 267
Motive for communication, 116
Motive for joining a group,
   142–143
Motorola, 4
Movements, 97
MoveOn.org, 39
Multifinality, 44
Multiple causes, 44
Multiple paths, 44
Myers, Isabel Briggs, 147
Myers-Briggs personality types,
   147–149
Myers-Briggs Type Indicator
   (MBTI), 147
Myths
   conflict, 252–56
   leadership, 283–286

**N**

N-geners, 164, 165

Name-calling, 266

NASA failures, 23, 45, 190

NBA Championship Finals (2004), 44

NCA Credo, 22–23, 35, 59–60, 135, 219, 259

Need step, 328

Negative synergy, 45, 46

Nestlé USA, 4

Net conference, 100–101

Net generation, 164, 165

Neutrality, 134

*New England Journal of Medicine,* 200

*New York Times,* 196

Newspapers, 196

NewsStand: CNN & *Time,* 45

*Newsweek,* 4

Nijstad, Bernard, 181

Nominal group technique, 268–270

Nonsummativity, 44

Nonverbal behaviors, 90
  appearance, 94–95
  defined, 90
  eye contact, 96–97
  facial expressions, 96–97
  functions, 91–94
  movements, 97
  principles, 90–91
  space and seating, 95–96
  timing, 98–99
  voice, 97–98

Norms, 124, 125. *See also* Group norms

**O**

Object, 295

Objective criteria, 272–273

Observing groups, A–1 to A–18
  content analysis procedures, A–5 to A–8
  evaluating individual participating, A–11
  feedback, A–2
  PMR forms, A–11, A–12
  questions to ask, A–3
  rating scales, A–8 to A–9
  role of observer, A–1 to A–2
  Seashore Index of Group Cohesiveness, A–10
  verbal interaction analysis, A–4, A–5

Oetzel, John, 143, 155

O.J. Simpson murder trial, 324

One-meeting groups, 13

Online support networks, 18–19

Open-ended questions, 198

Open-minded, 173, 191

Open system, 40–41

Opinion giving, 120

Opinions, 199, 200

OPT-MSU merger, 217

Oral presentations, 316–334
  audience analysis, 316
  body, 328–330
  canons of rhetoric, 332–334
  conclusion, 330
  delegating duties, 323
  introduction, 327–328
  language, 330–331
  method of delivery, 331–332
  organizational style, 328–330
  organizing stage, 322–330
  planning stage, 316–322
  presenting stage, 330
  supplemental logistics, 319
  types of group presentations, 319–322

types of speeches, 317–318
  verbal supporting materials, 323–324
  visual aids, 324–325

Organizational groups, 19

Organizational style, 328–330

Organizations as systems of groups, 46–47

Outputs, 35–36

Overgeneralization, 205

Overhead projector, 325

Ozarks Greenways, Inc., 179

Ozarks Public Television, 217

**P**

Packer, Arnold, 142

Panel discussion, 319–321

Partial-win/partial-lose style of conflict management, 260, 263–264

Participant-observer, 24, A–1

Participant-observer perspective, 24

Participating in groups, 6–8

Participating rating scale, A–13, A–14

Participating style of leadership, 289

Pataki, George, 321

Patient's Bill of Rights, 20

Paul Revere Insurance Group, 20

Paul, Richard, 04

Paulus, Paul, 181

Peer pressure, 126

People-oriented listener, 64–66

People-related functions, 286

Perceiver, 148, 149

Perceiving/judging dimension, 149

Personal appearance, 94–95

Personal notes of meeting, 303

Personality differences, 146–149

Persuasive speech, 318

PERT, 241, 243–244

PERT chart, 243

P&G, 20

Phases of group socialization 115–118

Photograph, 324

Picture, 324

Playing, 121

PMR forms, A–11, A–12

Poker face, 99

Policy questions, 87

Politicians, 132

Poole, Marshall Scott, 77, 29, 238, 263

Positional roles, 118

Positive synergy, 44, 46

Postmeeting reaction (PMR) forms, A–11, A–12

Postmes, T., 7

Powell, Robert, 8

Power, 278–280

Power distance, 152, 153

PowerPoint, 325

Presentation software, 325

Presentations. *See* Oral presentations

Preview, 328

Primary groups, 16–17

Primary tension, 108

Principled negotiation, 270–273

Printed sources of information, 195–197

Private chat rooms, 237

Probing questions, 192

Problem, 220

Problem census, 223, 225–226

Problem characteristics, 222–223, 224

Problem orientation, 134

Problem-solution pattern, 328–329

Problem solving, 220. *See also* Group problem-solving problems

Problem-solving rating scale, A–9

Procedural conflict, 257

Procedural model of problem-solving (P-MOPS), 228–247

choose best solution, 238–241

defined, 228

describe/analyze the problem, 229–232

evaluate possible solutions, 233–238

focus group, 232

generate/explain possible solutions, 232

GSS, 235–238

implement chosen situation, 241

PERT, 241, 243–244

pros/cons, 234–235

RISK technique, 240–241

using P-MOPS (sample outline), 245–247

Procedure questions, 88

Process loss, 45

Procter & Gamble (P&G), 20, 46

Program Evaluation and Review Technique (PERT), 241, 243–244

Pros/cons, 234–235

Provisionalism, 134

Pseudolistening, 65, 67

Public speaking. *See* Oral presentations

Published materials, 195–197

Punctuated equilibrium, 112–113

Punishment power, 279

Pushing people's emotional buttons, 166

Putnam, Linda, 37

**Q**

Quality control circles, 20

Questions

closed-ended, 198

discussion, 85–89

observation, A–3

open-ended, 111

oral presentation, 299

phrasing, 88–89

probing, 192

rhetorical, 327

scale, A–8

Quotation, 327–328

**R**

Racial epithets, 82

Racial groups, 156–159

Rails to Trails movement, 179

Rating scales, A–8 to A–9

Raven, Bertram, 278

Ray, John, 91

Reasoning errors, 205–207

Recording, 120

Red Ribbon Committee, 302

References, R–1 to R–12

Referent power, 279–280

Reflective observation learning style, 146

Reflective thinking, 227

Reich, Nina M., 159

Reinforcement, 238

Relational dimension, 60

Relationally oriented individuals, 143

Relationship, 159

Relationship questions, 88

Renz, Mary Ann, 263

Reward power, 279

Rhetorical question, 327

Rhetorical sensitivity, 266

Riddle, Bruce, 113

RISK technique, 240

Rituals, 174

Ritz-Carlton Hotels, 4

"Roasting" a colleague, 318

Robert's Rules for Committees, 238

Robert's Rules of Order, 12

Robert's Rules of Order Revised, 124, 297

*Roe v. Wade,* 254

Role, 118. *See also* Group roles

Roper Center for Public Opinion, 317

Rothstein, Amy, 263

Rules, 124

Rybacki, Karyn and Donald, 332

**S**

SAMM, 235, 236

SC Johnson, 4

Scale questions, A–8

Schutz, Will C., 16

Scientific information, 203

Seashore Index of Group Cohesiveness, A–10

Seating arrangements, 95–96

Secondary groups, 17–21

Secondary tension, 108, 233

Self-centered members, 121

Self-construal, 155

Self-managed work teams, 20–21

Selling style of leadership, 289

Sensing/intuiting dimension, 147–149, 148

Sensor, 147, 148

Sex, 160

Shaking, 91

Shaw, Marvin, 11, 141

Sherwin-Williams, 20

Short story, 328

Show me skepticism, 191

Showing solidarity, 120

Sidetracking, 67, 68

Siebold, David, 77

Sigman, Stewart, 117

Silent arguing, 65, 67

Situational leadership, 288

Skepticism, 191

Slang dictionary, 79

Slide shows, 325. *See also* Oral presentations

Small group. *See also* Group defined, 5, 12, 13

open system, as, 40

system, as, 32–43. *See also* Systems theory

Small group communication, 4, 61–62. *See also* Communication

Small group inputs, 33–34

Small group outputs, 35–36

Small group throughput processes, 34–35

Smith, Karl, 253

Social accessibility, 95

Social distance, 95

Social presence, 15, 101

Social tension, 109–112

Social tension management, 110–111

Socialization, 113

Socioemotional function, 107

Software Assisted Meeting Management (SAMM), 235, 236

Solution simplicity, 222, 224

Sources of information, 195–197

Space and seating, 95–96

Spatial order, 329

Speaking time, 98–99

Spears, Britney, 324

Spears, R., 7

Specialized indexes, 195

Speeches. *See* Oral presentations

Spontaneity, 134

Stage fright, 108

Standing committee, 19

Statistics, 323

Status seeking and recognition seeking, 121

Steil, Lyman K., 63

Stewart, John, 90

Stohl, Cynthia, 37

Strategy, 134

Striking quotation, 327–328

Striking statement, 327–328

Structuration, 77

Students for Alternative Medicine, 53

Study groups, 19

Style, 332, 333–334

Subgroup, 267

Substantive conflict, 257

Suggesting procedure, 120

Summarizing, 119

Superiority, 134

Support groups, 17–19

Supporting, 120

Supportive behaviors, 134

Supportiveness, 133–135

*Swann v. Charlotte-Mecklenburg Board of Education,* 310

Sweating, 91

Symbol, 50, 55–56

Symbolic convergence, 167, 168

Symbols, 174

SYMLOG, 169–173

defined, 170

Symposium, 321

Synchronous communication, 59

Synergy, 44–45, 46

Syntectics, 185–187

System, 32

Systems theory

communication, 34

closed system, 40

environment, 36–37

feedback, 43

Systems theory—*Cont.*

　inputs, 30–34

　interdependence, 31–32, 41–42

　multiple causes, 44

　multiple paths, 44

　nonsummativity, 44

　open system, 40

　organizations as systems of
　　groups, 46–47

　outputs, 35–36

　overview, 31–33

　throughput process, 34–35

**T**

Talkativeness, 98

Task difficulty, 222, 224

Task focus, 159

Task forces, 20

Task functions, 107

Task-oriented individuals, 142–143

Task-related functions, 258

Task roles, 119–120

Team, 13–14

*Team Rodent: How Disney Devours
　the World* (Hiaasen), 154

Technology. *See also* Computer-
　mediated communication
　(CMC); Internet avatar, 92

　chat rooms and GSS, 237

　cyborg groups, 15

　meeting environments, 15

　net conference, 100–101

　presentation software, 297

Telecommuting, 42

TelePrompTer, 332

Telling style of leadership, 288

Tension, 109–112

Tension relieving, 121

Tertiary tension, 108–110

Testimony, 323–324

The Beatles, 94

Theory, 30

Thesis statement, 328

Thinker, 148, 149

*Thinker's Guide to Fallacies: The Art
　of Mental Trickery and
　Manipulation,* 204

Thinking/feeling dimension, 149

Thomas, Kenneth, 259

Throughput process, 34–35

*Time,* 48

Time cues, 98–99

Time-oriented listener, 65, 66

Time-Warner, 48

Ting-Toomey, Stella, 167, 266

*Today Show,* 9

Topical organization, 329–330

Transactional, 56–58

Transformative leadership, 285

Transparency, 325

Trautlein, Ann Margaret, 11

Trigger words, 82, 83

Trust, 130–132, 303–304

TRW, 21

Tse, Lao, 282

Tuckman, Bruce, 112

Tuckman's Model of Group
　development, 112

Tucson Diamondbacks, 45

**U**

UNIX, 39

Unity Church, 150

Ury, William, 270

**V**

Value questions, 87

Velcro, 185–186

Verbal aggressiveness, 116

Verbal interaction analysis,
　A–4, A–5

Verbal interaction diagram, A–4

Verbal message. *See* Language

Videoconference, 100

Videotape, 324

Virginia Tech, 207

Virtual groups, 39, 100

Visual aids, 324–325

Vocal cues, 97

von Bertanlanffy, Ludwig, 30

Voting, 240

**W**

Wang, H., 126

Welch, Jack, 187

Westinghouse, 20

Wilmot, William, 252

Win-lose style of conflict
　management, 260, 261

Win-win style of conflict
　management, 260, 262

Withdrawing, 170

Womack, Estelle, 3

Wood, Julia T., 159

Workforce 2000 Report, 142

Wright, David, 15

Wright, Kevin, 19

**X**

Xerox, 20

**Y**

Yahoo! Groups, 239